THE Essentials of Early Education

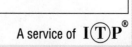

THE Essentials of Early Education

Carol Gestwicki

Central Piedmont Community College
Charlotte, NC

Delmar Publishers

I(T)P® International Thomson Publishing

Albany • Bonn • Boston • Cincinnati • Detroit • London • Madrid
Melbourne • Mexico City • New York • Pacific Grove • Paris • San Francisco
Singapore • Tokyo • Toronto • Washington

NOTICE TO THE READER

Cover Design: Brucie Rosch

Delmar Staff
Publisher: William Brottmiller
Senior Editor: Jay Whitney
Associate Editor: Erin J. O'Connor Traylor
Project Editor: Timothy Coleman/Marah Bellegarde
Production Coordinator: James Zayicek
Art and Design Coordinator: Carol Keohane
Senior Editorial Assistant: Glenna Stanfield

Copyright © 1997
By Delmar Publishers
a division of International Thomson Publishing Inc.

The ITP logo is a trademark under license.

Printed in the United States of America

For more information, contact:

Delmar Publishers
3 Columbia Circle, Box 15015
Albany, New York 12212-5015

International Thomson Publishing
Europe
Berkshire House 168-173
High Holborn
London, WC1V 7AA
England

Thomas Nelson Australia
102 Dodds Street
South Melbourne, 3205
Victoria, Australia

Nelson Canada
1120 Birchmont Road
Scarborough, Ontario
Canada, M1K 5G4

International Thomson Editores
Campos Eliseos 385, Piso 7
Col Polanco
11560 Mexico D F Mexico

International Thomson Publishing GmbH
Konigswinterer Strasse 418
53227 Bonn
Germany

International Thomson Publishing Asia
221 Henderson Road
#05-10 Henderson Building
Singapore 0315

International Thomson Publishing—Japan
Hirakawacho Kyowa Building, 3F
2-2-1 Hirakawacho
Chiyoda-ku, Tokyo 102
Japan

1 2 3 4 5 6 7 8 9 10 XXX 02 01 00 99 98 97 96

Library of Congress Cataloging-in-Publication Data

Gestwicki, Carol, 1940-
    The essentials of early education / Carol Gestwicki.
        p.   cm.
    Includes bibliographical references and index.
    ISBN 0-8273-7282-5
    1. Early childhood teachers—United States. 2. Teaching—
Vocational guidance—United States. 3. Early childhood education—
United States. I. Title.
LB1775.6.G47 1997
372.21—dc20

96-10995
CIP

CONTENTS

PREFACE

In this century, children have become cherished and recognized as our nation's future, at least rhetorically. The first years of life have been shown by research to be critical for later success in developing persons who live satisfying lives, and who make their own personal contributions to society. During those early years, children need adults—parents, other family members, teachers, and others—who support their healthy growth and development in many important ways. Most of us agree on these issues.

Why Was This Written?

This book is written from the author's strong conviction that the care and education of children in their earliest years must go beyond rhetoric, to provide optimum experiences and environments for real children in our very real world. Those who enter the early childhood profession find both enormous challenges and immense gratification as they nurture the healthy development of children and families. As child development research continues to discover the importance of the experiences, interactions, and environments that support children in the first years of their lives, it becomes increasingly clear that the adults responsible for children's care must have knowledge, attitudes, and skill to provide the best opportunities for children. As the need and demand for early education for children from birth through the primary years continues to expand in unprecedented dimensions, so too does the need for educated early childhood professionals.

This demand is related to a second strong conviction from which this book grows: not just anyone can, or should, work with young children, and moreover, young children do not need "just anyone." They need particular people, with specific characteristics, knowledge, skills, and attitudes, who have thoughtfully and deliberately prepared to enter into caring relationships with young children and their families. They need people who have committed themselves to following career paths in early childhood education, and who understand and accept the realities of the profession as it has evolved to this point. They need people who have decided to touch young lives, and are willing to stay the course.

Two Main Themes

These are the two main themes of this book: (1) that early education is important, meaningful, valuable work, supporting children and families during the most critical period of development; and (2) that only persons who are willing to accept the need for thoughtful and careful professional preparation will be able to help children reach their full potential. This book, then, proposes to examine the world of early education, and to assist the process of profession-al growth for those who are interested in considering it as their future, a future that impacts generations to come. It is assumed that students will use this text in a course that introduces them to concepts of early education, near the begin-ning of their academic programs of teacher preparation, whether in a two-year or four-year program. Because the text is designed for students who will con-tinue with other courses in a college program of early childhood professional preparation, the specifics of theoretical perspectives and of curriculum ideas and activities are left for those later courses.

Since the intention of the text is to help students begin active construc-tion of themselves as teachers, the style is both informative, so that students may truly understand the current field; and introspective, so that students may actively juxtapose their personal knowledge, goals, and experiences to con-sider the professional roles and possibilities of working with young children. So, however you as a student came to begin study of the essentials of early education, you are invited to reflect on the profession.

Coverage

Section One is entitled *The Starting Point,* because here you will be asked to consider early education and your own relationship to it.

Chapter One, *Decision-Making,* introduces the concepts of decision-making, to involve you in considering questions of importance to you person-ally, and to realize the variety of motivations that have brought other individu-als to this starting point.

Chapter Two, *Early Childhood Education Today,* defines the parameters of the field of early childhood education, and explores the diversity of program structures, of age-groups that early educators work with, of special population groups, and sponsors of programs. The social changes of past decades that have impacted early childhood education are identified.

Chapter Three, *What Quality Early Education Looks Like,* describes what quality looks like in early education. Some of the ideas here may be at odds with the images about working with young children, and you are encouraged to struggle and explore deeply the principles of quality presented here.

Chapter Four, *What Teachers Do,* explores the various roles of early edu-cators who work with children and families in a wide spectrum of opportuni-ties. You are urged to see how these fit with your personal goals and interests.

Section Two is entitled *Developing As a Teacher.* This section demon-strates that good teachers are not born but grow actively, with much personal effort and thought.

Chapter Five, *Why Become A Teacher?,* suggests answers to the question "Why become a teacher?", recognizing that the issues of personal satisfaction and needs are an important component in decision-making. You will need to find your own meaningful answers to this question to be satisfied as a teacher.

Chapter Six, *Growing Oneself as a Teacher,* considers the characteristics, skills, knowledge, and experiences that are important in creating oneself as a teacher. Three stories of early childhood teachers will be introduced, to help you understand the various paths individuals follow to enter the field. You will be asked to reflect on your own strengths and abilities in relation to teaching.

Chapter Seven, *Challenges for Early Educators,* examines some of the current challenges teachers face as they enter the contemporary field. It is important that you have a realistic and unsentimental understanding of the profession and its conditions, to juxtapose with your dreams and ideals.

Section Three is entitled *The Profession Comes of Age.* As we approach the end of the twentieth century, early education has come to an exciting time. It is the combination of seemingly unending need for quality child care, clear knowledge about what contributes to quality child care, and loud demands for professional standards and acceptance, that offer us positive directions for our immediate future.

Chapter Eight, *Roots of Early Education,* describes the roots of early education, or its heritage. In this chapter, you will see the multiple traditions and various philosophies and historic/social influences that have shaped the modern world of early education. Many of the names and events that you will have already read on the Timeline will appear in this chapter to describe our historical roots.

Chapter Nine, *The Modern Profession,* considers the current emphasis on professionalism, with the various components that have been created recently and that will shape your introduction to becoming a professional.

Chapter Ten, *Professional Education and Career Directions,* examines the various options in professional preparation, as well as some of the possibilities in career directions, within the classroom and beyond.

Chapter Eleven, *Current Issues in Early Education,* introduces the issues you will encounter within the profession and within classrooms today. As you read this chapter, you will see that the profession continues to evolve and define itself, and that there is challenging work for you to do as you proceed in teaching.

Chapter Twelve, *The Road Ahead,* leaves you with the challenge to become a teacher of young children, with the hope that you can now articulate the reasons you have decided to continue your preparation, to join with the thousands of teachers and caregivers who have determined that working with young children is the most important thing they can choose to do.

And make no mistake—we need and want you to stay. At no time in the history of our country have children and families needed more support, more care and early education than they do now. The social fabric of our nation is stretched thin; the youngest among us depend completely on adults who can nurture their growth and development and prepare them for a world we can't comprehend or even imagine. Together parents and teachers must form a circle of certainty within which children can become strong before encountering an uncertain world.

Yes, we welcome you to consider early education, thoughtfully and long. We hope that you and your fellow students will discuss these topics and issues in depth, and work through some of the additional readings and assignments at the end of each chapter. If you immerse yourself as fully as time allows in understanding early education *before* you move on into other courses, you will add to your knowledge base and deepen your theoretical understandings.

Features

You will find that each chapter features *learning objectives, review questions, suggested learning activities, quotes to contemplate,* and *suggestions for reading.* A *running glossary* will help you learn key terms by appearing in the margin where the word is introduced.

Timeline

Enjoy early childhood facts that spark discussion and thought, as they appear in a *Timeline* on the bottom of the pages throughout the book.

ECE Careers: *Theory Into Practice*

Watch for the *Theory into Practice* feature where you will meet a person working in the field of early education today, and hear some of their frustrations, joys, and advice to those entering the field. Use these profiles to explore early education deeply. And when it seems to you that you can wholeheartedly add your story to those of the teachers you will meet in this book, we urge you to add your voice, joyfully.

Full Color Art and Photographs

All the graphs, charts, and tables have been designed in full color. Numerous studies have established that students are at least 60 percent more likely to retain what they read when it is presented in color. A study at Loyola College found that color improves recall by 78 percent. The same researchers proved that color can improve decision-making, comprehension, accuracy, and retention.

All the photographs were taken on location at child care centers, schools, and hospitals and feature children who responded spontaneously, in order to provide accurate "snapshots" of real world early education.

The **NAEYC GUIDELINE** appears in Chapters Three, Four, and Nine where quality programs and excellence in teaching are described. The icon directs the reader to a very specific description of a component of quality as referenced in the NAEYC publication Developmentally Appropriate Practice in Early Childhood Serving Children from Birth to Age Eight edited by Sue Bredekamp, 1987. The reference with page number to the Bredekamp publication appears below each icon. EXAMPLE:

NAEYC GUIDELINE
Bredekamp, 1987, p.67

Acknowledgments

It has been my great good fortune over the years to hear the stories of many students, teachers, and colleagues who have made their own discoveries of the essential truths and pleasures of early education. This book is dedicated to them with thanks for their friendship along the way. I am especially grateful to three wonderful teachers and friends—Connie Glass, Annie Bryant, and Martha Huxster—who agreed to share their stories as early educators. I am also grateful to Christie Shamel, Connie Glass and Tracie O'Hara, some of Charlotte's fine model/mentor teachers, for sharing photos of their classrooms and children. Another thank you goes to the other teachers who agreed to share their faces, thoughts, and concerns with you: Harvey Bagshaw, Pansy Borden, Kim Brandon, Natasha England, Deborah Gordon, Lydia Ingram, Sheila Locklear, Sherry McIntyre, Tracie O'Hara, Michelle Pope, Kim Stevenson, and Debbie Wolfe. Watch for them in the "Theory Into Practice" feature in each chapter. A very special thank you to a good friend, Ed St. Clair, whose computer expertise rescued Chapter Two from disappearing into some black hole.

In addition, I appreciate the efforts and responses of the editorial and production staff at Delmar Publishers, and of the helpful comments and suggestions of reviewers:

Elaine Camerin
Daytona Beach Community College
Daytona Beach, Florida

Andrew Carroll
Georgia Southwestern College
Americus, Georgia

Jeri Carroll
Wichita State University
Wichita, Kansas

David Duerden
Ricks College
Rexburg, Idaho

Claude Endfield
Northland Pioneer College
Holbrook, Arizona

And, always, the support, assistance, and encouragement of my family has been important through this process.

A Professional and Life Choice

Gandini: *It seems that you made a choice to dedicate your life to the education and care of young children. When did you make this life choice?*

Malaguzzi: I could just avoid answering, as others have done before, by saying that when you don't ask me I know, but when you ask me, I do not know the answer anymore. There are some choices that you know are coming upon you only when they are just about to explode. But there are other choices that insinuate themselves into you and become apparent with a kind of obstinate lightness, that seem to have slowly grown within you during the happenings of your life because of a mixing of molecules and thoughts. It must have happened this latter way. But also World War II, or any war, in its tragic absurdity might have been the kind of experience that pushes a person toward the job of educating, as a way to start anew and live and work for the future. This desire strikes a person, as the war finally ends and the symbols of life reappear with a violence equal to that of the time of destruction.

I do not know for sure. But I think that is where to look for a beginning. Right after the war I felt a pact, an alliance, with children, adults, veterans from prison camps, partisans of the Resistance, and the sufferers of a devastated world. Yet all that suffering was pushed away by a day in spring, when ideas and feelings turned toward the future, seemed so much stronger than those that called one to halt and focus upon the present. It seemed that difficulties did not exist, and that obstacles were no longer insurmountable.

It was a powerful experience emerging out of a thick web of emotions and from a complex matrix of knowledge and values, promising new creativity of which I was only becoming aware. Since those days I have often reassessed my position, and yet I have always remained in my niche. I have never regretted my choices or what I gave up for them.[1]

[1]From *The Hundred Languages of Children: The Reggio Emilia Approach to Early Childhood Education* (p.49), by Carolyn Edwards, Lella Gandini and George Forman (Eds.), 1994, Norwood, NJ: Ablex Publishing Company. Reprinted with permission from Ablex Publishing Corp.

THE STARTING POINT

In this section, you are introduced to your active role in deciding to make a commitment to the early education profession. Chapter One will introduce the process of decision-making, and Chapters Two, Three, and Four will explore the parameters of early education, and teachers' roles in creating quality classrooms for young children. This general introduction to early education is necessary to clarify your expectations and images of what it means to be a teacher of young children.

C H A P T E R

1

DECISION-MAKING

OBJECTIVES

After studying this chapter, students will be able to:

1. **discuss various motivations for becoming a teacher.**

2. **describe the active role of decision-making.**

As you look around the room at your classmates in your Introduction to Early Education class, you may wonder how you all got here. Was there a common bond, idea, or experience that brought you together to become teachers of young children? You are probably seeing people who look very different from yourself, for teachers of young children may be of either gender, are of many ages, and have diverse ethnic and cultural backgrounds, as well as unique family and life experiences. In fact, what probably links you most to one another at this point, is that you are all exploring, wanting to know more about what it means to teach young children, and wanting to discover if this is the right place for you to be at this time. In this chapter, you will begin to understand the process of decision-making as you enter the early education profession. You must understand that much of this process is yours alone to do, that it is not something that can be graded as correct or incorrect, or measured as knowledge that you have achieved, as can so many other topics you will encounter during your professional preparation. Instead, decision-making includes juxtaposing your growing knowledge and experiences as an early childhood teacher with your introspective knowledge about yourself. At this beginning, you are urged to involve yourself, to collect your efforts in growing yourself as a teacher.

THINKING ABOUT TEACHING

Before you read any further, take a pen and paper and write down your reasons for why you are considering working with young children. You will meet other teachers and learn their reasons, but at the beginning it is important for you to identify your own reasons.

Robin M. could hardly wait for the first day of the semester. All her life she had wanted to be a teacher. Her mother was a kindergarten teacher, and Robin had grown up hearing funny stories about the children in her mother's classes, and watching her mother prepare materials. Her older sister had also studied early childhood education, and was now an assistant director in a child-care center. Robin wasn't sure what age-group she wanted to work with, but she knew with certainty that early education was the career for her (see Fig. 1-1).

Kim S. was rather apprehensive as she approached the first day of the semester in her education studies. Having just changed her major from nursing, where she had found the science courses too difficult, she was hoping that this would be an easier program, as the counselor had suggested. She knew she liked children, but had never been with a group of them all at the same time (see Fig. 1-2).

Mike D. was determined, but still feeling awkward as the first day of the semester brought him to his first early education class. His church work had convinced him that he was able to work with young children, but the strong opposition he had received from his parents and friends made him uncomfortably aware that others might wonder why he was here.

> *What else is there, finally, but one person making a difference to another?*
> —William Carlos Williams

Figure 1-1 **Some of you always enjoyed playing "teacher", and knew that early education was the career for you. (Courtesy of Connie Glass)**

1628
John Comenius, a Czech educator, writes *The School of Infancy,* referring to the "school of the mother's lap," in which a child from birth through age six would achieve the rudiments of all learning.

People become teachers for lots of different reasons. In most classes, a variety of motivations is present. Some of you knew instinctively and early in life that you wanted to help others learn. Your preschool teachers may have laughingly referred to you as "the third teacher" in the room, so anxious were you to tell the other children what to do, and report to the teacher if those other children did not obey. You played school with younger siblings and stuffed animals for hours on end, painstakingly using a pointer to emphasize the lessons

THEORY INTO PRACTICE

This is Tracie O'Hara. Presently a teacher in a therapeutic program for four-year-olds with behavioral problems, she has spent nearly twelve years in early education. With a background in special education, she has worked in several childcare centers, including centers where children with special needs were included with more typically developing children. A Model/Mentor teacher, she has also been active in her local professional organization.

What has been a significant frustration for you in early education? How do you deal with it?

A significant frustration for me has been apathy. It strikes different groups periodically–parents, teachers, politicians. I fight the frustration of wanting to *make* people see the importance of early childhood education by belonging to advocacy groups, like a local affiliate of the National Association for the Education of Young Children (NAEYC).

What is one thing you learned in classes that you really discovered to be true when you started working with children?

I am currently working on learning more about adult education and advocacy. It's important for teachers to see beyond the four walls of their classrooms to the overall quality of early childhood education.

What is an area you are working on now to learn more about?

It's really important to understand stages of development, and have knowledge of theories/theorists like Piaget and Montessori. The biggest gift teachers give their children is knowledge and understanding of where they are developmentally.

Why have you stayed in early education?

It's a growing, exciting field where new ground is breaking. We are writing the history books!

What is a comment or piece of advice you would give to those beginning to work in early childhood education?

Many early childhood professionals talk about "love" and "patience." For me, working with children and parents is about "understanding" and "respect." Patience, to me, says you grin and bear it. Understanding is knowing what to expect and using that knowledge. Love is important, but respect covers many more issues and will serve you and those you serve in many more ways. Early childhood in this country is in serious trouble if we don't learn to respect the children we profess to love.

Figure 1-2   **The demands of a group of children, all very different and interested in different things, is far different from playing with children one-on-one. (Courtesy of Tracie O'Hara)**

on display. Your future was assured, as you always quickly answered "a teacher" when grownups asked you what you would be when you grew up.

Others of you came less directly and deliberately to your teaching interest. Some may have found early work in child care in your community, an easily obtainable part-time job when going to school, a more interesting choice than flipping hamburgers or mowing lawns. You probably found that you genuinely enjoyed the company of young children, though frequently you may have been puzzled by the individual personalities or typical behaviors you encountered (see Fig. 1-3). Still, there was enough pleasure that you decided that this might be an interesting major or job choice to pursue, at least for a while. Some of you may have gained experience with children within your own families, looking after siblings, or nieces and nephews, and it seems only natural for you to continue this caring for children as a career.

Some of you are coming to teaching later in life, after experience with your own children has convinced you of the absolute importance of the

1641
Dame Schools are appearing in Massachusetts. Mrs. Walker, a widow, is paid one shilling and three pence by the town of Woburn, Massachusetts, for her annual salary, after taxes have been deducted.

As Confucius said, "A journey of a thousand miles begins with one step; but it is an unfortunate traveller who discovers after the first two hundred miles or so that he has been going in the wrong direction"
—Sybil Marshall

early years in nurturing healthy development and learning. As parents, some of you may have been drawn into your children's child care or early school classrooms as volunteers, and there discovered an interest and skill you had not recognized before. Others of you have become dissatisfied with the paths you took in college or in your career, and you have defined new goals that lead towards children. Some of you have been in related human service fields, and some are coming from unrelated fields. Some of you chose this field because you just like people, and recognize that you will constantly be working with families as well as children (see Fig. 1-4).

Some of you are here for very idealistic reasons, such as the desire to have an impact on the future and on the lives of children, or to make a lasting contribution to your communities. For some of you, teaching is a response to a strong religious orientation, and you feel the need to help young children become firmly rooted in your tradition. Some come for more practical reasons: assurance of job security, or long summer vacations, calendars, and hours that coincide with the needs of family obligations. And some of you come for a combination of these reasons.

Some of you have come to early childhood education because someone else has encouraged you to consider teaching. You might be following the path of a loved family member who is a teacher, and is a model for you. It might have been a teacher who took a special interest or formed a significant relationship with you, or one who became a symbol of what meaning teachers could have in the lives of others. It could have been a parent or coach who pointed out several talents or characteristics that could be beneficial for a teacher. Or, let us be totally honest here, it might have been at the urging of a parent or a high school guidance counselor who said in exasperation, to an undecided or lackluster

Figure 1-3	Individual personalities and typical age-level behaviors may be puzzling to beginning teachers. (Courtesy of Tracie O'Hara)

1642

The Massachusetts Bay Colony passes a law requiring parents to teach their children to read.

student, "Oh, you could always go into teaching little children. After all, just about anybody can do that!"

There is no one right reason for wanting to become a teacher of young children, but this last reason is surely the only wrong one. The misconception that teaching and caring for small children is easy, undemanding work is about as far from the truth as can be (see Fig. 1-5). Perhaps the misconception comes from the often-expressed idea that childrearing (parenting, mothering) comes *naturally* as a product of some instinct that magically allows adults looking after children to know exactly the appropriate thing to do and say (see Fig. 1-6).

Perhaps it is because much of parenting has, over history, been the work of women, and therefore carries the taint of being less important than the more obvious products of men's labors. Indeed, the important task of helping children grow and develop to their fullest potential consists of subtle actions, and is a long process that yields evidence of its worth only after much time. But whatever the reason for the misconception that teaching young children is easy, nonstressful work that can be done by almost anyone, this idea is harmful to the early education profession, and to children themselves. All too many young children today are being cared for by persons who do not understand the awesome responsibility of laying foundations for all later development. When this sobering idea takes hold,

Discovering the truth about ourselves is the work of a lifetime, but it's worth the effort
—Fred Rogers

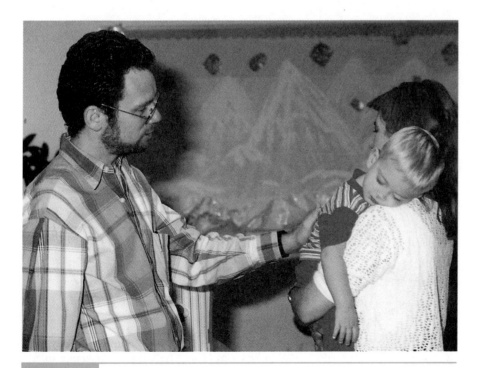

Figure 1-4   **Working with families may be a motivation for some of you.**

1647

Old Deluder Satan Act passes in Massachusetts Colony, requiring that towns with at least 50 households establish schools for young children, making education compulsory for every child to develop the ability to read the Bible.

Figure 1-5   **The challenges of meeting the needs of individual children within a classroom setting is *not* something just anyone can do. (Courtesy of Tracie O'Hara)**

Figure 1-6   **There is no magic instinct allowing adults to know exactly what to do or say in any situation. Challenge a classmate to interpret this picture, and know what to do and say!**

1693
John Locke, in England, writes *Some Thoughts Concerning Education.*

adults accept the need for developing their knowledge and skills to the fullest extent.

So if you have come to this point with this last reason in your mind, you are welcome to stay to learn what the profession and its roles are all about. At some point along the line, you will undoubtedly come to the realization that this is *not* easy work, and *not* just anyone can or should do it. If you perceive this, and then still want to stay, you are as welcome as if your initial motivation had been one of the others (see Fig. 1-7).

Some of you may be here to make a decision about whether or not to pursue a career in early childhood education that you have already begun. Others of you are hoping to decide which, if any, aspects of early childhood education *fit* what you want to do in the not-so-distant future.

Have you seen yourself anywhere in this discussion of the motivations to teach? You should understand that this is not merely an author's rhetorical question. It is a real question, one that many of you will read, yet it is meant to stop your reading and begin your serious contemplation. (One suggestion that might be helpful for students using this text would be to maintain a notebook of your written responses and personal reactions to the material. The notebook would be for your eyes only, and not to be handed in for a grade, although occasionally you might be asked to discuss some of your reactions with others, or pull from the notebook in your public writing.) Think about your own motivation for teaching, which may or may not have been included earlier (see Fig. 1-8).

Figure 1-7 **Children need adults trained to create interesting learning experiences, and to support children's exploration. (Courtesy of Connie Glass)**

1762
Jean Jacques Rousseau writes *Emile* in France.

Figure 1-8   **Have you seen yourself, and your motivations, here?**

THE PROCESS OF DECISION-MAKING

It is from many different paths that you have come together to examine the profession of early education. The desired outcome of this examination is a clear and strong commitment to become an early childhood educator. This career is not something that can be entered into lightly or tentatively, but will demand your energy, your effort, and your clear-eyed persistence. As you have come by different paths, so your continuing professional development will be unique to your own circumstances. "The good teacher's life is not an orderly professional pathway; rather it is a personal journey shaped by context and choice, perspective and values" (Jalongo and Isenberg, 1995, p. xvii). From your own context, you will make your own choices; your perspective will come from your own values.

So this course, and this textbook, will require your active participation. No doubt you have encountered learning situations where your role is defined as being a member of the audience, accepting and learning the material that you are presented. Your success in such endeavors is measured by how easily you can recollect the information on tests, or perhaps apply the facts you learned to a practical problem. In this textbook, the ideas and information are presented to increase your understanding of the profession of early education. But the information is not intended to stand alone as the ultimate end. In order to make a decision that is based on realistic conditions rather than vague images, you will need to take this information and process it by considering your own reactions. So your role must be that of an active participant, continually taking the new information

1815

The first Maternal Association is established by a group of minister's wives in Portland, Maine, to encourage the moral and religious training of children.

Figure 1-9 **Trying on roles mentally, and reflecting on them, will help you decide about early education as a career. (Courtesy of Connie Glass)**

and matching it to what you know of yourself. This active introspection–the first step to becoming a "reflective practitioner" (Schon, 1987)–may be a new student role for you. Yet it is the only way that you will ultimately be able to make a firm commitment to a career in early education, to proceed confidently in your professional growth, and to prepare to make your ultimate contribution.

Your own knowledge of your characteristic attitudes and responses should be applied at each point of learning new information. This helps you begin to understand how you would react to the joys and hassles of teaching. When the book talks about teacher roles, picture yourself carrying out those real activities, and determine how you would respond (see Fig. 1-9). When the text helps you learn the current efforts of the profession to increase compensation and status, imagine yourself involved in those attempts. As you read about issues that presently affect classroom practice, ask yourself whether these are issues about which you are also curious. By such continual reflection, you will come to a point where you can decide whether this is indeed the career for you, or whether it is not.

Such a realistic and strong commitment is essential, for as you will learn, there is a complicated journey ahead in entering the teaching profession. This journey includes learning much new information, and gradually developing the skills and dispositions of an effective teacher. It happens over time, and in the midst of conflict, uncertainty, and challenge. This is demanding work, and you must be convinced that it is the way you want to spend your working time in your life. One author suggests that "Three motivations help people decide on the kind of work they will do and whether or not they will stay with a given job: task, power, and relationship" (Manfredi/Petitt, 1993, p. 40). Your job is to find out what the profession offers in the way of tasks to do, power to have or share, and relationships with others, and also whether this will be satisfying to you.

Work is a major part of life, and it gives individuals much of their identity and self-esteem. The particular kind of work that you choose to do influences your relationships, your opportunities for personal growth, your place in the community, and the available resources for other aspects in your life. Choosing one's life work is not a decision that can or should be taken lightly. It cannot be done without a full understanding of what is involved in the work and a realistic appraisal of one's capacity to respond to it. This is your task, then, to take your self-knowledge and juxtapose it to a realistic perspective of the profession. Only then can your decision lead you to the career that will provide your life with meaning and satisfaction. Understand that the purpose of this text is not to convince you to become a teacher of young children; that is for you alone to decide. The book is to help you understand the breadth and depth of the profession, and to encourage you to consider your capacities in relation to the profession, as you work towards your decision.

You rarely have time for everything you want in this life, so you need to make choices. And hopefully your choices can come from a deep sense of who you are
—Fred Rogers

1816
Robert Owen establishes an infant school providing care for children of mill workers in Lancaster, England.

Figures 1-10   **Early childhood teachers may choose to work with different age groups.**

Components of Decision-Making

Who am I and how did I get there? opens the door for asking Who will I be and How will I get there?
—Mary Jalongo

In order for you to make an informed decision about early education as a career, there are certain questions that you will need to answer. You will find it essential to learn about the profession by finding out:

▶ What is the scope of possible work, including potential employers and age-groups to work with? (See Fig. 1-10.)

▶ What are the required tasks and roles in teaching?

▶ What are the working conditions and environments?

▶ What are the professional and legal requirements for various choices within teaching?

▶ What knowledge, skills, and educational levels are required?

▶ What are the personal characteristics of effective teachers?

▶ What are the possibilities for advancement and related career choices?

▶ What are the salary ranges?

▶ What are the professional supports and frameworks? and

▶ What are the advantages and disadvantages of the profession?

1819
Johann Pestalozzi, a Swiss educator, becomes the first recognized early childhood teacher in Yverdon, Switzerland.

Figure 1-11 **Some teachers find that the opportunity to get outdoors is important to them.**

All of this information is included in subsequent chapters. You have likely begun this study with initial impressions of what teaching young children is all about. As a basis for comparison with your later expanded and realistic understanding, it would be useful to stop at this point and write a brief account of what you assume it would be like to be a teacher of young children. What would you do each day? What would be the parts you would especially like? What about things you would find less attractive about the work?

In addition, your personal self-awareness will give you answers to:

▶ What are your values, goals, ideals and motivations?

▶ What are your ideas about what is important to you in life?

▶ What is your personal style in relationships?

▶ What is your temperament, and what are your characteristic responses?

▶ What are your preferences in work conditions, such as supervision and environment? (see Fig. 1-11.)

▶ What are your strengths and limitations? and

▶ What is your image of what you want out of life?

These may not be things that you have thought about, so you are encouraged to take as much time as needed to develop your self-knowledge. This

Dreams are a living picture in the mind generating energy. They are at once direction finders and sources of power
—Sylvia Ashton-Warner

1822
Robert Owen moves to New Harmony, Indiana, and establishes an infant school and day care center as part of the community.

Figure 1-12   **Welcome to the world of early education. (Courtesy of Connie Glass and Tracie O'Hara)**

reflection is absolutely essential in helping you decide what is right for you, and for you alone. Make an initial entry in your notebook in response to these questions listed above. Later questions and exercises will take you further in this self-exploration.

At various points, you will be encouraged to talk with other teachers. These conversations will certainly be helpful in giving you firsthand information and insights about real working conditions. You will discover that you are welcomed as a newcomer to the profession. But you are again reminded that individual reactions are completely unique, and what seems right or difficult for one person may be quite opposite for another. (You are also reminded that the conversations and observations you make in the course of this exploratory study are to be treated professionally. That is, it is appropriate to discuss your findings with peers within the classroom, but not to use the information for light gossip within the community.) In this book you will meet and hear the insights and experiences of many teachers. They are all real: either they are teachers with whom the author is acquainted or teachers you will *meet* in subsequent chapters. You will recognize the diversity of opinion and experience, and it may be helpful in striking resonance within your own thinking. Watch especially for the teachers in the "Theory into Practice" feature in each chapter, as well as the teacher stories in Chapters Three, Six, and Ten.

It is at once exciting and daunting to be told that your decisions are important, and that the decision you make about your work will affect the course of your life. But it is in the spirit of this cautious exhilaration that you are welcomed to the study of early education (see Fig. 1-12).

The hardest thing in life to learn is which bridge to cross and which to burn
—David Russell

> A life in teaching is a stitched-together affair, a crazy quilt of odd pieces and scrounged materials, equal parts invention and imposition. To make a life in teaching is largely to find your own way, to follow this or that thread, to work until your fingers ache, your mind feel as if it will unravel, and your eyes give out, and to make mistakes and then rework large pieces. It is sometimes tedious and demanding, confusing and uncertain, and yet it is often creative and dazzling: surprising splashes of color can suddenly appear at its center; unexpected patterns can emerge and lend the whole affair a sense of grace and purpose and possibility (Ayers, 1993, p. 1).

Perhaps you will decide to make your life in teaching. Those of us who have already come will do everything we can to welcome and support you. Welcome to the journey.

1823
First private normal (teacher training school) is established in Concord, Vermont.

SUMMARY

Though students may begin a teacher education program with diverse motivations, all are encouraged to reflect on the information presented about early education as a profession. Decision-making about work is serious, and it demands self-knowledge as well as information to define a realistic view of the profession.

QUESTIONS FOR REVIEW

1. Discuss several of the motivations to teach discussed in this chapter. How do these compare to your own motives?
2. Describe the interaction between knowledge concerning the profession and self-knowledge that results in firm commitment and decision-making.

ACTIVITIES FOR FURTHER STUDY

1. As suggested in the chapter, begin to record your responses and reflections in a journal.
2. Draw up a chart that contrasts what you currently know about early education as a profession, and what you know about your personal goals and characteristics.
3. Interview early childhood educators to determine what motivated them to teach, as well as what characteristics they feel are necessary to be a successful teacher. How do these compare to you and to the information in the text?

REFERENCES

Ayers, William. (1993). *To teach: The journey of a teacher*. New York: Teachers College Press.

Jalongo, Mary R. & Isenberg, Joan P. with Gloria Gerbracht. (1995). *Teachers' stories: From personal narrative to professional insight*. San Francisco, CA: Jossey-Bass Publishers.

Manfredi-Petitt, Lynn A. (1993, November). Child care: It's more than the sum of its tasks. *Young Children*, 49, (1), 40-42.

Schon, Donald. (1987). *Educating the reflective practitioner: Toward a new design for teaching and learning in the professions*. San Francisco, CA: Jossey-Bass Publishers.

SUGGESTIONS FOR READING

Bateson, Mary C. (1989). *Composing a life*. New York: Atlantic Monthly Press.

Cruikshank, D. (1987). *Reflective teaching: The preparation of students of teaching*. Reston, VA: Association of Teacher Educators.

Goffin, Stacie G. & Day, David E. (Eds.). (1994). *New perspectives in early childhood teacher education: Bringing practitioners into the debate*. New York: Teachers College Press.

2

EARLY CHILDHOOD EDUCATION TODAY

Millions of young children, from tiny newborns to children in the **primary** grades in school, will be leaving their homes today to be educated and cared for by people other than their families. As they are strapped into carseats or loaded on school buses or vans, these children will be heading to centers and classrooms to spend most of their waking hours in group situations with other children and with adults designated as "teachers" and "caregivers." Some of the older ones will go to a location that offers their parents the opportunity to leave them before the regular elementary school opening hours.

After six or so hours of classroom tasks, they will return to another after-school care setting so that parents can complete their full work day before picking up their offspring. (Actually some may travel most of the way with Mom or Dad, being enrolled in a center sponsored by their employer.)

Some of the youngest children will be passed still sleeping from parent to caregiver, and tucked into cribs to finish their sleep before waking to be fed. Some will be going to buildings that look very much like schools, with multiple classrooms, while others may be going to small programs in someone else's home. Some whose parents do not require care during a full working day can sleep a little later before leaving for their part-day program. Still others, because of affluence or parental choice, may remain in their own homes to be cared for by someone hired for child care.

All of these children participate in situations that fall into our definition of early childhood education programs. Those who become teachers and caregivers of young children can choose to work in a variety of settings and with children in several distinctly different developmental phases. In this chapter we shall examine the many facets and faces of early childhood education.

OBJECTIVES

After studying this chapter, students should be able to:

1. define early childhood education.

2. describe what is meant by various terminologies used to designate kinds of programs and populations served in the early years.

3. explain the factors in families and society that currently impact on early childhood education.

Primary: The first years of elementary school, often reckoned to be kindergarten through grade three, or sometimes five.

EARLY CHILDHOOD EDUCATION DEFINED

Let's start by meeting some individuals currently working in the field of early education.

Towanda K. is an assistant teacher in a class of four-year-olds at the local Head Start program, which uses classroom space in a large church in the community. In this same church, Chrissy P. works in the child care program as a floater, substituting in all of the classrooms as she is needed. This means that some days she is working with infants as young as six weeks, and other days with two-year-olds, three-year-olds, and so on, since the program includes children from infancy up to kindergarten age. The church also sponsors a part-day nursery school program, in which Rachel F. teaches three-year-olds. Some babies come just one day a week, for the Mom's Day Out program.

Down the street, there is a large center operated by a national child care chain that cares for children of these same ages. The center also offers before- and after-school care for children through twelve years of age who ride the school bus from the center to their elementary school, and who return at 2:30 p.m. Michael D. works with the oldest children in this program. When he leaves work, he goes to pick up his two-year-old niece to take her home. She spends her days with Maureen P., who operates a small family child care program for five toddlers in her home, including her own child.

The last early educators to meet are Kathy M., who teaches a kindergarten-first grade combination in the local elementary school, and her sister Traci, who teaches a small group of children ages two to four in a program for children with developmental delays (see Fig. 2-1).

Since every one of these teachers whom you have just met works in the field of early childhood education, this suggests that this term is quite inclusive of a variety of educational programs. Let us examine this current definition of early childhood education to see the scope of the term. NAEYC defines early childhood education as inclusive of:

National Association for the Education of Young Children (NAEYC): Largest early childhood professional organization established in 1926. Current membership over 90,000. Source of position statements on Developmentally Appropriate Practice, Code of Ethics, etc.

Early Childhood Education: Also early education. The variety of education and care settings that exist for children from infancy through at least eight years of age.

Figure 2-1   **Early education includes teachers who work in settings as different as these two classrooms. (Courtesy of Tracie O'Hara)**

1826
Friedrich Froebel writes *Education of Man,* describing the kindergarten system.

any part- or full-day group program in a center, school, or home that serves children from birth through age 8, including children with special developmental and learning needs. This definition includes programs in child care centers, both for-profit and nonprofit; private and public kindergarten programs; Head Start programs; family child care; and kindergartens, primary grades, and before- and after-school programs in elementary schools. These programs are operated under a variety of auspices and rely upon different funding systems, different regulatory structures, and different mechanisms to prepare and certify individuals to work with young children from birth through age 8 (*Young Children,* 1994, p. 69).

While this offers us a sense of the variety of structures encompassed by the term "early childhood education," it is by no means exhaustive. For example, does family child care include a recent graduate of an associate degree program in early childhood education, whose first employment was as a nanny jointly shared by two professional couples, and who cared for two children from one family and one from the other, in the home of one of the families? Or what about the after-school care not offered in an elementary school, but available for the elementary-aged child who takes the school bus to a family child care home that is also attended by four preschoolers and one baby?

THEORY INTO PRACTICE

This is Pansey Borden. After a career in banking, Pansey decided to return to college to prepare to teach young children. She has been a Head Start teacher for five years. After becoming a Model/Mentor teacher, this year she has advanced to become Education Assistant/Trainer for Head Start, while beginning to work on a graduate degree.

What has been a significant frustration for you in early education? How do you deal with it?

It is frustrating for me when I am unable to stimulate the involvement of parents in the thrilling discoveries of their children.

What is one thing you learned in classes that you really discovered to be true when you started working with children?

It is really true that play offers a natural way for children to learn, and I enjoy playing with my children.

What is an area you are working on now to learn more about?

I am working on enhancing my skills and knowledge in the area of diversity.

Why have you stayed in early education?

I have stayed in early education to share the excitement and wonder of the learning adventures of children.

What is a comment or piece of advice you would give to those beginning to work in early childhood education?

My piece of advice to beginning teachers is, don't worry if you can't answer all their questions, because the children will love you anyway.

I like unpredictability and variation; I like drama and I like gaiety; I like peace in the world and I like interesting people, and all this means that I like life in its organic shape, and that's just what you get in an infant room

–Sylvia Ashton-Warner

Infants: Children from birth through the first year of life.

Toddlers: Children from the time they become independently mobile (about age one) through their third year (age three).

Preschoolers: Generally refers to children from ages three to five years.

Primary-Aged Children: Children in kindergarten through third grade.

Temperament: Inborn characteristic ways of behaving.

Cooing: The first open vowel sounds made by infants, generally beginning around two months.

Babbling: Combinations of vowel and consonant sounds made by infants from three to twelve months.

No doubt you and your fellow students can think of other unique configurations within your own community experience. What the definition does convey, however, is the concept that the term "early childhood education" includes various care structures that meet individual needs for different families with children who are babes in arms, to those who have already achieved some permanent teeth and are deeply into reading, math, and softball. It is also obvious that it is important to include the concept of "care" when defining early childhood education.

In a later chapter, we will uncover the historical roots of early childhood programs that were derived from both education and social welfare concerns, and that defined a need for young children to receive care outside of their families. All good programs for young children provide educational activities to encourage children's skill development, and the care to assist children with personal routines in safe, healthy, and nurturing environments (see Fig. 2-2). This joint function of early childhood programs does not fully reflect the term "early childhood education." However, this definition helps us see that we must think broadly when we consider the topic.

In this chapter, we will take this definition apart phrase by phrase, to increase our recognition of the designations commonly used. We will begin with considering the separate populations who are designated by the definition, and with whom you could choose to work. In later courses, you will study the stages of development and have opportunities to observe children of various ages, and you will discover in detail the typical specific characteristics of **infants, toddlers, preschoolers**, and **primary-aged children**. This discussion is thus a brief introduction to begin thinking about your choices.

DEVELOPMENTAL STAGES IN EARLY CHILDHOOD

Infancy

As you will notice from the Timeline, currently in the United States, a majority of mothers of infants return to work before their babies have reached their first birthday. Many return to the job after only a few *weeks* of maternity leave. Infancy includes the period from birth until the baby begins to walk—generally about the first year of life. During this time, infants show a unique **temperament** and move from relative helplessness to become increasingly social, vocal, and mobile creatures, actively exploring the world around them. They begin life weighing only a few pounds, after enormous growth in the nine months before birth. By their first birthday, they have tripled their birthweight—a rate of growth never again to be duplicated. From the blank stares they direct towards everything and everyone at first, they develop strong and definite preferences for a few special people who are rewarded with large, delighted grins of excited recognition whenever these few people appear. From only a cry, they produce infinite varieties of **cooing** and **babbling** sounds, and then work on first words. From being barely able to lift their heads, they develop amazing control over their small bodies—rolling, sitting, scooting, and standing—and can maneuver even the smallest object to their

1836

Massachusetts passes the first child labor law (seldom enforced) in the United States, prohibiting children under 15 from working in factory mills unless they had three months of schooling in the previous year.

Figure 2-2 There are aspects of both care of physical needs, and routines and education for skill development in early childhood education. (Courtesy of Tracie O'Hara)

mouths for further exploration (see Fig. 2-3). Infancy amazes us with its rapid development. When we have not seen a baby for a week or so, we will notice new feats and accomplishments.

But all of this marvelous growth does not occur in a vacuum. Infants grow because of their relationships with caregivers (Honig, 1993). Indeed, without caring adults, infants fail to grow and thrive physically and every other way. At the very beginning of their lives, these youngest children depend on adults to care for them, from the most basic cleaning and changing of their soiled diapers and frequent feedings, to changing their positions and soothing their distress. But beyond the meeting of physical needs, babies depend on adults to help them feel loved and secure, to feel predictable responses, and see joyful faces. They need adults who won't hesitate to give them "dominion over their bodies" (the phrase is from Alice S. Honig) as they form strong and trusting **attachments**. They need adults who touch them and talk to them with respect, and who know each child's style and preference in interaction. They need adults who realize infants' needs for **sensory** stimulation and interesting objects to explore safely. These adults know that babies are learning every moment, through every interaction and encounter.

Infant caregivers are in the very special position of being able to support the new family unit, as parents and babies adapt and respond to each other in what will become lasting attachments. They adapt to differences in need and style of babies and adults, creating a warm and secure environment. The unending tasks of physical care and routines are seen as meaningful opportunities for personal contact (see Fig. 2-4), rather than jobs to be hurried through. Infant caregivers know that the **curriculum** of infancy is embedded within such daily encounters, filled with sensory stimulation, language, and predictable patterns. This is not just baby-sitting, but laying important foundations.

Listen to the words of Maria, an infant caregiver:

Attachment: A major developmental task of infancy. Attachment refers to the forming of strong, mutual, affectionate relationships between adults and infants, enduring over time.

Sensory: Using any or all of the five senses. A primary method of learning about the world in early childhood.

Curriculum: Every learning experience that happens in the classroom, including planned and spontaneous activities and interactions.

1837
First public normal school is established in Lexington, Massachusetts.

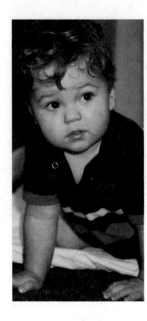

Figure 2-3   **Infants develop amazing control over their bodies during the first few months.**

This job is more than changing diapers. I think it's the base for these little babies. When they grow up, they will have a good feeling, a base of love. They will have something to give. They shouldn't start with problems. They should start with love and good care. They have to start with something positive. For them it is a hard problem if we do nothing but just change their diapers and feed them and didn't care about them. They're not going to have anything, not even if they're clean and if they're fed. They're not going to have anything to give, because it's nothing. It's not a base (p. 85).

I think I am doing something good for people, little people. I feel satisfied with my work because I love it and I'm trying to do my best. I think I'm doing something for these kids. Someday they are going to be grown up. They are going to have had something in their life when they were little, even though they'll never know me when they're grown. But I know I give this love when they need it, because their parents are working and cannot be with them the whole day. Nobody is going to notice, not even the babies, because they're so little. They're going to forget about me. But I know I give this love for them. That is something really nice for me to know. [1]

Read more about Maria and her work with infants in *Scenes from Day Care,* by Elizabeth Balliett Platt (1991).

Toddlerhood

There is an exuberant energy that flows from toddlers, little ones in their second and third years of life. Having discovered the freedom that comes with independent mobility and the dawn of language, toddlers seem bent on learning about everything in their small worlds, firsthand, and indeed, taking control of it. They are in nearly constant motion, as they walk, run, jump, climb, throw, dump, and drag large objects around with them. Power is an important issue with them, as they struggle to do things for themselves, to climb to new heights (quite literally), and to test every new ability they acquire. Without many words to express their needs, wants, and large plans—at least until quite late in toddlerhood—this can be a time of violent frustrations for these small children. Toddler temper tantrums have received quite a lot of bad press. With social skills and self-control still to be acquired, and with absolutely no sense of sophisticated concepts like property ownership, it is not surprising that toddlers

I believe there's no time in life when stability is more important than it is in early infancy. That's because there's no time, either, when the world is so new, so unfamiliar, seeming to change so constantly, and no time when we as infants have so little experience to bring to its understanding. Fortunate infants find the stability they need in the constancy of a face, the face of a constant caregiver

—Fred Rogers

---

[1] From *Scenes from Day Care: How Teachers Teach and What Children Learn* (p. 87), by Elizabeth Balliett Platt, 1991, New York, NY: Teachers College Press. Copyright 1991 by Teachers College Press. Used with permission.

1837
Friedrich Froebel establishes the first kindergarten (children's garden) for children ages three to six years in Blankenburg, Germany.

Figure 2-4	**The curriculum of infancy is embedded in meaningful encounters during routine caregiving.**

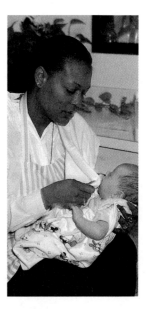

frequently run headlong into conflict with other people around them. There is exasperation from others who expect more signs of civilization, when toddlers rise to their hind-legs and begin to appear less babylike.

Having a group of individuals with like interests and characteristics together in the same room keeps toddler teachers busy safeguarding the rights and needs of all. It is the toddlers' limitations in thinking and understanding, as well as their indifference to the needs and wishes of others, that creates such challenges for teachers who constantly make decisions to strike a delicate balance (see Fig. 2-5): how to keep curious toddlers safe from physical dangers without thwarting their powerful curiosity; how to encourage independent exploration while recognizing that others will want to have the same opportunities (see Fig. 2-6); how to keep children who are continually on the move from literally bumping into each other; how to maintain necessary and realistic limits, recognizing that toddlers cannot yet control their own actions. And perhaps, most important, teachers must determine how to provide an environment rich with active learning possibilities and language, matched with the toddler style of learning on the move, without being tempted to "dribble down" to the second and third year the more organized group learning experiences traditional in the preschool or kindergarten.

This is indeed teaching, but as Dr. Burton White once called it, it is "teaching on the fly." Those who teach toddlers must have special skills and be thoroughly grounded in developmental understanding of toddlerhood tasks and abilities. Curriculum includes developing the important concept that "Mom will come back and that I can control my feelings of sadness when she leaves," learning to manipulate utensils at the lunch table, managing the whole bathroom process (see Fig. 2-7), and fitting giant pegs into the pegboard, as well as learning where to put them back on the shelf when the teacher sings the cleanup song. Discovering and delighting in personal competence is the learning that toddler teachers support.

A toddler teacher puts it this way:

> A teacher of toddlers . . . is mostly a mother substitute. By that I mean that what's important to very young kids is to be loved, to be safe, to be cared for, and that's what I do. The toddler curriculum is a curriculum of love and play. Those first months of being away from your parents can be terribly difficult, and we try to tune in to each individual child, to learn from them, to understand them so that we can help them discover that they are safe and known and cared for here. Then they can go about being with other kids, finding their friends as well as the materials that will interest and encourage them, because they are confident that this is their private space to be in, and that the adults here are their trusted friends (p. 24).

Children learn to care by experiencing good care
—James Hymes

1848

Interest in kindergartens is growing in Germany. Forty-four kindergartens are opened this year.

Figure 2-5   The challenge for toddler caregivers is to allow freedom for safe exploration, to avoid thwarting their strong curiosity.

Figure 2-6   Toddlers need opportunities for independent learning, without bumping into each other. (Courtesy of Tracie O'Hara)

Figure 2-7 **Learning to manage the bathroom process is a serious learning task for toddlers.**

In some ways I guess this is a hard age to be in a group, Anna says later. They're all so self-centered. But in other ways this is a good time to learn about others in relation to yourself. Alessia may bite or hit or push. We say, 'No, you can't do that. It hurts!' We comfort the victim and may involve Alessia in comforting too. But then when she's hit or pushed, we say and do the same things. We show each kid respect and even-handedness. Over time they see that we insist on a safe, happy environment for everyone and that we demand respect and fairness for each one" (p. 31).

"It's exhausting work," admits Anna. "But it's much more emotionally draining than physically exhausting because you have to be tuned in to some very important and basic human needs all the time. I try to keep things in perspective, to remind myself to focus on the kids themselves.²

Read more about Anna and her teaching of toddlers in William Ayers' *The Good Preschool Teacher,* 1989.

Preschoolers

When we encounter preschoolers, those three-, four-, and five-year-old children who are busy in the worlds of **imaginative play**, **creative art**, and

First grade need not be a black cloud that darkens all the days that precede it. Nor must children's essential nature be exploited in order to make intellectual gains, social gains, emotional gains or physical gains
—James Hymes

Imaginative Play: Also called dramatic play. The spontaneous pretend and fantasy play typical of preschool children.

Creative Art: Open-ended art, where children are free to select their materials, and use them to express their own ideas, without patterns or directions from an adult.

---

²From *The Good Preschool Teacher* (p 28), by William Ayers, 1989, New York, NY: Teachers College Press. Used with permission.

1854
New York Nursery and Children's Hospital is established. Called the "Nursery for the Children of Poor Women in New York City", this is recognized as the first child care program in the United States.

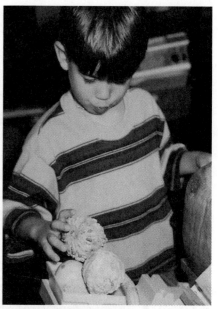

Figure 2-8	**Preschoolers are busy in the worlds of imaginative play, creative art, and discovery learning. (Courtesy of Connie Glass and Christie Shamel)**

Discovery Learning: The active learning where children construct their own understandings of the world through manipulation of materials and interaction with others.

discovery learning (see Fig. 2-8), we see what most of us have considered to be early childhood education—although as we are now seeing, this term encompasses far more than the blocks and dress-up clothes we may have more narrowly associated with the term before this chapter. Preschoolers, now adept with the language and their own physical skills, are truly ready for the social encounters and play with other children that form the base of active learning in their classroom and group experiences. (Preschoolers who have had limited

1856

Margarethe Schurz, a student of Froebel's, begins a small German language kindergarten for six children in her home in Watertown, Wisconsin.

play experiences up to this point may still start by exploring and playing alone before they move to playing with others.) Friendships now become meaningful and important, although they are often filled with the quick disagreements that occur when children are learning how to play with others such as, "You can't come to my birthday!" Learning occurs through interaction with other children and with materials, all carefully supported by adults. Such experiences help preschool children continue to construct an expanded understanding of their world (see Fig. 2-9).

Literally everything in the world is of intense interest to preschoolers, depending on the breadth of exposure they receive at home and at school. They may discuss knowledgeably subjects such as dinosaurs, weather, faraway places, and exotic animals, or more close-to-home topics like family and neighborhood crises and events. It is only when close attention is paid to these conversations that adults understand how far removed from logic preschoolers' understandings and concepts still are. Preschoolers are caught up in the wonderful excitement of actively learning about this world, its actions, interactions, and infinite possibilities, and to be a classroom teacher with them is to share this energetic excitement.

Preschoolers are working on developing a "sense of **initiative**," to use a term you'll learn more about later: a feeling of competence and confidence in their abilities. Their classroom world must provide opportunities to initiate (see Fig. 2-10).

Another **developmental task** of the preschool years is to become skillful at **self-help skills**; things like dressing, toileting, and caring for personal hygiene. Play is the absolute medium for initiation and exploration by these

> *It is all too easy for us adults to forget just how inexperienced infants and young children really are and how much they have to learn about the world that we have already conceptualized and now take for granted*
>
> —David Elkind

Initiative: The energy and ideas to undertake action. Initiative is a developmental task of the preschool years, so preschoolers need opportunities to initiate some of their activities.

Developmental Task: The accomplishments and learnings that are appropriate for a particular stage in development.

Self-Help Skills: Those skills children learn to care for their own personal and physical needs.

Figure 2-9   **Interaction with other children is an important method of learning for preschoolers.**

1860
Elizabeth Peabody begins the first English language kindergarten in Boston with 30 children.

Figure 2-10   **Preschool children are active learners, highly motivated when they select their own tasks and interactions. (Courtesy of Connie Glass)**

Abstract: Related to purely cognitive thinking, rather than related to concrete objects or experience.

youngsters. Preschool teachers are not fooled by the verbal facility and ready store of information of young children, and they do not believe that they should offer more **abstract** academic lessons. They know that during these years children's active involvement with materials and other people will allow them to continue to fine-tune their understandings and build their basic concepts, and that these foundations must not be rushed through. Preschool classrooms offer children attractive varieties of materials carefully chosen and arranged by teachers to help children move along in their activities and interests. Teachers plan events—"Happenings," to use James Hymes' description—that capture interest, involvement, and attention. They help children see connections between their experiences that start to make sense to them. They offer children unhurried blocks of time to build, create, construct, work, imagine, and talk, in a supportive atmosphere that values these undertakings. They see children as active learners, following highly motivated paths of learning, and benefiting from teachers who act as **facilitators** of their individual interests and needs.

Facilitator: One who supports and encourages learning. Early childhood teachers function as facilitators by commenting, questioning, reinforcing, providing materials and encouragement.

This image of the preschool teacher may dispel the stereotypical image of a teacher as a teller, a dispenser of information, a director of all classroom learning experiences, and the constant center of attention at the front of the room. Indeed, in a preschool classroom (as in good early education classrooms for all ages) there is no front of the classroom, but a busy swirl of activity that circles and fills the room. This is by no means to suggest that preschool teachers merely supervise unorganized chaos, but rather that the active nature of children's learning through play dictates teacher behaviors that are frequently less obvious than the traditional teaching roles. But these roles are far more comprehensive than this brief outline suggests, and will be discussed in more detail in Chapter Four. Rather than focusing on the purely cognitive aspects of learning associated with

1860
Child population of the United States is 17 million.

Figure 2-11   **Active learning experiences in kindergarten and the early primary years are just as important as they are for preschoolers.**

much later education, preschool teachers are concerned with the whole child. They recognize that development is indeed integrated and interrelated, and that it is an error to concentrate on only one aspect of the child.

A question may arise in your mind as you think about these play experiences for preschool children. We have defined preschoolers developmentally as three-, four-, and five-year-olds. Yet in the United States at this time, most five-year-olds are in **kindergarten** programs, that are supported with public education funds, usually located and integrated in elementary schools, and increasingly subjected to academic methods and requirements. (Indeed, increasing numbers of three- and four-year-olds are enrolled in similarly funded and located programs.) Their teachers are frequently leading them through many activities that are planned around traditional skill and drill, and teacher-directed learning. In many cases, this is to ensure that preschoolers can perform acceptably when they take the **standardized tests** at the end of the year. As you learn more about quality early education, you will discover how far from appropriate such widespread practices of **early academics** are, and the profession's recommendations that the early primary years maintain the continuity in active learning style discussed as appropriate for preschoolers (see Fig. 2-11).

Hear how a preschool teacher views her function of facilitating the development of the whole child:

> When someone asks me what I do, and I answer that I am a teacher of four-year-olds, I sometimes get the response: "What on

Kindergartens: Programs for five-year-olds, now generally operated in every school system, and originated by Frederick Froebel.

Standardized Tests: Assessment techniques with results that have been accumulated for large groups of children, producing standards or norms for evaluating children's successful learning.

Early Academics: The introduction of academic content and teaching methods to children before the primary grades.

The emphasis of our educational approach is placed not so much upon the child in an abstract sense, but on each child in relation to other children, teachers, parents, his or her own history, and the societal and cultural surroundings

–Carlina Rinaldi

earth can you teach them?" Many years ago I would have answered by describing some of the science projects or work with art materials I did with children. Now it is different. I feel more secure in my own position: I tell them what I really do. I teach children about the world they live in, about themselves, and their peers. And I teach children about adults, trust, and love. I work with attitudes. I hope to inspire a love of learning. This is what I teach. . . . I want children to know themselves and feel good about what they know. I want children to recognize that there are areas in which they need to grow. I want children to learn to express themselves, but I accept the fact that some are not able to do that yet and are still fighting the world with their fists. I want children to come to terms with themselves, whatever those terms may be. I want to help each child accomplish these things through my caring. . . .

I want children to know their teacher, to know her as a friend. I want children to know that adults are there to help them grow, to set limits, and to protect them. I want children to know that when they are sad or troubled, there is always a lap for them to climb on and receive comfort. I want children to know that nursery school is now a big part of their world and that they are an important part of this world. I want children to know that this is where they are supposed to be and that Mommy and Daddy want them to be here. I want children to know that next year they will be in a different place and that they will be ready to leave here and move on to kindergarten. This is what I teach. This is the hidden curriculum.[3]

Read more about Carol Hillman's ideas about teaching preschool children in her book, *Teaching Four-Year-Olds: A Personal Journey* (1988).

Primary Schoolers

Decode: Process of making sense out of letters and numbers.

Most of us remember our first experiences in "big school": the days spent sitting at desks, working through the tasks in workbooks and on the blackboard, struggling to **decode** the complexities of word recognition and math skills. When you visit primary classrooms today, you may find children engaged in settings and activities that do not look or sound much different from your memories. The teacher may spend much of the morning working with reading groups, while frequently reminding those working at their desks that they have work to do and are getting too noisy.

But you may find other classrooms where children are busy in small groups or individually, some sitting on the floor, others at tables or desks. You may hear quiet conversations or active debates about joint projects. You may see some working at activity centers on assigned tasks, others quietly reading, some drawing. When you look for the teacher, you may find him/her talking

---

[3]From Hillman, Carol B. *Teaching Four-Year-Olds: A Personal Journey.* Bloomington, Ind: Phi Delta Kappa, 1988. Used with permission.

1863

First American kindergarten text–*The Moral Culture of Infancy and Kindergarten*–is published by Elizabeth Peabody and her sister, Mary Mann, wife of Horace Mann.

Figure 2-12 **School-aged children become very interested in peers, and in developing literacy skills.**

with an individual child, working with a small group, or observing the work of several others. You may discover that children are choosing which task to do first, how and where to do it, and which friends to work with. You will notice that several things seem to be very important to this age-group: interacting with **peers** has become a major interest; becoming competent at the academic skills defined as important by society, parents, and teachers is compelling; the wider world is also of interest (see Fig. 2-12).

Later in the morning you may sit in on a class discussion where children are considering the fairness of classroom rules and the logical consequences of breaking them. During the morning when a conflict had arisen, you had noticed the teacher mediating as the children were brought together to discuss solutions.

The differences between primary classrooms derive from the debates and discussions about developmentally appropriate practice and teaching methods, about which you will read more in Chapters Three and Nine.

But for many primary-aged children, this classroom is not the only place they will spend their time today, with a teacher and as a member of a peer group. Because there may not be anyone at home who can supervise the child's care in the hours before and after school, many children may be enrolled in a **school-aged child care** program that provides both care and a variety of enrichment activities. (Unfortunately, a majority of school-aged children with working parents are "**latchkey**" children, caring for themselves in the hours before and after school.) School-age child care programs may be provided by the school system itself, employing certified teachers and assistants, in which case the program seems more like a continuation of the school day. They may also be provided by a variety of community agencies with interest in supporting child and family

Peers: Those who are age-mates or equals.

School-Aged Child Care: The provision of before- and/or after-school care for primary-aged children whose parents' work schedules necessitate care beyond the hours of the typical schoolday. Sometimes held under school system auspices, sometimes under for-profit or other nonprofit auspices.

Latchkey: Term used to refer to school-aged children who are under their own supervision in the hours before and after school.

1870
There are 10 German language kindergartens and one English language kindergarten in the United States.

needs, such as local churches or Y programs. Some for-profit programs also arrange for children to be part of their overall child care program.

Teachers of primary-aged children have many challenges in providing for the individual educational needs of a large group of children. Hear about one elementary school teacher's response to the many demands on her:

> Sometimes, at such moments, feeling altogether calm, Chris would think, "In my next life, I'm coming back as an air-traffic controller." But there was always a child somewhere in the room waiting for her. . . . Chris felt them waiting around her. She thought how much fun it would be to sit for a long time with Judith and discuss her novel. She glanced at the clock, up on the wall above the closets. Its minute hand stood still. She had a few minutes before science. But the minute hand was one of those which stored up time and then sprang the news on her all at once. It leaped. She absolutely had to help poor Pedro. "Slow learner" was the kindly term for many of these children. It implied what she knew to be true, that they *could* learn, but she also knew that in this time-bound world, a slow learner might not learn at all if she didn't hurry up. And if she didn't hurry, she wouldn't get to keep her promise to Arabella, who was waiting patiently for Chris to help her fix up her story about becoming a hairdresser someday.
>
> Usually Chris could manage to keep most of them busy, but that was pure engineering. They always had time on their hands, and she never had much to spare (pp. 38-9).
>
> Classroom management, as Mrs. Zajac practiced it, required an enlargement of sense. By now Chris could tell, without seeing, not only that a child was running on the stairs but also that the footfalls belonged to Clarence, and she could turn her attention to curing one child's confusion and still know that Clarence was whispering threats to Arabella, (p. 115).
>
> Even the most troubled children had attractive qualities for Chris. Even the most toughened, she always felt, wanted to please her and wanted her to like them, no matter how perversely they expressed it. She belonged among schoolchildren. They made her confront sorrow and injustice. They made her feel useful. Again this year, some had needed more help than she could provide. There were many problems that she hadn't solved. But it wasn't for lack of trying. She hadn't given up. She had run out of time.[4]

For a look at Chris Zajac's whole year as an elementary school teacher, read *Among Schoolchildren,* by Tracy Kidder, (1989).

Having looked at the major developmental divisions in early childhood education, let us now consider some of the other facets of our definition.

Everything I need to know I learned in kindergarten
—Robert Fulghum

---

[4]From *Among Schoolchildren* (p. 331), by Tracy Kidder, 1989, Boston, MA: Houghton Mifflin Co. Reprinted with permission. All rights reserved.

1871

Milton Bradley Company manufactures Froebel's gifts and occupations, becoming the first commercial company to sell materials for kindergartens.

Figure 2-13 **Children with special needs due to physical impairment likely need modification to their learning environments.**

SPECIAL DEVELOPMENTAL AND LEARNING NEEDS

The uniqueness of human development of all individuals is documented and accepted. Individual differences are created by variations in inherited potential and characteristics, and in environmental stimulation, experiences, and supports. In later coursework, you will study the basic principles and guidelines for recognizing typical development during various periods in early childhood. This will be helpful to you both in planning curriculum and teaching strategies for various age-groups, and in recognizing where children's development and learning lies beyond typical **norms**. When children's development and learning does not fit within the broad averages for **age-level norms** typical behavior and functioning that are called norms, they are said to have **special needs**.

For many reasons, which may include physical impairment, physical **disability**, or illness, cognitive functioning or limitation, or social-emotional conditions, young children may need special modification or care in their learning environments (see Fig. 2-13). They also may need the services of members of a team of professionals with specialized training, in addition to teachers. This team may include physical and occupational therapists, speech diagnosticians and therapists, psychologists, and so on. Parents today frequently have an array of available choices for the education and care of their children with special

Norm: An average or typical standard of development, derived from median or averages of research data.

Age-Level Norm: Behaviors or abilities typically associated with average or median numbers of children of a particular age.

Special Needs: When development and learning does not follow typical patterns, individuals are said to have special needs for intervention with modifications in the environment or teaching techniques to help them develop optimally.

Disability: Limitation, whether physical, mental, or emotional.

1871
First public kindergarten in North America is established in Ontario, Canada.

Home-Based Care: Program where services are delivered to children and families within their own home.

needs. These may range from professional support for **home-based care**, to specialized residential or day schools that concentrate on working with particular needs, to inclusion within programs for typically developing children. Thus, for example, a three-year-old who is hearing impaired may spend his days at home, with a sign language teacher coming in once a week to work with him and his parents, or in a part-day program for hearing impaired children, or in a classroom with children who hear normally, with an audiologist advising his teachers on techniques to work with him specifically.

Since the passage of PL94-142, the Education for all Handicapped Children Act in 1975 that guaranteed services for three- to five-year-olds, (see Timeline) and the Amendments in 1986 (PL99-457) that extended services from birth through age three, children from birth through age six have been guaranteed free public educational services in the "least restrictive environment." Generally, there is a national trend to decrease the number of specialized, isolated learning environments for children with special needs.

Mainstreaming: Placement of individuals with special needs within classrooms with typically developing individuals. This term is now less frequently used than *inclusion.*

Inclusion: Placement of individuals with special needs within classrooms with typically developing individuals, with special services provided within the classroom setting.

Special Education: Branch of professional study that centers on techniques of working with children with special needs.

What this has meant is that increasing numbers of children whose developmental functioning and learning needs may be far from typical are appearing in classrooms with children developing without the same challenges. At first called **mainstreaming**, now more usually called **inclusion**, this occurence has increased the diversity of children within many early childhood classrooms. Diversity is indeed an important current issue that we will discuss more fully in Chapter Eleven, but here we should note that the inclusion of children with special needs offers benefits for them and their families, as well as for children whose development follows more predictable patterns (see Fig. 2-14). And for teachers working with children who have special needs, there are also benefits as well as challenges. Some of the professionals working with these children have been prepared by specialized coursework and degrees in **Special Education**. But more frequently, early childhood teachers find themselves in need of additional support and training when learning to best meet the needs of these individual children. There is little doubt that the pattern of inclusion will mean that most early childhood teachers will at some point work with individual children who need specific adaptations and assistance. We will talk more about inclusion in Chapter Eleven.

KINDS OF PROGRAMS

Looking back at our original definition of early childhood education, we can see that we need to consider what is meant by a number of terms that describe the structure of different programs. Programs may be described by words that indicate: the length of time that children are cared for; the funding system for the programs; the specific populations served by the programs; and the specific focus, philosophy, and/or location of the program services.

Length of Time of Program

Part-Day: Refers to programs for children that only operate for a half-day, or for only several days a week.

Part-day programs offer educational and care programs to children for several hours, rather than during a full day. These programs also may not

Figure 2-14 **There are benefits for all when children with special needs are included in early childhood classrooms. (Courtesy of Christie Shamel)**

function during a full week, as for example a group of three-year-olds who come for classes from nine until noon, on Monday, Wednesday, and Friday mornings. Frequently, though not always, the parents of these children may not be working full-time, so they do not require care such as meals, naptime, and so on. The usual purpose of these programs is to offer stimulation, activities, and group experiences to help the children develop optimally. Many of these programs have their roots in the history of early nursery school or kindergarten education. Programs that are created to offer interventional stimulation for children whose later educational success is considered to be **at-risk**, and for children with particular special needs, also frequently operate on a part-day basis.

Full-day programs are generally offered to serve the needs of parents who work outside their homes and thus need supplemental care for their children during a full work day of eight hours or more. Many full-day programs operate from early morning—6:30 or 7:00 a.m., for example—until 6:00 p.m. or later, to allow parents to leave their children, put in their full work day, and include time to return to the center for pick-up. Many states require programs to contract with parents for specific hours, limiting the number of hours that a child may have care in a day to nine or ten. It should also be noted that some child care programs that serve particular corporations, hospitals, or businesses may operate several shifts of child care to accommodate needs of parents who work at times other than during the day. Some programs also operate on a full-day basis because of the transportation and organizational needs involved. Centers that operate on a full-day basis usually have staff scheduled to work at staggered times, to provide adequate coverage over the full period (see Fig. 2-15).

At-Risk: Concern about developmental delay due to negative environmental conditions or physical conditions.

Full-Day Programs: Programs that provide care for children through an entire day, including meals and sleep arrangements.

1873
Elizabeth Peabody establishes the journal *Kindergarten Messenger.*

Figure 2-15 **Parents who work require full-day care for their children, including meals and nap-time. (Courtesy of Tracie O'Hara)**

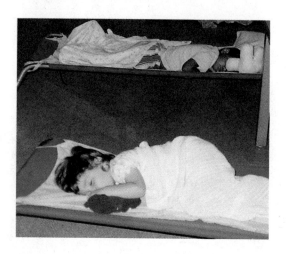

Funding Systems

For-Profit: Also call proprietary. Early childhood programs that are established with the goal of earning profit for the owners.

For-profit centers, also called proprietary centers, are established to provide specific child care services while the owners and managers aim to earn income from the business. Probably at least half of the nation's child care programs are for-profit, ranging from large chains that may operate hundreds of centers nationally or regionally (see Fig. 2-16), to local owners who may own only one center. There is enormous variation in the kinds of services offered, from care for infants and toddlers, to before- and after-school care, summer camps, and enrichment programs. There is also wide variation in the quality for children and working conditions for staff, as generally reflected in the typically much higher poor rating on programs, staff-child ratios, and higher **staff turnover** rate in for-profit centers (Doherty-Derkowski, 1995, pp. 102-106), with obvious exceptions to be found in many communities.

Staff Turnover: Refers to the rate at which practitioners leave their place of employment and seek other work.

A current trend is for proprietarial centers to contract with business and industry to operate employer-sponsored or on-site child care. The sheer visibility of these centers is often improving the quality of the programs. "Advocates of for-profit care claim that their dependence on parent satisfaction forces them to manage efficiently and to be especially responsive to child and parent needs" (Kagan and Newton, 1989, p. 4). Another kind of care that obviously comes under the heading of for-profit includes family child care homes. These will be dicussed more fully later in this chapter.

Nonprofit: Early childhood programs that are subsidized by government or agency funds, where any surplus funds are used for program improvements.

Nonprofit centers include the many thousands run by churches and other organizations or corporations within the community, to support family needs and welfare. These programs frequently receive free or subsidized space from the sponsoring agencies, thus reducing their costs and permitting budgetary expenditures for needed materials. Many are also eligible for some kinds of government funding. A significant number of NAEYC accredited centers are non-profit centers.

Prekindergarten: Term usually applied to publicly supported programs for children younger than five years of age.

Other programs that are nonprofit include those run exclusively with public funds, either local, state, or federal. These would include programs such as kindergartens and **prekindergartens** sponsored by school systems, Head Start

— The Exchange Top 100 —
The Nation's Largest Early Childhood Organizations

Organization	Type	Headquarters	CEO	Capacity*	Centers*
KinderCare Learning Centers	NC	Montgomery, AL	Tull Gearreald, Jr.	180,000	1,200
La Petite Academy	NC	Overland Park, KS	Robert Rodriguez	100,000	792
Children's World Learning Centers	NC	Golden, CO	Duane Larson	66,500	500
Children's Discovery Centers	NC	San Rafael, CA	Richard Niglio	21,000	215
Children's Services—Head Start	HS	Chicago, IL	Virginia Williams	20,000	370
Los Angeles County Office of Education	HS	Cerritos, CA	Andrew Kennedy	19,226	344
Agency for Child Development—Head Start	HS	Brooklyn, NY	Richard Gonzales	19,000	175
Childtime Childcare Inc.	NC	Farmington, Hills, MI	Harold Lewis	18,750	150
Tutor Time Learning Centers	FR	Fort Lauderdale, FL	Michael Weissman	13,000	65
YMCA of Greater Houston	YC	Houston, TX	Bill Phillips	10,500	217
Novel Education Dynamics Inc.	NC	Media, PA	A.J. Clegg	10,012	72
Primrose Schools	FR	Cartersville, GA	Paul Erwin	7,440	48
Kids 'R Kids International	FR	Norcross, GA	Pat Vinson	7,410	39
Bright Horizons Children's Center	EM	Cambridge, MA	Roger Brown	7,285	79
Neighborhood Services Head Start	HS	Detroit, MI	Carolyn Gray	6,833	101
Corporate Child Care Management Services	EM	Nashville, TN	Marguerite Sallee	6,401	48
East Coast Migrant Head Start	HS	Arlington, VA	Geraldine O'Brien	6,237	89
New Horizons Child Care	RC	Plymouth, MN	Susan Dunkley	5,957	48
CEO Head Start	HS	Cleveland, OH	Robert Moman	5,820	93
Redlands Christian Migrant Association	HS	Immokalee, FL	Barbara Mainster	5,642	65
Texas Migrant Council	HS	Laredo, TX	Oscar Villarreal	5,600	54
Gulf Coast Community Services Association	HS	Houston, TX	Ruth Marshall	5,585	58
Child Development Centers	LS	Campbell, CA	Vern Plaskett	5,300	79
YMCA of Metropolitan Dallas	YC	Dallas, TX	J. Ben Casey	4,999	87
Metro Dade CAA Head Start	HS	Miami, FL	Dorothy Davis	4,855	70
Creativity in Child Care	LS	Clearwater, FL	David Braughton	4,649	39
Creative World Schools Inc.	RC	Raytown, MO	Billie McCabe	4,100	43
Mississippi Action for Progress	HS	Jackson, MS	Bobby Brown	4,016	41
YMCA of San Antonio	YC	San Antonio, TX	Larry Crutsinger	3,933	94
The Sunshine House	RC	Greenwood, SC	Roseann and Dennis Drew	3,854	29
Out Wayne County Head Start	HS	Wayne, MI	Pat Horne McGee	3,700	23
YMCA of Greater Cincinnati	YC	Cincinnati, OH	Jerry Haralson	3,468	87
Minnieland Private Day School	RC	Woodbridge, VA	Jackie Leopold	3,465	39
Sunrise Preschools Inc.	NC	Scottsdale, AZ	James Evans	3,463	28
Children's Friend Inc.	RC	Warner Robins, GA	Dewayne Foskey	3,275	25
Young World Inc.	RC	Greensboro, NC	Robert Lennon	3,200	16
Prodigy Consulting Inc.	EM	Atlanta, GA	Gene Eidelman	3,019	17
YMCA of Greater Indianapolis	YC	Indianapolis, IN	April Nelson	3,000	102
Kama'aina Care Inc.	LS	Kailua, HI	Raymond Sanborn	3,000	25
Pinecrest Schools	RC	Sherman Oaks, CA	Donald Dye	3,000	11
Baltimore City Head Start	HS	Baltimore, MD	Carleathea Johnson	2,900	56
School District of Philadelphia	HS	Philadelphia, PA	Rosemary Mazzatenta	2,900	52
Childcare Network Inc.	RC	Columbus, GA	James Loudermilk	2,731	25
Kids at Work	EM	Troy, MI	C. Thompson Wells, Jr.	2,617	15
Bright Start Children's Centers	NC	St. Paul, MN	Jon Jacka	2,600	24
Human Development Corporation	HS	St. Louis, MO	Lois Harris	2,572	42
Greentree, Childcare by ServiceMaster	EM	Downers Grove, IL	Linda and Loren Oury	2,546	19
The Children's Courtyard	RC	Arlington, TX	Jim Mills	2,506	13
SCOPE	HS	Smithtown, NY	Leonard Kramer	2,500	50
CEDA Head Start	HS	Chicago, IL	Saundra Van	2,500	22
American Child Care Centers	RC	Tempe, AZ	John Broe	2,482	23
Action Day Nurseries/Primary Plus	LS/RC	San Jose, CA	Carole Freitas	2,300	17
Resources for Child Care Management	EM	Morristown, NJ	Robert Lurie	2,252	16
Shelby County Head Start Program	HS	Memphis, TN	Edward Mayhue	2,220	18
Mulberry Child Care Centers	EM	Needham, MA	Clark Adams	2,148	24
Storytime Learning Centers	RC	Dublin, OH	Jeffrey Roby	2,100	21
Clayton Child Care	LS	Fort Worth, TX	Frankie McMurrey	2,000	33
Jemcare Quality Childcare	RC	Fort Worth, TX	Joseph McCombs	2,000	12
The Goddard School for Early Childhood Education	FR	King of Prussia, PA	Joseph Scandone	1,885	18
Little People Day School Associates	RC	Norristown, PA	Robert Sprague	1,810	13
ECLC Learning Centers Inc.	NC	Providence, RI	Ronald Bates	1,788	12

Reprinted with permission from *Child Care Information Exchange*, P.O. Box 2890, Redmond, WA 98073, 1-800-221-2864.

Figure 2-16 **The nation's largest early childhood organizations include both for-profit and non-profit auspices.**

Largest Early Childhood Organizations Growing Again

Every year for the past nine years, **Child Care Information Exchange** has surveyed the nation to identify the 100 largest early childhood organizations (based on total licensed capacity). The 1994 listing, which appears on the following pages, includes seven types of organizations:

National for Profit Chains (NC). For all nine years of this survey, the largest four organizations have come from this category. While growth has slowed in recent years, look for a return to rapid expansion.

Head Start Organizations (HS). Nearly 20% of the nation's largest early childhood organizations derive most of their funding from the federal Head Start program. Expansion has been dramatic for the past three years.

YMCAs and YWCAs (YC) are fast becoming a major player in the early childhood world, not only in after school care but also in care for infants, toddlers, and preschoolers.

Franchise Operations (FR). For two decades, no one would touch franchising in child care. Now some of the fastest growing companies in the nation are franchisers.

Employer Focused Chains (EM). While centers operated for employers represent less than 1% of all early childhood organizations, nearly 10% of the largest organizations operate solely or primarily employer sponsored centers.

Regional For Profit Chains (RC). Still a major factor—about 20% of the largest 100 organizations are for profit chains operating in one state or metropolitan area.

Local Non Profit Systems (LS). Operated primarily, but less so recently, in the poorer neighborhoods in metropolitan areas, non profit systems represent about 10% of the 100 largest organizations, with few in the top 50.

Organization	Type	Location	Contact	Capacity	Sites
Child Care of Southwest Florida	HS	Fort Myers, FL	Rhea Mike	1,723	14
Tempe After School Enrichment Program	LS	Tempe, AZ	Jane Romatzke	1,653	18
YMCA of Metro Milwaukee Child Care Services	YC	Fox Point, WI	Karen Altman	1,590	54
YMCA of Metropolitan Washington	YC	Washington, DC	Herman Gohn	1,508	33
JCCEO Head Start	HC	Birmingham, AL	Gayle Cunningham	1,500	36
Greater Burlington YMCA	YC	Burlington, VT	Sue Luck	1,500	22
Do Re Mi Learning Centers Inc.	RC	Oak Park, MI	Lecester Allen	1,500	10
Kiddie Kare Schools Inc.	RC	Fresno, CA	Patricia Fisher	1,493	10
Rainbow Rascals Learning Center	RC	Southfield, MI	Patrick Fenton	1,440	18
Educo Inc.	RC	Reston, VA	Richard McCool	1,440	10
Creative Day Schools	RC	Greensboro, NC	Belvin Smith	1,436	8
Miami Valley Child Development Centers	HS	Dayton, OH	Marilyn Thomas	1,434	39
Summit Child Care Centers Inc.	LS	Summit, NJ	Anne Lachs	1,420	8
Kiddie Korner Day Schools	RC	Charlotte, NC	Sylvia Eagle	1,411	11
Next Generation Child Development Centers	EM	Carrollton, TX	Dr. Layton Revel	1,400	12
Lehigh Valley Child Care Inc.	LS	Allentown, PA	Judith Chase	1,396	19
Bobbie Noonan's Child Care Inc.	LS	Frankfort, IL	Roberta Noonan	1,390	12
Day Care Assocation of Montgomery County	LS	Ambler, PA	Fred Citron	1,388	20
North Kansas City Schools	LS	Kansas City, MO	Sherri Kuhn	1,392	19
Another Generation Preschool	RC	Plantation, FL	Renee Goldman	1,292	6
Tender Care Learning Centers	RC	Pittsburgh, PA	Frank Reabe	1,287	16
Enrichment Preschols Inc.	RC	Nashville, TN	Linda Tynes	1,258	9
Vermont Hills Family Life Center	LS	Portland, OR	Brenda Dengo	1,204	36
Hester's Creative Schools Inc.	RC	Greensboro, NC	Henrietta Hester Harris	1,160	7
Biederman Educational Centers	RC	Cleves, OH	Patricia Biederman	1,150	10
The Peanut Gallery	RC	Carrollton, TX	Pat Burgesser	1,146	6
Creative Child Care Inc.	RC	Hurst, TX	Gene Little	1,141	12
Child Inc.	HS	Austin, TX	James Strickland	1,136	21
Sheltering Arms Child Development	LS	Atlanta, GA	Elaine Draeger	1,130	12
Thomas Learning Centers	RC	Aurora, CO	Leon Thomas	1,125	18
Lit'l Scholar Academy	RC	Las Vegas, NV	Gary Vause	1,125	6
Children's Wonderland	RC	Agoura, CA	Debby Bitticks	1,120	6
Monroe County Community Schools	LS	Bloomington, IN	Wendy Perry	1,100	16
Children's Learning Centers of Amarillo	LS	Amarillo, TX	Tom Slatton	1,096	11
Children's Programs Inc.	LS	Brookfield, WI	David Linsmeier	1,051	22
YWCA of the Hartford Region	YC	East Hartford, CT	Julie Nichols	1,050	34
Playcare Child Care Centers	RC	Rochester, NY	Sandra Alexander	1,043	13
EPIC	LS	Yakima, WA	Ed Ferguson	1,040	13
KCAA Pre-Schools of Hawaii	LS	Honolulu, HI	Jimmy McCoy	1,034	7
Federation Day Care Services	LS	Philadelphia, PA	Norman Finkel	1,033	12

*Total licensed capacity for preschool and school age children of all sites or centers as of January 1, 1995. Based solely on information supplied by organizations. Organizations exempt from licensing have submitted estimates of what their capacity would be under state licensing requirements. This is an evolving list. If you believe your organization belongs on it, call Exchange at (800) 221-2864.

Figure 2-16   *(Continued)*

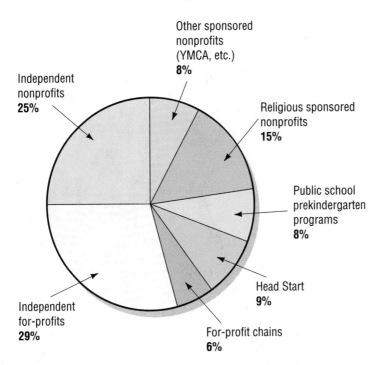

Adapted from *Reaching Full Cost of Quality* by Barbara Willer (Ed.), 1990, NAEYC.

Figure 2-17 **Child care has numerous sponsors in communities, including non-profit and for-profit organizations.**

and Even Start, as well as specific local initiatives. (See Fig. 2-17 for an indication of the variety of auspices for child care.)

Specific Populations Served

As discussed earlier in this chapter, many early childhood programs are designed to serve specific age-groups. There are specific centers and classrooms for infants, for toddlers, and for preschoolers. Local legislation and school authorities will have designated primary and kindergarten, and in some cases, prekindergarten, systems. Parental need will have dictated community programs for before- and after-school care.

In addition, individual communities may have determined for specific needs for early childhood programs. Many large cities today have early childhood programs for homeless children, both at the preschool and primary level. For reasons related to transience and lack of continuity, as well as real physical and social needs, these children may benefit from having specific programs with staff trained to provide stability and security in their lives (Klein, Bittel, and Molnar, 1993). Many adolescent mothers require child care to complete their education. Thus, many communities provide child care for infants and toddlers for young parents, along with emotional support and education for parenting,

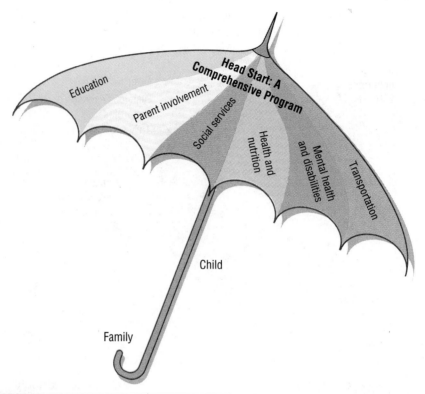

Education

Parent involvement

Head Start: A Comprehensive Program

Social services

Health and nutrition

Mental health and disabilities

Transportation

Child

Family

Figure 2-18   **Head Start is a comprehensive early childhood program, serving children and their families in numerous ways.**

A good program, no matter what its name or style, will be proud of the youngness of its children. It will be geared to honest, real-life children—the noisy, messy, active, dirty kind. . . . A good school enjoys youngsters as they are: Imaginative. Full of ego. Animal-lovers, lovers of heights and hideaways, lovers of all cuddlies. Devotees of sand and mud and water. Gigglers, fast-riders, wrestlers, talkers
—James Hymes

with parenting classes offered in the same building where they are completing their academic requirements. Shelters for battered women frequently provide child care programs, recognizing that parents will need supplemental care for their children while they try to make new plans for shelter, jobs, and counselling, and that children will benefit from the emotional support of trained caregivers at this stressful time in their lives.

Many communities have identified specific needs of families that require additional supports, such as non-English speaking or immigrant parents, or parents who have been caught in the cycle of abuse or neglect. Head Start has special programs for children from migrant families. Programs identified by the community and designed to meet the needs of children in specific populations have become part of the early childhood scene in modern America.

Specific Focus and/or Location of Programs

Some programs for early education are distinguished from others because of the rationale or philosophical basis for the program, or the physical location of the program. We will examine some examples of these distinctions.

1875

New York Society for the Prevention of Cruelty to Children is established, since the only available means to protect a child the previous year was under the Society for Prevention of Cruelty to Animals.

Head Start

  Head Start is a good example of an early childhood education program established with a particular focus. It was established in 1965 by President Lyndon B. Johnson as a part of his War on Poverty (see Timeline). From its inception, the Head Start program's focus has been to expose young children, who are being raised in poverty or with other special needs, to a variety of experiences designed to decrease their environmental disadvantages. The purpose of Head Start is to break the cycle of poverty by improving health and physical well-being, to develop physical skills, social opportunities, and cognitive functioning, as well as involving parents in their children's educational experiences. The mandate is for 90 percent of the children in the program to be from families that are at or below the federally determined poverty level. Since 1972, Head Start has also been mandated to include at least ten percent of children who have special needs.

  Head Start was designed as a comprehensive program (see Fig. 2-18) to include: high-quality educational experiences for three- to five-year-olds; medical, dental, and nutritional screening and services for children; and **social services** to their families. The program has served over 13 million children and families in the past 30 years, and it is currently funded at over 3.5 billion dollars per year, making it the major focus of federal attention to child care and education. Head Start programs exist in every state and territory, in rural and urban locations, and are administered by local community agencies. Several smaller alternative structures were created in the late 1960s and early 1970s to provide greater access. Parent Child Centers were created to work with parents and their children under the age of three; and Home Start offered home-based educational services to teach parents how to foster their children's learning and development. Some Head Start programs are part-day and some full-day, with wraparound services to assist working parents. Head Start currently serves

Head Start: Established in 1965, educational program for preschoolers in families below the poverty level. Comprehensive services include: education; family support through social services and parent education; medical, dental, and nutritional services for children.

Social Services: The branch of professional services that help provide for basic needs for families and individuals.

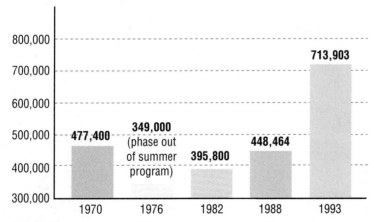

Adapted from *Children's Defense Fund, 1995.*

Figure 2-19 **Head Start Enrollment.**

1876
Philadelphia Exposition exhibits a model kindergarten in the Women's Pavilion.

nearly three quarters of a million children every year, though this figure is less than half of the children who are eligible nationwide (see Fig. 2-19). The goal was full funding by 1996. Unfortunately, with the Contract with America of the 1994-95 Congress working towards a balanced budget by the year 2002, funding for many programs for poor and low-income familes with children has been cut. Children's Defense Fund estimates that 340,600 children would lose Head Start early childhood services under the plan which would reduce enrollment by 46 percent.

With more than 30 years of experience and research, Head Start has taken a respected place in the early childhood community, and is recognized by the public and legislators as an essential force in providing opportunities that enhance later school success. In addition, Head Start has been beneficial to the early childhood profession, pointing out the need for teacher education. (See CDA in Chapter Ten, and more on what the history of Head Start tells us about federal involvement in early education in Chapter Eight).

Montessori Schools

Montessori Schools:
Schools based on the philosophy of Maria Montessori, including an emphasis on sensory learning, practical life skills, and didactic materials.

Other groups with a particular focus include early childhood programs that were established to follow a particular philosophy. **Montessori schools**, following the philosophical approach of Maria Montessori (see Chapter Eight) have proliferated in the United States since the early 1960s. Montessori schools use unique methods, materials, and specially trained teachers. Sequences of prescribed tasks, using precisely designed didactic Montessori materials, are presented to children in a designated order. Montessori teachers

Figure 2-20 | **Practical life activities are part of Montessori classrooms. (Courtesy of Countryside Montessori School, Charlotte, NC)**

Figure 2-21 **Beautiful materials that appeal to the senses and teach by self-correcting are found in Montessori schools. (Courtesy of Countryside Montessori School, Charlotte, NC)**

Sequential Steps: Refers to predictable patterns of development and learning that follow in order.

Practical Life Skills: Those skills used in daily life, such as washing dishes, and sweeping floors. A part of the Montessori curriculum.

Philosophy: One's beliefs and attitudes. Related to early education, one's ideas about how children learn and how teachers teach.

Absorbent Mind: Phrase used by Montessori to describe young children's active, natural learning style in their first years.

Didactic: Teaching, usually refers to materials that teach because their properties are inherently self-correcting. Montessori developed many didactic materials.

Sensitive Period: Term used by Montessori to indicate time of readiness for particular learning.

or "directresses" have received specialized training in an institution accredited for Montessori teacher training, with emphasis on observing children and presenting the directions in **sequential steps** for the activities for which they are ready. Montessori's philosophy included introducing children to varieties of **practical life skills**, such as washing dishes, sweeping floors, and watering plants (see Fig. 2-20). Other components of the curriculum included *sensorial,* providing materials to help children broaden and refine sensory perceptions; and *conceptual,* using concrete academic materials to introduce children to reading, writing, mathematics, and social studies.

There are particular terms that help explain the Montessori **philosophy**. Some of these include: **absorbent mind**, Montessori's description of the ease with which young children learn unconsciously from the environment; **didactic** materials, those that teach children directly by making errors in their use obvious to the child for self-correction (see Fig. 2-21); **sensitive periods**, the periods of learning during which children are particularly sensitive to particular stimuli. One abiding distinction of the Montessori philosophy is the respect for children and their abilities and accomplishments.

Many Montessori schools are for children ages two through six, although in some communities, Montessori education may continue through the elementary grades and beyond. In this country today are found Montessori schools that strictly follow the original techniques (Association Montessori International, AMI), and others that follow practices adapted to American culture and current thinking (American Montessori Society, AMS).

1878

The American Froebel Union is established by Elizabeth Peabody. This is the first professional association for those concerned with the education of young children.

High/Scope Preschool Key Experiences

Creative Representation
- Recognizing objects by sight, sound, touch, taste, and smell
- Imitating actions and sounds
- Relating models, pictures, and photographs to real places and things
- Pretending and role-playing
- Making models out of clay, blocks, and other materials
- Drawing and painting

Language and Literacy
- Talking with others about personally meaningful experiences
- Describing objects, events, and relations
- Having fun with language: Listening to stories and poems, making up stories and rhymes
- Writing in various ways: drawing, scribbling, letter-like forms, invented spelling, conventional forms
- Reading in various ways: reading storybooks, signs, symbols, one's own writing
- Dictating stories

Initiative and Social Relations
- Making and expressing choices, plans, and decisions
- Solving problems encountered in play
- Taking care of one's own needs
- Expressing feelings in words
- Participating in group routines
- Being sensitive to the feelings, interests, and needs of others
- Building relationships with children and adults
- Creating and experiencing collaborative play
- Dealing with social conflict

Movement
- Moving in nonlocomotor ways (anchored movement: bending, twisting, rocking, swinging one's arms)
- Moving in locomotor ways (nonanchored movement: running, jumping, hopping, skipping, marching, climbing)
- Moving with objects
- Expressing creativity in movement
- Describing movement
- Acting upon movement directions
- Feeling and expressing steady beat
- Moving in sequences to common beat

Music
- Moving to music
- Exploring and identifying sounds
- Exploring one's singing voice
- Developing melody
- Singing songs
- Playing simple musical instruments

Classification
- Exploring and describing similarities, differences and the attributes of things
- Distinguishing and describing shapes
- Sorting and matching
- Using and describing something in several ways
- Holding more than one attribute in mind at a time
- Distinguishing between "some" and "all"
- Describing characteristics something does not possess or what class it does not belong to

Seriation
- Comparing attributes (longer/shorter, bigger/smaller)
- Arranging several things one after another in a series or pattern and describing the relationships (big/bigger/biggest, red/blue/red/blue)
- Fitting one ordered set of objects to another through trial and error (small cup—small saucer/medium cup—medium saucer/big cup—big saucer)

Number
- Comparing the numbers of things in two sets to determine "more," "fewer," "same amount"
- Arranging two sets of objects in one-to-one correspondence
- Counting objects
- Space
- Filling and emptying
- Fitting things together and taking them apart
- Changing the shape and arrangement of objects (wrapping, twisting, stretching, stacking, enclosing)
- Observing people, things, and places from different spatial viewpoints
- Experiencing and describing positions, directions, and distances in the play space, building and neighborhood
- Interpreting spatial relations in drawings, pictures, and photographs

Time
- Starting and stopping an action on signal
- Experiencing and describing rates of movement
- Experiencing and comparing time intervals
- Anticipating, remembering and describing sequences of events

Reprinted with permission of High/Scope Education Foundation

Figure 2-22 **High/Scope Preschool Key Experiences.**

High/Scope

Another philosophical approach in current early childhood education is the **High/Scope** approach. This curriculum has developed under the leadership of David Weikart, whose earlier work was in the Perry Project, one of the best known intervention programs of the 1960s (see Timeline). The High/Scope curriculum is based on Jean Piaget's constructivist theories of child development. "The curriculum rests on the fundamental premise that children are active learners, who learn best from activities that they themselves plan, carry out and reflect on" (Epstein, 1993, p. 30). As with most good nursery schools, children learn in a variety of learning centers with plenty of appropriate materials. Teachers help children actively plan what they will do each day, then carry out their plan in a work time for the self-selected activities, and then review with the teacher what they have done—**"plan, do, review**." Teachers join in children's play, asking questions to extend their thinking skills. The High/Scope curriculum identifies five ingredients of active learning for young children:

1. Materials for the child to explore

2. Manipulation of materials by the child

3. Choices by the child about what to do with the materials

4. Language from the child and

5. Support from the adult (Epstein, 1993).

Teachers also use small groups to help children focus on **key experiences**, a set of eight concepts based on Piaget's ideas of the cognitive characteristics and learning potential of preschoolers. These concepts include: active learning involving children's initiation and use of sensory and manipulative materials; use of language; experiences that allow children to represent their ideas and experiences; opportunities for classification; opportunities for seriation; opportunities to promote understanding of number concepts; opportunities to understand spatial relationships, and understanding of time (see Fig. 2-22).

Teachers may study the High/Scope philosophy in short workshops and training institutes. Students who are interested in learning more about Montessori or High/Scope philosophies and training may use the addresses included at chapter end to obtain more information.

These are just three examples of early childhood programs based on particular philosophical orientations. With your classmates you may wish to learn more about others, such as **Waldorf Schools**, **open schools** related to British infant schools, the **Reggio Emilia** model from Italy, or schools following the **Bank Street Philosophy**, the precursor of our current model of **developmentally appropriate practice (DAP)**.

Location of Programs

The other categorization refers to the location of the early childhood programs. You may hear references to *on-site* or **employer-supported**

High/Scope Curriculum: Curriculum that is based on Piagetian cognitive principles, developed after the model of the Perry study by David Weikart.

Plan-Do-Review: The basic methods of the High/Scope cognitive curriculum, in which children make choices with teacher assistance, carry out the activity, and report on the activity.

Key Experiences: Term that describes eight important cognitive components of the HIgh/Scope Curriculum.

Waldorf Schools: The philosophy emphasized the whole child, with a goal of allowing children to become self-motivated. Play and interaction with others is emphasized, as are multi-sensory experiences and creative art. Teachers are "mother figures" who work to understand individual temperaments–staying with the same group of children over time.

Open Schools: A style of education developed in American progressive schools and in British infant schools, that is based on freedom of choice and individualized curriculum.

Figure 2-23 **Many employers now offer on-site child care for their employees. (Courtesy of NationsBank, Charlotte, NC)**

Reggio Emilia: Early childhood programs in Reggio Emilia, Italy, world famous for their child-centered and extensive project approach to learning.

Bank Street Philosophy: Principles of best traditional nursery school practice, as exemplified by the lab school and the college of education established by Lucy Sprague Mitchell, based on Dewey's principles of progressive education, linking theory and practice.

Developmentally Appropriate Practice (DAP): The standards defined by NAEYC that base teaching practices on developmental knowledge of age-level standards of children's abilities and observation of individual differences, including abilities, interests, and culture.

Employer-Supported Child Care: Early childhood programs that are often on-site at a work place, or provided for the convenience and financial support of employees. Also referred to as *on-site.*

Campus-Child Care: Programs based on college campuses, as a service for students and faculty, and frequently serving as a lab school for early education students.

child care, which usually refers to child care arrangements made by employers so that their employees' children can be cared for near their parents' workplace (see Fig. 2-23). You may hear about **campus child care**, which usually includes full- or part-time care available for students and faculty at a college or university, as well as for the general community. In addition, campus child care programs may frequently function as lab or model programs for early childhood education students. But probably the most widespread kind of programs distinguished by location are **family child care** programs.

Family child care

Family child care refers to the small groups of children cared for in a private residence by a child care provider. Often subject to different kinds of (or non-existent) licensing **regulations** than more formal child care centers, these operations usually care for fewer than twelve children in a home setting that often duplicates the appearance of a large extended family, often with children of several ages, including older school-aged children who come at the end of their school day. There are advantages to such a setting: there is often a small **adult-child ratio**; care may closely replicate homerearing and a homelike atmosphere, with consistent caregiving by the same person over a period of time; possible flexible scheduling to meet parents' needs; and close parent-caregiver relationships (see Fig. 2-24). There may also be disadvantages: there is frequently no regulation of these child care settings, putting children at possible risk for health and safety; often family child care providers have little or no training (although now there are conferences, a national association, newsletter, and an accreditation system); the center may provide more custodial care, as the provider concentrates on her household chores and children are not provided the kinds of stimulating experiences they need to thrive. And there are both advantages and disadvantages to the kinds of mixed-aged groupings that usually exist in family child care (Trawick-Smith and Lambert, 1995). But, whatever the pluses or minuses, this form of child care is still the most widely used

1880
There are over 400 kindergartens in 30 states.

Figure 2-24 **Family child care offers several advantages, including a home-like atmosphere. (Courtesy of Hope Valley Family Child Care)**

of any others in this country, with about forty percent of child care, especially for children under age three, being in family child care homes (see Fig. 2-25). Hear a family child care provider:

> It seems such an ordinary life. I live on a dead-end street in Oakland California, in a three-story wooden house, and every day in my home I take care of other people's children. From 9 to 5, five days a week, forty-eight weeks a year, I watch over them with enormous care. I am a daycare provider. I say this with pride, compassion, and a well-exercised sense of humor. It is not an easy task being a provider. But I love what I do and, as with any work that is lifelong and life-enveloping, I find my own equilibrium in it. I am able to be with these children fully and take my comfort from them (p. 1).
>
> Yes. Other people's children share my life and my home and I am daily inspired by them. At the end of each day I know I have done something important. Sometimes, of course, it is only that I've survived the day! (p. 2).
>
> That's why I love what I do. Creating good daycare is indeed like Christmas. It is a way of filling children with anticipation and dreams. It is a way of giving them a place where everything good has the possibility of happening at once. Brief quote from *Two to Four From Nine to Five* by Joan Roemer and Barbara Austin. Copyright © 1989 by Joan Roemer and Barbara Austin. Reprinted with permission of HarperCollins Publishers, Inc.

Family Child Care: Arrangements for child care within small groups (often less than six children) in homelike settings, usually the family child care provider's home.

Regulation: The supervision to ensure meeting standards set by each state for minimum requirements for licensed child care facilities within the state.

Adult-Child Ratios: The number of children of a particular age that may be legally (by regulation) or optimally (by accreditation standards) cared for by one adult.

1883
G. Stanley Hall publishes "The Content of Children's Minds" in the *Princeton Review.*

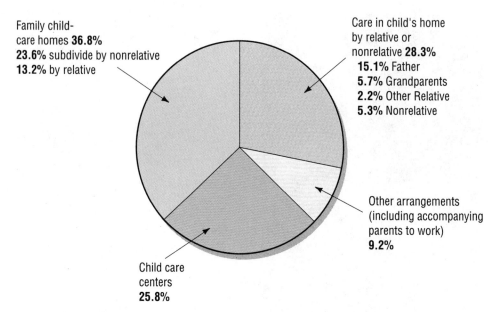

Family child-
care homes **36.8%**
23.6% subdivide by nonrelative
13.2% by relative

Care in child's home
by relative or
nonrelative **28.3%**
15.1% Father
5.7% Grandparents
2.2% Other Relative
5.3% Nonrelative

Other arrangements
(including accompanying
parents to work)
9.2%

Child care
centers
25.8%

Adapted from *Reaching Full Cost of Quality* by Barbara Willer (Ed.), 1990, NAEYC.

Figure 2-25 **Family child care is still the most popular form of out-of-home child care used by families.**

Greeting his pupils, the teacher asked:
"What would you learn of me?"
And the reply came:
"How shall we rear our children?"
"How shall we work together?"
"How shall we live with our fellow man?"
"How shall we play?"
And the teacher, pondering these words, sadly walked away, for his own learning touched not these things
—Author unknown

Read more about the experiences of a family child care provider in Joan Roemer's book, *Two to Four from 9 to 5* (1989).

FACTORS THAT IMPACT ON EARLY CHILDHOOD EDUCATION

Societal Value for Education

As you look at the Timeline, you will see that there has been a variety of forms of early childhood education in this country since its earliest days. The earliest public expenditures on children included funds for schools to teach primary academic skills. The public schools have since expanded to include the kindergartens that began as products of a particular philosophy about little children. With their inclusion into the public schools, kindergartens have undergone a series of changes in philosophy and format, and the debate about these changes is ongoing. The nursery schools that became part of the scene for middle-class American children from the 1920s on were a reflection of both the societal value on early education and stimulation, and the cultural acceptance of the importance of childhood. The prevailing public wisdom is that good, basic, early education is necessary in order to find a place in the complex contemporary work world.

While there is considerable current debate about a lack of a national philosophy or perspective to form a policy of support for children and families, most Americans believe in the ideal that the healthy development of children is a key to our future.

1884
The National Education Association establishes the Department of Kindergarten Education.

Concern About Quality of Education

As the Timeline repeatedly indicates, while American society has developed in relation to modern times and the world at large, the school systems have continually undergone examination as to their effectiveness. This may reflect both American values of competition and success, and concern with comparisons with other industrial nations (see Sputnik on the Timeline). The early childhood intervention programs of the 1960s—the main remaining example of which is Head Start—sought to start the learning process as early as possible, in the hopes that this would contribute to the overall attainment of goals, and to quality education. Prekindergarten programs supported by state funds are another effort to do this, as are early childhood programs based on particular philosophies that some feel represent optimum learning opportunities.

As you will see in our later discussion of issues, there are real issues about the quality of child care programs that have yet to be resolved; the most recent study indicates that we are quite right to still be concerned about the quality of early education in the United State. (see Fig. 2-26). There is a concern about quality, but a lack of public understanding about the necessary ingredients for quality in early childhood programs. As we will discuss further in Chapter Eleven, this constitutes a major challenge for early childhood professionals today.

A two-year-old is not a six-year-old, and a six-year-old is not an adult! That may seem like a simplistic statement, but I've seen people in all walks of life treat some two-year-olds, and some six-year-olds, as if they were adults

—Fred Rogers

Changing Social Patterns

Probably the greatest influence on trends in early childhood education today is the **demographic** data that portray changed patterns of family life and employment. In the past 30 years, two interrelated social patterns have appeared. One is the increasing breakdown of typical family patterns. With divorce now occurring in at least 50 percent of all marriages, and large increases in the numbers of children born to unmarried parents, there are enormous rises in the numbers of families headed by single parents. At the same time, census data reveal that the majority of all parents, whether in one- or two-parent families, are in the work force. This necessitates the use of some forms of supplemental child care for children from birth on, and changes the face of early education (see Fig. 2-27).

Demographics: The statistics of the population that indicate sociological information and trends.

> The repercussions resulting from the widespread movement of mothers into the labor force—and the concomitant adjustments to family and community life—are comparable in their importance to those resulting from the advent of the automobile, which changed the face of the earth. These effects may be even more significant, because they affect our most intimate family relations and patterns, and ultimately the structure of our society (Culkin et al., 1990, pp. 10-11).

One of the immediately obvious effects of the changing demographics of families and the workplace is the enormous increase in the amount of child care needed in most communities. According to current estimates by the U.S.

1885
The NEA recommends that kindergartens become part of the public schools.

Figure 2-26 | **Unfortunately studies show that many children are not in quality programs that offer safe, attractive playgrounds or selections of well chosen materials in good condition. (Courtesy of Connie Glass)**

Department of Labor, the projected job growth for preschool and kindergarten teachers needed by the year 2005 is an increase of 54 percent! But not only is the need increasing; so too is the discussion about how to respond to total family needs as the faces of families change. Community attention and debate is on how best to support these parents in their important task of childrearing. Various family supports are recognized as necessary for the well-being of children, families, and communities. Schools and child care programs are increas-

1886
Chicago Kindergarten College is established.

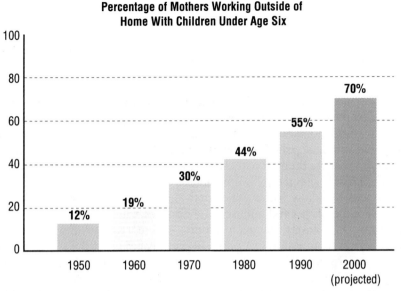

Adapted from *Reaching Full Cost of Quality* by Barbara Willer (Ed.), 1990, NAEYC.

Figure 2-27 | **The number of preschool children with mothers employed outside the home doubled in the years from 1977 to 1991.**

ingly asked to assume roles of helping parents by providing social support and education. The various components of the early childhood education system are now seen as a necessity for both the support of family needs and the care and early education of young children. Early childhood practitioners are in a vital position to provide this community support in a time of changing social patterns.

Importance of Choice

As Americans, we have always valued being able to choose among alternatives. The diversity in structure, philosophy, purpose, and administration of early childhood programs today indicates not only the different historical roots (see Chapter Eight), but also the varying needs for services and goals for children held by different families. Early childhood education in America today truly has something for everyone.

IMPLICATIONS FOR PROSPECTIVE TEACHERS

For prospective teachers, this examination of the definition of early childhood education may open new avenues of thought. Most of you had a specific image in mind when you took the initial steps of saying "I would like to teach little children." It may be that you assumed you would find employment in your local school system kindergarten classrooms—and it may be that will remain

Children have the right to have friends, otherwise they do not grow up too well.
Children have the right to live in peace.
To live in peace means to be well, to live together, to live with things that interest us, to have friends, to think about flying, to dream.
If a child does not know, she has the right to make mistakes. It works because after she sees the problem and the mistakes she made, then she knows
—Poster from Diana School, Reggio Emilia

1888
Lucy Wheelock establishes the Wheelock School (later college) in Boston to train kindergartners (kindergarten teachers).

your final goal. But in the meantime, it is useful for you to consider the wider variety of populations it is possible to work with, as well as the variety of potential employers.

Age-Group Considerations

In thinking about the variety of age-groups it is possible to work with, it is assumed that future development and curriculum classes will not only give detailed information about children at various ages, but also offer opportunities to observe and have **practicum** work with these children. It is only by actually being with real children, in real classrooms interacting with their teachers and caregivers that you can truly see the kind of work this would be for you. Such experiences will allow you to talk with the adults involved, and learn their perceptions of the pluses and minuses of their work with the specific age-groups. Take every opportunity you get to observe different age-groups.

There is no question that personal preferences and values enter into narrowing down one's choices. "I just can't take the aggressiveness of toddlers," you may think after a week or two in their classroom, although after a longer period you may find yourself admiring their single-minded drive and exuberant personalities.

(Babies) "I really love working with the little ones—it's so satisfying to watch them come to trust me. And the rate of development—always something new."

(Preschoolers) While another may sigh, "I do love the babies, but I find the parents' constant challenges hard to take. I'll be happier with the preschoolers' parents—they're so much more relaxed." "I can do so much more with the preschoolers—I get tired of a lot of the sameness that seems to go with the toddlers."

(Kindergarteners) "Give me school age kids every time—we really have some conversations. The younger ones are always worried so much about themselves. My second graders are interested in projects to help in the community."

(Toddlers) "Tattling! I don't have to deal with that with my little toddlers."

(Kindergarteners) "There's nothing like kindergartners. Watching them get so excited about being in school and learning so much is fun."

(Preschoolers) "I still feel that my preschoolers need me—when I taught kindergarten the kids were just too independent."

You can hear the very real differences in preference and motivation for working with various developmental stages in these teachers' comments. Obviously it is important to find a good match for your skills and temperament; your satisfaction in your work will depend on it.

Kinds of Employers

There are specific training and **certification** requirements for working in particular settings with different groups. We will look more closely at these in Chapter Ten. Here as we consider possiblities, it is important to recognize the

---

Practicum: Supervised opportunity for student teachers to obtain practical teaching experience in a classroom with young children.

A pedagogue is a man or woman who stands in a caring relation to children: In the idea of leading or guiding them is a "taking by the hand," in the sense of watchful encouragements. "Here, take my hand!" "Come, I will show you the world. The way into a world, my world and yours."

–Max van Manen

Certification: The process whereby each state indicates teachers qualified to teach in the public schools by meeting specific educational and student teacher requirements.

differences that may occur in working with various administrations funded by particular sources.

The programs run with public funding generally are tied to specific accountability requirements. This means that attention to regulations, guidelines, and paperwork may be a significant part of a teacher's responsibility. Nonprofit programs with minimal public funding may be less burdened to some degree by such requirements. In for-profit programs, teachers are generally tied to the particular owner's philosophical requirements. The advantage of family child care programs is the flexibility for the early childhood practitioner, including the opportunity to be with one's own children in the home.

As early childhood teachers recognize the relative importance of the **autonomy** to make decisions, or of being bound by regulations and specific guidelines and required reports, they may be influenced in their decisions about potential employers. These are all issues of personal preference for you to consider as you discover the essentials of early education. Find out what the possibilities are in your community for the kinds of programs discussed in this chapter.

Autonomy: The sense of being able to function independently of others, of being able to do things for oneself, of being a separate individual. Forming a sense of autonomy is an important developmental task of toddlerhood.

1889
Jane Addams founds Hull House in Chicago, including a kindergarten.

SUMMARY

The definition of early childhood education includes a wide variety of programs serving children from birth through age eight, or even older, in before- and after-school programs. These programs may serve both typically developing children and those with special developmental and educational needs. Programs may be: full- or part-day; nonprofit or for-profit, within school system programs, such as kindergarten and prekindergarten, and primary classrooms; Head Start; before- and after-school child care; or family child care. There are several factors that impact early childhood education today. These include: societal value of early education; concerns about the effectiveness of education; changing social patterns that require increased supplemental child care and family support; and the American regard for a variety of choices.

QUESTIONS FOR REVIEW

1. Define early childhood education.
2. Describe what is meant by each of the following terms: full-day care; part-day care; for-profit centers; nonprofit centers; family child care; special needs; Head Start.
3. Identify three of four factors that influence the forms of early childhood education today.

ACTIVITIES FOR FURTHER STUDY

1. Read one of the following books to get insights into working with a particular age group or in a particular setting. See "References" and "Suggestions for Reading" for bibliographic information.

Ayers, William. *The Good Preschool Teacher.* (This includes infant and toddler caregivers, family child care providers, kindergarten teachers, and a teacher of homeless children.)

Greenberg, Polly. *The Devil has Slippery Shoes: A Biased Biography of the Child Development Group of Mississippi.* (Head Start).

Hillman, Carol. *Teaching Four-Year-Olds: A Personal Journey.*

Wollman, Patti G. *Behind the Playdough Curtain: A Year in My Life as a Preschool Teacher.*

Roemer, Joan. *Two to Four from Nine to Five.* (family child care.)

Kidder, Tracy. *Among Schoolchildren.* (elementary school).

Ashton-Warner, Sylvia. Teacher. (preschoolers in New Zealand).

2. Talk with a variety of early childhood teachers from particular settings. Your instructor may invite some to class. Summarize their responses to the following questions: What contributes to their their job satisfaction? job dissatisfaction? What is their specialized training? What are three or four typical events during their day with the children?

3. Spend some time in the early childhood setting of at least one of the following: infant care; toddler care; a preschool classroom; a kindergarten classroom; a classroom of one of the early grades; a family child care home; a Head Start classroom. Listen to and discuss reports of others about their visits.

4. Check your phone book to see what child care and preschools are located in your community. What type of program do you suppose they are judging from their advertisement?

REFERENCES

Ayers, William. (1989). *The good preschool teacher.* New York: Teachers College Press.

Culkin, Mary L., Helbrun, Suzanne W., & Morris, John R. (1990). Current price versus full cost: An economic perspective. In Barbara Willer (Ed), *Reaching the full cost of quality in early childhood programs.* Washington, D.C.: NAEYC.

Doherty-Derkowski, Gillian. (1995). *Quality matters: Excellence in early childhood programs.* Reading, MA: Addison-Wesley Publishers Ltd.

Epstein, Ann S. (1993). *Training for quality: Improving early childhood programs through systematic inservice training.* Ypsilanti, MI: High/Scope Educational Research Foundation.

Exchange Top 100–The Nation's Largest Early Childhood Organizations (1994, November-December) Child Care Information Exchange (72).

Hillman, Carol. (1988). *Teaching four-year-olds: A personal journey.* Bloomington, IN: Phi Delta Kappa Educational Foundation.

Honig, Alice S. (1994, March). Mental health for babies: What do theory and research teach us? *Young Children. 48,* (3), 69-76.

Kagan, Sharon Lynn & Newton, James W. (1989, November). For-profit and nonprofit child care: Similarities and differences. *Young Children. 45,* (1), 4-10.

Kidder, Tracy. (1989). *Among schoolchildren.* Boston: Houghton Mifflin Co.

Klein, Tovah, Bittel, Calley, & Molnar, Janice. (1993, September). No place to call home: Supporting the needs of homeless children in the early childhood classroom. *Young Children. 48,* (6), 22-31.

NAEYC position statement: A conceptual framework for early childhood professional development. (1994, March) *Young Children. 49,* (3), 68-77.

Platt, Elizabeth Balliett. (1991). *Scenes from day care: How teachers teach and what children learn.* New York: Teachers College Press.

Roemer, Joan. (1989). *Two to four from Nine to Five.* New York: Harper and Row Pubs.

Trawick-Smith, Jeffrey & Lambert, Laura. (1995, March) The unique challenges of the family child care provider: Implications for professional development. *Young Children, 50,* (3), 25-32.

Willer, Barbara (Ed.) (1990). *Reaching Full Cost of Quality.* Washington, DC: NAEYC.

SUGGESTIONS FOR READING

Ashton-Warner, Sylvia. (1958). *Teacher.* New York: Simon and Schuster.

Greenberg, Polly. (1969). *The devil has slippery shoes.* New York Macmillan.

Wollman, Patti Greenberg. (1994). *Behind the playdough curtain: A year in my life as a preschool teacher.* New York: Charles Scribner's Sons.

Addresses: The American Montessori Society,
150 Fifth Avenue, Suite 203
New York, NY 10011.

Association Montessori International,
170 W. Scholfield Road
Rochester, NY 14617.

National Head Start Association,
201 N. Union Street, Suite 320
Alexandria, VA 22314.

High/Scope Education Foundation
600 N. River Street
Ypsilanti MI 48198-2898.

3

WHAT QUALITY EARLY EDUCATION LOOKS LIKE

Quality in early care and education takes many forms and has unique faces. Yet there are specific descriptions that can be applied no matter what the age-group or population served, or what the structure of the program. This may seem like a daunting task, to be able to describe and recognize factors that are found in quality early childhood programs. Indeed, it is a task that researchers, scholars, and position statement commissions have labored over for years, and their combined efforts still precipitate spirited debate. To some extent, the difficulty is that quality is often defined subjectively, with powerful and deep early sensory memories exerting unseen influences on our opinions. If you have visited sites of early childhood programs, you have likely been attracted to (or dismayed by) some space in the room or some activity that resonated with meaning for you, often for unconscious reasons.

But standards for quality must go beyond subjective opinion, to find their basis in concrete and observable phenomena that can be discussed and explained. In this chapter, we will explore some of the specific components found in quality early education, and describe how these components may be manifested. You will be asked to consider each component actively as we move through the discussion. This involvement is designed to help you as you begin to construct your personal understanding of quality early education. In later coursework, you will learn more about how teachers create the environments that allow for excellent education to occur; for now it is important that you begin to be able to evaluate learning environments as you make initial visits to early education programs.

THINKING ABOUT QUALITY

When parents are asked to describe what they are looking for in a program for their children, their first desires are usually for health and safety (Child Care Information Exchange, 9/93). Early childhood educators who are looking for excellence in a program, however, are more likely to define *high quality* as one that:

▶ "supports and assists the child's physical, emotional, social, language, and intellectual development; and

▶ supports and complements the family in its child-rearing role" (Doherty-Derkowski, 1995, p. 4).

Katz (1993) directs us to consider five different but interrelated perspectives as we consider quality in an early childhood program. The first is a *top-down* perspective that examines measurable and quantifiable characteristics, such as adult-child ratios and teacher training, that set the stage for excellent early childhood education to occur. While many of these things are defined and regulated by licensing law and credentialing systems to be discussed in later chapters, it is important to recognize the correlation between these factors and the discussion of quality in this chapter.

Second is the *bottom-up* perspective that describes the quality of life experienced by children within the program. This perspective is obtained when adults take children's perspective; propose whether program practices would help children feel individually welcomed and securely accepted within the center; and find engaging, challenging, and absorbing learning experiences. As we think about stories of children in various classrooms, we draw conclusions about how those classrooms would impact on children's lives (see Fig. 3-1).

Figure 3-1   **A bottom-up perspective allows adults to consider program practices from a child's viewpoint. These children seem to feel secure in their classroom, and are busy with absorbing activities. (Courtesy of Tracie O'Hara)**

1890
Six states have public kindergartens.

The *inside* perspective is from the viewpoint of the staff members involved in a school or center. Teacher job satisfaction and retention of qualified personnel over time has a major impact on related elements for quality. As we consider the components, think about how staff would perceive their lives if these components were either present or absent.

The *outside-inside* perspective considers the quality and impact of relationships between early childhood practitioners and families. The mutual respect and relationships that allow teachers to create classrooms that are individually responsive to their specific children, are crucial to quality.

The final perspective is the *outside* perspective, which is the relationship between the early childhood program and its community and the larger society beyond. As programs respond to community need and expectation, and as social decisions and support mesh, good things can happen for children and families. Be aware of these complex interrelationships of participants as we consider quality.

A BIRD'S-EYE VIEW OF QUALITY

Let's look at several early childhood classrooms to see if our quick glance can yield first clues about quality.

Robin's Family Child Care Home

What is essential is to realize that children learn independently, not in bunches; that they learn out of interest and curiosity, not to please or appease the adults in power; and that they ought to be in control of their own learning, deciding for themselves what they want to learn and how they want to learn it
–John Holt

Robin Ferguson, a thirty-two year old mother of two school-aged children and a three-year-old, cares for her own child along with another three-year-olds, one two-year-old, and two eight-month-old twins in her comfortable home in a small subdivision. She has cared for children at home since her older two were babies.

This morning finds the three-year-olds busy playing in the family room that adjoins the large kitchen. One of them is playing with baby dolls in an area with child-sized kitchen furniture, and one is stringing some beads and spools. That child wanders into the kitchen where Robin is feeding breakfast to one of the babies, while the other sits near her on the floor fitting cups into each other. Robin helps the bead-stringer tie the beads into a necklace. When the older child tries to slip the necklace onto the baby on the floor–who protests weakly–Robin redirects him in a conversation admiring the beads, and then changes the topic to the bird-feeder on the deck that they had filled the day before. The floor baby is still unhappy, and Robin gently talks with her as she continues to feed her brother. When this does not soothe the baby, Robin puts out some Cheerios for the baby in the high chair, rolls the high chair to the doorway where she can keep an eye on that baby, and scoops up the crying baby. She takes the baby to the changing table in the family room, commenting to the child playing with a doll that she has to change the baby, and wonders if she has to change her baby too. She keeps her eyes on the baby's face as she changes the diaper, although her soft conversation includes the older child, as well as the other older child who has wandered back into the room. At Robin's suggestion, he comes over to join her as she sings to the baby, who is now grinning cheerfully.

1892

At a meeting of the National Education Association, in Saratoga Springs, New York in July, the International Kindergarten Union is organized. This will later become the Association for Childhood Education International.

THEORY INTO PRACTICE

This is Harvey Bagshaw. Harvey has worked in the field for four years, beginning as a kindergarten resource teacher, continuing with a year in first grade, and now two years as a kindergarten teacher.

What has been a significant frustration for you in early education? How do you deal with it?

Time is a big frustration for me as a teacher. There never seems to be enough time for all the things we would like to do during the day. I have found that you just work with the time you have by choosing those activities that the students will get the most out of. To help manage my time I have a general scope for my topics to be taught. I use student checklists to monitor the objectives that are being mastered and those that still need work. I also re-teach and re-evaluate throughout the year. This is the one thing that helps me the most with time. There are many skills that I don't get hung up on because I am constantly reteaching them. The more connections you make to something, as well as the many opportunities you provide to students, help to reinforce what you are teaching.

What is one thing you learned in classes that you really discovered to be true when you started working with children?

The one thing I learned in my college classes that I have discovered to be true is that *all* children can learn. Children learn at different rates and in many different ways. As a teacher it is my responsibility to find what works for each child and help them grow as much as they can to become positive lifelong learners.

What is an area you are working on now to learn more about?

I am continually working on making my classroom a more child-centered environment in which there are many open-ended activities for them to engage. Providing students with open-ended activities allows for all children to be challenged to learn at their level and to feel successful. It is very important to meet the needs of all the students. My goal is to help students develop problem solving strategies both academically and socially.

Why have you stayed in early education?

I have stayed in early education because teachers play an important role in developing a child's life. Children should learn to be problem solvers and risk takers. They need to have a positive self-concept. I want them to explore their creativity. I want them to investigate and question the world around them. I want them to tap into their areas of interest so they can grow into well-rounded individuals. School for them should be a place where they can't wait to go and learn. It is in teaching that I feel I can make a difference.

What is a comment or piece of advice you would give to those beginning to work in early childhood education?

My advice to beginners is to get into the classroom as a volunteer. This is the best way to get a true feeling for this profession. Work in as many classrooms as you can. It will help to see the different learning styles of children as well as the different teaching styles of teachers. Remember to be open-minded when you are volunteering. Always find the positive in any situation and make it work for you. You can learn something from these experiences whether they are good or bad. They will all help you grow as a teacher. It wasn't until I volunteered during college that I began to see the real picture of teaching. It was then that I started making connections between my studies and my real experiences. I'm still learning every day. It could be from a student in my class or from a teacher at another school. In this field you never stop growing as a teacher. I hope that when you become a teacher you too will continue to try new ideas to find what works best for children.

Sam Cooper's K-1 Classroom

Sam Cooper teaches in a class that includes five- through seven-year-olds in a public elementary school. During the few minutes that we are in his large, attractive classroom, we see a number of groups containing three to five children busy in several areas in the classroom. Three children are talking to each other as they puzzle over a computer game. Four boys are sitting at a round table, busy with notebooks, crayons, pencils, and markers. One boy explains to us that they are writing in their journals. Sam arrives at that point, and responds to one child's comment about his work with a specific and enthusiastic response that indicates his familiarity with the child's story. He encourages another child to share his idea with another, and suggests to a third child that his friend might help him figure out his spelling for the word he asked about.

Sam's glance searches the room, and he moves over to two girls who are in heated discussion about balancing objects on the scale. Sam does not interrupt, listening seriously to each contribution, nodding thoughtfully and supportively, then asking a question. As the girls seem to move into cooperative activity, Sam looks around at other busy children. He notices a child standing by the bookshelf, moves over to discuss his selection, and speaks with him quietly, finally leaving him after a pat and a smile. A child and adult enter the classroom. Sam moves over to greet them both, and engages in relaxed conversation with the parent, who seems equally relaxed with Sam. Sam gives the children a prearranged signal to gather at the meeting carpet; the parent has been invited in advance to conduct a minilesson about American sign language, since the children are so interested right now in different methods of communication.

Maia Chen's Toddlers

Maia Chen is one of two teachers for a group of ten children ages fourteen to twenty-four months in a church-sponsored child care center in a large city. We find them playing outdoors right now. Maia has added several large, sturdy cartons to their usual playground equipment of climber, low slide, large sand area, and three small swings. Four of the toddlers have climbed into the biggest box; Maia sits near them, commenting on their activity. "You climbed right in the big box, didn't you, Justin. Sarah's in the box with you. Oh my, here comes DuJawn, he's climbing in with you. D.H. thinks there's room too—maybe if you scoot over a bit. Look at that—four children in the box. And jumping, too. It's a jumping box." The children laugh with excitement, and Maia joins in. A shriek from the sandbox gets her immediate attention. "Oh Derek, that looks uncomfortable. I think Jennifer's trying to tell you that you're crowding her (as one toddler attempts to sit where another child already is.) How about we find a space for you to dig over here? There—now you both can make big holes. Let me see—oh that hole *is* getting big." Meanwhile Maia's coteacher is pushing three children in the swing, and another climbs repeatedly up the steps and slides down the slide, never far from Maia's gaze and encouraging smile. Maia reaches in her pocket and pulls out a notebook in which she jots down two

The creation of a community of caring people, big and little, is the most important goal in child care. People who care about each other help each other grow and learn

—Elizabeth Jones and Gretchen Reynolds

1893

Model day nursery at Chicago World's Fair cares for 10,000 children of sightseeing parents.

words of a brief observation that she will expand later, before turning to the children who are now pushing the boxes around the playground.

Three early childhood programs, three teachers and their children, all briefly serving to illustrate some of the things that indicate excellence. Some fundamental concepts lie behind the practice of each of these teachers. Think about it–what do you identify that each has done that seems excellent to you?

Standards for quality early childhood programs have been defined by several professional organizations. In the References section, you will find listings for their position statements on appropriate practice. These are important resources with which to become familiar as you begin to learn about early education.

Later in this chapter we will return to the **position statement** published by the NAEYC (1987), since this is the most widely acknowledged standard for quality in accrediting early childhood programs. But here we will discuss our personal perspective on the components that exist in the programs just described. Those same components will be found in any excellent early education program.

Position Statement: Statement of philosophy of a professional organization, that is used to guide practice of professionals.

COMPONENTS OF QUALITY

The basic components that we will discuss separately here include: respect for uniqueness of individuals; relationships as crucial to learning; **reciprocity** of learning interaction; interrelationship and integration of learning experiences; environments that are prepared for active learning; and an underlying developmental understanding of children's abilities, interests, and learning style. And, by the way, this is already an oversimplification. In quality programs, these components are so interrelated that they are virtually inseparable and indefinable as separate entities. But we shall try to identify them individually. As we go through this chapter, keep your pencil and notebook handy. You will be asked to think about your personal knowledge or experience with the components of quality. Take your time to see what you already know about good early childhood programs.

Reciprocity: Mutual give-and-take.

The central element in quality early care and education is the teacher and what he or she believes and knows, and is, as a person (see Fig. 3-2). This is an important idea to state at the outset, because all of the other dimensions in a classroom radiate from this basic premise. No matter how good the administration, the education system or philosophy, or the community support is, everything of crucial importance in the learning environment comes from the decisions and actions of the teacher involved. Some of these components are particular attitudes, values, and ideas, and some are areas of knowledge. But *all* translate into specific teacher actions and arrangements in the classroom that have far-reaching implications for everyone involved. What an astonishing, humbling thought for all of us drawn to consider the act of teaching.

In any center for young children, a teacher learns as well as teaches, so do the children
—Catherine Landreth

Respect

To respect is "to show esteem for, to honor, to show consideration for, to avoid violation of" (*American Heritage Dictionary*). All of these phrases sug-

1895
Lilliann Wald founds the Henry Street Settlement House in New York City.

Figure 3-2   **The teacher in a quality early childhood classroom is a key to appropriate interaction and experiences.**

The secret to education lies in respecting the pupil
—Ralph Waldo Emerson

N A E Y C
GUIDELINE
Bredekamp, 1987, p.2

Association of Childhood Education International (ACEI): The oldest early childhood professional organization in the United States. Originally associated with the kindergarten movement.

gest that respect is a genuine recognition of, and sensitivity to, self and others. How does this manifest itself in a classroom?

Respect for Children and Families

There are several key considerations about respect for children. The principles of developmentally appropriate practice as enunciated by NAEYC (1987), **Association of Childhood Education International (ACEI)** (Moyer et al., 1987 and Isenburg et al. 1988), NASBE (1988), as well as other early childhood organizations, emphasize the uniqueness of the individual child as being a crucial determinant in teacher considerations for curriculum and care. The different interests, abilities, talents, and styles of learning, the range of developmental differences within children, as well as the pace with which children move through development, are particular for each child, and deserving of teacher sensitivity and response.

Quality programs for young children show this respect for individuality in every decision that is made about children's care and curriculum, from considering what to do about naptime for toddlers to choosing materials for the art table so that preschoolers may find something to whet a particular interest, or guarantee certain success. This is a good time for you to consider and note down practices you are aware of in early care and education settings that demonstrate respect for individuality in children, or the opposite condition,

1895
G. Stanley Hall holds a child development seminar for kindergarten teachers, explaining a new, scientific, psychological approach to education. Most teachers are upset and leave.

| Figure 3-3 | **When children are busy with their self-initiated activities, teachers are free to observe individual learning progress.** |

where program decisions fail to demonstrate this component, and that treat all children as if they had the same needs and interests.

Such respect demands of teachers, first of all, knowledge of specific individuals, knowledge that goes far beyond merely learning age-level norm characteristics. Such constantly growing knowledge demands continual observation and communication, as well as the ability to avoid hasty conclusions that they "know the children." Teachers who truly respect children's individuality find themselves always in a suspenseful state of not-quite-knowing, always being open to new perceptions and evidences of growth and change. Thus it follows that excellent programs for young children are structured, in **environment** and curriculum, so that teachers are able to observe children continually (see Fig. 3-3). What are some of the things that you think of in environmental arrangements, curriculum methods, and teacher functioning, that would allow teachers to do abundant observations on the children in their care? Specific practices such as encouraging individual exploration or small group interaction rather than whole group teacher-led activities, providing **open-ended** materials that do not require adult instruction or assistance, or defining observation and recording as an important teacher role come to mind. What else can you add?

Respect for children also implies a particular image of childhood as a time and state in which children are recognized as capable and interesting, as they are right now, even as they are also filled with the potential and desire to learn, to grow, and develop. Teachers listen carefully to children, recognizing that their insights are valid and their questions are important. They talk with children individually, about things that are of interest and consequence to both child and adult. These are genuine conversations that follow the same rules of

Bredekamp, 1987, p.3

Environment: Everything that surrounds the individual that impacts on their lives. Environments include physical arrangements of time and space, materials and activities within the environment, and the people available for interaction.

Open-Ended: Activities, materials, or communication that permits a variety of responses and reactions, rather than one fixed correct response.

Bredekamp, 1987, p.9, 10

1896
John Dewey begins an experimental lab school at the University of Chicago, for four- and five-year olds, called subprimary rather than kindergarten.

Figure 3-4   **Respect means that child-like exploration is accepted. (Courtesy of Tracie O'Hara)**

Self-Control: Ability to regulate one's own behavior, based on understanding of what is appropriate and inappropriate.

Self-Esteem: A sense of self-worth, or value placed on the image of self.

Diversity: The variety of differences that exist in a classroom, community, culture, or country. Diversity may refer to ability, gender, age, race, culture, etc.

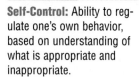

Bredekamp, 1987, p.11

Self-Identity: Image of self, constructed by feedback from others and cognitive understandings of gender, race, ability, and the cultural messages about these components.

Bredekamp, 1987, p. 7

Bredekamp, 1987, p. 11

communication that are used with adults, not just "pop quizzes" or questions such as, "What color is the ball?" or "How many bears do I have in my hand?" They talk with children, not at them.

Children are enjoyed as people, rather than seen as just slightly entertaining because of their less developed abilities and understanding of the world. (*Not* as in "Did you hear that? Isn't that cute; he called the lobster a 'monster.'") Their feelings and social interactions are accepted with seriousness, even as adults also recognize children's need for guidance and assistance in moving towards greater **self-control**. (*Not* as in, "It's nothing to get upset about. He probably doesn't even understand much about moving to another state.") This need for help and guidance is not seen as a defect, but understood as a necessary assistance in the progression of learning. (*Not* as in "I'm sick and tired of hearing toddlers yell.") Respectful guidance of young children means that techniques and communication that safeguard positive feelings of **self-esteem** are used. Discipline methods that humiliate or cause feelings of shame and doubt are not seen in excellent programs.

Adults with this kind of respect for childhood are not in a hurry to move children on prematurely to more advanced learning or behaviors that they are not yet ready for. Instead, they recognize that childhood has an importance of its own, not just as a preparation stage for a later time. This is an important question to consider: How do adults convey to children that their childlike abilities and characteristics are appreciated, enjoyed, and accepted? (see Fig. 3-4.)

Respect for individuality in children is also offered when teachers help children learn to recognize and comfortably acknowledge the **diversity** of race, culture, religion, socioeconomic experiences, gender, and physical ability that exists within American communities and in classrooms. Classroom materials, visitors, activities, and conversations all help children accept their **self-**

1896

Susan Blow is at Teachers College representing the Froebelian point of view, and Patty Smith Hill represents the newer developmental approach.

Figure 3-5 **When parents work in partnership with teachers, they help create curriculum that is responsive to their individual goals for their children.**

identity and that of others. Each child bears a personal identification, with an individual family and its background. As teachers interact with children's parents, welcoming them into communication and collaboration, children perceive that their own family culture is respected. When parents are drawn into partnership with early childhood educators, they are able to help teachers truly understand their children, and to guide teachers in creating curriculum that is responsive to their individual needs and goals for their children (see Fig. 3-5). Without such dialogue, teachers are in constant danger of overstepping the boundaries of individual appropriateness in the **multicultural** world in which we live. Respect for individuality includes this acknowledgement of individual family needs and preferences, and the active attempt to work with them. Genuine respect comes when parents and teachers recognize that each has a role in children's lives, roles that are very different, but complementary, rather than the cause for antagonism. What are some of the practices in early childhood programs that convey respect for individual cultures, and show attempts to reach out for collaboration with families?

To capture the essence of respect, it can be said that programs and teachers are **child-sensitive**; that is, that uniquenesses are noticed, acknowledged as important, and form a significant basis for planning in the total program. This

Children value themselves to the degree they have been valued
—Dorothy Briggs

Multicultural: The awareness of the diversity of cultures and cultural experiences.

Child-Sensitive: (Also child-centered) Those programs whose practices are responsive to knowledge and observations about children.

1898
National Federation of Day Nurseries is organized, in an attempt to promote better standards for child care.

may be a more descriptive term than the frequently-used *child-centered*, which may seem rather one-sided or totally indulgent of children. Respect demands both sensitivity and responsiveness.

Respect for Self

Teachers who have respect for self recognize the right and personal obligation to be authentic to the values and principles that drive their lives. This begins as teachers consider the philosophy and practices of potential employers, to determine whether these are compatible with their own deeply held personal convictions. Nothing more quickly destroys personal or professional joy of life than to have to function in a setting that calls for dissonance with self. Sometimes teachers feel they can make compromises that would allow them to keep their job while balancing with their principles. It is definitely true that there are, as yet, few perfect worlds, and that teachers will likely have to live with some situations that are less than ideal. Nevertheless, to be able to maintain congruent feelings of personal and professional integrity, teachers will need to identify those ideals and issues for which there is no room for compromise.

Such insights sometimes come slowly, after experience, such as the young teacher who left her first job after several months, saying ruefully, "I didn't realize how strongly I felt about teamwork. I now know that being part of a supportive community of adults and children is necessary for my ability to grow and see myself as a real contributor in the small world of the child care center. I will never again take a job that doesn't emphasize that feeling of community." There may be teachers who want to be able to express their deep religious beliefs in their daily work; they will need to find programs that permit them to do so. Or teachers who believe so strongly in being able to espouse particular life-styles that they would be uncomfortable working with other adults who deem them unacceptable. Teachers must identify their defining principles.

Beyond self-knowledge and self-awareness, self-respect is dependent on teachers having a mature sense of valuing the worth of their ideas and abilities. Jersild (1955) spoke of humility being an important attribute of a professional, to prevent the kind of overbearing dominance that would preclude establishing positive relationships with others. But this is not a self-effacing humility; rather, it is a confidently accepting recognition of one's strengths and capabilities, coupled with an understanding of the need to join with others for maximum effect. This is the idea that teachers do not have to be all-knowing, all-answering to any question, but can draw on the strengths of others, both adults and children. Thus teachers who value their worth are confident in knowing they have a contribution to make in early care and education. They know that their passions and ideas are worth sharing, that their presence is valuable. Such teacher confidence leads towards excellence.

Relationships

Quality early childhood programs recognize that learning takes place in the context of relationships. Much time and effort go into building and sustaining significant relationships. These relationships form complex webs that extend in

> *Whenever we become inattentive to the fact that children are people in their own right, with their own needs, their own special abilities, and their own learning priorities, we are likely to engage in miseducation*
>
> —David Elkind

1898
Nearly 3,000 kindergartens now exist, with an enrollment of 200,000 children.

many directions: from teacher to child; child to child; teacher to parent; teacher to teacher; parent to parent; and, of course, the most important, parent to child. The ultimate statement on the importance of relationships in early education comes from the late Loris Malaguzzi, of the Reggio Emilia programs in Italy.

> Although (from our experience in Reggio Emilia) we know how strongly children represent the center of our educational system, we continue to be convinced that without attention to the central importance of children and families, our view of children is incomplete; therefore, our proposition is to consider a triad at the center of education–children, teachers, and families. To think of a dyad of only a teacher and a child is to create an artificial world that does not reflect reality.
>
> . . . We strive to create an amiable school where children, teachers, and families feel a sense of well-being; therefore, the organization of the school–contents, functions, procedures, motivations, and interests–is designed to bring together the three central protagonists–children, teachers, and parents–and to intensify the interrelationships among them (Malaguzzi, 1993, p. 9.).

Intensify the **interrelationships**: what a strong image. Those who offer good early childhood care and education make procedural and environmental decisions based on their potential for encouraging relationships to flourish. The current practice of assigning **primary caregivers** for the youngest children is based on this concept as are **multi-age groupings** (where children remain together and with the same teachers over periods of time) that many schools and programs are exploring for continuity. How different this is from making decisions based on efficiency, such as if a teacher had a feeding table device that allowed her to feed six infants simultaneously. Time might be saved, but the quality of personal and physical interaction that promotes the development of an emotional attachment would likely suffer. Or, what if the time-honored custom of encouraging kindergarten and primary children to "do your own work", working in solitary silence at separate desks, were changed to providing tables that allow children to face each other and encourage interaction and **cooperative learning** situations? Or, what about the effect of the traditional staffing policy of having the fewest staff members available at the beginning and end of the day were changed to permit time and opportunity for parent-teacher and teacher-teacher conversations? What other specific decisions in the procedures, functions, and environment of early childhood settings can you imagine that could enhance the quality of the multiple relationships within programs?

Of the variables that can be regulated (that is, standards can be set to produce them), two that affect positive child outcomes in early childhood programs include group size and ratios of adults to numbers of children (*Young Children*, Jan. 1993). The reason is obviously related to the quality of relationships that can be formed. (See Fig. 3-6 for recommended ratios for quality, and effects when these ratios are not met.) The same study shows that quality is also related to the nature of interaction between caregivers and parents, and between caregivers and children. Relationships *matter.*

Interrelationships: The connections, as between one aspect of development and another, and between people.

Primary Caregivers: Caregivers assigned to primary responsibilty for a small sub-group of children within a larger group.

Multi-Age Groupings: Arrangements that group children across several ages, and frequently keep them together for two or more years, rather than separating them by chronological age.

Cooperative Learning: Learning where environments and activities are structured so children can work together.

Bredekamp, 1987, p.38

1899

John Dewey publishes *The School and Society,* outlining his philosophy of progressivism, that education was a means of social reform.

NAEYC Recommended Child-staff Ratios and Group Sizes

Age of child	Group size										
	6	8	10	12	14	16	18	20	22	24	28
Birth to 12 months	3:1	4:1									
12 to 24 months	3:1	4:1	5:1	4:1							
24 to 30 months		4:1	5:1	6:1							
30 to 36 months			5:1	6:1	7:1						
Three-year-olds					7:1	8:1	9:1	10:1			
Four-year-olds						8:1	9:1	10:1			
Five-year-olds						8:1	9:1	10:1			
Six-to eight-year-olds								10:1	11:1	12:1	
Nine- to 12-year-olds										12:1	14:1

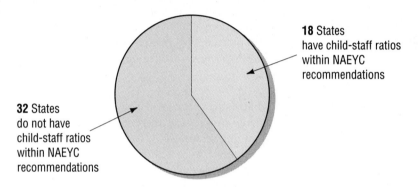

18 States have child-staff ratios within NAEYC recommendations

32 States do not have child-staff ratios within NAEYC recommendations

Percent of Classrooms with Good and Inadequate Practices Based on Those with the Most Children per Adult (Highest Ratios) and Fewest Children per Adult (Lowest Ratios)

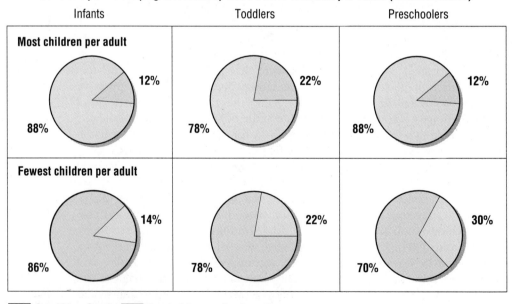

Infants — Toddlers — Preschoolers

Most children per adult
- Infants: 88% / 12%
- Toddlers: 78% / 22%
- Preschoolers: 88% / 12%

Fewest children per adult
- Infants: 86% / 14%
- Toddlers: 78% / 22%
- Preschoolers: 70% / 30%

Good/Very Good   Barely Adequate/Inadequate

Figure 3-6   Recommended ratios for quality programs. Compare this with the standards in your community. Notice the connection between adult-child ratios and quality. (From information in *Young Children*, *48* (2) p. 65-67, January 1993.)

| Figure 3-7 | **Children construct their own understandings of the world by interaction with materials and people in their environment.** |

Reciprocity of Learning

If teachers believe that learning takes place in the context of many complex adult-child relationships and does not result solely from one-way pronouncements and instruction, learning becomes a reciprocity where the responsibility is shared by every participant within the system. Most teachers find this concept rather exciting, removing from them the burden of being the sole resource for learning.

Children construct their own increasing understanding of the world by interaction with materials and people in their environments (see Fig. 3-7). Quality programs understand this principle of individuals constructing their own reality, with all participants playing both teaching and learning roles. The excellent teacher studied by Margaret Yonemura (1986) said, " 'We all have some learning to do from each other,' expressing her underlying view that we are all resources with practical knowledge. . . . the 'all' was inclusive of all children and adults" (Yonemura, 1986, p. 50).

Bredekamp, 1987, p.3

The image that conveys the concept of a *non*-reciprocal learning environment is that of a pitcher whose contents are being poured into an empty cup. The teacher is the pitcher, the cup is the child, and the action is all one-way, with the child taking in knowledge from the teacher and nothing being given back to the teacher, and no one else involved in the *transaction*. Instead, the image that could exemplify a reciprocal learning environment, where learning is multi-directional rather than following a single line, is that of a game where many balls are being thrown at random around a group. A ball leaves one hand, flying across the room to another hand, crossed by the flight of another that goes from a different hand to still another. Another ball suddenly surprises the

1900
Montgomery Ward catalog now offers kindergarten materials.

Figure 3-8 **Children who work together, or watch others at work, teach each other and learn from each other.**

first thrower, and so on. The possibilities of connections and combinations is limitless. This is the richness of a reciprocal learning environment, where all participants can teach each other and learn from one another, in *interaction*.

What would a reciprocal learning environment be like, from a teacher's point of view? One of the best descriptions of a teacher learning from children comes from Vivian Paley. In her work she continuously marvels at how she learns from the children themselves how to present ideas that they can comprehend. Her mistakes with using adult logic are gently changed as she listens carefully to the children, and has new insights to the world they have constructed. And, as we discussed in the previous section, remember that the web of relationships is providing other sources for reciprocal learning. As Paley also points out, the children learn from each other in ways she cannot teach them. Here she is reflecting on a child's words:

> Samantha's explanation, "You're really a helicopter really but you're pretending a baby" could never be used by a teacher. The statement can only be made by another child, because it must stay within the child's context of reality . . . In this single exchange between two young children there are important implications for classroom teaching at all levels. Children are able to teach one another best if they are permitted to interact socially and playfully throughout the day (Paley, 1990, p. 136).

What I hear, I forget. What I see, I remember. What I do, I understand.

—Chinese proverb

Read some of Paley's work–*Mollie is Three* (1986); *Bad Guys Don't Have Birthdays* (1988); *The Boy Who Would be a Helicopter* (1990)–and grow into your own understanding of how good teachers learn from children (see Fig. 3-8).

And Janet Gonzalez-Mena reminds us, in *Multicultural Issues in Child Care* (1993), how teachers can change their limited perspectives as they come

1903

Conflict within International Kindergarten Union is so disruptive that the Committee of Nineteen is established to "formulate contemporary kindergarten thought."

to learn reciprocally by listening to parents who have very different views about raising children.

One of the most important, and often undeveloped, reciprocities in early childhood programs is the reciprocal relationship that should exist between co-teachers and colleagues. Professional growth and learning does not take place in a vacuum. Opportunities for supportive dialogue and shared reflections, for joint observation and goal-setting provide for teachers' stimulation and challenge. Excellent programs provide encouragement and environmental supports for forming real collegial systems. Reciprocal learning is only possible when teacher attitudes of respect for all are present, and when the importance of relationships is recognized and nurtured.

Think about this concept of reciprocity in good learning environments. What examples or evidences of reciprocity have you encountered in your own learning experiences?

These first three components to be found in quality programs depend largely on attitudes and philosophy that translate into discernible kinds of interaction and communication. The next components are more directly related to the child development knowledge base of the teachers involved in the program.

Integration of Learning Experiences

In quality programs, children are seen as whole children, meaning that there is equal attention paid to needs and growth in all domains of development: **physical**, **cognitive**, **emotional**, **social** and **moral**. Physical competence, both **gross motor** and **fine motor**, and skill, emotional development or control and needs, social development skills, and intellectual development are all recognized as important aspects occurring simultaneously in young children. Simultaneously does not mean at an equal or parallel level; rather, it means that all of this learning is occurring in the same child at the same time. Furthermore, what is happening in one aspect of development is interrelated and has an effect on what is happening in other aspects. For example, success in learning some of the cognitive curriculum of the early elementary years can be predicated on the child's comfort in social situations, and ability to respond to the directions and guidance of a new adult. Infant language development parallels the acquisition of motor abilities to explore the world firsthand. Toddler frustration and temper outbursts may be directly related to limited vocabulary for expression, and so on.

The **whole child** is also seen as a part of the child's family, rather than in isolation in the classroom. The world at a school or center comprises only a part, and a small part, of a child's life experiences. The family's life is included in the classroom's, and the child is recognized at all times as a family member and participant.

Because the wholeness of children is recognized, those who sponsor good programs know that they cannot expect children to learn in a fragmented way, with learning or subject matter broken into individual, isolated lessons. Imagine the nonsense of planning an infant day to include a time to practice physical skills of crawling on the mat, followed by a short time of language instruction, with an experience in emotional closeness and bonding to come

Physical Development: Related to growth and coordination.

Cognitive Development: Related to mental functions of thinking, knowing, perceiving, and learning.

Emotional Development: Related to the feelings, and expression of them.

Social Development: The steps of learning appropriate social interaction, with peers and adults.

Bredekamp, 1987, p.3

Moral Development: Related to developing a sense of right and wrong behavior, and the ability to control one's actions by these internalized standards.

Gross Motor: Related to the whole body and to the larger muscle movements, such as legs, arms, trunk.

Fine Motor: Related to the smaller muscles of the body and limbs, such as fingers, toes, face, sphincters.

Whole Child: Recognizing the various separate and interrelated aspects of the individual: the domains of physical, cognitive, language, emotional, and social development.

1903
Of 175 public normal schools, 40 offer kindergarten training.

Figure 3-9   **These children, exploring materials, are learning many different things in an integrated curriculum.**

Integrated Curriculum:
Curriculum that centers on activities in which many aspects of development and knowledge are developed, rather than separating curriculum into separate subject or skill areas.

N A E Y C
GUIDELINE
Bredekamp, 1987, p.13

Assessment: An evaluation, as of abilities, skills, knowledge when referring to persons, or components when referring to environments.

next! Instead, caregivers sit near babies crawling on the mat, smiling, talking, encouraging, interacting. Development in all domains is being nurtured simultaneously–learning is integrated.

In the same way, good curriculum for older children consists of **integrated curriculum**, whole activities, rather than separate subject lessons. Not language period, followed by math and then science, but participation in a cooking activity that allows children to learn all of those concepts in a meaningful activity, as well as develop and use the skills involved (see Fig. 3-9). What thoughts or experiences with integrated learning have you had? What questions do you have about it?

Integrated learning for children in high quality programs does not happen by chance. Teachers who observe children continually come to know their abilities, their strengths, and the areas of development that need particular support. They assess individual development in the light of their knowledge of the predictable sequence of developmental abilities, so that they have for each child a sense of where the child is now, and what the next steps will be. These **assessments** are always enhanced by the teacher's dialogues with parents, so that objectives and goal setting is based on the best available information. So in good programs for young children, teachers have a clear sense of direction to guide them in planning the most appropriate learning experiences for individuals. The learning may look spontaneous and involve choices and action on the child's part, but it is part of a careful overall plan for each child, and it is not haphazard.

Another factor that contributes to whole rather than fragmented experiences for children and families is the wholeness of the early childhood program itself. Such wholeness is only achieved when a clearly articulated common philosophy connects all participants to an understood framework that is translated

1904
America has 166 day nurseries for low-income working families, according to the census report, of which 113 are in four states–Massachusetts, New Jersey, New York, and Pennsylvania.

Figure 3-10 | **Quality environments allow children to make choices of their activities.**

into daily actions. Defining common beliefs is crucial to full participation for both staff and families, so that adults knowingly commit themselves to the stated fundamental beliefs that will bind them. Quality programs have clearly stated and understood philosophies to guide their decision-making.

An Environment Prepared for Active and Cooperative Learning

Programs designed for children to learn through their interaction with materials and people indicate this orientation by decisions that structure the time and space environment for active learning. Classroom environments reflect teacher beliefs about children and how they learn, about the form and content of curriculum, and about the importance of social connections. When environment is seen as an important component of quality, teacher attention is given to physical arrangements for opportunities that encourage "encounter, communication, and relationships" (Gandini, 1993, p. 6).

Because teachers know that children learn through direct manipulation, play, and work with varieties of materials, furniture is used to display the available choices in a logical and organized way, encouraging children's choices and productive use. The environment is organized into logically separated **interest centers**, so that children may decide to work or play alone, with a few other children, or with a larger group. The coherence and unspoken messages of invitation, challenge, and order allow children to feel a measure of control over their learning activities and methods. In quality learning environments, children have opportunities to make choices: about which activities they are interested in; about how they will structure their learning activity; about whom they will play and work with, and where (see Fig. 3-10).

Bredekamp, 1987, p.3

Interest Centers: Also learning centers. Areas in classroom arranged for particular activities for children's choice. (Examples include an art center, a block center, a book center, etc.)

1906
G. Stanley Hall publishes *Youth,* the first consideration of adolescence as a separate period in development.

Figure 3-11   **What message does this book area give to children?**

Environment does convey messages. It can say, "This is a place where you can decide some things that you are going to do today," or "The teacher will always be the one in charge of telling you what to do." It can say, "Work with a friend if you like," or "Stay in your seat and work by yourself." It can say, "Here are some things that will allow you to succeed," or "This stuff is really hard and the teacher thinks you won't be able to learn it without her." It can say, "They care about your work here," or "What you do isn't really very important." It can say, "What you do, think, and communicate with your play is significant," or it can say, "After you play then we'll do the important things." It can say, "Your rights to work undisturbed and undistracted will be protected," or it can say, "This is not a peaceful place." It can say, "Childhood is valued and appreciated as a separate and distinct time of life," or it can say, "That childhood is seen as superficially cute." It can say, "You can do as much as possible for yourself here," or it can say, "You'll need to depend on grownups to do things for you." It can say, "There are some limits on things that aren't safe or acceptable," or it can say, "You'll have to make mistakes and then we'll stop you." It can say, "You belong here as a member of this classroom community," or it can say, "Your individuality is not respected." Think about it—in what specific ways can the design and placement of classroom furniture and materials, the decoration on the walls, or the classroom schedule and routines reflect these messages? What about other messages that you have been aware of in physical environments? (see Fig. 3-11.) Programs that understand children's active involvement

1907
Maria Montessori establishes a school for young children (Casa dei Bambini) in the slums of Rome.

Figure 3-12 **What are some of the "loose parts" in this water play situation, allowing children to explore, invent, combine, and communicate? (Courtesy of Tracie O'Hara)**

in discovery learning support this activity with the way time and space is arranged.

Quality programs for young children emphasize materials and experiences, knowing that children learn through doing, not through being just told about concepts. As James Hymes once put it, learning for young children comes through "Happenings."

> A Happening is always a verb. When the children are baking or buying or cooking or playing or painting or digging or washing or making or selling–this is a Happening. Science is not a Happening. Mathematics is not a Happening. Nor are the units found so often in kindergartens and in some nursery schools: The Seasons, Transportation, The Home, The Farm . . . . These are all nouns. Young children need verbs. Events. Action (Hymes, 1974, p. 85).

Excellent classrooms show themselves by the enticing materials that invite touching, the variety of "loose parts," to use Nicholson's phrase referring to open-ended materials (Nicholson, 1974), that allow children to explore and invent, to combine, create, and communicate (see Fig. 3-12). Materials are in good repair, safe, and readily used with the children's level of manipulative ability, and have been carefully selected for the learning

1908

London School Clinic is established by the McMillan sisters in response to concern that British children were not arriving at school age healthy enough to learn.

Figure 3-13   **Quality programs allow time for children's involvement in routine activities.**

environment because of the teachers' goals and children's interests. Think of some of the materials that have been part of any good early childhood program you know. What were some open-ended items that were used in interesting ways by the children?

If learning is to be organized around *Happenings,* large blocks of uninterrupted time are needed for children's meaningful involvement in them. The daily schedule will be organized to permit participation, practice, and repetition as children's repertoire of skills and knowledge grows, rather than letting institutionalized necessities fragment the day into multiple pieces, with many confusing **transitions**. When programs recognize that children's self-esteem and confidence as learners result from meaningful, personal involvement in activities, the daily plan permits such involvement (see Fig. 3-13).

Quality programs for young children recognize the importance of environmental decisions and create environments that support interaction and activity.

Underlying Developmental Understanding

When care and education programs for young children make their decisions based on facts and **theories** from child development knowledge and research, they are using standards of developmental appropriateness. The question is always: is our practice supported by what we know to be true about children in general, and these children in particular? While recognizing that the quality of an early childhood program is affected by many factors, NAEYC states that a major determinant of program quality is the "extent to which knowledge of child development is applied in program practices" (Bredekamp, 1987, p. 1).

Teachers in quality programs work from a child development knowledge base that has taught them much about children's abilities and interests at vari-

Transition: Period of change. The daily schedule in a classroom contains several transition periods, and children undergo transitions when they change from classroom to classroom.

Theory: Set of ideas, principles, or explanations to explain phenomenon, as in child development.

Bredekamp, 1987, p.1

Figure 3-14 **Classroom activities and themes are created because of children's interests. After noting the children's excitement with the construction next door, the teacher planned materials and activities to explore the theme of "construction." (Courtesy of Tracie O'Hara)**

ous stages. Thus they are able to structure learning experiences in which children can find their own developmental level, guaranteeing success without fear of failure. Recognizing that the individual children, even within a particular chronological grouping, may be far apart in their actual developmental ability, they provide materials that can be used with increasing levels of sophistication and skill. Children's freedom to make choices, coupled with teacher support and challenge, helps them find the activities they are ready for. Have you seen examples of children being able to choose the activities and materials that match their developmental readiness?

Appropriate curriculum in good classrooms is created through the interaction of children and all the involved adults, including parents, and through teachers' careful observation of children, and knowledge of developmental tasks and goals. That is, teachers are acutely aware of the direction they will help children move toward because of their recognition of the sequence of development in all domains. The actual activities, themes, and projects are created because of children's interests (see Fig. 3-14).

Because teachers recognize that young children's learning styles are active and hands-on, the strategies they use to support active learning may look quite different from what many think of as typical teaching behaviors. Teachers in good programs for young children will not be found instructing or lecturing from the front of the room; indeed you should have a hard time finding a front to the room! They interact with individuals or small groups busy at work or play. Embedded in their interaction may be chal-

N A E Y C
GUIDELINE
Bredekamp, 1987, p.4

N A E Y C
GUIDELINE
Bredekamp, 1987, p.4

The object of teaching a child is to enable him to get along without his teacher
—Elbert Hubbard

1911
Rachel and Margaret McMillan establish the Deptford School, an open air nursery school in London, inventing the term "nursery school."

lenges or suggestions of new directions to take in exploration, questions that may stimulate more activity or extend thinking, comments that reinforce or provide information. This is subtle and supportive teaching, adapted to each individual situation. Occasionally you will see teachers working with the whole group, but there is much less direct instruction even in this form, as children and adults interact together. As they listen to children's responses and ideas, teachers are continually assessing the progress and seeing what new learning they can facilitate. Teaching styles and strategies are shaped by developmental knowledge of how young children learn. In the next chapter we will discuss more about teacher roles and techniques. How does this description of teacher strategies match your image of what you would do as a teacher of young children?

POSITION STATEMENTS

All of the components of quality programs that have been discussed in this chapter are discussed in some detail in the most comprehensive professional organization position statement *Developmentally Appropriate Practice in Early Childhood Programs Serving Children From Birth Through Age 8,* published by NAEYC in 1987. That statement represents a consensus of the thinking of many early childhood professionals about appropriate and inappropriate practices in programs that span the time from infancy through the early elementary years. It was created in response to a need for a clearer definition of developmentally appropriate practice that arose when centers were applying criteria for accreditation (see Chapter Nine.) In the opening position statement, NAEYC affirms that a "high-quality early childhood program provides a safe and nurturing environment that promotes the physical, social, emotional, and cognitive development of young children while responding to the needs of families" (NAEYC, 1987, p. 1). Guidelines are presented in the position statement that describe how principles of developmental appropriateness can be applied to four components of early childhood programs: curriculum; adult-child interactions; relations between family and program; and developmental evaluation of children. Specifics of integrated components for appropriate and inappropriate practice for infants, for toddlers, for three-year-olds, for four- and five-year-olds, and for children ages five through eight years are described. These are all specifics with which you should become familiar and able to explain as an early childhood practitioner. It would be useful to discuss them with your classmates now.

When NAEYC accredits centers for quality (you will learn more about the accreditation process in Chapter Nine), it evaluates ten factors that include: the physical environment, health and safety, nutrition and food service, administration, staff qualifications and development, interactions among staff and children, staff-parent interaction, curriculum, staffing, and evaluation, with specifics defined in each factor (Bredekamp, 1990) (see Fig. 3-15). This suggests yet another standard for examining the quality in any given situation. As you examine various statements about quality (see Caldwell and Hilliard, 1985; and Phillips, 1987; NASBE, etc.), you will discover that they all include and incorporate the basic ideas discussed in this chapter.

Teachers teach for the wrong reasons most of the time. We teach what we've been taught, what will keep children busy, or what's easy for us. But we have no business interrupting a child unless we have reason to believe we're meeting that child's needs and interests
—Sydney Gurewitz-Clemens

N A E Y C
GUIDELINE
Bredekamp, 1987, p.3-13

Figure 3-15	**NAEYC accreditation standards evaluate physical environment, including the outdoor play area.**

If a child is to keep alive his inborn sense of wonder. . . he needs the companionship of at least one adult who can share it, rediscovering with him the joy, excitement, and mystery of the world we live in

—Rachel Carson

NOT FOUND IN QUALITY

Before we finish this discussion about what quality early childhood programs look like, it may be useful to identify in general what you will not see, if the program is developmentally appropriate (see Fig. 3-16).

Institutionalization

When decisions in programs are made to fit adult need or preconception, children are often expected to behave and learn in ways that fit with the requirements of the institution, rather than in ways that nurture their growth and development. What do we mean by this? As you search your memory for early childhood education experiences, you may recall occasions when children have had to do things that were not necessarily good for them, their learning, or their self-esteem, but because these were deemed necessary for the good of the institution. Examples of this might include: keeping exhausted toddlers awake so they can eat their lunch at the time convenient for the kitchen staff; insisting that first graders eat a silent lunch, so they can finish in twenty minutes and allow the next group to use the cafeteria; demanding that three-year-olds all sleep on their tummies at naptime, so they won't look around the room and prolong time for falling asleep; insisting that entrance to the two-year-old group has a prerequisite of giving up all pacifiers and "lovies," and so on (see Fig. 3-17).

Sometimes inappropriate practices exist because "That's the way we've always done it," and no one is applying the test of developmental appropriateness to it. Sometimes inappropriate practices exist because the adults in

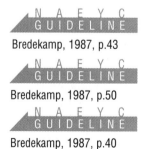

N A E Y C
GUIDELINE
Bredekamp, 1987, p.43

N A E Y C
GUIDELINE
Bredekamp, 1987, p.50

N A E Y C
GUIDELINE
Bredekamp, 1987, p.40

1911
Mothers' Pension Act provides pensions for mothers of young children with no source of support.

> ### WHAT IS QUALITY CHILD CARE ABOUT?
>
> It's about warmth and caring and interesting things to do. It's about high self-esteem and genuine concern about the quality of everyone's day. It's about playing games and singing songs and playing house and holding and laughing and having a nice time. It's about everyone being accepted and respected without reservation—and telling each other this in lots of ways. It's about overlooking transgressions so we can get on with things that really count. It's about children and adults spending the day together and looking forward to spending tomorrow together, too.
>
> ### WHAT IS POOR QUALITY CHILD CARE ABOUT?
>
> It's about criticism and harsh voices and stern faces and frowns. It's about battles of will between children and adults. It's about threats and time-outs for *everything*. It's about too many rules and bribery and adults who always stand up and no one can sit in their laps. It's about not much that's interesting going on and waiting for time to go home and wishing you didn't have to come back tomorrow.
>
> From "Caregiver's Corner," by Jeanine Allen, 1991, *Young Children, Vol.* 46(6) p. 18. Used with permission. National Association for the Education of Young Children.

Figure 3-16   **What is quality child care about, and not about?**

> *This is the essence of education: to facilitate a person's learning, to help that person become more in tune with his or her resources so that he or she can use whatever is offered more fully*
> —Fred Rogers

Readiness: State of being ready. Used in early childhood education to indicate child's ability to learn particular tasks. When used as *readiness tests,* frequently indicates tests used to determine readiness for academic learning of kindergarten and/or first grade.

charge are thinking about adult convenience, efficiency, time, or budgets. Sometimes they exist because the adults are lacking in child development knowledge or current thinking about appropriate practices. And sometimes they exist because adults have particular views about children needing to endure negatives to strengthen character, or to emphasize adult power. But whatever the reason, practices that do not nurture development and learning through emphasis on support and acceptance of individuals are bad for us all, and dehumanize society.

Failure

If early childhood schools and programs stand ready to adapt to individual needs and achievements of children, there will always be opportunities for children to find their comfortable learning level and style and thus, to succeed. But when programs apply their own arbitarily drawn standards for success to children at various ages, there are too many occasions when children will have to fail, since arbitrary standards allow no room for individual timetables. For example, readiness testing before gaining admission to kindergarten is going to exclude some children who have failed to meet the school system's standard for **readiness**. Proof of having completed toilet training before moving on to the next preschool classroom will negatively characterize those children who are

1912
The Children's Bureau is created by the federal government, and given the responsibility to investigate child health and labor.

Figure 3-17 There is *no* evidence of institutionalization here as these busy two year olds engage in a home-like activity of washing chairs. (Courtesy of Tracie O'Hara)

not yet ready. Not yet being ready to move from two to one nap per day may mean that some young toddlers will be denied moving on to the wonderful stimulation of the next class. Standardized testing at the end of second grade will find those children deficient who are learning at a less standardized rate. As long as schools and programs apply firm and arbitrary standards with no room for individual needs or developmental patterns, children will fail, and they and their parents will be burdened by a negative evaluation that may have lasting impact on future successful learning and development (Kamii, 1990).

Bredekamp, 1987, p.76

Indifference

Quality programs for young children depend on adults who have visions of wonderful worlds to support children and families, who are not willing to accept mediocre facilities, policies, or curriculum as the way it has to be. When teachers and caregivers are either not knowledgeable enough to be able to know mediocre from excellent, or when they become overwhelmed by the discrepancies between what they know should be and what is, indifference to lack of quality permits too many less than wonderful situations for children to exist. Indifference is an enemy to good early childhood education.

This is a good time for you to consider other conditions that you believe you should not find in good schools and centers for young children. Write them down for later discussion. Recognizing the opposite to excellence in early education will help you define your personal standards.

Jerome Bruner has said that one thing that happens in school is that children are led to believe they don't know or can't do something that they knew, or could do, before they got to school
—John Holt

SUMMARY

NAEYC and other professional organizations have described standards for developmentally appropriate practice. These include specific criteria for curriculum, adult-child interaction, home and school relationships, and evaluation of children's developmental progress in programs that serve children from birth through age eight. In this chapter, we elaborated on the attitudes and knowledge that are components of quality early education. These include: respect for the individuals involved; emphasis on developing relationships among all participants; reciprocity of learning for all participants; integrated learning experiences; environments to facilitate active learning; and developmental knowledge as the basis for curriculum content and teaching strategies. Components not found in quality programs include institutionalization, failure, and indifference.

QUESTIONS FOR REVIEW

1. Describe several components to be found in quality early childhood programs. Why are these necessary?

2. For each component described above, discuss several practices that might be included in program structure or function.

3. Identify what is meant by the NAEYC position statement on developmentally appropriate practice.

4. Identify several components not found in quality programs. Why should these practices be avoided?

ACTIVITIES FOR FURTHER STUDY

1. In small groups, discuss with classmates the statements and experiences you reflected on and recorded in your notebook throughout the chapter. Identify experiences that seem to corroborate the components discussed in the chapter. Identify experiences that seem at variance with the chapter. Identify the additional ideas discussed by the participants.

2. Write a personal statement of your belief or philosophy of early childhood education, based on your thinking and reading to this point.

3. Prepare a statement to deliver at a school board meeting that discusses whether or not to exclude five-year-olds that do not make a specific score on a readiness test given before admission.

4. Prepare answers to these questions from parents:

   a. Why do the children spend most of their time playing in your classroom?

   b. Why are some of the two-year-olds beginning toilet training and some are not?

   c. Why doesn't my four-year-old bring home artwork every day, like my next door neighbor's child does?

   d. What I don't get is, why do you call it teaching when you're not doing reading or math lessons or anything like that?

5. Read the NAEYC position statement on developmentally appropriate practices. What are the key words you find in these guidelines?

REFERENCES

Author. (1993). The effects of group size, ratios, and staff training on child care quality." (1993, January). *Young Children, 48,* 2, 65-67.

Author. (1993, September/October). What parents want. *Child Care Information Exchange, 93,* 63-67.

Bredekamp, S. (Ed.). (1987). *Developmentally appropriate practice in early childhood programs serving children from birth through age 8.* Washington, D.C.: NAEYC.

Bredekamp, S. (1990). An overview of NAEYC's criteria for high quality in early childhood programs. In Barbara Willer, (Ed.). *Reaching the Full Cost of Quality in Early Childhood Programs.* Washington, DC: NAEYC.

Caldwell, Bettye M. & Hilliard, III, Asa G. (1985). *What is quality child care?* Washington, DC: NAEYC.

Doherty-Derkowski, Gillian. (1995). *Quality matters: Excellence in early childhood programs.* Reading, MA: Addison-Wesley Publishers Ltd.

Gandini, Lella. (1993, November). "Fundamentals of the Reggio Emilia Approach to early childhood education." *Young Children, 49,* 1, 4-8.

Gonzalez-Mena, Janet. (1993). *Multicultural issues in child care.* Mountain View, CA: Mayfield Publishing Co.

Hymes, James L., Jr. (1974). *Teaching the child under six.* 2nd. Edition. Columbus, OH: Charles E. Merrill Publishing Co.

Isenberg, J., & Quisenberry, N. (1988). Play: A necessity for all children. *Childhood Education, 64,* 3, 138-145.

Kamii, Constance, (Ed). (1990). *Achievement testing in the early grades: Games grown-ups play.* Washington, DC: NAEYC.

Katz, Lilian. (1993). *Five perspectives on quality in early childhood programs.* Perspectives from ERIC/EECE. [Monograph series, 1], Urbana, IL: ERIC Clearing House on Elementary and Early Childhood Education.

Malaguzzi, Loris. (1993, Nov.). For an Education Based on Relationships. *Young Children, 49,* (1), 9-12.

Moyer, J., Egerston H., & Isenberg, J. "The child-centered kindergarten." *Childhood Education, 64,* 235-242.

NASBE. (1988). *Right From the Start.* Alexandria, VA: Author.

Nicholson, Simon. (1974). How not to cheat children: The theory of loose parts." *Alternate Learning Environments.* In G. Coates. (Ed.), Stroudsberg, PA: Dowden, Hutchinson and Ross.

Paley, Vivian Gussin. (1990). *The boy who would be a helicopter.* Cambridge, MA: Harvard University Press.

Phillips, Deborah A, (Ed.). (1987). *Quality in child care: What does research tell us?* Washington, DC: NAEYC.

Yonemura, Margaret V. (1986). A teacher at work: professional development and the early childhood educator. New York: Teachers College Press.

SUGGESTIONS FOR FURTHER READING

Author. (1995, March). "Reaffirming a National Commitment to Children." *Young Children, 50,* (3), 61-63.

Balaban, Nancy. (1990, March). Statement to the Montgomery County Council. *Young Children, 45,* (3), 12-16.

Bredekamp, S., & Rosegrant, T., (Eds.). (1991). *Reaching potentials: appropriate curriculum and assessment for young children.* Washington, DC: NAEYC.

Christie, J.F., & Wardel, F. (1992, March). How much time is needed for play?" *Young Children, 47,* (3), 28-32.

Greenberg, Polly. (1990, January). Why Not Academic Preschool? (Part 1) *Young Children, 45,* 2, 70-80.

Greenman, Jim. (1994, November). Institutionalized childhoods: Reconsidering our part in the lives of children. *Child Care Information Exchange,* 63-67.

Honig, Alice S. (1989, May). Quality infant/toddler caregiving: Are there magic recipes? *Young Children, 44,* (4), 4-10.

Kamii, Constance. (1985, September). Leading primary education toward excellence. *Young Children, 40,* (6), 3-9.

Katz, Lilian G. (1994, November). What should young children be learning? *Child Care Information Exchange,* 23-25.

Kelman, Anna. (1990, March). Choices for Children. *Young Children, 45,* (3), 42-45.

NASBE. (1991). *Caring communities: Supporting young children and families.* The Report of the National Task Force on School Readiness. Alexandria, VA: Author.

NAESP. (1990). *Early childhood education and the elementary school principal: Standards for quality programs for young children.* Alexandria, VA: Author.

Sava, Samuel G. (1987, March). Development, not academics. *Young Children, 42,* (3), 15.

WHAT TEACHERS DO

When children play school, they often demonstrate an interesting portrayal of their perceptions of what it is that teachers do. Whether these images have their roots in real life experiences, or in traditions taught by older children, or in partial understandings of a distant adult world, children's play of school usually indicates the exercise of power of an adult who controls and dominates the learning situations, often firmly chastising the unfortunate players who go against the "teacher's" will. This central role of clear and direct instruction is often the larger society's image of the word "teacher". And it is likely that many beginning early education students also are consciously or unconsciously influenced by this idea.

Yet this image associated with teaching is at once limiting and misleading when we consider teaching young children. It is limiting, because there are many more roles that teachers play in addition to direct instruction. Some of these roles are played openly, and are obvious as we follow teachers through their daily lives; others are less evident, often occurring behind the scenes as teachers create the framework for good programs and curriculum, and create linkages between their classrooms and beyond. This image is also misleading, because the dictionary definition of the word "teacher" may suggest a narrower scope of function than exists today for the adults involved in the early years of children. As Lilian Katz points out, "The younger the child, the greater is the range of his or her functioning for which adults must assume responsibility" (Katz, 1995, p. 141).

OBJECTIVES

After studying this chapter, students will be able to:

1. identify several distinct roles played by early childhood teachers.

2. describe the rationale for each of the roles, and discuss component behaviors.

3. discuss the interrelationship of the various teacher roles.

In fact, the word "teacher" itself may be part of the problem. The adult's role and functioning in programs for young children suggests more complexity: "What proportion of the role is educational? How much is health-related? How much emphasis should be put on care?" (Katz, 1995, p. 140). There have been attempts in recent years to replace this term with its implied limitations, but nothing seems to have quite worked. "Caregiver" implies too custodial a function, and quite overlooks the important attention to the development of knowledge and skills. Bettye Caldwell (1990) suggested the designation "educarer" to combine the two concepts of teacher and caregiver, but it has not been widely used. Bernard Spodek et al. (1988) suggests that "early childhood practitioner" might be comprehensive enough, but others feel it may be too generic to have much meaning except to those initiated into the profession.

As the search for appropriate terminology continues, it is most important that you who are entering the field understand the complexity and interrelationships of the various roles involved in the care and education of young children. In this chapter we will explore those separate roles, and allow you opportunities to reflect on your own involvement in them.

> Before I stepped into my first classroom as a teacher, I thought teaching was mainly instruction, partly performing, certainly being in the front and at the center of classroom life. Later, with much chaos and some pain, I learned that this is the least of it–teaching includes a more splendorous range of actions (Ayers, 1993, p. 4).

Let us consider that "splendorous range."

IDENTIFYING THE ROLES

Professional: A practitioner that has met the standards of knowledge and performance required by the profession.

When we refer to teacher *roles,* we are referring to the particular functions and behaviors that teachers are expected to perform and exhibit. If you were to ask experienced early childhood **professionals** what hats they wear on any given day, they might respond with a list of nouns that are associated with particular actions. That list might include: parent, housekeeper, nurse, diplomat, artist, musician, judge, cook, friend, bookkeeper, entertainer, and instructor; the more facetious might include labels such as liontamer or Pied Piper. A beginning teacher said she alternated between police officer and ringmaster (Dollase, 1992). They might add some specific skills that have been handy: repairing toys, detecting guilt or sources of strange odors, restoring physical order from chaos, washing paint from favorite T-shirts, unstopping toilets, or determining fair solutions to playground conflicts. Or they might get right down to the nitty-gritty of everyday situations, describing nose-blowing, endless amounts of shoe-tying, table-cleaning, and taking out the trash. But in this discussion on roles we want to look beyond those specific categorizations to the larger aspects that are included in our concept of providing support for the growth and development of young children in the kind of excellent programs we have discussed in Chapter Three.

Without truly radiating and receiving joy, an adult cannot foster an atmosphere where children can invent and create
—Loris Malaguzzi

Read the following brief scenarios and see if you can identify the roles that the early childhood teachers are involved in: what are the various things that they are doing that all relate to their function of helping young children grow and develop? Be aware that some scenarios may suggest more than one role to you.

THEORY INTO PRACTICE

This is Deborah Gordon, a child care provider in her large family home that has received national accreditation. A mother of a six-year-old and a three-year-old, she has been involved in child-care for eight years. She has taken numerous courses in an associate degree program in early childhood education, as well as much workshop training.

What has been a significant frustration for you in early education? How do you deal with it?

A frustration for me is knowing some children are in unhealthy situations and not being able to do anything about it. I deal with it by providing the child with the best environment while he is in my care. I try to make sure parents know I am available whenever they may need to talk.

What is one thing you learned in classes that you really discovered to be true when you started working with children?

Each and every child truly is a unique individual—just as different as fingerprints.

What is an area you are working on now to learn more about?

Right now I'm working on learning more about discipline techniques that will enable me to help preschoolers solve their own problems.

Why have you stayed in early education?

I stay because it is a rewarding challenge when I can make a positive difference in a child's life.

What is a comment or piece of advice you would give to those beginning to work in early childhood education?

I would tell new teachers to have a strong commitment to making life better for children, to continue to receive as much training and education as possible, to join professional organizations and associations and actively participate when possible. Because the work can be long, hard and tiring with low wages, if you discover it is not for you, don't stay in the field.

Sarah James is spending her Saturday morning as she usually does, visiting all the yard sales in her part of town. She is particularly delighted with two puzzles and an unopened game she found, and is considering going back to one house that offered a small table for sale.

Rosa Sanchez has spent the evening stuffing envelopes at the local election board. School bond issues are on the ballot at the upcoming local election.

Thomas Finch has spent an hour talking with the speech therapist who regularly visits a child in his classroom. Later he discusses the earlier conference with his teacher assistant.

Barbara Schulz cradles tiny Jonathan as she feeds him his bottle. She notes that he is sucking strongly, but also that his congestion is undiminished. She decides to call his grandmother, since she knows his mother is in class.

Anne Mahoney invites her director to sit in on a scheduled conference with Rickiya's parents, since she feels they may be upset with the discussion of difficult behaviors that is planned.

Sheila Berkowitz sits near a group of children building in the block area, occasionally asking a question and listening carefully to their responses. From time to time she makes notes on a pocket notepad.

Patrick Porter takes a child who has been at loose ends off to one side of the classroom for a quiet conversation. After a few minutes he gets the child started on an activity creating patterns from small colored cubes, first demonstrating the concept from the activity card.

SuHai Nguyen leads a group discussion after she has read a folktale to the class. After a few minutes of discussion, she records the children's comments on a wall chart.

Tomeka Jeffries picks up a screaming toddler who was trying to grab a toy from another child, and takes him over to the rocking chair. After a few minutes of calming, she interests him in a waterplay activity.

Janelle Hawkins strips the dramatic play dressups from the hooks and stuffs them in bags for the parent who will wash them this weekend. She reorganizes materials on the shelves, matching them to the picture cards that show where materials belong.

Rachel Jacobs takes the boys who are arguing about turns at baseball over to the picnic benches and helps them to discuss their difficulties and find a solution.

Jane Meyers talks with her coteacher about rearranging the children's playground time to allow for longer periods to work on indoor projects.

Georgia Wilder listens carefully to the child who is talking with her, gently asking another child who interrupted to please wait until she's finished talking with Cara.

Debbie Miller sits quietly at the end of the day, making notes in her daily log.

All of these adults work in classrooms that serve children from birth through the early school years. All of them are performing the various roles that are part of a teacher's daily life. Discuss with your classmates the names that you gave to the separate teacher activities. You may have identified them with your own words, but see if you can find activities that match the following

> *When you are dealing with a child, keep all your wits about you and sit on the floor*
>
> —Austin O'Mally

1913
Report of the Committee of Nineteen reflects so much diversity that three reports are given: conservative (Froebelian), liberal (Deweyan), and liberal-conservative (combined viewpoints).

| Figure 4-1 | **Nurturing includes the one-to-one contacts that are essential for healthy personality development in young children. (Courtesy of Tracie O'Hara)** |

teacher roles: nurturer; observer; organizer of environment; collaborator with parents; collaborator with colleagues and other professional staff; provider of resources; setter of limits of behavior; facilitator of learning; advocate for children and families; model of appropriate behavior; evaluator/assessor.

From this introductory activity, you can see that teachers of young children perform various roles that all support children's growth and learning. The roles played are generally the same, whether you are talking about working with infants, toddlers, preschoolers, or school-aged children, and no matter what the setting. The precise activities discussed under each role may look a little different depending on the age-group served, but the roles themselves are constant. As we go on to organize and discuss these roles more fully, think also about yourself performing these roles. Are these the activities you want to be involved in during your daily professional work?

Teacher as Nurturer

Nurturing means supplying the support that children need to grow and develop. Physical as well as social and emotional needs must be met for healthy development. With the youngest children, the warm physical contact and responsiveness that accompany the providing of physical needs is an interrelated and inseparable kind of nurturing that is essential. That is to say, the gentle stroking and soft crooning that accompanies the cleansing bath, the warmly enfolding arms that hold the baby when being fed the bottle, are both nurturing to overall development. Young children's healthy social/emotional development is dependent on involvement in warm and supportive relationships with caring adults. The most important relationships, of course, are with their parents and family members. But the other adults involved in their care also hold key roles in healthy personality development (see Fig. 4-1).

Bredekamp, 1987, p.25

Nurturing: Providing the care and fulfilling needs to promote development.

1913

The number of public normal schools that offer kindergarten training has increased to 71 out of 146.

The role of *teacher as nurturer* involves the support of this development. Often early childhood professionals are the first people outside the family with whom children have caring relationships. As more and more infants and toddlers spend large portions of their time with adults paid to care for them, they are dependent on those relationships for the emotional nurturing that would in the past have been available through parenting. And the need for warm and emotionally based relationships does not disappear after toddlerhood; preschoolers and children in the early elementary years also look for love and affection from their teachers.

There are both similarities and differences between the teaching and mothering roles (Katz, 1980), and all early childhood teachers must be wary of being drawn into usurping any aspects of parenting and becoming too intimately involved in children's lives. Nevertheless, teachers should recognize and accept the centrality of warm, individual relationships between themselves and the children in their programs. Teachers have to be able to identify and try to fulfill individual children's needs for physical warmth and contact as well as for emotional support and security. No one who feels unable to respond to children's needs for affection and attention should consider the profession of early childhood education.

A word of caution as you consider this point: individuals vary in the degree of demonstrativeness with which they are comfortable. Some students worry, saying, "I've just never been a touchy-feely person. I'm not real comfortable doing a lot of hugging or kissing. And furthermore, in this day and age, I'm not sure that people want others physically close to their children. Does this mean I won't be a good teacher for young children?" The answer to this is no. Just as adults vary, so do children. Some children enjoy a lot of physical contact and others do not. Warmth and emotional responsiveness can be demonstrated to children in many ways: in gentle smiles and personal eye contact; in a warm tone of voice; in personal attention and shared moments. The exact manner of nurturing is quite individual. Children know when they are genuinely cared for, even though the message may come in different ways.

Nurturing looks like many different things, depending on the age and needs of the children in the teacher's care. For babies and toddlers, it may include being "smoothers of jangled feelings . . ., comforters, . . . facilitators of parent-child separations" (Balaban, 1992, pp. 69-70), as well as rockers, singers, and tummy-kissers. For preschoolers, it may include touches on the arm when passing, moments of quiet conversation, a special hug for good morning. For school age, it may be offering a joke that the child can appreciate, teasing gently about private secrets, a personal wink or thumbs-up sign. All of these tell children that teachers know and like them as unique individuals.

It is also important that teachers realize that it is beyond their power to help a child feel completely loved if the child perceives opposite messages elsewhere. Sometimes in the role of nurturer, teachers find themselves in the position of nurturing parents who may have unfulfilled emotional needs and thus have difficulty adequately providing for their child's needs. Here again, because of the professional relationship involved, teachers must recognize realistically that they will be unable to provide for everyone's needs. But as they recognize the need for

1913

Caroline Pratt, frustrated with the Froebelian-based teacher preparation at Teachers College, begins an experimental school for five-year-olds in New York City.

supportive relationships, they may be able to help parents find other sources for their own emotional growth and health that will ultimately benefit children.

As we will discuss in Chapter Five, just loving children in some vaguely superficial sense is certainly not enough to qualify one as an early childhood teacher. But it is important to realize that creating nurturing relationships that allow children to trust and feel comfortable in their center or school is an essential role of the teacher.

Nurturing also implies providing for the essential meeting of physical needs, or **caregiving**. Even elementary teachers find that they must meet children's health and hygiene needs, as they make sure children have opportunities for nutrition, elimination, rest, and to learn health habits. Teachers of younger children will find much more primary responsibility for diaper-changing and cleansing, for feeding children or helping children learn to feed themselves, for serving food and cleaning up afterwards, for helping with hand-washing and face-wiping, and changing clothes after spills or accidents. Through such commonplace daily acts, children experience adults' gentleness, and demonstration of skills that they can learn to do themselves eventually. And also through such caregiving activity, curriculum is taught, developing skills by sharing language and concepts. Teachers of the youngest children recognize that the caregiving aspects of their work are important times for building relationships and for teaching, and as such they do not rush through them to get to something judged to be more important.

> **Caregiving:** Refers to the physical nurturing and protection of young children.

Teacher as Researcher

A teacher role that surrounds and undergirds much of effective teacher practice is the role of *teacher as researcher*. Effective teachers are continually in the process of learning more about educational theory and practice in general, and in particular, more about the children and families with whom they work. They see themselves as continually and actively constructing their own understanding of teaching and learning, helping themselves change and learn. As researchers, they collect data, analyze information, and test hypotheses (see Fig. 4-2).

This idea of teacher as researcher may surprise you when listed as a primary role for early childhood teachers, and you may think at first that it is not clearly linked to supporting children's learning, but it is, in several distinct ways.

The first connection is in the importance of teachers' feeling that they are growing in their understanding of where they have been, where they are now, and what they are about, in order to be truly effective in their work.

> *The goal of observation is understanding, not some imagined objectivity*
> —William Ayers

I have spent thousands of hours in schools and one of the first things I sensed was that the longer the person had been a teacher the less excited, or alive, or stimulated he seemed to be about his role. It was not that they were uninterested, or felt that what they were doing was unimportant, or that they were not being helpful to their students, but simply that being a teacher was on the boring side. . . . What would be inexplicable would be if things turned out otherwise, because schools are not created to foster the intellectual and professional growth of teachers. The assumption that

1914
Caroline Pratt designs first set of unit blocks.

Figure 4-2 **An important teacher role is observing and recording information on individual children's progress and areas of interest.**

teachers can create and maintain those conditions which make school learning and school living stimulating for children, without those same conditions existing for teachers, has no warrant in the history of man (Sarason, 1972, pp. 123-124).

Every experienced early childhood teacher recognizes the truth that there is a danger of becoming complacent and vaguely disinterested in the daily scene of classroom activities. The danger becomes lessened when teachers begin to define themselves as "field researchers in child development" (Carter and Curtis, 1994, p. 90). When teachers identify subjects and questions about which they are genuinely curious, they focus their attention on finding answers in their own classrooms, with their own children. Teachers are learners, and by becoming learners, are themselves involved in active and dynamic processes within the classroom.

For example, Patrick Porter decided this year to see if children can learn the reading and writing skills required by the end of the year competency tests, by using their skills for in-depth projects that *they* select. He's doing more informal small group and individual instruction as he and the children see the need for a particular skill to use in their project work. "It certainly is keeping me on my toes," he laughs, "because I can't just use the teacher's guides and preplanned lessons, but instead I really have to know where each child is and what they're working on and need. My guess is, they're learning these skills just as well as the old way, if not better, but it's going to be fun to see at the end. It's been interesting for us all. And we've got some amazing projects going." This doesn't sound like a bored teacher, because he has defined his interest and is actively pursuing it. Teachers working with all ages make their own discoveries, testing hypotheses and theories, and the learning environment actively brings together children and energized adults, who have a renewed appreciation of children's play and learning styles.

We always have to act on too little information, but at least the information is collected methodically every day. We try to stay flexible in the face of our fantasy as to who the child is, reversing and turning corners as new data comes in. To refine the guessing mechanism through logging makes a good teacher better
—Sydney Gurewitz-Clemens

1914
U.S. Public Health Service publishes first edition of *Infant Care.*

Obviously a key function of the teacher as researcher is the teacher as *observer*–being "listeners and watchers" (Balaban, 1992, p. 69). **Objective** observation, done systematically over periods of time, helps teachers focus on children. Regular observation allows teachers to know specifics about each child–likes, dislikes, style, abilities, and needs. These specifics are useful in forming relationships. Indeed, one piece of advice that most teachers have received is that focused observation is a useful strategy when dealing with a child that the teacher finds difficult to like. Paying close attention to the child will usually help a teacher find things that are positive that may have been previously overlooked. Specific insights on children's development also allow teachers to support children's individual learning most appropriately. Regular observing and recording (Jones and Reynolds [1992] call this role "scribe") allow teachers to assess individual patterns and learning styles. Thus they can formulate meaningful individualized goals for children, based on their knowledge of sequential steps and individual capabilities. "A teacher working with many human knowers can guide their learning only within a learning environment in which attention is paid to what is happening for each learner. In such a classroom the teacher becomes, not primarily someone who tells and corrects, but someone who watches" (Jones, 1993).

Setting specific goals for supporting children's development and learning based on regular objective observations, compared with the norms of child development research (as well as on the subjective interpretations that teachers can make as they discover more about individuals), gives teachers the structure that allows them to explain their practice to others, as well as to evaluate the effectiveness of their actions. Saracho (1988) refers to this teacher role of observer and assessor as *diagnostician,* but this may suggest a clinical expertise that is beyond the true scope of the teacher as researcher.

Teachers who know their children intimately through observation and recording have the ideas and insights that allow them to generate appropriate curriculum activities and projects that have real meaning to their particular groups of children. Such curriculum–sometimes termed "emergent" (Jones and Nimmo, 1994)–is grounded in teacher observations and dialogue with the children and adults involved in a program, and teacher reflection. **Emergent curriculum** can only occur in a particular place, at a particular time, with a particular group of children (Cassidy and Lancaster, 1993). Teachers who are playing the role of observer and researcher are able to create this meaningful curriculum (see Fig. 4-3). Thus, although early childhood educators are continually planning, the role of planning is not discussed separately here, since the planning is interwoven inextricably with observing, goal-setting, assessment, and the daily lives and conversations that stimulate thinking. These roles are also cyclical, with observing leading to initial goals and starting plans, and subsequent observation informing the direction of plans that follow.

Teachers who are carefully observing and recording examples of children's play and learning are able to deepen children's learning experiences by helping children represent and recreate their learning for themselves and others. Discussions and evaluations with children, other teachers, and parents become more productive when teachers have recorded specifics that indicate

Objective: The ability to base conclusions on observable fact.

Bredekamp, 1987, p.5

Emergent Curriculum: Curriculum that develops out of the particular interactions and interests of the individuals in a particular setting at a particular time.

1915
Maria Montessori has an exhibition classroom at the World's Fair in San Francisco.

Figure 4-3   **Meaningful curriculum is created by teachers who know their children's interests and abilities.**

patterns of growth or particular needs that require attention. Observing and recording–doing real and practical research by asking and attempting to answer specific questions about groups of children and individuals–is an ongoing teacher role that influences literally every other role that we will discuss. In later courses and practicums, you will work on developing observation techniques and skills.

Teachers as researchers push themselves continually into finding new and unknown territory in their work with children. This makes it a learning and growing experience for themselves, and allows their teaching to more likely match the children they work with. As one teacher put it:

> I work in a state of uncertainty because I do not know where the children will arrive to, but it is a fabulous experience!. . .It is as if we are starting off together on a voyage. It could be short; it could be long. But there is an eagerness in doing it together (Laura Rubizzi, quoted in Edwards, 1994, p. 159).

Teacher as Set Designer

This is the designation for the role that teachers play when they organize and create the environment for children's active learning. Set designer seems to be a comprehensive enough term to include the many facets of environmental decisions and arrangements that teachers need to make. It is also broad enough

A good teacher of young children needs to take great pleasure in setting up a classroom that allows children to explore, to question, to work alone, in a group, or with an adult

–Carol Hillman

1915

First parent cooperative nursery school is established by a group of faculty wives at the University of Chicago.

to include the family child care home provider who arranges play and rest areas within her own home, the infant caregiver who has to provide for individual mobility patterns as well as unpredictable baby schedules for eating and sleeping, and the elementary teacher who is using learning centers as well as traditional desk arrangements in his classroom. The term also implies the importance of this teaching role; anyone who has ever experienced the difference between the bare-staged running through of lines and the play seen against a full and suggestive backdrop, complete with appropriate props and effects, realizes how much is conveyed and enhanced by this behind-the-scenes work. *Teacher as set-designer* requires careful thinking and planning about the desired product and the roles children will play, combining two of the teacher roles defined by Saracho (1984): organizer of instruction and manager of the environment.

Some authors (Hillman, 1988; Carter and Curtis 1994) have referred to the teacher role of *architect,* to describe the ways that teachers use and adapt space to fit children's play and activity needs. In fact, many teachers faced with creating a learning environment in an old school or church basement have often wished they could truly be architects, knocking out walls that crowd or creating doors and windows where light and access would expand the possibilities. But since most teachers come on the scene after the architectural decisions have been made, it is probably more accurate to describe a set designer role. By the arrangement of furniture and materials, teachers send the kind of specific environmental messages about children and learning that we discussed in Chapter Three. Their attention to the environment helps give emphasis to the kinds of curriculum and learning possibilities that can go on. The children-as-players who enter the set immediately grasp their roles and set about the activity.

What kinds of decisions do teachers make in their role of set designer? They decide on the aesthetics of the place, creating a look that invites, attracts, warms, comforts, and says who belongs (see Fig. 4-4). They decide on the order and organization of the place, placing objects where they will attract notice and can be used most effectively. They create methods of ensuring that the players have ready access to the props and materials they will need for their work. To continue the "theatrical" model and metaphor, teachers decide on and gather the props, after careful consideration of what kinds of materials will enhance the learning environment for the particular players. (Think back to the role of teacher as researcher to see how it connects with this role.) And good set designers are always ready to improvise, adding other props as the play proceeds and they discover what could be helpful additions. (This could be seen as a subcategory: teacher as prop manager [Carter and Curtis, 1994]). The provisioning of stimulating, meaningful materials for learning is an extremely important facet of set design.

Teachers as set designers create careful groupings and scenes to prevent the players from crowding one another, while they also permit interaction and freedom of movement. And they set a stage that prevents accidents, carefully safeguarding children's activity by removing potentially hazardous materials or circumstances. The play will be able to proceed smoothly because the players

N A E Y C
GUIDELINE
Bredekamp, 1987, p.7

1916
Lizzie Merrill-Palmer leaves funds in her will to establish the Merrill-Palmer School (later Institute) in Detroit, to teach girls to be mothers.

Figure 4-4 | **With a beanbag chair and shower curtain, the teacher in the role of "set designer" created a listening cave that invites participation.**

clearly understand the plan for their functioning within the environment. Some of the materials on the set will be very familiar to the child's play.

As you understand, when we talk about "the play" we are not talking idly about theatrical matters here, but we are aware that teachers make many behind-the-scenes decisions that *do* impact the quality of learning and interaction (see Fig. 4-5). One last thing teachers decide that also controls opportunities for learning is the time-frame–the **schedule** and **routine**–for the environment. The play is not allowed to drag out long after the interest has waned, or is interrupted before full involvement develops. A sensitive pacing allows for active involvement, quiet interludes, intermissions such as restroom visits and snack times, and individual levels of participation.

In the role of teacher as set designer, teachers often find themselves doing creative scrounging and production of materials, since most early childhood programs do not come readily equipped with everything a teacher would like to have. They frequently find themselves arranging and preparing materials outside of their regular classroom hours, since much of the stage manager function is done behind-the-scenes to be ready and waiting when the players arrive on the scene. The environment is critical to the learning that will take place there. In schools that realize the importance of the environment, it is seen as "educating the child; in fact, it is considered as the 'third educator' along with the team of two teachers" (Gandini, 1994, p. 148).

Schedule: The order of daily events in the program.

Routines: Repeated components of the daily schedule, often associated with care of children and environment, such as snack time and cleanup time.

1916

Lucy Sprague Mitchell and Harriet Johnson begin the Bureau of Educational Experiments in New York City. The Bureau is later to become the Bank Street School of Education.

Figure 4-5 | **The behind-the-scenes decisions that created this attractive dramatic play area have an impact on the quality of play and interaction that take place here.**

We value space because of its power to organize, promote pleasant relationships between people of different ages, create a handsome environment, provide changes, promote choices and activity, and its potential for sparking all kinds of social, affective and cognitive learning. All of this contributes to a sense of well-being and security in children. We also think that the space has to be a sort of aquarium that mirrors the ideas, values, attitudes, and cultures of the people who live within it (Malaguzzi in Gandini, 1994, pp. 148-9).

Teacher as Facilitator of Learning

The dictionary definition of *facilitate* tells us that it means to make easier, to aid, or assist. This conveys the full meaning of *teacher as facilitator* of children's active learning, as a resource person to help children as they construct their own continually shifting knowledge of the world. Teachers of young children facilitate development and learning by providing them with time, space, materials, and support for active exploration. They carefully choose opportunities based on their knowledge of individual children, child development, and family and society goals and needs. They allow and encourage children to become active learners, and match their teaching strategies to what is required to best assist a child's learning. Another term that has been used to describe the process of helping children reach new levels in their understanding is *scaffolding* (Berk and Winsler, 1995). This term was used by the Russian psychologist Lev Vygotsky (see Chapter Eight) to describe the kind of assistance that adults

Bredekamp, 1987, p.10

1917
Caroline Pratt's Play School (later to become City and Country School) is growing. Lucy Sprague Mitchell is one of its teachers.

Figure 4-6 | **Teachers as facilitators support active exploration with their interest and open-ended questions.**

Each time one prematurely teaches a child something he could have discovered for himself, that child is kept from inventing it and consequently from understanding it completely
—Jean Piaget

give children in their learning. "If the children have gone from [point] A to B and are getting very close to C, sometimes to reach C, the child needs to borrow assistance from the adult at that very special moment" (Filippini, quoted in Edwards, 1994, p. 153). In helping the child make the next step, the adult functions rather like a scaffold framework that allows the child to reach further than would be possible unassisted. Facilitation of learning is a supportive relationship; it is done with a child actively, not just information that is given to a passive child.

To return to our "theatrical" metaphor, facilitating is what happens after "the teacher writes the play, gathers the props, sets the stage . . . and, once the play has begun, assumes the role of stage manager. Stage managers see to it that the play goes on. (Directors, on the other hand, tell the players what to do and how)" (Wasserman, p. 27). Facilitating keeps the learning action–and the play–moving, by using a variety of teaching strategies.

What are some of the teaching strategies that a teacher uses in the role of facilitator? These include: asking questions to help children clarify or extend their learning; making suggestions or providing materials that lead children further in their explorations; encouraging and sustaining effort with their presence; supporting as children struggle with new challenges; demonstrating and teaching new information and skills that children need to proceed; and reinforcing learning by providing opportunities for children to practice or communicate about their learning (see Fig. 4-6). All of these strategies are choices for teachers to make as they select the most appropriate response in the situation. The goal of all learning strategies is to help children to "improve, extend, refine, develop, and deepen their own understandings or constructions of their own worlds" (Katz, 1995, p. 6).

1918
Public assistance is available to mothers in thirty-nine states.

Teachers learn that good questions can help children focus and think about their activity and learning, or can challenge them to further exploration. They learn that good questions are those that encourage thinking and communication, rather than those where children merely focus on trying to give the teacher the right answer that is apparently expected. Good questions are generally open-ended, or **divergent**, and cause children to really question also (Rogers, 1990). Learning comes from posing continually harder puzzles to the individual. Teachers are genuinely curious about the answer to good questions, not just trying to test what the child has learned from the teacher. For example, "What other words that you know does that remind you of?" could be a helpful and unpressured question for a child, suggesting that prior knowledge could help the child figure something out; "What color is that?" implies that the teacher expects and knows the correct answer. Good facilitators learn to formulate good questions.

Teachers can enrich and deepen learning experiences by offering suggestions for additional activity or by adding materials that can support new directions. A teacher may say, "You know, you could put some of the plants where they'll get lots of light and some where they won't get any if you wanted to see whether they really do need light to grow." This offers the children a meaningful experience that will teach, rather than simply listing on the board the essentials for plant growth. Similarly, when the teacher sees that the children are interested in discussing heavy and light objects, the addition of a scale to the science center will likely lead to much weighing and discovery.

When teachers freely move around the classroom to observe and interact with children busy at work and play, their actual presence encourages and sustains children's efforts.

> [An] answer. . . about what produced prolonged concentration in play
> rather took us aback. It was the presence of an adult. I do not mean an
> adult "over the shoulder" of the child, trying to direct his activity, but one
> in the neighborhood who gave some assurance that the environment
> would be stable and continuous, but would also give the child reassur-
> ance and information as, if, and when the child needed it (Bruner,
> 1991, p. 80).

Classrooms where the environment and curriculum emphasize individual and small group learning free teachers to interact in individualized ways. This not only allows them to give specific instruction and assistance as needed, but also to encourage children who are struggling at particular moments. It is a mistake to generalize that teachers who work with young children do not provide direct instruction or demonstration, for they certainly do as they find it is needed. Rather, this is not their sole teaching strategy, nor necessarily one that is used more than others. They recognize that learning does not happen only as a result of their talking. Elementary- and school-age child care teachers also recognize that strategies other than direct instruction may be equally important, rather than falling into the "lecture" mode too prevalent in the upper grades.

Divergent Thinking: Thought that does not center on finding correct answers, but is flexible and moves in creative directions.

N A E Y C
GUIDELINE
Bredekamp, 1987, p.5

Making peace is the most difficult work of all
—Hanan Mikhail Ashrawi

1919
Margaret McMillan publishes a book titled *The Nursery School.* Her sister Rachel had died in 1917.

| Figure 4-7 | **Good facilitators know that children need to repeat activities to build confidence. This child has done this puzzle six times this morning. What might a facilitator do to encourage a next step?** |

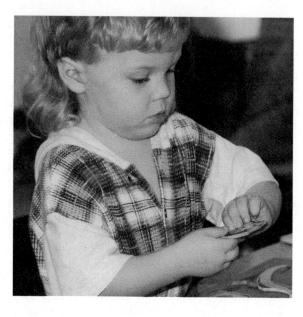

In facilitating learning, early childhood teachers recognize the need for children to repeat and practice using newly acquired abilities and knowledge. They provide activities and opportunities that allow children to enjoy their new level of competence, and to be able to communicate their learning with others. They support the need for practice and repetition, and then offer suggestions to see if children are yet ready to move to extensions of this learning (see Fig. 4-7).

Listen to this teacher of four-year-olds as he watches a child wrapping a package in the dramatic play area. "Hey neat, that's a good idea. I see you've got it all wrapped now. Looks almost ready to be mailed. Anything else to go on it? Oh sure, there's some string in that drawer if you'd like to put it around." Back in another few minutes he comments, "It *is* hard to tie it up and hold it on at the same time. Could my fingers help yours? Yeah, tying is hard. Show me how you're trying it. Hm. Would you like me to show you another way to tie? Let's try this." He demonstrates, then unties it and encourages the child to try. "That's it, put that end over the other one. Great, now pull it a bit tighter. All right–that should do it. Good job. We can put some shoes out here if you'd like to practice tying some more." How many facilitating strategies do you find that the teacher used here? What might be less constructive ways of responding to the child?

Being a facilitator of learning is very much like being a partner in a dance. If the teacher as facilitator tries to go too quickly and does not choose teaching strategies that follow the lead of the child, it will not be a successful match. Here again, knowledge of child development as well as observation of the child's needs and interests are prerequisites for facilitating.

> *The routine, the boundaries, the expectations need to be clear and make some sense to me and to the kids. There's freedom within the organization, and freedom within the control. That sounds funny, but it's true. Once the limits are clear there's a freedom kids can handle*
> —William Ayers

Teacher as Limit-Setter

Young children slowly understand what acceptable behavior is in their schools and homes. This is an understanding that gradually becomes internal-

N A E Y C
GUIDELINE
Bredekamp, 1987, p.11

1919
Harriett Johnson establishes the Nursery School of the Bureau of Educational Experiments.

ized to help children control their own behavior. In the meantime, they need adults who understand how difficult a process this is, and who can guide them positively and effectively as they learn to live within limits. From babyhood on, teachers and caregivers help children come to see that there are reasons for acting in certain ways. Children feel secure in a classroom or home that is predictable in its expectations of behavior, and that gradually helps children assume more and more control over their actions.

This role of the *teacher as setter of limits* for behavior may look very differently from the memories you may have of the sometimes punitive and stern adults you may have encountered in early school days. Most everybody has heard and seen the effects of the advice that many teachers were given as they began their teaching careers: Don't smile until Christmas! (Ryan, 1970). Somehow it was felt that such unrelenting grimness would portray the teacher as a powerful disciplinarian whose word would be law. But if you also recall unhappy children being sent out of the classroom or given a variety of **punishments**, you can see that the grim **authoritarian** approach had little lasting positive effect on children's behavior. Katz (1995) defines authoritarianism as the "exercise of power without warmth, encouragement, or explanation" (Katz, 1995, p. 7).

Instead, young children need to have around them adults who are **authoritative**–using their power with warmth, support, encouragement, and good explanations of the limits they must impose, and impose respectfully. As early childhood educators base their guidance and discipline decisions on their child development understandings of how children think, learn, and develop impulse control, they are more likely to guide as a firm and friendly adult who is neither terribly surprised nor upset by children's mistaken behavior in the early years. Within the context of caring relationships, children come to trust that adults will help them control their impulsive behaviors, while protecting their rights to be safe. Then they will come to identify with the adult, and want to please and be like the adult in behavior. Good early childhood teachers guide with gentle words and helpful suggestions (see Fig. 4-8). They do this by their use of both direct and indirect guidance.

Indirect guidance refers to the behind-the-scenes arrangements that teachers make in the environment that not only prevent problems from occurring, but also help children learn appropriate behavior. Teachers' use of indirect guidance actually reduces the number of conflicts or problem situations that will arise, making the atmosphere more positive and necessitating less direct teacher intervention. In later courses you will learn much more about indirect guidance, but in this context it is appropriate to consider several examples of the powerful influence of indirect guidance on children's appropriate behavior.

When Thelma Reynolds noticed that she was having frequent outbursts and biting encounters in her toddler room in the period just before lunch time, she changed some of her plans. Rather than having her coworker busy herself with setting the table and going for the lunch cart while she was trying to change diapers and wash hands and faces, she asked the other teacher to sit with the children in a cozy area of carpet and pillows, playing soft music and looking at books with them. Then, after diapers were changed, she had several

Punishment: Negative response and penalty for undesirable behavior.

Authoritarian: One who exercises power absolutely, without regard to others' responses.

Authoritative: One who exercises control with confidence and warmth, as well as awareness of others' responses and of when to share power.

Indirect Guidance: The arrangements teachers make in the time and space environment that impact on children's behavior, both preventing problems and creating positive learning environments.

1920
The School of Motherhood and Home Training opens at Merrill-Palmer.

Figure 4-8 | **Effective teachers are firm and friendly adults, guiding children gently towards self-control.**

of the children help her with the table, and several others remained on the carpet while the other teacher went for the lunch cart. The result was relaxed toddlers who were not at loose ends without adult attention. Result? No more occasions that required adult intervention and time-out for the impulsive behaviors that disappeared.

The reading activity and game area in Jim Phillips' first grade classroom is extremely popular. A lot of the arguments seem to begin as children crowd each other there, or insist on getting a turn. Jim has instituted a sign up planning board and kitchen timer system that the children could control, allowing equal access, as well as creating another game area in his room. Result? No one has been tattling lately about the unfair practices or words of their peers.

Susan Jordan had noticed that there was a lot of rough play occurring in the large central area of her four-year-olds' room, where children frequently brought many toys to play from various centers in the room. To solve the problem, she created several clearly separated and defined smaller areas to play, eliminating the large open space that seemed to invite roughhousing when children clumped together there. The centers have toys stored on shelves with tables nearby, thus subtly suggesting places to use the materials. Result? No more fights and chaos in the middle of the room.

Attention to the space and time in which children have great difficulty in controlling their behavior may help teachers create environments that prevent discipline problems.

But it is inevitable that teachers will also have to use **direct guidance**–their full repertoire of verbal and nonverbal skills–to communicate with children. Thus

Direct Guidance: The direct teaching of adults to children about appropriate behavior. Direct guidance may include either verbal or nonverbal messages. Another term for direct guidance is discipline, which unfortunately has more negative connotations.

they can understand what the children's limits are, the reasons for them, and more appropriate behaviors the children can learn. Teachers learn to communicate clearly, in terms that children can concretely understand. They are careful to use words and techniques that teach without shaming or demeaning children, because they recognize that children's positive feelings about self are critical to their healthy development. They are less concerned about merely stopping undesirable behavior, or punishing it, and more concerned with asking themselves the question, "What can I be teaching here?" (Katz, 1984). For they realize that there is much for children to learn about behavior. Children need to discover that their behavior affects the way others respond to them, and that they cannot hurt other people or ignore their rights. They need to learn that their own and others' feelings are respected, but that some ways of expressing feelings are unacceptable, especially when they infringe on others. They need to learn that they can discuss differences and disagreements, and do not have to rely on physical force to solve problems. They need to learn that adults will keep them safe while helping all the children in the group learn to live within limits. They need to learn that adults believe that children want to, and can gradually learn all these things, and take over more of their own self-control.

Early childhood teachers who are helping children learn these important lessons about social skills and emotional control recognize that this is a vital area of their curriculum, not just troubling interruptions to their teaching. They realize that understanding and slowly internalizing these lessons for self-control is a slow and gradual process, and that even elementary-aged students are still struggling with self-control. They recognize that children's mistaken behaviors may result from many causes, so they are continually trying to learn as much as possible about each child, to help in the ways they need help. They communicate with families, to understand individual cultural values and the discipline children are accustomed to. Thus they do not arbitrarily apply prescriptions or systems to children, ("The first time you interrupt, your name goes on the board. The second time, you miss outdoor play time. The third time. . ."), but respond thoughtfully in each situation. They observe, hesitating before they intervene to see if children can manage without their help–as long as no one's safety is at risk (see Fig. 4-9).

Teachers encourage children to resolve their own conflicts, and they act as mediators, providing words of support such as, "You can tell him, 'I'm using that.' You don't have to hit him." "What could you two do, if there's only one red trike and you both want a turn? I believe you can work it out." They help design **logical consequences**, so children can experience the results of their behavior. Most of this teaching they do spontaneously, as the need arises, talking individually with children. Sometimes they plan group discussions or meetings about children's common social/emotional concerns; for example, leading a conversation about people getting hurt feelings when left out of classroom activities, or reading a book about friends taking turns. Gradually, children learn these **prosocial behaviors**.

Early childhood teachers find their own guidance style by reading and discussion with other teachers, by studying and supporting their school or center discipline philosophy, and by remembering and working through some of their

Logical Consequences: Guidance technique whereby adult helps child follow through on activity to experience the logical result or recompense for a mistaken behavior.

Prosocial Behaviors: Those behaviors associated with empathy and caring for others.

1921
Patty Smith Hill begins a lab nursery school at Columbia Teachers College.

Figure 4-9   **The teacher is monitoring this situation closely to ensure safety, while seeing if the children can work out their own problems of regulating turns.**

It is not an easy thing for children in groups to control their impulses. What helps them feel comfortable is knowing there are adults in charge who will take charge by providing the control they need

–Fred Rogers

N A E Y C
GUIDELINE
Bredekamp, 1987, p.41

Model: (also role model) To demonstrate behaviors for another to imitate.

childhood memories about powerful adults. They discover that there is no "magic bag of tricks" to find instant discipline solutions, but that their confidence and skills will grow gradually, much like children's self-control. See Fig. 4-10 for a list of positive guidance techniques that teachers use instead of punishment. You will learn much more about guidance as you study early education.

Teacher as Model of Behavior

Much important learning goes on everyday within the context of the relationships between adults and children. Adults are truly the most important and influential people in the lives of young children. Who those teachers are as people, and how they act, teach far more loudly than any spoken lesson. In the role of *teacher as model* of behavior, early childhood professionals can exert greater influence than they often realize. "One of the most important things we adults can do for young children is to **model** the kind of person we would like them to be. Living together . . . at school gives teachers that opportunity" (Hillman, 1988, p. 54). Young children need to associate with adults who demonstrate the personal qualities we want them to acquire. Children absorb uncritically and unconsciously the attitudes and characteristics of the adults they encounter. Indeed, so powerful is the adult's behavior that it is the behavior that is imitated and retained, even if the adult directly teaches a different lesson. For example, if the caregiver tells children to treat each other gently, but is herself rough in her handling of children, they will more likely treat each other roughly also. You likely have a memory of some teachers who exerted a powerful influence

1922

Abigail Adams Eliot, having studied with Rachel McMillan in London, begins the Ruggles Street Nursery School and Training Center in Roxbury, Massachusetts; this is one of the first schools to train teachers in early childhood education.

THE MAGIC LIST

Alternatives to Punitive Discipline.

Anticipate trouble	Overlook small annoyances
Give gentle reminders	Deliberately ignore provocations
Distract to a positive model	Reconsider the situation
Inject humor	Point out natural or logical consequences
Offer choices	Provide renewal time
Give praise or compliments	Give hugs and caring
Offer encouragement	Arrange discussion among the children
Clarify messages	Provide discussion with an adult

From *Please Don't Sit on the Kids!*, by Clare Cherry (1983), p. 64.

Figure 4-10   **Strategies for non-punitive guidance.**

---

on your behavior. The teachers may have been unaware of how their model of behavior influenced you.

There are many different areas in which teachers model behavior. This discussion is to begin your thinking about this role, but is by no means exhaustive. Teachers demonstrate respect for others when they speak to children and adults with courtesy, offer to help, and use "please" and "thank you". Therefore, children learn manners. They show concern when others are hurt physically or emotionally, and children learn about compassion. They describe and express their own emotional responses in constructive ways, and children learn to release their own feelings without hurting themselves or others. They challenge unfair practices or biased thinking, and children learn that they can respect diversity and fight prejudice. They demonstrate their own active curiosity and involvement in learning, and children see that learning is a lifelong activity (see Fig. 4-11). They negotiate solutions and plans with parents and coteachers, and children get vivid examples of cooperation. What other important lessons do children learn from teachers as models?

Sometimes teachers deliberately model behaviors to teach children useful skills. The obvious kind of examples that come to mind here include showing pat-a-cake to an infant, nose-blowing to a toddler, cutting with scissors to a preschooler, and letter formation to a primary-aged child. But the most skilful modeling is involved in demonstrating play skills to new young players. Jones and Reynolds (1992) call this teacher role "player," and suggest that the most appropriate times to take on this role occur when children come to school "unfamiliar with its materials, language, or play scripts . . . , when children are still short on ideas for play in the school setting and/or skills for playing with materials and each other" (Jones and Reynolds, 1992, p. 41). Sensitive early childhood teachers realize that overinvolvement in children's play is disruptive and teaches children to rely too much on adult direction of their play. So they

There was a child went forth every day
And the first object he look'd upon, that object he became
— Walt Whitman

1922
Edna White begins a nursery school at the Merrill-Palmer School.

Figure 4-11	This teacher is modeling gentle treatment of animals as well as curiosity.

move in and out of play, to model role-playing *with* ("Let's see if they have some cereal we can buy in their store") or *for* ("Could I have some coffee, please? Hm, that's pretty hot") children, taking their cues from the children about when their modeling will be useful. Sometimes they talk aloud as they demonstrate thinking through a solution to young children: "Let's see, the problem seems to be that the tower won't stand up. I wonder what could help. Maybe if we tried . . ." Sometimes they intentionally make mistakes: the tower falls again. "Oops, oh dear. We'll have to try something else."

In the role of teacher as model, there are many powerful lessons taught.

Teaching that impacts is not head-to-head, but heart-to-heart
—Howard G. Hendricks

Teacher as Collaborator

Teaching may appear to you to be a fairly solitary activity; often teachers act alone in their centers or classrooms, or sometimes with another adult. And there is something a little wistful about this; as one author put it, "quality child care can be such a quiet accomplishment" (Poelle, 1993, p. 124). But the role of *teacher as collaborator* recognizes that good teaching depends on support and communication from other adults: other teachers, administrators, and, also very importantly, parents.

True collaboration depends on a belief that teachers are learners, "acknowledging their uncertainties as they construct for themselves an understanding of children's development" (New, 1994, p. 222). While this attitude goes against the grain for many adults who have been influenced to believe that professionals should function independently of others, it is crucial to becoming able to collaborate fully. As learners, teachers actively look for multiple perspectives, exchanging points of view with all other adults involved in the children's care and education. Teachers recognize they have much to give and to

1923

Abigail Adams Eliot begins a parent cooperative school based on the McMillan principles of nursery education in Cambridge, Massachusetts.

receive in their collaboration with colleagues and parents. The strength of partnership allows teachers to accomplish things that would otherwise be impossible without collaboration.

One roadblock to *collaborating with other teachers* is the common complaint of staff in child care centers or elementary schools that there is simply not time to form the relationships and to communicate with others. But they discover, when they find the time, that their work load is actually made easier with the help of others' ideas, and that they find satisfaction in new ways. Hear a teacher comment:

> "It also helps that we have a team of teachers," says Anna. "We need each other. We can step back from something that's difficult to deal with and help each other out. You need to have a supportive, communicative staff. It's a bit like a good marriage, having someone to share the joy and also the problems, someone to bounce the emotions off of." (Ayers, 1989, p. 28).

When administrators organize environments and create an atmosphere that supports a team spirit, all staff benefit, no matter what their level of education or experience. A first essential for team work is the development of a sense of trusting one another. Efforts to support this are vital in any healthy school or center. As staff come to know each other, including their individual **interpersonal** styles and personal needs, they develop a "common vision" for committing their efforts and energy. Identifying the strengths and contributions of others allows teachers to focus their attention on positives, rather than geting caught up in the petty differences often bred in day-to-day living. The same principles of accepting and respecting differences that teachers learn to use with children are equally important when working with adults of often quite different backgrounds.

Important to the concept of collaborating as a staff member is learning to communicate openly about beliefs and practices. Collaboration demands careful listening and clear speaking. But most important of all is the desire to learn from others, and to help them learn, to be part of a dynamic organism. So what might collaboration with other teachers look like? It might be the infant teacher who visits other classrooms to get ideas for creating a more interesting environment. It might be the toddler teachers who meet to discuss common problems such as biting, and decide to put on a workshop to discuss their experiences with other teachers. It might be several preschool teachers who talk regularly about their common observations of their children, and brainstorm to create meaningful curriculum. It might be the small group of family child care providers who communicate regularly by telephone to discuss common concerns. Or it might be the staff of a school-age child care program who are studying their discipline philosophy, and coming to consensus about the parts to keep and the parts to discard. Teamwork is also something you will learn more about later. For now it is just important to consider this role as part of your future professional functioning. From this collaboration with other teachers, everyone benefits: parents, children, and the teachers themselves.

N A F Y C
GUIDELINE
Bredekamp, 1987, p.35

Interpersonal: Refers to the relationships between people.

1923

Yale University, the University of California, the University of Minnesota, and Columbia University are centers of child development research, using funds provided by the Laura Spelman Rockefeller Memorial.

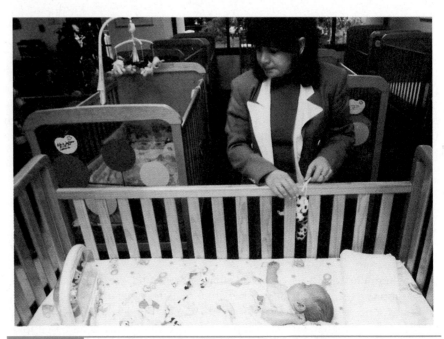

Figure 4-12 | **Parents have their own goals for their children, and must be invited into active collaboration with teachers.**

It is important for parents and children to realize how much work teachers do together. They must see how often teachers meet to discuss, sometimes peacefully and other times more loudly. They must see how teachers cooperate on research projects and other initiatives. . . . All of this represents for the children a range of models that make a deep impression. They see a world where people truly help one another (Malaguzzi, 1994, p. 64).

Bredekamp, 1987, p. 12

Becoming a *collaborator with parents* is an extension of this idea that teachers have much to learn. As people who play the key roles in their children's lives, both long before and long after teachers do, parents have information and vision that must influence teacher practice and goals. Though they come from different directions and therefore have different perspectives and emotional involvement, teachers and parents have a common purpose, of wanting to help children grow and develop. This shared purpose must be the impetus for teachers to ensure inclusion of parent ideas and values (see Fig. 4-12).

Collaborating with parents is vital to creating excellent early education programs that are truly responsive to the families they serve. When adults of diverse educational and cultural backgrounds come together, the challenge is to recognize and accept the differences without being overwhelmed or threatened by them. Working to include parents in their children's programs will never be an easy role for teachers, but it is vital. Teachers must recognize this truth, and develop the skills and attitudes that facilitate inclusion of often diverse expectations and experiences.

1923
Arnold Gesell writes *The Preschool Child.*

Teachers who collaborate with parents may arrange frequent ways to communicate, face-to-face and in other ways, such as newsletters and bulletin boards. They may include parents in classroom activities with children or other parents. They solicit their ideas about individual goals for their children, and share their own perceptions about children's growth and development. Together they learn about a child's development and work to support children's optimum development, and the parent-child relationship.

> Family participation requires many things, but most of all it demands of teachers a multitude of adjustments. Teachers must possess a habit of questioning their certainties, a growth of sensitivity, awareness, and avail-ability, the assuming of a critical style of research and continually updated knowledge of children, an enriched evaluation of parental roles, and skills to talk, listen, and learn from parents (Malaguzzi, 1994, p. 63).

This goes beyond the more traditional view that early childhood teachers are parent educators, but is instead the concept of learning together with par-ents. In later coursework, you will learn much more about understanding life from a parent's viewpoint. You'll also learn how this understanding will help you build methods of reaching out to them and involving them in their chil-dren's classroom lives, and to become advocates with teachers for issues impor-tant to them (Gestwicki, 1996).

The role of collaborator with other colleagues and parents takes teachers beyond the classroom into societal and cultural surroundings, where creative conflict and dissonance helps to define the knowledge and goals for all partic-ipants. As Malaguzzi (1994) put it, "Such relationships are and should be com-plicated."

Teacher as Advocate

The role of *teacher as advocate* is also played beyond the classroom walls, and perhaps jointly as collaborator with other teachers and parents. Kagan suggests that advocacy in child care and early education has three main rationales: to safeguard what has been achieved; to increase the capacity to pro-vide services; and to make important changes (Kagan, 1988). In the current cli-mate of decentralization, deregulation and budget cuts, these will continue to be powerful motivations for early childhood educators to include advocacy as one of their roles.

Advocacy has not always been considered a role for early childhood pro-fessionals. Earlier in this century, true professionals were led to believe that their main responsibility was to practice within the classroom. But more current con-cern for the welfare of children and families demands that teachers become knowledgeable about and involved in the social, political, and economic devel-opments in communities that impact families. Less stable communities and eco-nomic conditions, and shifts in family makeup and parental roles bring strains on the family unit. The community at large is polarized in the debate about what sup-ports for children and families are legitimate concerns of government, to say

Advocacy: The act of defending or stating the cause of another. In early education, this means sup-porting the ideas and issues of the profession.

1924
Lawrence Frank, administering the Rockefeller Foundation grant, is the first to begin using a multidisciplinary approach to studying children at Columbia University.

Figure 4-13   **Teachers must look beyond their classroom walls to become advocates for children and families.**

nothing about how involved private business should or should not be in family matters. Decisions are made by legislators and business and other community leaders that impact the care and education of children, and the quality of life of their families. Children are often a powerless and voiceless minority who need advocates to protect their rights and argue for their needs (see Fig. 4-13).

Because of their education and experience, teachers must lead the way to become advocates for children and families. Those who have a child development knowledge base have an obligation to share their expertise with laypersons who will need it to make informed decisions. Often in the name of accountability, fiscal economy, and efficiency, policies are made that can be harmful to children's optimum development. Examples of this include high adult-child ratios in child care centers or primary classrooms, decrease in regulations that require policing, or increasing numbers of standardized tests. Teachers need to voice their concern about the impact of such mistaken policies on child development. In addition, teachers who recognize the primary importance of the **nuclear family** unit advocate for support systems that strengthen and bolster the ability of parents to function fully. Until recently, teachers have also been reluctant to advocate for themselves, for the wages, benefits, and working conditions that convey societal recognition of their professionalism and contributions to society. But as the clear connections are made between quality programs and teacher training and retention in the profession (Whitebook et al., 1989), advocating for early childhood professional recognition and adequate compensation for worthy work is part of advocating for excellence in early education and care (Bloom, 1993). We will talk more about the Worthy Wage campaign in Chapter Eleven (see Fig. 4-14).

Nuclear Family: The separate family unit, consisting of parent(s) and offspring.

1924
The professional journal *Childhood Education* is published by the International Kindergarten Union.

Figure 4-14   **When teachers advocate for worthy wages for worthy work, they are advocating for quality programs for children. (Courtesy of Tracie O'Hara)**

In their role of advocate for children and families, early childhood educators may be found visiting the state legislature to talk with local legislators about pending bills, attending a local meeting where candidates for office discuss their views on child and family issues, organizing a media campaign to draw community attention to child care needs, or writing a letter to a state representative to discuss support for developmentally appropriate kindergarten curriculum.

Teachers must overcome feelings of powerlessness, lack of knowledge and skills, as well as the exhaustion of answering the day-to-day demands of their other teaching roles, to assume this important function of advocate. As one early educator put it: "If we won't–who will? Or can?"

WHAT IS THIS TEACHER DOING?

Before we leave this discussion of roles, it will be useful for you to read the following story of a family child care provider, and identify the various roles she is playing in her morning of interaction with her group of children. While all the roles just discussed are not represented in this account, it is useful for you to see the integration of the roles in a typical scenario of good practice, and, not incidentally, representations of the excellent practice we discussed in the preceding chapter.

Puzzle, a Picnic, and a Vision: Family Day Care at its Best

Not long ago I was fortunate enough to be present during an extraordinary drama between a family day care provider and the children in her care.

We teachers—perhaps all human beings—are in the grip of an astonishing delusion. We think that we can take a picture, a structure, a working model of something, constructed in our minds out of long experience and familiarity, and by turning that model into a string of words, transplant it whole into the mind of someone else

—John Holt

1925
Sigmund Freud's theory of personality development, stressing the importance of the early years and relationships, is published.

It was late morning. A three-year-old and a four-year-old were racing small, cast-iron cars along a homemade highway running from the arm of a comfortable chair to the living room wall. A willing toddler retrieved the cars that had met their demise on the moulding. A mobile eight-month-old infant followed in his wake.

In the kitchen, oblivious to the noise and excitement, Joel, a four-year-old boy, sat at the table, intently working on a 100-piece puzzle.

After some 60 cars had wrecked themselves on the wall, the older children tired of the game. Hungry and ready for lunch, they advanced toward the kitchen table.

Absorbed in the puzzle, Joel was unaware of the danger headed his way; but the caregiver could see what was about to happen. Scooping up the infant, she placed herself between the group and the kitchen. "Joel is working at the table," she said. "I'll go and see how he's doing. You wait here."

She stood over the boy a moment before she said, "The other children are hungry. Are you ready to stop for lunch?"

Joel looked up, but only for an instant. "I'm not," he said.

Passing me on her way to the children, the provider explained, "He worked on a different puzzle for over an hour yesterday. When he was finished, he picked out this one to do today."

To the children she said, "Joel is still working on the puzzle." She gave out the information evenly, the way someone might read a telephone number from the phone book.

"So?" asked the four-year-old.

"Let's take a minute and think about what we should do." The caregiver released the infant and sat down on the floor with the children. "Let's see. We could wait and give Joel time to finish what he's doing."

"We're hungry now!"

"Well, then that won't work. What else could we do?"

The infant shrieked, but no one else said anything.

"I can think of things," the caregiver said in the kind of voice that lets children know something special is about to happen.

"Like what?"

"Well, we could fast. We could skip lunch for today and see how we felt." The provider dangled this as bait, but the preschoolers knew enough not to bite.

"All right, we could make Joel stop. We could tell him it isn't fair for him to keep working when we're hungry. We could mess up his puzzle because he's kept us waiting."

Unaware of the momentousness of this suggestion, the infant and the toddler were making their way back to the cars. Transfixed, the older children held their breath.

"We shouldn't do that," the four-year-old finally said.

"I agree, Sara. I'm glad you said that." The caregiver smiled at Sara and then, with a flourish, pulled the rabbit out of the hat: "We could have a picnic, instead, in the living room."

"A picnic! A picnic! We want the picnic!"

1925
Twelve percent of the nation's preschoolers are in kindergarten programs.

Looking down from his observation post in his high chair, the infant watched as the caregiver, the toddler, and the two preschool children spread a blanket, a plastic tablecloth, sandwiches, milk, and fruit on the rug.

When everyone was seated, Joel left the table and joined the group.

"How come he gets to have a picnic with us?" the three-year-old asked.

"Why?" the caregiver returned the question.

"Because he wasn't finished with the puzzle."

"Is it finished now?" she asked Joel. She couldn't see the table top from the floor, where she was kneeling.

"Not yet."

"You'll be able to work on it again later, after the picnic, if you want to," she said.

"Yeah. Because we're having a picnic and you didn't have to move it!" the three-year-old exclaimed.

This whole drama took no more than five minutes, and yet, so inspired was this caregiver's nurturing, the moment lives with me still. She had a vision of what a child–a person–could become. She nurtured the children's highest qualities–the ability to listen to their own conscience, the ability to talk about their feelings, the ability to correct their mistakes and go on. She was looking for more than good behavior from them; she had a commitment to the human spirit.

She knew intuitively how to guide them. "We could mess up Joel's puzzle," she said in a voice so beguiling it caused my heart to skip a beat. Only a moment before, the children had been on their way to do just that. But the caregiver knew what she was doing. The children didn't take off for the kitchen; they paused and considered. "We shouldn't do that," Sara said. And this time Sara knew that she was right.

The same skill is evident in the provider's conversation with Joel. She could easily have decided whether or not to let him continue with the puzzle. But more is at issue here than lunch. It is important for Joel to learn to recognize his feelings and speak on his own behalf. And so the caregiver invites him to consider the problem. His answer reveals her nurturing–he knows that he matters.

As I left this home, I thought of how fortunate these children were to have this adult for their caregiver. Her vision was profound, her instincts were true, and her touch was light. Child care can't get much better than that.[1]

Consider the effectiveness of the various roles this teacher played. These are the roles you will play as you become an early childhood professional.

---

[1]From "A Puzzle, A Picnic, and a Vision: Family Day Care at its Best" by Amy C. Baker, 1992, *Young Children, 47*, 5, pp. 36-38. Used with permission.)

1925

Patty Smith Hill holds a preliminary conference of nursery school advocates at Columbia University, inviting 25 people.

SUMMARY

As you proceed to study early childhood education, you will learn more about the separate roles that teachers in various programs and schools integrate in their daily lives. These include the teacher as: nurturer; researcher; set designer; facilitator; setter of limits; model of behavior; collaborator with teachers and parents; and advocate.

QUESTIONS FOR REVIEW

1. Identify several of the various roles of early childhood teachers discussed in this chapter.
2. Discuss briefly your understanding of the rationale for each role, including specifics about what that role might look like in particular settings.
3. Discuss the interrelationships among the various roles.

ACTIVITIES FOR FURTHER STUDY

1. Identify the various teacher roles that you find in the following examples. Remember that the various roles are interrelated, so that you may find more than one role.

   a. A family child care provider writes a newsletter describing some of the children's recent learning activities. In the letter, she includes a copy of her discipline philosophy, and invites parents to comment on it. She also solicits donations of old kitchen utensils.

   b. A second grade teacher organizes a trip to the recycling center for her class, since this is a subject she feels strongly about.

   c. An infant teacher makes a display of family photos, under Contac paper, above the baseboards in her room.

   d. A preschool teacher prepares for her fall conferences with families by organizing the anecdotal observations made by the two teachers in the room on each child, and noting questions that she wants to ask each parent.

   e. A kindergarten teacher clips out newspaper articles on pending local legislation that will affect adult-child ratios in child care centers, and posts them on her parent bulletin board, along with the addresses of local representatives.

   f. A Head Start teacher arranges for her director to observe a child in her classroom who frequently hurts other children.

   g. A toddler teacher creates a cozy area in her classroom with piles of soft pillows and stuffed animals. She frequently sits here with children.

   h. A first grade teacher helps several children find words in a picture dictionary for writing in their journals.

   i. A kindergarten teacher adds several new containers of objects to his counting center.

j. An infant teacher rocks a fussy baby, then places him on a mat with some colorful objects just out of his reach. He's been crawling for a week now.

Discuss your ideas with your classmates.

2. Go back to the scenarios that began this chapter. Now what roles do you find?

3. Complete the following statements: When I first thought about becoming a teacher, I thought that teaching meant: . . .

Now I'm beginning to think that teaching also means: . . .

One teaching role that appeals to me a great deal is: . . .

One teaching role that concerns me at this point is: . . .

4. Observe in an early childhood center for a morning. Take detailed objective notes on one scenario. Later label each teacher role and define its purpose.

REFERENCES

Ayers, William. (1989). *The good preschool teacher.* New York: Teachers College Press.

—. (1993). *To teach: The journey of a teacher.* New York: Teachers College Press.

Baker, Amy C. (1992, July). "A puzzle, a picnic, and a vision: family day care at its best." *Young Children, 47,* (5), 36-38.

Balaban, Nancy. (1992, July). The role of the child care professional in caring for infants, toddlers, and their families. *Young Children, 47,* (5), 66-71.

Berk, Laura E., & Winsler, Adam. (1995). *Scaffolding children's learning: Vygotsky and early childhood education.* Washington, DC: NAEYC.

Bloom, Paula Jorde. (1993, March). Full cost of quality report. "But I'm worth more than that!" *Young Children, 48,* (3), 65-68.

Bruner, Jerome. (1991). Play, thought, and language. In N. Lauter-Klatell (Ed.) *Readings in Child Development.* Mountain View, CA: Mayfield Publishing Co.

Caldwell, Bettye M. (1990). "'Educarer': A new professional identity." *Dimensions, 16,* 3-6.

Carter, Margie, & Curtis, Deb. (1994). *Training teachers: A harvest of theory and practice.* St. Paul, MN: Redleaf Press.

Cassidy, Deborah J., & Lancaster, Camille. (1993, September). The grassroots curriculum: A dialogue between children and teachers. *Young Children, 48* (6), 47-51.

Dollase, Richard H. (1992). *Voices of beginning teachers: Visions and realities.* New York: Teachers College Press.

Edwards, Carolyn. (1994). Partner, nurturer, and guide: The roles of the Reggio teacher in action. *The hundred languages of children: The Reggio Emilia approach to early childhood education.* In Carolyn Edwards, Lella Gandini & George Forman (Eds.) Norwood, NJ: Ablex Publishing Corporation.

Gandini, Lella. (1994). Educational and caring spaces. *The hundred languages of children: The Reggio Emilia approach to early childhood education.* In Carolyn Edwards, Lella Gandini and George Forman, (Eds.), Norwood, NJ: Ablex Publishing Corporation.

Gestwicki, Carol. (1996). *Home, school, community relations.* (3rd ed.) Albany, NY: Delmar Publishers.

Hillman, Carol. (1988). *Teaching four-year-olds: A personal journey.* Bloomington, IN: Phi Delta Kappa Educational Foundation.

Jones, Elizabeth, (Ed.). (1993). *Growing teachers: Partnerships in staff development.* Washington, DC: NAEYC.

Jones, Elizabeth & Nimmo, John. (1994). *Emergent curriculum.* Washington, DC: NAEYC.

Jones, Elizabeth and Reynolds, Gretchen. (1992). *The play's the thing: Teachers' roles in children's play.* New York: Teachers College Press.

Kagan, Sharon L. (1988, May). Dealing with our ambivalence about advocacy. *Child Care Information Exchange,* (61), 31-34.

Katz, Lilian. (1980). Mothering and teaching–Some significant distinctions. In L. Katz, (Ed.), *Current Topics in Early Childhood Education, 3,* Norwood, NJ: Ablex Publishing Corporation.

Katz, Lilian. The professional early childhood teacher." (1984, July). *Young Children, 39,* (5), 3-10.

Katz, Lilian. What is basic for young children? (1995). In *Talks with teachers: A collection.* Norwood, NJ: Ablex Publishing Corp.

Malaguzzi, Loris. (1994). History, ideas, and basic philosophy: An interview with Lella Gandini. *The hundred languages of children: The Reggio Emilia approach to early childhood education.* In Carolyn Edwards, Lella Gandini & George Forman, (Eds.), Norwood, NJ: Ablex Publishing Corporation.

New, Rebecca. (1994). Cultural variations on developmentally appropriate practice: Challenges to theory and practice. *The hundred languages of children: The Reggio Emilia approach to early childhood education.* In Carolyn Edwards, Lella Gandini, & George Forman, (Eds.), Norwood, NJ: Ablex Publishing Corporation.

Poelle, Lisa. (1992). I'll visit your class, you visit mine: Experienced teachers as mentors. *Growing Teachers: Partnerships in Staff Development.* In Elizabeth Jones, (Ed.), Washington, DC: NAEYC.

Rogers, Dwight L. (1990, Fall). Are Questions the Answer? Enhancing Young Children's Learning. *Dimensions, 19,* (1), 3-5.

Ryan, Kevin, (Ed.), (1970). *Don't smile until Christmas: Accounts of the first year of teaching.* Chicago: University of Chicago Press.

Saracho, Olivia N. (1988). Cognitive style and early childhood practice. In *Professionalism and the early childhood practitioner.* Bernard Spodek, Olivia N. Saracho & Donald L. Petus, (Eds.). New York: Teachers College Press.

Sarason, S.B. (1972). *The creation of settings and the future societies.* San Francisco: Jossey-Bass.

Spodek, Bernard, Saracho, Olivia N., & Petus, Donald L. "Professionalism, semi-professionalism, and craftsmanship. In *Professionalism and the early childhood practitioner.* Bernard Spodek, Olivia N. Saracho & Donald L. Petus, (Eds.). New York: Teachers College Press.

Wasserman, Selma. (1990). *Serious players in the primary classroom.* New York: Teachers College Press.

Whitebook, M., Howes, C., and Phillips, D. (1989). *Who cares? Child care teachers and the quality of care in America.* Final report of the National Child Care Staffing Study. Oakland, CA: Child Care Employee Project.

SUGGESTIONS FOR FURTHER READING

Benjamin, Ann C. (1994). Observations in early childhood classrooms: Advice from the field. *Young Children, 49,* (6), 14-20.

Bergen, Doris. (1994, Summer). Developing the art and science of team teaching. *Childhood Education, 70,* (4), 242-243.

Bredekamp, Sue. (1993, November). Reflections on Reggio Emilia. *Young Children, 49,* (1), 3-16.

Duckworth, Eleanor. (1987). *The having of wonderful ideas and other essays on teaching and learning.* New York: Teachers College Press.

Feeney, Stephanie & Chun, Robyn. (1985, November). Effective Teachers of Young Children. *Young Children, 41,* (1), 47-52.

Klass, Carol S. (1987, March). Childrearing interactions within developmental home- or center-based early education. *Young Children, 42,* (3), 9-13, 67-70.

Powell, Douglas R. (1986, September). Effects of program models and teaching practices. *Young Children, 41,* (6), 60-66.

Rogers, Dwight L., Waller, Cathleen Boggs, and Perrin, Marilyn Sheerer. (1987, May). Learning more about what makes a good teacher good through collaborative research in the classroom. *Young Children, 42,* (4), 34-39.

Saracho, Olivia N. (1988). Cognitive style and early childhood practice. In *Professionalism and the early childhood practitioner.* Bernard Spodek, Olivia N. Saracho & Donald L. Petus, (Eds.). New York: Teachers College Press.

Spodek, Bernard, Saracho, Olivia N., & Petus, Donald L. "Professionalism, semi-professionalism, and craftsmanship. In *Professionalism and the early childhood practitioner.* Bernard Spodek, Olivia N. Saracho & Donald L. Petus, (Eds.). New York: Teachers College Press.

Stephens, Karen. (1994, January). Bringing light to the darkness: A tribute to teachers. *Young Children, 49,* (2), 44-46.

From *The Good Preschool Teacher*

For these six women, teaching involves a search for meaning in the world. Teaching has become for each a life project, a calling, a vocation that is an organizing center of all other activities. Teaching is past and future as well as present, it is background as well as foreground, it is depth as well as surface. Teaching is pain and humor, joy and anger, dreariness and epiphany. For these six, teaching is world building, it is architecture and design, it is purpose and moral enterprise. Teaching is a way of being in the world that breaks through the boundaries of the traditional job and in the process redefines all life and teaching itself.

"Teaching as identity" is the clearest theme to emerge in this inquiry, and "teaching as identity" is the frame through which each portrait makes sense. In these portraits, there is no clear line delineating the person and the teacher. Rather, there is a seamless web between teaching and being, between teaching and person. Teaching is not simply what one does, it is who one is. Teaching is a life, a way of being in the world, an intentional circle for these six outstanding teachers (p. 130).

There are, of course, teachers who are narrower in their concerns and more clearly bounded in their jobs than these outstanding teachers are. And yet, teaching is the kind of activity that calls out strongly for an investing of oneself. For many, perhaps most, teachers, the sense of calling exists. It may be only a flicker of memory or a feeling dulled by years of bureaucratic maneuvering, endless demands, and excruciating complexity; it may exist now only as a shadowy palimpsest, that little erasure that leaves tracks on the page. But somewhere along the way, teaching called out to teachers as a chance to love children, to make a difference in their lives, to remake the world. Teachers somewhere, sometime felt called to teach.

From *The Good Preschool Teacher.* (p. 131), by Williams Ayers, (1989).

DEVELOPING AS A TEACHER

In Section I, we examined the organization of the early childhood field, the descriptors of excellence in early childhood classrooms, and the various roles of early educators in the care and teaching of young children. From this framework, it is time to move to specific understandings of why individuals choose to become teachers, and to make early childhood education a career. Chapter Five will examine the motivations of particular teachers in deciding to teach young children. Chapter Six will explore the personal characteristics and attitudes that are important for teachers to possess. Chapter Seven will juxtapose the positive aspects of teaching with the less attractive realities; it is important that you be able to accept the challenging aspects of the profession along with the attractions. Be prepared to think honestly about yourself in relation to teaching. Could this be your life?

5

WHY BECOME A TEACHER?

OBJECTIVES

After studying this chapter, students will be able to:

1. identify and discuss ten motivators for individuals who enter early education.

Many thousands of women and men enter the field of education every year, working in child care centers, kindergartens, Head Start Centers, elementary classrooms or after-school enrichment programs, or in their own family child care settings. And the truth is, many thousands of others leave their teaching jobs to find other employment. Why do they come or decide to leave? The answer lies in motivation, in answering the question, "Why teach?" Having examined the appearance of excellence and the teacher roles involved, we recognize the inadequacy of the old cliché, "Those who can't do, teach." Clearly teaching demands much of those who accept the task. So education of young children is not an endeavor that can be entered into casually or accidentally–or at least, not if the teacher is going to remain satisfied and productive, and remain physically in the field.

Your involvement with this book represents your own intention to examine issues of early education with some seriousness. As you read about teachers who decided to work with young children, think carefully about your own motivations and expectations of what teaching as a career can offer you.

What is there in teaching that could attract and keep you?

MOTIVATIONS

When individuals begin to think about the world of work in which they will earn their living and spend their time, they want to consider those occupations that will answer the particular questions that are personally relevant at the time. What are these questions? The questions are unique to the individual, and will likely change for the individual from time to time, during various stages of adult development. Broadly, the questions likely relate to the meaningfulness of the work, the conditions, tasks, and demands of the work, the necessary preparation and qualifications for the job, and the expectations of what this work would provide for one's life. People ask different questions at different stages of their life cycle. Some younger adults may be pursuing questions that relate to their ideals and dreams; some older adults may be trying to reconcile the realities they have experienced, while many questions transcend life cycle distinctions. Those new to the world of work may ask questions related to possibilities for entry without experience, where more experienced workers may be wondering about opportunities for advancement or job security. Some of you may be considering teaching for the first time, as you newly enter the world of work. Others may be considering reasons to stay, or to continue to develop skills. Some of you may be thinking about teaching as an early life commitment, before moving on to do some other work, and some of you may be contemplating a career commitment in early childhood education. Whatever your circumstances as you read this section, it is important that you isolate and identify your own particular expectations and hopes that you will want to be fulfilled by your choice of work. Take some time now to write down the issues that will motivate you as you decide on meaningful work. What do you want from your work, from a career? This decision is yours alone. If you were to discuss these ideas with others, you would likely find both similarities and differences; the concept of motivations and expectations for particular work is highly personalized. As you read about people who have made the choice to teach, you may find insights to assist you in making the decision to commit yourself to early education as a career.

The purpose of this chapter and this section is not to convince you that you ought to become a teacher of young children. As discussed earlier, that decision is yours alone to make. Rather, here is the opportunity to consider how well this career is suited to you. Take these opportunities to be introspective about your important questions, needs, and characteristics. The world of early childhood education needs people who have made a genuine commitment to its realities.

It takes an entire village to raise a child
—African proverb

Motivators

Motivators towards a given profession are both large and small. Some are related to human characteristics, meaning the emotions and meaning for the individual, and others to structural aspects, being the way the profession itself is organized. We will consider the human motivators first.

Three motivations help people decide on the kind of work they will do and whether or not they stay with a given job: task, power, and relationship.

1925
Franklin Public School Nursery is established in Chicago, the first public nursery school.

Every person needs a different combination of the three–the ability to get things done (task), the ability to have control over her or his life (power), and the ability to develop social connections (relationships). Every adult balances these three motivators in one way or another no matter what professional focus they choose. The way in which different professions attract people motivated in certain ways becomes easy to see when we consider the combination of tasks, power, and relationships (Manfredi-Petit, 1993, p. 40).

All three of these ideas relate to human needs and satisfactions. Manfredi/Petit goes on to state that:

highly relational people thrive in the child care business. . . . The promise and adventure of authentic, long-term relationships encourage many people to consider spending their days with children for a living. The high relationship component compensates those who stay" (p. 41). (See Fig. 5-1.)

THEORY INTO PRACTICE

This is Kim Stevenson. A mother of two preschoolers, she entered the community college early childhood certificate program a year ago, as a means of moving to a job other than restaurant management. During her first practicum placement, she was offered a full-time teaching position. Since that time, she continues coursework, now towards an associate degree in early childhood education, while teaching (and mothering) full-time. This is her first year teaching, in an NAEYC accredited, church-sponsored child care program, in a mixed age grouping of three-, four-, and five-year-olds.

What has been a significant frustration for you in early education? How do you deal with it?

I get frustrated when children are not respected and cared for like they need to be. I try to give all the children I come in contact with the attention and love they need and/or want.

What is one thing you learned in classes that you really discovered to be true when you started working with children?

I have discovered how important it is to give children respect and trust them to make their own decisions.

What is an area you are working on now to learn more about?

A current challenge is to learn more about special needs children and how to involve them in a regular classroom setting.

Why have you stayed in early education?

I love children. Helping them to accomplish tasks that are important to them gives me a feeling of accomplishment. It makes me feel that I am making a difference.

What is a comment or piece of advice you would give to those beginning to work in early childhood education?

Our children are our future leaders. We need to nurture them so that they will feel confident in who they are. Respect them and love them as if they are your own children.

| Figure 5-1 | **Highly relational people thrive in early education.** |

Early childhood educators have opportunities to form relationships with the children they teach, their families, and colleagues in the field.

Enjoyment of Children

For most teachers, the fact that they genuinely enjoy being with young children is the main reason they consider the profession, and definitely the reason they stayed.

Motivation is what gets you started. Habit is what keeps you going
–Jim Ryun

"What other job can you have that lets you play with kids, and watch them playing? They're great–I mean really fun. Amazing things come out of their mouths. They know so much, and they're learning so much. And never, I mean never, boring. Kids are so real." Connie G., teacher of 4's.

"I'd never really paid much attention to children until I had my own. Then I was blown away. There's these little people, and every single day they find something new. And the world is really brand new for them, and their eyes are so wide, taking it all in. And I get to look at it all again too, because I'm with them. It's like getting a second chance at the world." David J., co-owner of a family child care home.

"I just like being with kids. They're honest and funny, and smart and they love your singing even if nobody else does. I can just let myself go and be silly right along with them. Nothing else is so much fun." Laura V.

"Hutch was a year old and my first day with him I was hooked . . . Hutch was just a joy to be with.. . . I remember one time early on, it just happened that I had Hutch and Eric on the same day because their moth-

1926
Jean Piaget publishes *The Language and Thought of the Child,* outlining the four periods of the growth of intelligence.

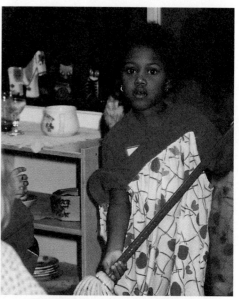

Figure 5-2   **The enjoyment of being with children at play is strong motivation for many teachers. (Courtesy of Tracie O'Hara)**

ers asked me, and I was fascinated by the interaction between them. It
wasn't some kind of underdeveloped, superficial play that you might read
about. I was amazed at how full and engaged it was." JoAnne W. (Ayers,
1989, pp. 66-67). (see Fig. 5-2.)

"Loving kids means I want to physically take care of them, make
them safe and comfortable. And also, I enjoy being with them. I enjoy
their personalities. I like this age especially because I love watching them

1926
Patty Hill's early childhood conference becomes the National Committee on Nursery Schools. At this second meeting of the
conference there are 295 representatives from 24 states, the District of Columbia, Hawaii, and England.

learn to walk and talk. It's so formidable, so awesome, that it keeps me going through some of the rougher times. They take off so fast, and then they're gone. It's mind-boggling, and it gives me a lot of hope." Sally (Ayers, 1989, p. 33).

A deep and genuine enjoyment of children and a desire to be with them is a primary motivator for teachers. These teachers recognize that children are interesting and valuable in their own right, and don't approach them primarily as persons in need of change and instruction. It is the pleasure from being in the daily company of young children that will fill some of the human demands for teachers.

This enjoyment is beyond the sentimental view that is frequently phrased as "I just love children, they're so sweet." Those of us who have been involved in early education for some time have probably heard this pat answer too many times not to roll our eyes and grit our teeth when it is uttered. The reality is that this idealized expression usually has nothing to do with flesh-and-blood children, and certainly would not keep people very long in the profession. Hear a teacher who has taught preschoolers for fifteen years:

> Indeed, I believe what happens in my house is important and worth sharing—but it is not because I am a woman who poetically loves other people's children. I don't really. I am no different from any other mother, who, to a large extent, can take or leave other people's children but adores her own. I didn't get into this work because of some romance. I certainly wouldn't have stayed in it all these years. And frankly, I don't trust people very much who go around saying, "I just love kids, don't you?" (Roemer, 1989, p. 2).
>
> Loving children in general is no help when dealing with nine or nineteen or twenty-nine flesh-and-blood children. What happens when someone is changing her fortieth diaper of the day? Or when a teacher meets a child she doesn't love? Or when she is in an unlovely situation where the children are treating neither her nor one another well? What good does abstractly loving idealized children do her then? (Ayers, 1989, p. 32).

Teachers can enjoy young children, while still being quite realistic about their developmental characteristics. These characteristics may include stubbornness, illogical thinking, uncontrolled outbursts, and a large propensity not to care very much about other people's needs or rights. They recognize that real-life children are not always sleeping angelically, or sweetly smiling, but that they scream, kick, and are frequently smelly and sticky (see Fig. 5-3). If your motivations have begun with the I-just-love-children declaration, it is important that you get plenty of firsthand experiences to be sure that you still enjoy them, while recognizing them for who they are, right now. Try it out; get right in there and get some experience with children, whether by baby-sitting, participating in community or church programs, or volunteering in classrooms. If you are a parent who has discovered your fascination with children through your experiences with your own, get involved with other peoples' children too, by forming play-

Children need adults who are convinced of the value of childhood. They need adults who will protect them from the ever-ready molders of their world. They need adults who can help them to develop their own healthy controls, who can encourage them to explore their unique endowments. . . Children need adults—in every walk of life—who care as much for children as they care for themselves

—Fred Rogers

1926

Parents (called for the first two years *Children*) is published by Parents Magazine Company, as the first magazine designed to give information to American families.

Figure 5-3	**Real life children may have uncontrolled outbursts and get messy and sticky. How "lovable" would you think these children are right now? (Courtesy of Tracie O'Hara)**

groups or participating in your child's early education program. As Joann Roemer pointed out, you may be wild about your own, but less enthusiastic about those of others. Have you explored your feelings about children?

Enjoy Working With People

The relational aspects of teaching are not confined to relationships only with children. Teachers are in the position of being able to work with a variety of other adults, including assistants and coteachers, colleagues in the center or school, administrators and board members, as well as the adults in the families they serve. As discussed in Chapter Four, collaboration with other adults may support teacher efforts and personal growth. The social recognition and personal fulfillment they receive within these relationships may also be highly motivating for teachers.

As you progress through your courses to prepare you for early education, you will discuss and learn the skills that will make working with other adults easier and productive, so it is not important at this point whether or not you necessarily have the skills for these relationships; what is important is to consider whether you enjoy working with a variety of people.

Darlene works a lot with parents. "A lot of the women are angry, of course," she says. "And it's not easy. I try to build up a sense of trust first. They're supposed to fill out a lot of forms, but I try not to start with that. I try to start with a kind word or just talk about the kids." Darlene M. (Ayers, 1989, p. 101).

Teachers who enjoy being with adults as well as children find satisfaction in the opportunities for these contacts.

1928
John Watson publishes *Psychological Care of Infant and Child,* which suggests that parents not hug or kiss their children, or let them sit on laps.

How do you feel about the prospect of working with adults as well as children?

Making a Difference in Children's Lives

Another primary motivating force for most teachers is that they get tangible evidence that they are making a difference in children's lives.

> You watch a child struggle, really struggle, because reading is made such a big deal, he knows he's supposed to learn it, and he can't and he's scared and worried. And you encourage him, and give him the clues and help him along, and suddenly he starts to get it. It's amazing to watch him relax, and know that he's going to be OK, and you helped him, you really did. Cathy M., first grade teacher.
>
> What I like best about teaching is seeing kids puzzled, engaged, and challenged. There's a certain intense look that can follow that puts me on a cloud. It can happen to whole groups of kids or to individuals working alone. That's the reward of teaching for me. There's also a satisfaction at being in on the beginning of things and of having kids come back and say, "This was the best." I look at older kids and think that so much is already settled. I like the little ones. Michelle W. (Ayers, 1989, p. 94).
>
> I like seeing kids achieve. That's the reward for me. I like being right there when it happens. I like the here and now of intimacy." Darlene M. (Ayers, 1989, p. 102).
>
> To see the kids growing, that's all I need. If I see a kid take a step in the right direction, that makes it all worthwhile. You may beat your head against a brick wall for months, and then they move forward a little and it's like "Yea!" I get as much from the kids in the room as I give them. It's always a two-way street. That's exciting. It's nice to put in and put in and put in—and then see them grow. Lynda K. (Raphael, 1985, p. 31).

As teachers watch the progress children make in their growth and development on a day-by-day basis, they are thrilled by realizing that their attention and support have helped children make these important steps. They get concrete evidence that their efforts mean something, and make a difference (see Fig. 5-4). They watch a child stop hitting other children to get his way, and try using words to negotiate with others. They see a child learn to manage the complicated tasks of elimination control on her own, with a proud grin of accomplishment. They watch a six-year-old participating in a playground game with physical skill that slowly developed under their watchful assistance. They accept the first tentative writings of a newly literate child, knowing their teaching has helped the love of reading develop.

In some cases, teachers know they are the only adults from whom that child may get a smile or gentle touch that day. An early childhood teacher once expressed this as the knowledge that for many of her children, the only good thing that would happen to them that day was something at school. In others, they know they are among the group of adults that nurture a particular child,

You are looking outward and that above all you should not do now. . . There is only one single way. Go into yourself. Search for the reason that bids you write [or teach], find out whether it is spreading out its roots in the deepest places of your heart
—Rainer Marie Rilke

1928

Survey by the National Society for the Study of Education lists 84 nursery schools in twenty-three states and the District of Columbia.

Figure 5-4   **Knowing he has helped this child develop physical coordination is rewarding to this teacher.**

but that their efforts are still unique and special. Sometimes early childhood teachers are motivated to make a difference in children's lives because of the disparity they perceive between the warm and comfortably secure childhood in their memories, and the reality they see in contemporary children's lives.

> I remember when I was a little girl lying under the tree looking up. I would lie there for hours and dream and dream. My daycare children do the same thing. They get under the tree and spread their arms and all their thoughts. They think about every little detail and imagine all the wonderful things to come. And each day they play out all their beautiful dreams. That's exactly what I believe good daycare is—a place where children can spread their arms and thoughts and dreams. Joan R. (Roemer, 1989, p. 293).

> Anna can remember and relive being a baby and a child. . . . when she holds a child she remembers that sense of safety that comes with being in the strong arms of a friendly giant. When she comforts a crying child, she remembers the wonderful sense of relief and well-being that can follow sadness, sorrow, falling apart. . . . "My grandmother in Cuba was very open and very loving," says Anna. Anna T. (Ayers, 1989, pp. 24-25).

Anna wants to nurture as she was nurtured. Conversely, sometimes it is precisely because they have less than happy childhood memories that teachers want to make a difference in the lives of children.

> As a child I was often frightened and confused, and she [her mother] was often withdrawn. My mother acted like I couldn't get my life together, and she never trusted me, although I don't remember giving her any reason for not trusting me. . . . As a child I turned to my teachers, who liked me and let

With the continually changing world children are growing into, teachers must help children inquire *more than they* acquire
—Margie Carter and Deb Curtis

1928
Thirty-two percent of American cities are providing public kindergartens.

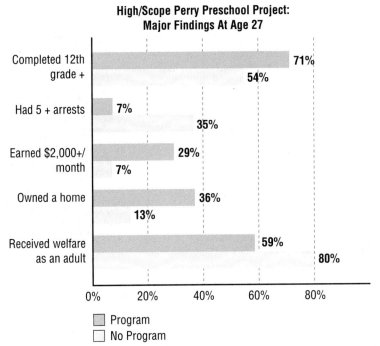

**High/Scope Perry Preschool Project:
Major Findings At Age 27**

Completed 12th grade +: 71% / 54%

Had 5 + arrests: 7% / 35%

Earned $2,000+/month: 29% / 7%

Owned a home: 36% / 13%

Received welfare as an adult: 59% / 80%

0% 20% 40% 60% 80%

☐ Program
☐ No Program

Adapted from *Changed lives, significant benefits: The High/Scope Perry Preschool Project to date* by L. Schweinhart and D.P. Weikart, 1993, Summer, *High/Scope Resource, 12,* (30), 1, 10-14.

Figure 5-5   **The differences in social factors found in the Perry Preschool Project illustrate the real and lasting effects of early education experiences.**

me be a safety patrol, a messenger, or a monitor. I remember several of my early teachers vividly because I adopted each of them, and they replaced my mother in my affection. JoAnne W. (Ayers, 1989, p. 69).

     I sometimes wonder if I'd be a different person today if I'd had the kind of mothering I give to my [child care] kids. I'm happy now, but I still wonder how my life might have been different. Darlene M. (Ayers, 1989, p. 101).

Every teacher knows of some specific impact that they have had on specific children, and that impact has a lasting effect on these children's entire lives. Teachers know it–and research proves it. **Longitudinal studies** that have followed children show that the effects of early education contributed impressively to success in later schooling and social adjustment. Lazar et al. (1982) demonstrated that good early childhood education programs had enabled children to progress satisfactorily through later grades without failure or need for special assistance. The Perry Preschool Project of Ypsilanti Michigan has followed participants of several different models of preschool education through their twenty-seventh year (Schweinhart and Weikart, 1993), as well as contemporaries who did not have the benefit of early education programs. There were

Longitudinal Studies:
Studies that follow the same individuals over a period of time, to learn results over time.

1929
The National Committee on Nursery Schools becomes the National Association for Nursery Education.

| Figure 5-6 | **Making a difference in an individual child's life is a major factor that keeps teachers feeling positive about their work.** |

noteworthy differences not only in school success, but also in social factors such as involvement with crime, adolescent births, marriage, job and salary levels (see Fig. 5-5). The researchers found specific positive correlations between participation in early childhood learning experiences and later positive accomplishments. *"It was the development of specific personal and social dispositions that enabled a high-quality early childhood program to significantly influence participants' adult performance"* [italics added] (Schweinhart and Weikart, 1993, pp. 11-12). These and many other studies show real effects of early education intervention in children's lives (see also Powell, 1986).

As you are deciding about teaching as a career, you might like to read more about what research shows about the lasting effects of positive education experiences in the early years. And talk with teachers; every one will undoubtedly have real stories about children whose lives they have touched and changed. When they tell those stories to you, their eyes will shine as they recall the difference they know they made. It is making that difference in children's lives that keeps many teachers in the classroom, year after year. It is this that gives teachers a satisfaction that far exceeds monetary rewards, that makes the work feel worthwhile (see Fig. 5-6).

> The Whites' gratitude reminded me of why I was still in this job after nearly twenty years. It was to help the children. Patti W. (Wollman, 1994, p. 137).
>
> I get so much from these kids. You don't have to have the best program or the most expensive materials, but if you sit down with them–it's what they need most. It's good to see them when they're laughing and having a good time. Then you know that they're learning, whether they

1929

There are approximately twelve industrial day care programs in the United States.

know it or not. Fulfilling their needs fills my need. Laura Beth C. (Competence, March 1995).

What greater reward could there ever be than the privilege and responsibility of trying to make a permanent difference in the life of a child? Janice C. (Kane, 1991, p. 31).

There is no question that in making the difference in children's lives, teachers also find some of their own needs met. However, as satisfying as this is, the real importance is in the difference it makes to children.

There are different personalities in kids which meet almost every need an individual could have. There are kids in here that are bright, and they meet one need; there are the kids that are slow that meet a whole other need. Those are the kids that really need you to be there to help them, to encourage them. That makes you feel good, even important. . . .You get all this feeling into one individual in one classroom and it's like . . . I don't know why it's not something that everybody wants to do. Lynda K. (Raphael, 1985, p. 27).

As a child, how did a particular adult make a difference in your life? As an adult, have you experienced the knowledge that you have been able to touch a child's life with lasting impact? How was that important to you?

Teachers often have no inkling that they have made a difference in a child's life, even if it has been a dramatic one. It's an interesting idea to consider, that they may never fully know the good they have done, even as they do get some indications of the difference they have made.

Supporting the Lives of Families

The family is recognized as the primary unit in society. Strong and stable families make for healthy communities. Early education teachers reach beyond the confines of their classrooms to touch and enrich the lives of families, so that their influence is indeed comprehensive. Parents of the youngest children need information and emotional support to optimally nurture their children's development. They need the security of knowing they can leave their children in the hands of trusted and competent caregivers while they go to work. They need connections with the community resources that will help them perform all the tasks of parenting. They need to trust teachers to help their children become interested in learning and in school. They need to be welcomed into the center or school, to feel that they have something to contribute in their children's lives away from home. They need to feel respected by other adults, and by society for their primary importance in their children's growth and development (see Fig. 5-7).

Early childhood educators are on the front-lines, between parents and the society at large. They are often the first people outside the family that have prolonged contact with children and parents. Their support and relationships may be crucial determinants in families' optimum functioning. They have the power to help parents understand and accept their children, and to support parent-

Anything child-care providers or preschool teachers can do to preserve the essential bond between parent and child during the preschool years will help preserve the emotional health of our country
—Fred Rogers

1930
International Kindergarten Union changes its name to Association for Childhood Education International.

Figure 5-7   **Many teachers see their importance in supporting parent-child relationships to help make strong families.**

child relationships. Working with the entire family, and knowing the importance in our society of strengthening families, may be a motivator for teachers.

> I glanced once more around the cool, quiet room. It seemed so dull without the children. All at once, I realized that there was more reason to be happy than to be sad. I felt victorious: Cathy and I had accomplished our goal. We had enriched the lives of thirteen families who would never be the same. Patti W. (Wollman, 1994, p. 280).

What are your concerns about contemporary families? Would the opportunity to work with the whole family, as well as specific children, be important to you? Why or why not?

Making a Contribution to Society

Teaching is considered to be one of the "helping professions," one that is helpful to individuals and to society at large. Every culture in the history of the world has had teachers to instruct the young, and caregivers to ensure their nurturance. The importance of the early years is recognized and documented. Our government and community leaders speak repeatedly about the importance of early education and care, not only for children's development, but as a support for the essential structure of families to build a healthy society. While the actual realities of the current conditions of early childhood teachers may appear to conflict with this statement about the social values placed on teaching, many still feel that their desire to give something to the larger society is accomplished by teaching (see Fig. 5-8). Individuals express this by saying things like: "I feel I need to give something back"; "I want to know that my work has had some impact on the world"; "I want to know that I've done something that could be written on my tombstone."

1930
America has 262 nursery schools for children younger than school age; thirteen of these are public nursery schools.

Figure 5-8 **Getting children off to a healthy start allows teachers to feel they are contributing to the larger society.**

Why I am here, and take such extraordinary care with the children left to me each day, is because I believe in that old idea that we can change the way we are in the world through our children. I believe that we are not merely fostering children here, but, rather, helping create wonderful adults. And that my being with children in the way that I am, matters. It matters a great deal. I began my daycare out of this belief. Joan R. (Roemer, 1989, p. 3).

For many, teaching is an activity that has been particularly sanctioned for them by family reverence for education, or by personal experiences during schooling that clearly indicated teachers' contribution to society.

I grew up in a context that esteemed education. In my family, TEACHER is spelled with capital letters. . . Miss Harper was strict. . . We knew she liked us. . . . but I think she especially took care of the black kids, a mission I feel I continue in my work today. . .Miss Harper was different. She fought the system in a quiet way. She fought for kids to make it. So in the fifth grade I decided to become a teacher. There were no chance factors involved, no accidents of fate. It was as deliberate and planned as anything can be, and I pursued it right up to the present. . . I liked the idea of being as important to people as Miss Harper was to me. Michelle W. (Ayers, 1989, p. 91).

The drama is the struggle to teach, to do it better, to get it right
—William Ayers

What was the attitude in your family about the importance of education, of teachers? How do you see the influence of these attitudes in your consideration of a career in early education? What are your memories of any teacher who seemed to be making a difference to society?

It seems clear to many that teachers' influence extends beyond a particular classroom at a particular time.

1930
There are now 48 million children in the United States.

MOMENTS IN AMERICAN FOR CHILDREN

- Every 5 seconds of the school day a student drops out of public school.
- Every 10 seconds a teenager becomes sexually active for the first time.
- Every 26 seconds a baby is born to an unmarried mother.
- Every 30 seconds a baby is born into poverty.
- Every 34 seconds a baby is born to a mother who did not graduate from high school.
- Every 59 seconds a baby is born to a teen mother.
- Every 104 seconds a teenage girl becomes pregnant.
- Every 2 minutes a baby is born at low birthweight.
- Every 2 minutes a baby is born to a mother who had late or no prenatal care.
- Every 4 minutes a baby is born to a teenage mother who already had a previous child.
- Every 4 minutes a child is arrested for an alcohol-related crime.
- Every 5 minutes a child is arrested for a violent crime.
- Every 7 minutes a child is arrested for a drug crime.
- Every 2 hours a child is murdered.
- Every 4 hours a child commits suicide.
- Every 9 hours a child or young adult under 25 dies from HIV.

Children's Defense Fund, The State of America's Children Yearbook 1994, Washington, DC: CDF, 1994.

Figure 5-9   **Every community has children living under difficult conditions who need the help of caring adults outside their family.**

Ashley Montague calls early childhood teachers the "unacknowledged legislators of the world." Teachers can indeed make a whole world of difference.

Just think how the world would be different today if Saddam Hussein had had a caring, loving first grade teacher, or if Michael Milliken had attended an NAEYC accredited child care center.

The long term impact on society of the effective performance of one teacher is phenomenal. Roger Neugebauer (Gordon and Browne, 1993, p. 173).

The times in which we live create many concerns about society. Statistics on family breakdown, educational failure, economic uncertainty, rising crime rates, and increasing polarization of separate groups within our communities are both sobering and frightening (see Fig. 5-9).

It is this reality of change, complexity, plurality, fragmentation, conflict, and contradiction of beliefs, values, faiths, living conditions, aspirations, and life-styles that makes the lives of young people today an experience in contingency (van Manen, 1991, p. 2).

Watching children contend with the changes in society, and watching society worry about the effects of the changes on the children, is a fact of modern life. Individuals who feel the need to do something besides worry about the negative changes in our communities may be drawn to work with the most vulnerable, supporting families where they need the support. If making a contribution to society is important to you in the work that you do, this may be a motivation to consider early education.

Need for Variety and Challenge

There are individuals who want their daily work lives to follow predictable patterns, to know without question what they will be doing at 10:15 on any given morning. They want to feel assured that their skills and abilities are equal to the job demands, and therefore want no unexpected demands or events. There are others, however, to whom that description sounds numbingly boring. These individuals are attracted to work that is never quite predictable, in which challenges and questions arise continually, where each day is predictable only in that it will probably be unlike any other. Life in centers and classrooms with children from birth through the primary school years answers this latter description—and then some.

> Plus teaching is never boring. It's different from day to day, regardless of whether you are doing the exact same thing. Kids' reactions to each other, to me, to what they're doing, are always changing. For me, that's really exciting. It keeps my energy level up. I like the constant change, and the fact that it never gets routine. Lynda K. (Raphael, 1985, p. 27).

As you read the descriptions of quality programs in Chapter Three, you probably realize that the individualization and creation of active, hands-on learning events that are required means that early childhood teachers live in a world of movement, noise, choice, and activity of separate members of a group, whether the group members are a few months or a few years old. In such an environment, there are infinite numbers of tasks that call simultaneously. A typical scenario may be four children splashing water in the water table, while another needs assistance in the bathroom and yet another is crying quietly in the book area, when the phone rings, and an upset-looking parent walks in the door. After you studied the various teacher roles in Chapter Four, you probably realized that these roles would often be demanded at the same time, as the previous example indicates. Teaching young children demands all the energy, knowledge, patience, and creativity that most people have available to them, as well as a capacity to be flexible in the face of diverse demands.

Much of the variation in a teacher's day comes from the "clients," who are the children themselves and their families (see Fig. 5-10). With rapidly developing children, change is the operative word; it is impossible to be sure at any one time how children will react and behave, and what their specific needs will be. The diversity of **inherited** potential environmental experience offered by each individual family means that a classroom full of three-year-olds may all have stunningly different interests, needs, and ideas. When children walk, or are carried, through the door on any given morn-

Everyone wants to feel that he or she has something to offer. The most depressing feeling in the world is the feeling of having nothing to offer—nothing that's acceptable

—Fred Rogers

Inherited: Refers to those characteristics that are directly transmitted from genetic combinations from the parents.

1933-35

Establishment of about 2,000 WPA nursery schools, in every state except Delaware, to provide employment for out-of-work teachers, social workers, nutritionists, and nurses during the Great Depression, and serving close to 75,000 children from poor families.

| Figure 5-10 | **Some teachers enjoy the challenges of unpredictability, that working with children offer.** |

ing, teachers are never sure just who is coming in, and what they will have to adapt to. Hear one example:

> The next day, I wondered how Jeremy would behave. Faced with a trauma, children sometimes act out their anger or guilt in class by being hostile or destructive. Sometimes they are so sad that they withdraw for a while. Often, they use the classroom therapeutically, making pictures about the event or reenacting their story as they build with blocks or Lego.
>
> Frequently, the classroom is an oasis. The child drops his trouble at the door, and plays contentedly. It is good to have a place where he or she doesn't have to think about the trouble. I didn't know Jeremy very well; which way would he choose? Patti W. (Wollman, 1994, p. 11).

Early childhood teachers have to develop the skills and intuitions to learn how to adapt to a great many unknowns in the course of a day. Some of them are small events that indicate larger happenings: the six-month-old baby who seems unusually fussy today, until the caregiver discovers a new tooth about to pop through; the six-year-old who cries when he's forgotten his library book, until he reveals he left it in his Dad's car when Dad picked him up from Mom's house after the weekend visit. Some of them are the adjustments that need to be made as teachers learn children's individual styles and idiosyncrasies: Barbara is getting whiny, so that indicates to the teacher that it is time to get her involved in a quiet activity; Sam is getting wild, which means that free play period had better come quickly to an end.

According to one famous piece of research, a classroom teacher must make about two hundred unpredictable "personal interactions" during each hour of working with a group of children (Kidder, 1989, p. 33) (see Fig. 5-11). Just think what that implies about diverse situations, interactions, and adaptability on the teacher's part. That's challenge enough, surely–and more!

The flexibility and adjustments that are a part of every early childhood teacher's day come with experience and observation, and are assisted by the development of the teacher's skills:

> All I had were the tools of my trade. I used my detective skills to find out what was the matter, and my diplomatic skills to keep the parents at bay until I had concrete suggestions for them. I needed every ounce of my policing skills to keep the kids from hurting each other, and every drop of acting talent to beguile them into wanting to come each day despite the chaos around them. Patti W. (Wollberg, 1994, pp. ix-x).

In the following excerpt, a teacher describes some events in her classroom day near the beginning of the school year with three- and four-year-olds.

1942

Passage of Lanham Act, to fund child care centers for children of mothers working in factories to support the war effort in World War II. There are 944 nurseries caring for over 38,735 children, often functioning through twelve to eighteen hours.

| Figure 5-11 | **Two hundred or so unpredictable "personal interactions" every hour can offer great challenge to a teacher.** |

Picture the knowledge and skills that are demanded of her, and then acknowledge that this scene illustrates that early educators are involved in work that offers them both diversity and a challenge to use all of their energy, creativity, and abilities.

> The children are just beginning their work period—it's the time we call free play. Jenny, Sharon, Cory and Lee are chatting at the playdough table (conversation is the usual by-product of playdough or clay). Jason, Benjamin and David are in the block corner, considering their options. Jeremy is painting at the easel and Amanda is watching him. Mary Ann and Louisa are looking at books.
>
> In walks Harris with his mother in tow. She kisses him good-bye, waves at us and leaves the room faster than I thought was humanly possible. Harris does not kiss her and shows no emotion when she leaves. He doesn't even look in her direction. (Since this is an uncommon way of dealing with separation from a parent, I take notice. It does not augur well.)
>
> Harris immediately runs over to Jason, who is playing quietly. "Let's play house!" he shouts with such enthusiasm that Jason immediately gets up. They go over to the house and loft area, followed by Lee, who knows a good thing when he sees one. Teachers have a sixth sense of disaster: I am not far behind.
>
> The boys begin to take out the dishes and set the table. So far, so good—but so far is only two minutes. Without warning, Harris picks up a piece of plastic fruit and hurls it to the floor. "Ha!" he yells. Lee and Jason immediately follow suit. Lee's banana hits the loft and Jason knocks over a

Great changes in the destiny of mankind can be effected only in the minds of little children
—Herbert Read

1943

Private industries also support child care centers, including two excellent centers run by Kaiser shipyards in Portland, Oregon, directed by Lois Stolz and James Hymes.

pot with a flying red pepper. I announce the rule–"We do not throw things in class." This stops no one at all. You'd be amazed at the number of objects which can be thrown in the one minute it takes me to move the boys away from the table.

Now, I've got three culprits, all needing discipline, but none needing the same kind. Lee is not yet three (what's he doing in my three-four's class–he's still in Pampers!); he needs to be told the rules. Three-year-old Jason knows the rule but cannot control his impulses. He needs to learn that objects do not exist only for his pleasure–to be thrown or eaten at will. If I didn't know this from their ages, I would know it from their faces: Lee looks perplexed and Jason chagrined. What I see on Harris' face is nothing–none of his past enthusiasm, no anger, just nothing at all. Whatever is making this kid tick is not in good working order.

As these thoughts are running through my mind, the rest of the room suddenly erupts. (Why not? Kids get nervous when there's a lot of *Sturm* and *Drang*.) Sharon yells "ICK!" She has tasted the playdough. Jeremy has finished his painting and wants to wash his hands. Amanda wants us to take Jeremy's painting off the easel so she can begin. Both are calling our names insistently. In the reading area, Mary Ann and Louisa start to fight over the same book. Louisa shouts over and over "She isn't sharing!" while Mary Ann starts to cry. At the same time, Cory falls off her chair and begins to wail.

Cathy looks at me, already busy with the three boys and unable to help her. We both start to laugh, helplessly. "Any suggestions?" she asks, in her wonderful, low-key manner.

I have no choice. "Tell Jeremy and Amanda to wait *one* [italics added] minute and go handle Mary Ann and Louisa. I'll take Sharon and Cory."

Leaving the boys with a feeling of trepidation, I hurry to pick up Cory. My first priority is to check for injury, but she's just scared. I walk over to Sharon with Cory in my arms and explain that we don't eat play-dough. Even if it looks like a cookie, it's not. I tell her to go get a drink of water. Then I head back to the boys.

Although I've only been gone two minutes, I'm too late. Jason is crying. "Harris bit me!" he sobs, and shows me his hand. There are the tooth marks, sure enough, and there is Harris, impassive as a stone.

Welcome to Pandemonium. Patti W. (Wollman, 1994, pp. 1-3).

Even for an experienced teacher, such a morning is somewhat daunting–and this teacher has assured us that it is all true! But at the same time, it is challenging to all one's skills and abilities, and then rather exhilarating, to find oneself equal to the tasks called for.

I feel productive in teaching. I can see my work has results. It's stimulating because I have to keep thinking and creating. I have to keep my mind active. I'm in good physical shape working with little children. . . . Each new group of children brings new and exciting chal-

Companies recall faulty airplanes and poisonous food, but we can't recall children. They have only one chance to get an education

–Joan Ganz Cooney

1944

In July, Lanham centers were operating at its peak: 3,102 children's centers with average daily attendance of 129,357 children.

lenges. Here's all these new personalities. What will they be like? What will we discover? How will we grow as people and as a group? I find that exciting. I don't feel that the work is repetitive because I don't do anything exactly the same. Each day is different. The year starts, and it's a whole new beginning. Here I go again. Maya D. (Ayers, 1989, p. 125).

"No two days are ever the same." Laura Beth C. (Competence, March 1995).

Opportunities for Growth

The last section you read suggests that early childhood teachers are continually challenged to learn new things, and develop and use new skills. The profession itself is in a state of continual growth and challenge, something you will learn more about in Chapters Nine and Eleven. Within each early childhood center or school, there are continual opportunities to work with new groups or ages, new colleagues. The related job opportunities (See Chapter Ten) within the field offer additional occasions for teacher growth.

Perhaps because those who work with young children are constantly encountering beings who are becoming, they themselves are challenged to continue to grow. If a chance for personal and professional growth is one of your career motivators, you could find it in early education.

Hear one very good and experienced teacher who described herself as "unsatisfied, striving for something more":

I've become more able to support children as they initiate and sustain their own growth and learning. I'm more attentive to the ways children think and make sense of the world. I'm more sensitive to their quest, and therefore I'm better at what I do. At the same time I find that I feel an even more urgent need to 'perfect' the classroom, to make it more nurturing and more stimulating simultaneously, an environment that supports and encourages inquiry. Michele W. (Ayers, 1989, p. 95).

She is a good teacher already; she sees her own growth, and she is challenging herself for more. How does this appeal to you?

Need for Trained Caregivers and Early Educators

One motivator for individuals concerning a particular occupation or field is the availability of job opportunities; that is, the need for employees in the profession. The good news about early care and education is that there appears to be no end to the demands for trained professionals in the field (see Fig. 5-12). Whether you are drawn to work with school-aged children or with younger ones, there are many opportunities in every community. In the country's school systems, estimates are that only half of the number of teachers is available for the number of positions projected for the last years of this cen-

1945

50,000 children are cared for in 1,500 Lanham nurseries in 41 states.

GROWING JOB SECTORS IN U.S.
Projected job growth in selected fields by the year 2005

Home health aides	+ 138%
Computer systems	+ 111%
Special education teachers	+ 74%
Preschool, kindergarten teachers	+ 54%
College, university faculty	+ 26%
Restaurant cooks	+ 46%
Waiters, waitresses	+ 36%
Forest conservation	+ 22%
Truck drivers	+ 28%
Architects	+ 20%
Health technicians	+ 40%
Forestry (logging)	+ 2%

Source: U.S. Department of Labor

Figure 5-12 **It is projected that job growth in early childhood will continue to increase.**

tury (Duke, 1990, p. 31). This does not accurately give us the deficit number of kindergarten and primary teachers, but, combined with statistics on teachers who leave the school systems each year, implies continuing need. In most communities, surveys of numbers of latchkey children–those who go home to empty houses at the end of their school day to care for themselves until working parents return–continue to mount, indicating that after-school care is a large unmet need.

There are clear figures that convey the urgent need for preschool teachers and caregivers. The need for employees in programs for young children nearly doubled between the mid-80s and mid-90s. As women continue to enter the work force in record numbers, with well over fifty percent of mothers of preschoolers and infants working, the demand for child care continues to multiply. And, in addition to working parents, 30 percent of non-employed parents also use early care and education programs to offer social and educational benefits to their preschool children (Morgan et al., 1993, p. 2). Because of these demands, the number of available positions for children in centers and family child care homes has almost reached the saturation point (Morgan et al., 1993). Government and business leaders recognize that they must support community efforts to expand and improve available child care services. Congress passed a new **Child Care and Development Block Grant** in 1990 and 1991 (see Timeline) to increase funding for Head Start and other child care services, and to continue support for improvements in child care. The first national educational goal–"By the year 2000 all children will start school ready to learn"– has increased the urgency to establish quality early childhood programs and support services. A growing number of corporations are ready to

Child Care and Development Block Grants (CCDBG): Federal funds made available to the states since 1991, to improve quality and availability of child care.

1945

Because of restricted travel during World War II, no NANE conference is held. Instead, a mimeographed Volume 1, Number 1 *Bulletin of the National Association for Nursery Education* is set to members.

Figure 5-13   **Without teachers trained in child development, studies show that the quality of early education programs suffers.**

support these initiatives with expenditures of large amounts to support improvements in early education in their communities. These combined private efforts and public initiatives have turned public attention towards expanding child care needs.

This concerned press for expansion in turn increases the demand for early childhood practitioners with relevant, specialized training. One 1988 estimate was that "all the graduates of the 1,650 four-year colleges and two-year associate programs in the United States that offer degrees in early childhood education would constitute barely enough staff for the existing early childhood centers in Massachusetts and New York" (Morgan et al. 1993, p. 3). The National Child Care Staffing Study (1989, 1993) indicates that the child care field continues to be plagued by high rates of turnover and individuals leaving the field each year. (We'll explore reasons for that, and efforts to counteract it, in Chapter Eleven.) An impressive body of solid research indicates that, without teachers who possess the specialized child development training, the quality of early care and education programs, and ultimately children's growth and development, will be at risk (see Fig. 5-13).

Clearly the demand for people trained to work with young children is a pressing need. Investigate the need for trained teachers and caregivers in your own community. You could be an important part of meeting that need. Although job availability alone should not be the sole motivator for choosing to enter a career, it is important to know that demand will continue to exceed the supply of professionals in this field. This pressing need will help draw social recognition to the importance of this work, and hopefully improve the employment conditions for early childhood educators.

Teaching is a human activity, constrained and made possible by all the limits and potential that characterize any other human activity
—William Ayers

1945

Attachment theory is discussed by Réné Spitz in "Hospitalism: An Inquiry into the Genesis of Psychiatric Conditions in Early Childhood."

There's always too many kids and too few resources. . . . There's always a job that can be done, but that's what I'd change. Michelle W. (Ayers, 1989, p. 94).

Autonomy in Work

Much of what teachers and caregivers do is according to their own skill, knowledge, and decisions. Within their own classrooms, they have a fair amount of autonomy. Although within public school systems, decisions about curriculum and school policy are made by administrators; within their classrooms, teachers control a good deal of power. "To a degree shared by only a few other occupations, such as police work, public education rests precariously on the skill and virtue of the people at the bottom of the institutional pyramid" (Kidder, 1989, p. 52). There is a certain amount of pre-ordained structure in many programs that receive public money, and church-sponsored programs may ensure that their teachings are maintained and supported; still, teachers can usually follow their personal inclinations in many classroom decisions. Autonomy is even greater in family child care settings or for-profit ownership settings, where individuals have created the programs to match their philosophy, goals, and needs.

Autonomy is sometimes a mixed blessing that leaves teachers and caregivers to be the "only arbiter of their own conduct" (Kidder, 1989, p. 52). Until teachers become experienced, they also depend on the support and wisdom of others. Autonomy can also feel rather lonely. But, with these disadvantages aside, many individuals look for a measure of freedom to practice independently in their work, to feel that they have some control over their lives, and the early childhood practitioner certainly has this (see Fig. 5-14).

How appealing is it to you to have some freedom to make decisions in your work?

Other Structural Characteristics

While structural considerations are relatively minor motivators, it is still worth noting that the way the profession is structured may offer some advantages to some who are considering it. One of these advantages is that early education is a relatively easy profession to enter. No matter which facet of early care and education the individual is attracted to, most areas do not require extensive preservice education. Indeed, for many of the positions with preschool children, teachers may begin with minimal training, getting experience as they work on credentials through in-service training. While we will see that the demands of providing quality programs require a solid knowledge base, the profession recognizes that some of its practitioners have combined experience with formal education. The hurdles of special examinations or apprenticing systems that make other professions more difficult to enter do not impede in this career.

There is an inclusiveness in the area of early education which extends to its practitioners; issues of social class, status, gender, age, or disability are not seen as barriers to employment in this profession. This goes beyond the earlier

1946

Six months after the end of the war, the Lanham nurseries are no longer funded. States are permitted to continue them, but most are disbanded, with notable exception of centers in California.

Figure 5-14 **Early childhood teachers have a good deal of autonomy in managing their classrooms and curriculum.**

understandings that certain professions demanded that its practitioners assume middle-class values and life-styles. The attitudinal barriers that some men find will be discussed in Chapter Seven.

There are some who choose to work in those portions of the early childhood field that are structured to operate on the traditional nine- or ten-month school year, attracted by the long summer vacations. While some find the decrease in annual salary an unattractive feature of employment in these settings, others–usually parents with school-aged children–are attracted by this element. As discussed in Chapter Two, many family child care providers choose to work from their own homes for the convenience of their other family responsibilities. Again, these structural considerations should be less important motivators than the human factors discussed earlier.

> Teaching is an act of hope for a better future. The rewards of teaching are neither ostentatious nor obvious–they are often internal, invisible, and of the moment. But paradoxically, they can be deeper, more lasting, and less illusory than the cut of your clothes or the size of your home. The rewards are things like watching a youngster make a connection and come alive to a particular literacy, discipline, or way of thinking, or seeing another child begin to care about something or someone in a way that he never cared before, or observing a kid become a person of values because you treated her as a valuable person. There is a particularly powerful satisfaction in caring in a time of carelessness, and of thinking for yourself in a time of thoughtfulness. The reward of teaching is knowing that your life makes a difference (Ayers, 1993, p. 24).

1946

Arnold Gesell, doing child development research at Yale, establishes the first descriptions of children at different chronological ages, using normative data.

SUMMARY

In this chapter, students have been asked to consider the relative importance of ten different motivators as they considered the answers to the question, "Why teach?" (see Fig. 5-15). These motivators include:

1. **Enjoyment of children;**
2. **Enjoyment of working with people;**
3. **Making a difference in children's lives;**
4. **Supporting the lives of families;**
5. **Making a contribution to society;**
6. **Need for variety and challenge;**
7. **Opportunities for growth;**
8. **Need for trained caregivers and early educators;**
9. **Autonomy in work; and**
10. **Other structural characteristics.**

Of all the questions in this text, "Why teach?" may be the most crucial for you to find satisfactory answers to before making your decision. If you have found some answers here to the motivating questions you defined for yourself, you may now be ready to look more closely at your personal characteristics and values, to know whether you are suited to this career.

QUESTIONS FOR REVIEW

1. Identify, and discuss, at least six of the motivators described in this chapter.
2. Which of these motivators has personal meaning for you?

ACTIVITIES FOR FURTHER STUDY

1. Pull out the list of motivating questions/issues you defined for yourself at the beginning of this chapter. Write a brief paper titled "Why should I teach? (or not teach?) Share this with another classmate. Find similarities and differences.
2. Interview early childhood educators about why they chose this field, and what has motivated them to stay. Ask them also about the characteristics they feel are needed for individuals in this work, and about things they dislike about the field, or their job. This is information that will be helpful to you as you think about the next two chapters.
3. Design a tombstone for yourself. On it, place a phrase or accomplishment for which you'd like to be remembered.
4. With your classmates compile a list that incorporates all of the motivators that you listed in Question #1. Then make a survey, and hand it out to several teachers, asking them to rank the factors in order of importance to them. Discuss your findings.

REFERENCES

Author. (1995, March). CDA profile: Laura Beth Colonna. *Competence, 12,* (1), 3.

Ayers, William. (1989). *The good preschool teacher.* New York: Teachers College Press.

Ayers, William. (1993). *To teach: The journey of a teacher.* New York: Teachers College Press.

Connolly, Janice. (1991). Don't waste your time with those kids. In Pearl Rock Kane, (Ed.), *The first year of teaching: Real world stories from America's teachers.* New York: Penguin Books.

Duke, Daniel Linden. (1990). *Teaching: An introduction.* New York: McGraw-Hill Publishing Co.

Gordon, Ann & Browne, Kathryn W. (1993). *Beginnings and beyond: Foundations in early childhood education.* (3d Ed.). Albany, New York: Delmar Publishers Inc.

Hendrick, Joanne. (1987). *Why teach? A first look at working with young children.* Washington, DC: NAEYC.

Kidder, Tracy. (1989). *Among schoolchildren.* Boston: Houghton Mifflin.

Lazar, I., Darlington, R., Murray, H., Royce, J., & Snipper, A. (1982). A report from the consortium for longitudinal studies. *Monographs of the Society for Research in Child Development, 47* (2-3, Serial No. 195).

Manfredi-Petitt, Lynn A. Child care: It's more than the sum of its tasks. (1993 November). *Young Children. 49,* (1), 40-42.

Morgan, Gwen, Azer, Sheri L., Costley, Joan B., Genser, Andrea, Goodman, Irene F., Lombardi, Joan, McGimsey, Bettina. (1993). *Making a career of it: The state of the states report on career development in early care and education.* Boston: Wheelock College.

Powell, Douglas R. Effects of program models and teaching practices. (1986, September). *Young Children. 41,* (6), 60-67.

Raphael, Ray. (1985). *The teacher's voice: A sense of who we are.* Portsmouth, NH: Heinemann.

Roemer, Joan. (1989). *Two to four from nine to five.* New York: Harper and Row Publishers.

Schweinhart, L. & Weikart, D. P. (1993, Summer). Changed lives, significant benefits: The High/Scope Perry Preschool project to date. *High/Scope Resource, 12,* (30), 1, 10-14.

Schweinhart, L, Weikart, D. P. & Larner, M. (1986). Consequences of three preschool curriculum models through age 15. *Early Childhood Research Quarterly, 1,* 15-45.

Wollman, Patti Greenberg. (1994). *Behind the playdough curtain: A year in my life as a preschool teacher.* New York: Charles Scribner's Sons.

van Manen, Max. (1991). *The tact of teaching: The meaning of pedagogical thoughtfulness.* Albany, NY: State University of New York Press.

SUGGESTIONS FOR FURTHER READING

Greenberg, Polly. (1992, November). Making the most of it: Expanding professional horizons. *Young Children, 48,* (1), 58-61.

| Figure 5-15 | **Generally teacher answers to the question "Why teach?" cannot be found in books, but in consideration of relationships with the children themselves.** |

GROWING ONESELF AS A TEACHER

Frequently in introductory textbooks on teaching, there is a section that includes a list of necessary characteristics and competencies for teachers to possess. It is a little disconcerting to encounter these lists, for it suggests that the essence of good teaching can be somehow reduced to the sum of the words on those lists. It is also likely rather intimidating to beginning student teachers to consider those lists. Anxiously scanning them is like checking the published names of those with unpaid taxes to make sure that their particular name or personal characteristics has not been publicly proclaimed as unfit! Instead, this chapter will focus on helping students explore the concept that teachers teach from within the context of the lives they create for themselves. Teaching itself involves a process of becoming, and the life experiences of the individual are the ingredients in that process. Teachers need to bring their "examined" lives into their classrooms, and this chapter is to facilitate that personal examination. In addition, teachers go through stages of development in their professional lives, just as they pass through stages of development in their personal lives, and this chapter will help you understand those stages, and how you can actively participate in creating yourself as a teacher. Remember that teaching is highly personal; your journey to becoming a teacher will be quite unlike that of another person.

CONSIDERING PERSONAL AUTOBIOGRAPHY

"A good teacher is first and foremost a person, and this fact is the most important and determining thing about him" (Combs et al. 1974, p. 6). If you think back on the good teachers you have known, you will likely confirm the truth of this statement. No doubt each one stands out in your mind as a unique individual, with a particular personality, values, beliefs, methods, and techniques. Think about their characteristics, and list these in your journal. Probably they were all competent, but likely they were competent in ways that made them quite unlike every other teacher you encountered. Good teachers teach with their whole being. The complete person who walks into the classroom each day, is not only the sum of the accumulated knowledge and techniques learned to use while working with children.

Good teaching is also intensely personal. It is the sum of experiences, emotions, thoughts, and learning that have occurred in one's life up to this point, interacting with the particular world in which one teaches (see Fig. 6-1). Since the self is the tool with which teachers fulfill the teacher roles, it is vital that both new and experienced teachers come to a deep level of self-awareness

When you know where you came from, you know where you're going
—Frances Brock Sturms

Figure 6-1 | **Good teaching is the sum of experiences, emotions, thoughts, and learning that have occurred in your life up to this point, interacting with the world in which you teach.**

1946
The American Baby Boom begins.

and self-acceptance. Rather than measuring themselves up against a defined standard for what a good teacher should be like, teachers need to be active in uncovering the truth about what they themselves *are* like, and what this will mean in their teaching practice.

Examining their personal lives, including the experiences that have helped shape their values and the ways they live and relate with others, is an important ongoing process for good teachers. A phrase that is frequently used about teachers who take the time and effort to analyze their actions and evaluate their effectiveness is "reflective" practitioners (Kochendorfer, 1994). It is important to extend this concept to reflecting about one's whole life as a means of being an effective teacher.

THEORY INTO PRACTICE

This is Sheila Locklear, who has been in the field of early education for over ten years. After beginning as a nanny, she moved to work in a child care center, and is currently the teacher of a class of four-year-olds. She completed her assocate degree in early childhood education just over two years ago, by taking coursework in evening classes.

What has been a significant frustration for you in early education? How do you deal with it?

A significant frustration for me has been getting financial support from the general public, to maintain needed materials for children, teachers, and support staff. I have dealt with this by getting creative, having fund-raisers, making my own teaching tools. Teachers I work with often share materials and look for outside resources such as the library and the resource and referral agency lending library. Parents often are great resources for material which can be recycled, as well as being teaching tools themselves.

What is one thing you learned in classes that you really discovered to be true when you started working with children?

Every child really does develop differently, and each child should be thought of as an individual, and respected for who they are. Each stage of development is important, although one stage my influence one child more than another.

What is an area you are working on now to learn more about?

I continually work on learning ways to balance discipline, learning, and fun in a classroom.

Why have you stayed in early education?

What keeps me here is the small rewards—a smile that says "I can do it;" a parent who tells you you have made a difference in their child's life. The day to day challenge to stay in the field against the public's odds.

What is a comment or piece of advice you would give to those beginning to work in early childhood education?

Advice to beginners: Get to know *every* child in your care. Respect the whole child and his/her family. This helps you balance what you want to teach and what the child needs to learn.

Listen to these words of a supervisor of child care workers talking to a new employee:

> You will learn nothing from others, . . . Nobody can teach you anything until you come to know that you are already the expert on the subject that lies at the heart of all learning . . . the subject of you. . . . You will learn nothing at Willoughby House unless your primary interest is in you and your ability to take charge of your life. If your curiosity is here then all of us, kids and staff, can share and contribute, but always with the knowledge that you are the expert on the subject of you. Charlotte (Fewster, 1990).

William Ayers (1989), in his fine book already referred to in this text, worked with six preschool teachers to try to uncover the "meaning of their life stories as those stories influenced their teaching" (p. 6). Using a variety of interviews, observations, and interpretive activities, Ayers worked to help the teachers take part in a process of "self-discovery and self-construction through autobiography" (p. 126), while also attempting to discern whether there were qualities and patterns that were common to good teachers. The entire book is thought-provoking and revealing in what we interpret about the nature of good preschool teaching, but perhaps a primary insight is that autobiography helps the individual practitioner to look beyond the self-portrait "for linkages with what we know of the larger social realities of teaching" (Ayers, p. 126). Before you proceed with this chapter, this might be a good opportunity to begin work on your own autobiography to increase your self-knowledge. Through this self-understanding, you will be able to find the uniqueness that you bring to teaching, and the ways in which you will be able to answer teaching's demands upon you. "The challenge of teaching is to decide who you want to be as a teacher, what you care about and what you value, and how you will conduct yourself in classrooms. . . . It is to name yourself as a teacher" (Ayers, 1993, p. 23). It is time to begin to name yourself as the person who will be the teacher.

Noise, noise, noise, yes. But if you don't like noise don't be a teacher. Because children are noisy animals. . . . But it's a natural noise and therefore bearable
—Sylvia Ashton-Warner

> The person I am is partly constituted by my life memories. Past experiences have been consolidated in me such that memories may unexpectedly appear in changing situations and circumstances. The past may have been forgotten, but it may also suddenly confront us again when the past becomes relevant for the present. The power of childhood and life memory attests to the fact that we are historical beings: we have life histories that give permanence and identity to the present we are (van Manen, 1991, p. 22).

In your **journal**, begin to write a story about yourself; you may want to add to this as thoughts occur to you later. Your autobiography will reflect your unique history, and will be unlike anyone else's. If you have already had some experience teaching, you will find some questions here that you can answer from that experience; if you have not yet had teaching experience, you can answer those questions when you rethink your autobiography. Here are some questions to get you started; go ahead and write about any other issues that seem to you to be pertinent or come to mind after you think about these questions.

Journal: Notes for the individual. In early education, used to document individual progress of children and teacher.

1946
The *Common Sense Book of Baby and Child Care* is published by Dr. Benjamin Spock.

What early influences made you the person you are today? Who were the important people in your life? What picture comes to mind as a place you liked to be? What were you like when you were ten? Who gave you your name, and why?

What strong childhood memories do you have? How do these memories influence you as you think about working with children? Do you see an influence from your family on your decision to teach? How have you been influenced by any colleagues or mentors? What outstanding teachers do you remember? What were their central teaching ideas/styles?

When did you decide to become a teacher? What was it about teaching that attracted you? Are there any chance factors that led you to consider teaching? How did you feel after you had made the decision? What are your goals for children?

What is important to you beyond teaching? What do you do about it? What concerns you most about the state of the world, and about the state of children and families? What have you read recently that was important to you? What do you see yourself doing five or ten years from now?

For experienced teachers: How have you changed as a teacher over time? Can you remember when you felt comfortable as a teacher? Is teaching pretty much what you'd expected? Did your training prepare you for what you found in your classroom? What is rewarding for you in teaching? What have your favorite times been? Least favorite? Have you considered leaving the profession? Why do you stay? What would you change in your work, if you could? Why do you teach as you do? Which children do you find most appealing? Most difficult? What else is important in describing who you are and will be as a teacher? (Some of these questions adapted from Ayers, 1989, pp. 8-10.)

THREE TEACHERS

In the section that follows, you will hear the stories and self-revelations of three real teachers of young children. These teachers agreed to participate with you to see how who they have become in their lives, influences their everyday practice of teaching. In each autobiography, we see not only what they've been made, but what they've made of what they've been made (Ayers, 1989, p. 126). As we listen to them talk, we will discover some truths about how teachers can become more active participants in their own reflective practice, and how this will affect their teaching (see also McLean, 1993; and Ambrose, 1993).

Connie's Story

Connie has been a teacher in a halfday preschool program for fifteen years (see Fig. 6-2). Now 50, she was raised with the idea that her role would be a wife and mother, and she was sent to college so she "would have something to fall back on." Because her mother had always been a "kid-person," she was too, so elementary education seemed like a plausible major for study. But when she taught first grade after graduation, it was in a traditional school with the traditional style of teaching, and she hated it. "It wasn't true to me and what

Figure 6-2 **Meet Connie Glass.**

Figure 6-2 **Meet Connie Glass.**

I believed about kids." After three children, when her youngest daughter was two, she began to look for a part-time job to earn a little extra money. (And as she said at a recent Worthy Wage Rally, "That's what I got–a *little* extra money!") Her son had had special needs in his development and learning, and she had been exposed to a lot of on-site training and education by working with his specialists, so by that point she felt she'd "figured out how to parent." Her daughter had accidentally left behind a sweater at a church they had visited, and when Connie went to retrieve it she was intrigued by the school. She purchased and immediately read a book written by the founder of the school (Riley, 1979), and went right back in to apply for a job. In her first year of working with three-year-olds, Connie felt overwhelmed. The director was also in her first year, but when Connie needed help, the former director was there to observe in her room and make suggestions. Because of this, Connie felt supported, rather than discredited for her lack of skill–in effect, mentored. Even though it was a difficult year, she felt there was no question that this was what she was meant to do. She felt she was in control by the third year of teaching. She left the school for a brief period, when the director left to establish a full-day program elsewhere. But after a year of teaching at that new school, Connie returned to the original school. She found the full–day program to be so very different from half-day, including her discovery that she resented having to work with other peoples' children, when her own were home on a snow day and she couldn't be with them. The needs of the children who were in full-day care took "a lot of my emotional reserve"–for example, the child who came in crying every day. She was mature enough not to take it personally, but found it draining.

She smiles as she recounts a story about when she really learned what "discovery learning" was all about. "I had put out red paint, then later yellow. And I was just poised for someone to discover that together they made orange. I saw one little fellow staring with fascination down into the paint jar, holding his brush that had been dipped into the other color. So I crept closer, waiting to hear the magic words. And I did, but not 'Look I made orange'; he said, 'Look Connie, I'm making swirls.' So I learned a lot about how kids could make their own discoveries."

She thought of the teaching as a part-time job at first, though she loved it. Gradually she moved into thinking of herself as a professional, knowing the children and families more intimately, and knowing herself as a teacher. Her feelings of success come when she sees children work out their own differences–"then I feel I've been rewarded, even though it doesn't always happen on the teacher's time schedule." What does she want for them? "I want them to think for themselves. I like it when they look at something and get something different from what others do."

Outside of teaching, for a long time Connie put her efforts into an organization called Beyond War, consistent with her feelings that the biggest need in this world is for individuals to resolve their conflicts peacefully. Now those

1948
World Organization for Early Education (OMEP) is founded, to meet every third year around the world.

Figure 6-3   **Meet Annie Bryant.**

Mentor: An experienced individual, who can support a less experienced individual.

efforts go into the classroom learning, to help children celebrate and accept diversity and differences. When asked what she'll be doing five years from now, Connie replies with certainty, "I'll be here." She feels called to teach, and this is her reason for doing it. She needs to be with children, feeling gratified as she sees them grow. One of the best things about teaching is having a coteacher to run things by. Connie comments that she recalls the long afternoons as a young parent, with nobody to share ideas with, and she remembers feeling lonely. She also recalls the first scary feelings of teaching, when everything is new and different, and beginners feel nervous and afraid. This is probably one of the factors in her entering the model/**mentor** training program in her city, to help beginners get a new start. "All of the professional moves currently in early childhood education are positive—we need to educate people a lot." Connie is here to continue making her contribution.

Annie's Story

Annie was raised in a large extended rural Southern family, by a mother who had three children at a young age and worked, so much of the rearing was assisted by uncles and aunts (see Fig. 6-3). Children were "not particularly valued—meant to stay in their place." She felt she was not smart. The space between her front teeth meant she told lies, she was told, and the schools she attended did nothing to help with feelings of nurturing. Annie remembers harsh discipline, and cultural biases, with teachers clearly singling out African-American children with "kinky hair and raggedy clothes—both of which I had." No teacher made a difference in her life. She also remembers accompanying her mother to do housework in the home of a white family, and being told she had to stay in the kitchen, rather than go in to other parts of the house to play with the family's children. As she talks about these memories, Annie sees clear connections with her goals for the children with whom she works. "I worry about the effects on children of others' responses to them. These things stay with them forever. That's why it's so important to pass on to the people in my life, to make children feel better. I don't remember adult love, and I want these children to remember it."

Annie had assumed she would be following a career in business, after courses in business administration. The negative side to her jobs as secretary and office manager was feeling confined to the office. After marriage and moving to Baltimore, Annie became involved in a Head Start Parent-Child program when her eleven-month-old daughter was found to have developmental delays with speech and physical development. Immediately she became involved in talking with therapists, and was required to attend parenting classes, which included volunteering hours in the classroom. Despite her initial feeling that she didn't particularly like being with the children, she got drawn in to the Head Start work, serving on committees, on the parent advisory board, and going to

1950
Erik Erikson publishes *Childhood and Society,* outlining his theory of psychosocial development.

a national convention. She was offered a job as a Head Start teacher, and began to like the work, initially because it gave her freedom and variety outside of an office. During this first time teaching, she saw a lot of "wrong things done to children, by both teachers and parents. The teachers who did right motivated me; I was learning a lot about my child and about myself and my potential."

Annie remembers two of the professional staff in particular. One, an education specialist, brought her in for a discussion, questioning her about how she responded when her daughter indicated she wanted something without speaking. "She grilled me–I took offense." She told Annie that the reason her child was not talking was because she was not being made to talk; with everything being given to her, she wouldn't be able to speak for herself. Annie got angry, then got over it and went back to her to thank her, saying the advice had been valuable. A physical therapist also advised her not to give in to her daughter, but to let her try herself to the maximum. Annie thought–the child was so determined *not* to use her walker, maybe she could be equally determined about walking herself. "She got to be two and was still not walking, and this forced me to knock on doors and ask questions. All of this got me started into children, learning their development, what was right, about discipline, nurturing. I could have had a spoiled child, but all of those professionals helped me learn." Annie was associated with the Head Start program for three years. Then, when her marriage broke up, she returned to her hometown and moved in with her family to get help with her daughter's care. She began cleaning offices at night, but "didn't last a week," she says with a grin. At the local community college, a counselor basically chose the early childhood curriculum for her, Annie says, on the basis of her low test scores and the CDA courses she had completed with Head Start at the University of Maryland.

She got a part-time job working with after-school care while she completed her two-year degree, then taught for Head Start for a year after she graduated, feeling she owed them a debt for getting her started. Then she applied for a job in a church-sponsored child care center, for the first time feeling enough confidence to bargain over salary. "I now knew the value of my degree and my education. My family was so proud of me, and I was proud of me."

After several years in the classroom, Annie was nominated by a parent to receive the award for the child care teacher of the year. Recently she has become the director of the center, though she admits this is not something she feels really good at yet–"I should have listened more in my day care administration course"–and still prefers teaching. When asked what she'd like to be doing five years from now she replies, "Still training, and maybe something for parents. I'd like to make a difference in parenting–that's where it started for me. Somebody had to tell me. I don't see any child as being a child who can't learn. I know I have made a difference in children's lives, whereas I don't know anybody I can go back and hug the way they come back to hug me. I got conned into it by a couple of college instructors who believed in me, enough to give me all the push I needed. Now I know I can do it, but then I didn't. Everybody needs somebody who can believe in you–like my baby. I needed to believe in her enough to trust her and let go. My heart goes out to parents, they're so torn."

Anti-bias training of teachers is important to me. Everybody deserves a chance–lots of kids can't develop to their fullest potential. I've been on both

I have come to a frightening conclusion. I am the decisive element in the classroom. It is my personal approach that creates the climate. It is my daily mood that makes the weather. As a teacher, I possess tremendous power to make a child's life miserable or joyous. I can be a tool of torture or an instrument of inspiration. I can humiliate or humor, hurt or heal. In all situations it is my response that decides whether a crisis will be escalated or de-escalated, and a child humanized or dehumanized

–Haim Ginott

1950
Fourteen percent of mothers of children under five years old are employed outside of the home.

Figure 6-4   **Meet Martha Huxster.**

sides; now I get teased about 'talking white.' My strength is I can relate to those who have had very little education. We've got to start somewhere. Somebody has to do it. It keeps giving me experience. When I stop, they'll be putting dirt on me. The mentoring course has given me even more strength: I never thought I'd be able to get up in front of a group." Annie was thoughtful after our long conversation. She summed it up: "Teaching is not something you get into for the money. It has got to be something you believe in and you live."

Martha's Story

Martha followed her older sister into child care (see Fig. 6-4). Her sister had begun volunteering, then working, at a nearby program when in high school, and Martha went along to help. Immediately she decided this was it, this was what she wanted to do. Education was important in her family—both parents were college-educated—and she has wonderful memories of nurturing, loving teachers early in her life. Martha herself began to work while still in high school for the same center. The center was one of five for-profit centers that was owned by an overtly successful woman, who Martha took as a model and mentor, wanting to be like her. Martha planned to one day have her own center, since one could obviously make a good deal of money doing this work that she enjoyed so much. For three years during high school and through all four years of college during the summers, Martha worked for the same center, and was paid minimum wage, with no raise for seven years. The owner said two memorable things that stay with Martha as things she has now learned differently; one was that it didn't matter how many children she was given to care for–if she was a good teacher, she could handle it. The other was that if employees didn't do what they were asked, there were people lined up outside the door to get the position. Martha now realizes how many corners were being cut, to make things cheaper and profits higher. When finally she asked for a raise, she was given five cents an hour. She said this was like a slap in the face, and she decided: "Never again!" She had been thinking things would get better, and they didn't. Martha sees this as stimulating her active interest in advocacy, and her current efforts in the Worthy Wage campaign.

Martha still had the goal of owning her own center. The practicum experiences and opportunities to observe other teachers in her degree program really helped her understand quality. For the experience, she took a position as assistant director in a center operated by a large national chain. For two years, she struggled with knowing that the center really was not offering quality care, and visiting a friend's excellent program confirmed this. She decided she needed more education, but when she applied to the university for a master's degree in Early Childhood, she was told that because her undergraduate degree was in child and family development and not teacher certification, she would need an additional 51 hours before beginning the master's.

Her next position was in a half-day preschool program, that "really allowed me to cut loose on creativity with the children." Unfortunately, there were no benefits, including no workmen's compensation. So when she got hurt in an accident at work, and the employer wanted to use her own health insurance—which she did not have for over four years of employment—she took a position in a center that did offer health insurance. A trainer from a local resource and referral agency saw her in action in the classroom and asked her to do a workshop. Martha did, and loved it, thinking, "This could be it." She began training other teachers more regularly, and entered the model mentor training program. (You'll hear more about mentoring programs later.) Although she enjoyed the classroom teaching, she still felt she needed more money, and the wider educational opportunities piqued a lot of interest for her, as she realized how much could be done with advocacy. Martha then took a position as a child development specialist with the YWCA, assisting with training at four centers. She recounts a story of going in to work with a teacher with 20 years of teaching experience, of slowly empowering the older teacher to understand the reasons for doing the things, like lesson plans, that no one had ever helped her understand. This has been satisfying for her to acknowledge how much other teachers need help.

Presently Martha has taken the position as director of one of the Y's more challenging centers. And at the same time, she and her sister have begun an organization that holds training conferences for teachers four times a year. Martha says, "I want to share, to tell teachers my experience, to help them grow, to get more opportunities." Five years from now she sees herself still training, and she also still dreams of finding funding for her own program, a "really unique preschool program. I would love to trash the current system. Teachers can't maintain that high level of energy eight hours a day to be truly available to kids. It would be such a good preschool program, people would be drawn to it like magnets." She smiles, recalling her past ideas of making money. "It might not make a profit, but it would make a difference."

What do we learn from these stories of lives in progress? Are there common patterns and continuities in the stories that can help us think about how teachers grow? Obviously these are three very different individuals, with quite unique experiences. Take your time to think about and note down some thoughts you have after hearing these accounts. Then together we'll move to a consensus on the qualities of good teachers.

It has taken me a lifetime of learning from children to begin to know these things: how to stop the waste, how to channel the precious forces of children

—Caroline Pratt

QUALITIES OF GOOD TEACHERS

Process of Becoming

Good teachers of young children recognize that the preparation for their work and their lives is an ongoing, never-ending process.

Teaching is not something one learns to do, once and for all, and then practices, problem-free, for a lifetime, any more than one knows how to have friends, and follows a static set of directions called "friendships"

1950
Four percent of children are born to unmarried mothers.

Figure 6-5   **Good teachers continue to remain open to new learning and growth.**

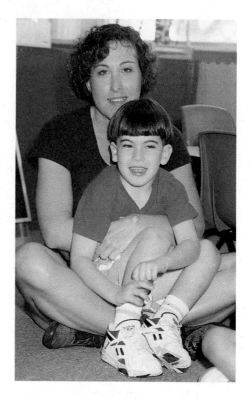

through each encounter. Teaching depends on growth and development, and it is practiced in dynamic situations that are never twice the same. Wonderful teachers, young and old, will tell of fascinating insights, new understandings, unique encounters with youngsters, the intellectual puzzle and the ethical dilemmas that provide a daily challenge. Teachers, above all, must stay alive to this (Ayers, 1993, pp. 127-128).

A good teacher is not produced once and then forgotten: a good teacher is re-created day-by-day (Raphael, 1985, p. 13).

Just as they recognize that their work with children is a process of facilitating development over time, rather than achieving specific, easily observable and quick goals, so too teachers acknowledge that they continue to create their teaching, their understanding of what they do and how they do it, and their personhood. They continue to question, to puzzle, to set goals, to remain open to new learning (see Fig. 6-5). In so doing, they model for children the active process of becoming, human beings. "The good teacher is not a finished product, but a human process" (Combs et al., 1974, p. 144).

This is evident in the words of Carol Hillman, a teacher of four-year-olds you met earlier in this book.

Because I have been teaching four-year-olds for many years, I am called a "Master Teacher." But longevity of the job is not what has earned me this title. Longevity can mean doing the same thing year after year. But there is

1952
John Bowlby publishes *Maternal Care and Mental Health.*

little challenge in that or little satisfaction either. Rather, I am a Master Teacher because of the depth of experiences I have had over the years–experiences that have made me the person and teacher I am. Central to those experiences has been an attitude of wanting to grow, to continue learning. More than anything else, this attitude has sustained me in my work with young children (Hillman, 1988, p. 3).

Being committed to self-discovery allows teachers to grow. This implies curiosity. Therefore, teachers must recognize their constant state of growth and change, that they do not yet know what lies ahead, and what directions they will take. This uncertainty is not daunting, but intriguing with its wealth of possibilities and unknowns. Good teachers are curious about themselves, as well as much else in their worlds. In addition to curiosity, teachers need an ability to engage in self-criticism, to uncover the new challenges and demands that call for growth. The capacity for growth, change, and new horizons was evident in each of the three teachers whom we just met.

"Teachers must understand that even as they teach, they will also be taught; even as they help others develop, they will themselves change and grow" (Ayers, 1993, p. 80).

Feelings of Adequacy

While teachers recognize the unfinished nature of their lives and their development as teachers, they nevertheless accept themselves, and feel comfortable with their adequacy as people. Basic feelings of adequacy allow teachers to perform their daily tasks with a level of confidence and a mature ability to focus on the job at hand, rather than constantly evaluating their ability to perform it, or others' responses to them. It is necessary for teachers to feel basically adequate as people, in order to be able to transcend their own needs and to pay attention to those of others. Being in the classroom is not about meeting teachers' needs for attention and affection. This is not to say that there are not emotional rewards for teachers from their interaction with children and others; rather, these emotional rewards are not sought after to adjust teachers' feelings of inadequacy. The teacher functions at a deeply personal level with children and adults, but this is not deeply personal to be self-indulgent of personal needs. The purpose of teaching is other-directed; the primary goal is to foster a healthy self in each child being served, not to strengthen inadequacy of self in teachers (see Fig. 6-6).

How might these feelings of adequacy manifest themselves in everyday classrooms? When a teacher sees that the children are coming to be fond of the new coteacher and greet her every morning with joyful cries and hugs, she does not feel compelled to ask "Where's my hug too?" and create feelings of rivalry; instead she comments that she is delighted the children now have another adult to trust. Or when a parent says to a caregiver, "I don't know how you do it–I can't seem to get him to take a nap," she uses this as an opportunity to reassure and support the parent ("It *is* hard, and he probably feels so comfortable at home that he tests you a lot more than me"), rather than bolster her own ego ("Well, I've got so much more experience than you!").

The cellist Yo-Yo Ma was once asked to give his opinion of Pable Casals' exquisite interpretation of Bach. He pointed out that the beauty lay not in one note he played but in the combination of notes. Similarly with teaching, adding up the "notes" or parts only partially revealed its effectiveness. How the parts combined into a unified whole must be considered
—Margaret Yonemura

1953
Arnold Gesell publishes *Infant Development.*

Figure 6-6   Teachers who feel adequate as persons are able to focus on children's needs and development, to foster a healthy self-concept in children.

Sometimes "maturity" appears in the list of personal characteristics required for teaching. This word is vague in its meaning, often being different things to different people, but the likely intent is the capacity to accept oneself as one is—feeling OK about oneself, so that the needs of others are not ignored.

Understand also that this sense of basic adequacy is separate from the initial or occasional uncertainties that less-experienced teachers frequently feel. Notice that Annie, an experienced classroom teacher, is feeling less than adequate at the moment in her new role as director. But her past experience has led her to believe that she'll be able to learn the skills. Shortly we will discuss the recognized stages of teacher, and student-teacher, development, so that you can see that questions about functioning in the early childhood classroom are very common in early experiences of teaching. But adequacy of the person means that new teachers recognize they are basically capable, and believe they will be able to develop the necessary teaching skills, over time.

To silence enthusiasm at anytime is absolutely wrong
—Sri Chimnoy

Flexible Thinking

Every day, early childhood teachers are required to make hundreds of decisions, both large and small. They have to select responses and methods that are appropriate to complex and unique circumstances. Often they are faced with situations that they have not encountered previously, with behaviors that require the teacher to adapt existing ideas and techniques to fit complicated circumstances. Without relying completely on a history and authority dictated by others, teachers must create their own answers to real and immediate questions, and move beyond the purely theoretical to find appropriate responses to concrete conditions and feelings, to real-live children and adults.

This demands of teachers a predisposition to depend on their own problem solving ability, rather than resorting to a "cookbook " approach that has been previously learned, or resorting to the authority of others' decisions. Resource books and others may be consulted to assist teachers as they work through particular knotty problems, but they are not used as the final authorities—not, "This says I should" but "Hm, wonder what would happen if I tried this idea?" Individuals who are preoccupied with order, or classifying and using the "right" answer, are unlikely to be able to frame relevant responses. This means looking beyond trying to get a universally applied solution to, for example, biting. Instead, teachers try to choose from many known alternatives, what seems to best fit what is known about a specific child's reasons for biting, at this time. Flexible does not mean that the teacher is not working from a solid knowledge base, and is grasping at straws, as it were; rather, it implies fitting the knowledge of children, philosophy, and goals to the immediate conditions, and discovering the best course of action at this time. It also implies a quality of confidence in one's ability to make good decisions, and to be able to change course when the decision no longer seems good without feeling bound to the earlier direction. Flexible thinking means deciding not to stick with finishing the story because that is what is written on the lesson plan, but instead cutting group time short and taking restless children outdoors to play (see Fig. 6-7).

1954
B. F. Skinner publishes *Science and Human Behavior,* applying behaviorist theory to parenting and education.

Figure 6-7 | **Flexible thinking means watching these children engrossed in waterplay discovery, and deciding to extend the play period.**

Pedagogy: Related to the study and teaching of children.

Max van Manen has written an interesting book on the subject of "**pedagogical** thoughtfulness" (1991), in which he states that it is possible to learn all the techniques of instruction and still be "pedagogically unfit as a teacher." Merely learning knowledge and skills will not allow teachers to learn that which he claims cannot be taught formally: "the most personal embodiment of pedogogical thoughtfulness" (p. 9).

> So a new pedagogy of the theory and practice of living with children must know how to stand in a relationship of thoughtfulness and openness to children, rather than being governed by traditional beliefs, discarded values, old rules, and fixed impositions. The pedagogy of living with children is an ongoing project of renewal in a world that is constantly changing around us and that is continually being changed by us (van Manen, 1991, p. 3).

Sometimes lists of required characteristics include "creativity." Not only does this make many of us who feel limited in artistic ability feel nervous, but it is also a narrow descriptor of the ability to think in a divergent way, consider multiple possiblities, and select one to act upon. Flexible thinking also helps teachers see many learning possibilities, in particular materials and activities, and to realize that there are many ways to teach a particular concept or skill to match many different learning styles. Remember Connie and her story about how the child made a discovery that was quite different from what she had thought he would learn. Flexible thinking implies being experimental, curious, optimally uncertain. Interesting classrooms result from teachers with flexible thinking.

1955
United States ranking in infant mortality is 6th in the world.

Autonomy

Individuals who have developed autonomy are able to function in the flexible manner described above. They are not heavily dependent on others' opinions to guide their actions or decisions. They understand their own goals and motivations, and feel comfortable functioning independently. Teachers "finally decide what goes on in classrooms. When the door is closed and the noise from outside and inside has settled, a teacher chooses" (Ayers, 1989, p. 5). To be able to make those choices, teachers must have a healthy sense of autonomy that allows them to accept ultimate responsibility for their work and their decisions. Autonomy does not necessarily mean solitary, however. Teachers can assume responsibility and leadership, while still being able to work interdependently with others as a member of a team. In most situations with parents, teachers must be the ones to initiate communication and relationships; taking initiative comes from a sense of autonomy.

In the beginning, to be sure, teachers need the support and reassurance of others as they discover their "own personal idiom" (Combs et al., 1974, p. 8), but a basic component of the personality of successful teachers is the ability to function autonomously. There is a degree of self-confidence involved in the concept of autonomy; past experiences have led teachers to see themselves as people who can function independently.

An autonomous teacher will schedule parent conferences without having to be told to by her director, and when she perceives the need. Another would recognize his responsibility to discuss with the director his concerns about possible abuse in a family in his classroom, not waiting for others to take the lead. Another would suggest that the next staff meeting might be a good time to discuss the need for a late policy, rather than silently fuming about chronically late parents. Martha, in her active efforts on behalf of the Worthy Wage Campaign, has taken autonomous action that was borne out of her own frustration.

Autonomy, a healthy sense of one's own power, is critical in teachers who are trying to empower the children and parents with whom they work. When adults are still struggling to feel they have some control, it is difficult to create environments that free others; adults without autonomy often try to control the children in their care, and others within their sphere of influence, to bolster their own sense of power.

Empathy

Good teachers require the ability to identify with others, including the children with whom they work, their parents, and the teachers' other team members. This empathy has roots in an understanding of the complexity of human development, and in respect and concern for individual personalities and feelings. Empathy grows as teachers are able to focus on others' needs and feelings, an ability that arises from the teacher's maturity and willingness to transcend issues of self. It allows teachers to be really tuned in to children and adults, to recognize and accept deep individual differences. This knowledge about individuals comes through effort in observing and making connections to allow individuals to reveal themselves (see Fig. 6-8).

The ethical imperative underlying both child rearing and early childhood education is caring. Adults who choose to work with young children are, for the most part, people who enjoy children and who believe, on the basis of their own positive or negative experiences, that the quality of childhood matters. In this experience lies the source of empathy that is essential to caring
—Elizabeth Jones and
Gretchen Reynolds

Figure 6-8 | When a teacher has empathy, she is able to understand a child's feelings of insecurity, and support the child as she enters a new situation.

When most people say that teachers of young children need "lots of patience," they probably really mean the kind of gentle acceptance that comes with this ability to identify genuinely with the conditions and circumstances of the other. That is, it is not merely a patient tolerance that allows teachers to take the time to calm a child upset by a parent's departure from the classroom, but rather the empathy that lets them experience the depth of the child's sadness. Remember Connie's comments about the child who cried every morning.

Empathy means that teachers are not quick to judge and condemn those whose values, perspectives, and decisions are different from their own. Rather, when faced with a parent who is reluctant to have a child evaluated for a speech delay, for example, they recognize the emotions of fear and denial involved, and help parents express those feelings, rather than becoming impatient or angry when the parent does not immediately agree. Because of Annie's experiences as a parent, she can recognize the deep emotional experiences of the parents with whom she works.

Empathy prevents teachers from exhibiting biases or prejudices; teachers are able to get past narrow thinking, as they take another's perspective, rather than shying away from others who are different. Empathy is a vital component of the communication skills that good teachers develop; empathy helps teachers listen with a "third ear" to the unspoken messages that lie beneath behavior and spoken words. Good teaching is not "maudlin" (Combs et al., 1974, p. 84), but it is deeply caring. Empathy, the ability to identify with others, is the basis of that warm and caring involvement.

1957

Sputnik is launched by the Soviet Union (U.S.S.R.), precipitating much discussion about the effectiveness of American education.

Big Picture

Teachers who will be able to grow as persons and as teachers are those who are more concerned with large than with small issues. Those who have a philosophy that connects their teaching practice to the important issues in their lives are able to find meaning and congruence, and not to get bogged down in the minutiae of daily care. You will recall that Connie's personal involvement in an organization working for peace helps guide her goals for children in resolving their own conflicts and accepting diversity. This larger philosophy is likely what Almy (1975) referred to in her list of important personal characteristics of early childhood teachers as "world-mindedness," an interest and view that extends beyond the walls of the school or center, and connects the teacher to webs of deeper meaning and social relevance. Thus, the first grade teacher is less preoccupied with this Friday's spelling test than he is with considering the relative merits or harm on children of the system of standardized testing currently used in his school district. And the infant caregiver is less concerned with the exact number of disposable diapers left in a baby's cupboard for the week, than with exploring with parents alternatives for diapers that provide good hygiene as well as community environmental protection. This world-mindedness also allows teachers to bring the largeness of the world into the lives of their children. The teacher who is involved with activities for environmental preservation and concern awakens ecological interests in her children; the teacher who visits preschools in other areas has new ideas and resources to enrich his classroom life. Teachers who work for peace and justice in their communities can help their children understand these concepts in action. When teachers understand the values and themes that are important in their lives, they find ways of embodying these ideas in their classrooms and practices (see Fig. 6-9).

Being connected to a big picture suggests that good teachers do not choose teaching only as a job, or even as a career or profession. "It is to choose teaching as a project or a vocation, something one is called to do . . . (with) a vital link between private and public worlds, between personal fulfillment and social responsibility" (Ayers, 1993, p. 23). As Connie said in this chapter, quite humbly, "I am called to be a teacher."

Values are intensely personal products of our own experiences, our upbringing, our early learning, and our lives to this point in time. In the activities at the end of this chapter, you will have opportunities to uncover and describe your own values. It is important that you take time to do this, to see the sources that drive your own "big picture." In your teaching experiences, you will work with other adults whose values may be similar to yours, and those whose values are quite different. You will need to be able to identify those ideas that are important to you, and to articulate them to others, so that you can communicate with others who come from different directions. When values are unclear to you or not yet defined, you can feel discomfort and unhappiness, without clearly understanding the reasons for those feelings. For example, imagine the disquietude if, as a result of your own early childhood experiences, you feel strongly that children need a sense of order and predictability in their lives, and you are paired to work with a teacher who strongly values the ability to be spontaneous and free-floating in the daily routines. Being able to identify and clarify the rea-

He who learns by finding out has sevenfold the skill of he who learned by being told
—Arthur Guiterman

1959
The federal government establishes the Department of Health, Education, and Welfare.

Figure 6-9	**Because this child's teacher is involved with concerns about the environment, he becomes involved in her interests of exploring the natural world.**

sons for your values to others allows you to be able to discuss important issues, and to be able to hear their points of view, without compromising on those ideals–the "mountains you have decided to die on." Decide what you feel passionately about, for these are the ideas that define you. Indeed, identifying those crucial components of your big picture may help you avoid getting into teaching situations that would be untenable for you. An example of this would be the conflict experienced if a teacher took a position in a preschool that used a workbook-based curriculum that stressed academic achievements and long directed work periods for children, when her experiences, training, and intuitions all insist on children's active interaction in an environment designed for play and exploratory learning. In Margaret Yonemura's description of an excellent early education teacher, she points out that one of the hallmarks of the teacher's practice is "her continual analysis and assessment of her work to ensure consistency with her educational beliefs and intentions" (Yonemura, 1986, p. 45). The efforts to uncover one's own values are important to good teachers (see Fig. 6-10).

Self-Disclosure

By now you will have noticed the interrelationship of many of these important components for good teachers. Connected with understanding and communicating one's "big picture," one's sense of adequacy, and empathy, is the ability to reveal oneself to others. Recall Martha telling us how she wanted to share her story with other teachers, so they could see how they could also grow. Good teachers do not conceal their true selves behind some kind of pro-

Figure 6-10 **Teachers translate their values into classroom practices. Try to identify a value of the teacher in this room.**

fessional mask, relating in some two-dimensional way to the children and adults with whom they work. Instead, they are willing to be genuine, to be authentic (Moustakas, 1966), to be self-revealing.

> I have come to believe that the most important quality of all is being authentic. More than anything else I want to be believable. I want to be real. I want to be an adult in whom children have trust. . . . The most important thing to remember is that by being authentic, by being yourself, you will earn the trust of young children (Hillman, 1988, pp. 97, 99).

Lilian Katz describes an experience of visiting a preschool where the children were happily involved in traditional creative play activities, but where something seemed to be missing. As she reflected, she decided that if she were a child in that setting, she might say that the adults were always kind, friendly and warm, saying nice things, but "inside of them is there anybody home?" (Katz, 1995, p. 137). When serious, thoughtful responses are missing because encounters have become automatic and routinized, the question is indeed whether children see teachers as real. Being authentic and genuine, and avoiding the institutionalized responses that can come too easily, is an important part of self-disclosure.

Self-disclosure occurs in relationships of trust that come through a building process, where the individuals respond to one another, over time, consistently and caringly. Trust comes when individuals show themselves open to learn from each other, and to listen to one another without any preconceptions. Trust comes when individuals approach events in a positive spirit, with optimistic expectations, rather than assuming the worst of others. In these conditions, people feel free to reveal their true selves, without fear of rejection.

1960
Seventy percent of school districts in America have kindergartens.

Genuine questions emerge from meaningful relationships and experiences, and teachers have a responsibility to act as one important source of these experiences, and in the process, contribute their passions, values, and beliefs

—Elizabeth Jones and
Gretchen Reynolds

Self-disclosure implies being able to make and reveal personal mistakes and uncertainties; what a wonderful thing to let children know, that adults make mistakes also, and are able to admit them and rectify errors. "I'm sorry," says the teacher. "I forgot I said you could have the next turn. Let me write myself a note so you can be first tomorrow," and she does. Teachers don't have to be superhuman; they just have to be tolerant of human error and frailty, in self and others, rather than fearful of making mistakes. Humility is called for, to have the courage to admit what teachers don't know. Almy (1975) used the phrase "tolerance for ambiguity" as a prerequisite for early childhood teachers, which suggests many things, among them the concept that there is no state of perfection in people or situations. As teachers recognize this, they take the pressure off themselves of being some plastic model teacher, and allowing themselves to expose their real nature to others. Yes, this is the personality characteristic of honesty and integrity, and more—a positive and accepting environment that allows for everyone's growth.

It is not until teachers open themselves to others fully that the potential for growth of all is realized. Good teachers risk, and risk disclosing themselves. Part of the ability to risk, comes from not-taking-everything-as-deadly-earnest, as implied on lists of desirable characteristics that suggest teachers must have a sense of humor. Being able to grin at the ironies and complications of daily life in centers and schools for young children comes when teachers can recognize, accept, and reveal the imperfections in the human condition.

> Teachers needn't reveal themselves completely; few people do this, even among good friends. But they need to be seen as real people who care, have strong beliefs, live fully in the world (Perrone, 1991, p. 31).

Other Dispositions for Teachers

A "disposition", as the word is used by Lilian Katz and Carter and Curtis, is an attitude or tendency to behave in a certain way. As you read, you have probably been thinking about other words that you would use to characterize good teachers. Often the lists that are compiled outline what we intuitively expect from adults who will spend their days teaching young children. Many of them suggest warmth of personality, love for children, kindness, patience, as well as reserves of physical energy. Obviously this makes sense to anyone who recognizes the demands of teaching. To this list, some experienced teachers add their own suggestions. Hillman lists, "positive, supportive, enthusiastic, curious, patient, interested, calm, fair, experimental, humorous and sometimes even a bit poetic" (Hillman, 1988, p. 97), along with "all-seeing rather than all-knowing, a good listener rather than a constant talker" (p. 28). She also offers the words "spirit of willingness" (p. 28), which suggests positive attitudes as well as openness to learning and to change.

Gordon and Browne (1996) list "dedication, compassion, insight, flexibility, patience, energy, and self-confidence" along with being happy and fair-minded (p. 157). Feeney et al. (1996) list "sensitivity to others and a positive

1960
Of mothers of children under age six, nineteen percent are in the work force.

Figure 6-11 **Seeking collaboration and peer support is an important disposition for teachers.**

sense of self" as essential requirements, along with openness to new experiences and self-knowledge and acceptance (pp. 42-43).

An interesting discussion by Carter and Curtis (1994) builds on the thinking and writing about teacher education done by Lilian Katz. They discuss seven teacher *dispositions,* or habits of mind and attitudes, that characterize master teachers and are the desired outcomes of teacher training and education. While these may not necessarily be your attitudes as you enter a program of teacher preparation, these are the attitudes that you will want to consciously develop as you learn more about early childhood education.

The first disposition is that of delighting in and being curious about children's development. Rather than pursuing personal teacher agendas, good teachers stop and marvel at what children are doing, and try to discover what children's questions are. The second disposition is to value children's play, truly recognizing how children construct their understandings of the world and themselves through play. The third disposition is to expect continuous change and challenge. Such an attitude will enhance your ability to respond to classroom demands with creativity rather than resistance and stress, and to support spontaneous learning for your children and yourself.

The fourth disposition seems related to the third: it is to be willing to take risks and make mistakes. You will recall that we discussed this attitude earlier. The fifth disposition is to provide time for one's regular reflection and self-examination. As you are encouraged to do throughout this book, reflection is part of recognizing the teacher as in a dynamic process of continual growth and learning. This time is essential to deepen one's insights. A sixth disposition is to seek collaboration and peer support (see Fig. 6-11). Such collaboration allows teachers to keep their eyes on "bigger pictures," and to have colleagues with whom to gain strength and enlarged visions.

The seventh disposition takes us back to a discussion of the role of advocate in Chapter Four: it is to be a watchdog and whistle-blower. As you learn more about developmental theory and appropriate practices, this attitude will

1960
ASPO/Lamaze (The American Society for Psychoprophylaxis in Obstetrics) is established.

help you to resist pressure to accept less than optimum conditions in early childhood programs or schools. This list of desirable dispositions for teachers is worth remembering and coming back to at various stages in your teacher education.

NECESSARY TEACHER KNOWLEDGE AND EXPERIENCES

In addition to having desirable qualities and dispositions, teachers in the early years prepare for their work in a number of important ways. In Chapter Ten, we will examine the various career paths and educational requirements for various career choices, noting where specific certification and training requirements exist. We will also examine the core knowledge that has been defined as necessary for professionals in early education. In this chapter it is important to note that life experiences, personality characteristics, and values mesh with a professional knowledge base to help teachers continue to offer optimum experiences to young children. In addition, abundant experience helps teachers refine their skills and their practice. "Teaching is an eminently practical activity, best learned in the exercise of it and in the thoughtful reflection that must accompany that" (Ayers, 1993, p. 12).

Each of these learning opportunities will enable you to understand yourself in relation to becoming a teacher. Think about your progress through your early childhood programs not only as requirements for a degree or certificate, but as real opportunities for your own growth and development. And think of it also as only the beginning; completing a teacher education program is just a starting point of your journey as a teacher. Becoming a teacher is a process; accept the challenges.

A good teacher of young children needs to be willing to be the same kind of learner that she expects each child in her class to be

—Carol Hillman

STAGES OF TEACHER DEVELOPMENT

As you are at the beginning of your teaching preparation and career, it may be interesting for you to realize that some study has been done on the various sequences of professional development and growth patterns of teachers. Recognizing the common emotions and experiences, and their needed supports, at the various stages may be helpful. Katz (1995) discusses four distinct phases, with unique developmental tasks and training needs. The stages are linked very generally to experience acquired over time.

Stage I Survival

During this period, which may last at least a year, teachers are mainly concerned about whether they can survive–get through the day or week in one piece, without doing something dreadful; do the work; be accepted. Many teachers feel inadequate and unprepared as they face the realities of a classroom of energetic, developing children. Teachers in this stage need direct help with specific skills, as well as encouragement, reassurance, comfort, support, and understanding, as they develop basic concepts of what young children are like and what to expect of them.

1961

Pampers disposable diapers are introduced in a test market, along with an advertising campaign to promote their usage.

Figure 6-12   **It takes a lot of experience for teachers to reach a comfortable level of confidence in their own abilities.**

Stage II Consolidation

After a time, teachers believe they will survive the immediate crises and stay in the profession. They are now ready to consolidate their overall achievements, and to concentrate on learning specific new skills. They begin to focus on individual children and situations that are troublesome, and to look for answers to questions for individuals whose behavior departs from the norm. Teachers in this stage benefit from discussion with more experienced colleagues about possible alternatives for action and resources.

Stage III Renewal

Frequently, after several years of teaching, teachers get tired of doing the same old things, being quite disinterested in doing the same activities for successive groups of children. They begin to be interested in learning about new developments in the field. It is often useful for teachers at this stage to meet colleagues from other programs, to attend local and regional conferences, to read more widely, and to set new learning goals for themselves. Supports for all of these educational endeavors are helpful.

Stage IV Maturity

After several years of teaching, many teachers have reached a comfortable level of confidence in their own abilities (see Fig. 6-12). The questions they ask are deeper, more philosophical and abstract. Teachers in the stage of maturity search for insight, perspective, and realism. These teachers are ready to interact

1961
J. McVicker Hunt, in *Intelligence and Experience*, states that deficits in early stimulation can be corrected by early education.

with other educators working on problem areas on many different levels. See more about these stages in Katz, 1995.

AN EXPANSION ON THESE STAGES

Payne (in progress, personal communication) has recently expanded on these stages.

Stage I Survival

Teachers' primary concern is with controlling the group, avoiding injuries and misbehaviors, and fitting in with the other teachers at the center. They manage the classroom by maintaining control, creating many classroom rules, and using punishment to eliminate unwanted behaviors, with habitual responses to varying situations. They think of children as a group, requiring them to have similar experiences. They often use whole group activities and much teacher-directed time, since free choice is "just play" and not as important.

Stage II Internalization

After a time, teachers who have had good support and assistance begin to feel less overwhelmed and more able to focus on program planning and the individual needs of children. The focus of their energy turns from managing panic to planning programs. Teachers now maintain control by keeping children actively engaged, are interested to learn new strategies to manage behavior, and can think of several responses to situations. They create attractive classrooms and theme units, but rely heavily on teacher direction and teacher-made displays.

Stage III Maturity

Teachers are always, in the last analysis, thrust back upon themselves as the inventors of their own efforts and the authors of their own teaching texts
—William Ayers

After more time, teachers become more introspective and interested in the philosophy of teaching young children. They begin to see the value of child-initiated activities, enjoy observing and evaluating the meaning of play, and understand that children can be taught to resolve their own conflicts (see Fig. 6-13). They demonstrate respect and sensitive support to children and families, with whom they work as partners. They understand the impact of environmental arrangements on children's behavior, and know that behavior is an indicator of developmental stages. They seek out other teachers for support, and they learn from them. They want to share their knowledge with others, and are interested in improving conditions for children outside their own classroom.

STAGES OF STUDENT TEACHER DEVELOPMENT

You may also be interested to know that someone has organized some typical patterns that student teachers often experience. It might be comforting

1962
Jean Piaget publishes *Play, Dreams, and Imitation in Children,* in English.

Figure 6-13   **Mature teachers understand that children can learn to resolve their own conflicts.**

to know that you are not alone when some of these feelings and situations occur during your first practicum and teaching experiences. If you read through them all, you will see that there *is* light at the end of the tunnel, even though on some student days, that seems doubtful.

Phase I: Anxiety/Euphoria

▶ Easily identifies with children–because it is important to be liked by them.

▶ Making friends is an important early step in developing the authority relationship necessary in teaching.

Phase II: Confusion/Clarity

▶ "I don't know anything about planning curriculum."

▶ What are rules?

▶ How should routines proceed?

▶ When to intercede between/among children?

▶ Sometimes avoid situations out of fear or not knowing whether it is the teacher's role.

1962

The Perry Preschool Project in Ypsilanti, Michigan, is established by David Weikart and associates. This is the most famous of the early preschool programs established for early intervention, because of the extensive longitudinal follow-up on the children in the program. Other well-known early intervention programs include. . .

Phase III: Competence/Adequacy

▶ Triumph in guiding children.

▶ A good idea during planning.

▶ A hug.

▶ Need strong reinforcement from supervisor. Focus on positive.

▶ Even though progress has been made you still feel everyone around you seems to "know it all."

▶ There's so much to learn.

▶ Will I ever be that good?

▶ Still difficult to be a controlling figure or disciplinarian.

Phase IV: Criticism/New Awareness

▶ "If it was my classroom, I would do it differently."

▶ Imperfections become clear.

▶ Starts to find fault with practicum teacher.

▶ To question is part of the growth process.

Phase V: More Confidence/Greater Inadequacy

▶ Greater level than Phase III

▶ Students no longer question–they have acquired a sense of stability.

▶ They know they'll make it.

▶ Successes are more frequent.

▶ Wanting more responsibility.

Phase VI Loss/Relief

▶ Departing from children to whom you've become close.

▶ Standards of performance in proper perspective. Returning to classes somewhat difficult. (Caruso, 1977)

You will notice that individual variations during the various phases may range from success and confidence to discovering that this may not be the field that best matches student capabilities. Many student teachers find that keeping a journal during their experiences helps them identify and express their feelings, and keep track of their learning experiences (Surbeck, 1994.)

This was written in 1920 by Jessie Van Stanton, later director of the Bank Street Nursery School, after one year of teaching at the City and Country School. It was an assignment for Lucy Sprague Mitchell–about whom you will read more in Chapter Eight–to write an exposition about the ideal teacher. She says she wrote it while "oppressed by a sense of dreadful inadequacy, convinced that I could never learn to be a teacher."

THE "IDEAL" TEACHER AND HOW SHE GROWS

The teacher of young children should have a strong physique and a strong well-balanced nervous system. She should be plump and round and have curly short hair. Her cheeks should be rosy and her teeth pearly white. She should have a pleasing personality and a quiet firm manner. She should be poised and of a high moral character. She should have sentiment but not sentimentality. She should be gentle but not sloppy; strong but not impetuous when bitten or scratched.

She should have a fair education. By this I mean she should take a doctor's degree in psychology and medicine. Sociology as a background is advisable.

She should be an experienced carpenter, mason, and plumber and a thoroughly trained musician and poet. At least five years practical experience in each of these branches is essential.

She should be a close observer and a judge of character and should be able to deal with young and old. She should be able to hypnotize the parents of her young pupils and to cause them to change life-long habits of thinking in two mothers' meetings.

Tested at birth and found to have an I.Q. of 150, she was taken from her parents and brought up in totally disinfected surroundings. She was given a cold bath and a globule of gland each morning and her health was carefully watched.

From early childhood she was given every sort of tool and taught to practice close observation. She spent every morning seeing and sawing. In the afternoons, her time was spent on music, hearing, howling, and handling. She spent her evenings practicing manners, masonry, mechanics, mesmerism, and musing on metamorphosis. Thus she acquired early in life the inestimably useful habit of using every second to its highest capacity. *Now, at 63 she is ready!*

But, added to all the virtues and attainments for a teacher, the ideal director should have a spine of steel–to stand the long hours and the trememdous demands made upon her. Her spine must bend easily, however, so that she can crawl under radiators with the cleaning man to dig out the dirt–or put away blocks for two-year-olds on shelves close to the floor. She should have feet of iron so that she can go up and downstairs tirelessly all day long from kitchen to roof to classroom to office.

Now she has studied, Now she has taught. *Now, at 83–she is ready to direct!*

[1]From *The Ideal Nursery School Teacher* by Jessie Stanton. (1990). Reprinted in *Young Children, 45,* (4), 19. Used with permission of New York State AEYC. Originally published in Winter 1954 in *New York Nursery Education News*)

Figure 6-14	**Written by an early leader in the field of early childhood education, this summary recognizes that there is no one ideal for a teacher.**

1963

. . .IDS Harlem Project established by Martin and Cynthia Deutsch in Harlem.

SUMMARY

One idea about teaching that has long been discussed is whether good teachers are born, not made. Rather than being a question with an "either/ or" answer, this chapter suggests that good teachers are people who do have certain personal dispositions and personal characteristics that allow them to grow as teachers and as persons. These attributes include: being a growing person; feelings of adequacy; the ability to think flexibly; a sense of autonomy; an ability to empathize; values and philosophy that enable teachers to focus on a big picture; the ability to disclose self to others; as well as other dispositions. It should also be recognized, that contrary to the facetious entry in Fig. 6-14, there is no one ideal standard for teachers. In addition, knowledge and skill development will enhance teacher effectiveness. Areas of core knowledge and opportunities for practice in the field will be discussed further in a later chapter. In growing teachers–and student teachers–common problems and feelings are experienced at different stages.

Growing teachers is different from training them. Oddly, we more often think about growing plants than about growing people. People, especially the young, are to be domesticated–trained as dogs and horses are–to make them reliable, responsible members of society. . . . An alternative to domestication is liberation (Freire, 1970). Teachers, like other people need some of both (Jones, 1993, p. xi).

QUESTIONS TO REVIEW

1. Discuss your understanding of why self-knowledge is important to the development of a teacher.

2. Describe several attributes that are important for teacher growth and optimum functioning.

3. Describe several characteristics of the various stages of teacher, and student teacher, development.

ACTIVITIES FOR FURTHER STUDY

Many of the following questions are for your consideration in your private notebook or journal. Some are appropriate to share with a partner.

1. List ten words that you would use to describe yourself, to yourself only. List ten words that someone who knows you well would use to describe you. List ten words that an acquaintance would use to describe you. List ten words with which you would *like* to be described. Reflect on these lists. What do the similarities and differences mean?

2. How have you changed in the last three years? What would you like to accomplish in the next three years? What thing that you don't know how to do right now would you like to learn in the future?

3. What is your favorite thing to do alone? With others? What is something that is special to you that you would like to share with a child?

4. Discuss one value that is extremely important to you. Try to identify where this value came from.

5. Complete these sentences:

   I want to be a teacher who . . .

   I want to be a teacher who believes . . .

   I want to be a teacher who feels . . .

   I don't want to be a teacher who . . .

   I don't want to be a teacher who believes . . .

   I don't want to be a teacher who feels . . .

   I feel most competent when . . .

   I feel most unsure of myself when . . .

It really bothers me when children . . .

I love it when children . . .

6. List the five most important things you would like to accomplish with the children under your care. Number them one to five, with first being the most important. Compare your list with another classmate. Where are you similar? dissimilar? Explain to your partner why you value these ideas so highly, and listen to your partner's reasons in turn. Now do you find any common ground–can you agree on a common list? (It is all right if you can not. Just be able to explain why you can not give up anything from your list.)

7. When former students come back to visit, what is the one thing you hope they will say about your classroom that they remember from years before? What is the one thing you could not agree to do, even if asked by your supervisor or a parent, in an early childhood classroom?

8. Describe your classroom as you would hope it would be two years from now. What would it look like, what would be happening, what would children be gaining?

9. In what stage of teacher or student teacher development do you think you are at this time? What makes you think so? What would be most helpful to your growth as a teacher right now?

REFERENCES

Almy, M. (1975). *The early childhood educator at work.* New York: McGraw Hill.

Ambrose, Richard P. (1993). "Personal Narratives and Professional Development." *Childhood Education, 69,* (5), 274-276.

Ayers, William. (1989). *The good preschool teacher.* New York: Teachers College Press.

Ayers, William. (1993). *To teach: The journey of a teacher.* New York: Teachers College Press.

Carter, Margie, & Curtis, Deb. (1994). *Training teachers: A harvest of theory and practice.* St. Paul, MN: Redleaf Press.

Caruso, Joseph J. (1977, November). "Phases in student teaching." *Young Children, 32,* (1), 57-63.

Combs, Arthur W., Blume, Robert A., Newman, Arthur J., Wass, Hannelore L. (1974). *The professional education of teachers: A humanistic approach to teacher education.* (2nd ed.). Boston: Allyn and Bacon, Inc.

Feeney, Stephanie, Christensen, Doris, & Moravcik, Eva. (1996). *Who am I in the lives of children: An introduction to teaching young children.* (5th ed.). Columbus, OH: Merrill Publishing Co.

Fewster, Gerry. (1990). *Being in child care: A journey into self.* New York: The Haworth Press.

Gordon, Ann, & Browne, Kathryn Williams. (1996). *Beginnings and beyond.* (4th ed.). Albany, NY: Delmar Publishers Inc.

Hillman, Carol B. (1988). *Teaching four-year-olds: A personal journey.* Bloomington, IN: Phi Delta Kappa Educational Foundation.

Jones, Elizabeth (Ed.). (1993). *Growing teachers: Partnerships in staff development.* Washington, DC: NAEYC.

Katz, Lilian. (1995). *Talks with teachers of young children.* Norwood, NJ: Ablex Publishing Corporation.

Kochendorfer, Leonard. (1994). *Becoming a reflective teacher.* Washington, DC: National Education Association.

McLean, S. Vianne. (1993). Learning from teachers' stories. *Childhood Education. 69,* (5), 265-268.

Moustakas, Clark. (1966). *The authentic teacher.* Cambridge, MA: Howard A. Doyle Publishing Co.

Perrone, Vito. (1991). *A letter to teachers: Reflections of schooling and the art of teaching.* San Francisco: Jossey-Bass Publishers.

Raphael, Ray. (1985). *The teacher's voice: A sense of who we are.* Portsmouth, NH: Heinemann.

Riley, Sue Spayth. (1979). *How to generate values in young children.* Los Angeles, CA: The New South Company.

Surbeck, Elaine. (1994, Summer). Journal Writing with Preservice Teachers. *Childhood Education, 70,* (4), 232-235.

van Manen, Max. (1991). *The tact of teaching: The meaning of pedagogical thoughtfulness.* Albany, NY: State University of New York Press.

Yonemura, Margaret V. (1986). *A teacher at work: Professional development and the early childhood educator.* New York: Teachers College Press.

SUGGESTIONS FOR READING

Bowman, B. (1990). Self-reflection as an element of professionalism. *Teachers College Record, 90,* (3), 444-51.

Brand, Susan. F. (1990). Undergraduates and beginning preschool teachers working with young children: Educational and developmental issues. *Young Children, 45,* (2), 19-24.

Greenberg, Polly. (1992, November). Making the most of it: Expanding professional horizons. *Young Children, 48,* (1), 58-61.

Han, Eunhye. (1995). Reflection is essential in teacher education. *Childhood Education, 71,* (4), 228-230.

Heiss, Gayle. (1989, May). Preschool teaching priorities: Reflections of a former home morning care provider. *Young Children, 44,* (4), 31-36.

Humphrey, Susan. (1989, November). Becoming a better kindergarten teacher: The case of myself. *Young Children, 45,* (1), 16-22.

Katz, Lilian. (1990, February). *On teaching.* Child Care Information Exchange, 3-4.

CHALLENGES FOR EARLY EDUCATORS

As you hear the words and stories of early childhood teachers who find fulfillment and satisfaction in their work, it may seem to you that this profession could offer you the opportunity to achieve your personal and professional goals. But it is important to be completely realistic about the less attractive aspects that are also involved with the occupation. There is no question that the work is important and necessary, and the field needs many new teachers every year. But it is also vital that those teachers who are entering the profession understand some of the challenges they will face, along with other early childhood teachers. Thousands of teachers leave classrooms every year, burnt-out and disillusioned. Rather than have this happen to you, it is important that you evaluate those challenges and how they might affect your ability to remain and grow as a teacher in early education.

Some of the challenges to be discussed in this chapter have to be accepted and dealt with, taken as part of the territory that cannot really be changed. Yet you must consider whether you can learn to coexist with these conditions. Others of the challenges are slowly being remedied by the combined efforts of those in the profession who see it as part of their role to change the perceptions and conditions that are troubling them. So it is your task, while studying this chapter, to consider the impact of the existing challenges and conditions, and your own ability to contend with these factors. The early childhood profession needs and wants those individuals who have made the decision after clear-eyed examination of the actual status and issues of the profession. Before you start reading this chapter, think of the responses of those close to you when you told them you were considering early childhood education as a career. Write these in your journal.

OBJECTIVES:

After studying this chapter, students will be able to:

1. **identify and discuss ten challenges for those working in early education.**

2. **describe several helpful supports for teachers facing challenges.**

WHAT ARE THE CHALLENGES OF EARLY EDUCATION?

When Christie S. announced to her friends and family that she would major in early childhood education and plan to be a preschool teacher, she was dismayed by their responses. Rather than congratulating her on her choice of doing meaningful, important work as she saw it, her parents kept asking "Why?" And the specific meaning implied by their question seemed to her to be "Why do this work when you obviously have a good deal of intelligence and could do something more important?" And "Why be a teacher of young children, when other work could be far more profitable for you?" Her father put it rather bluntly: "I'm afraid I'll still have to support you after you are finished with college." And one friend said, "You call that teaching–what can you possibly teach those little kids?" Perhaps these have been responses that you have also encountered; they are indeed discouraging, since they imply an absence of respect for the work that you have decided is meaningful and important to you. And even more discouraging, these questions reflect some of the issues and attitudes that trouble the early childhood profession today.

When Christie turned to teachers who were already employed in early childhood centers and schools for reassurance and support, she was dismayed to discover that there too were numerous rumbles of discontent. One teacher spoke to her of his frustrations with the gender bias he encountered; another complained of the stress related to too many conflicting needs, and unmet goals. Several stated that they would be moving on to work that allowed them to earn the kind of salaries that were reflective of their education. It took a number of conversations with a teacher who had also experienced the frustrations and stress, and still decided that the satisfactions of the work were strong enough to outweigh the negatives, before Christie was reassured that her decision was a good one. She continued with her plans to become a preschool teacher, knowing that there would be emotional and social hurdles ahead. Together now we will explore the basis for early childhood teacher discontent, so that you too will be able to decide whether the positives outweigh the negatives.

It is interesting to note that some of the advantages that were discussed in earlier chapters also contribute to the stress and frustration that teachers of young children experience. You will recall that Almy suggested that teachers would need a "tolerance for ambiguity" (Almy, 1975). This implies that, as part of this ambiguity, the same characteristic of the work that makes it attractive, also makes it difficult. And ambiguity also suggests that tolerance for stress is a highly individual and subjective response; what is intolerable to one person may provide interest and excitement to another. That is why your personal evaluation of your habitual responses is important here.

We will begin by examining some of these characteristics of the work that bring both attractive and unattractive aspects into teachers' lives.

> *Disequilibrium is a predictable outcome of diversity: people with different world views and styles of being in the world keep challenging each other's assumptions*
> —Elizabeth Jones and John Nimmo

Variety and Unpredictability

You will recall those teachers who spoke earlier of the fact that no two days were alike, and that there was constant change in their work with young

1963

Bing's studies indicate that specific factors in the home, such as maternal warmth, high level of emotional involvement and interaction, and paternal interest are possibly associated with children's achievement.

| Figure 7-1 | **Adapting to a variety of needs and tasks simultaneously can be both physically and emotionally exhausting.** |

children. While a moderate amount of variety is stimulating and exciting to most people, a constant barrage of unpredictable events may result in psychological overload. The need to adapt continually may be exhausting both physically and emotionally, even while it is exhilarating (see Fig. 7-1).

Imagine the adjustments needed when a teacher discovers that her coteacher has had a car break down and is running late; that two of the children in her class have just been diagnosed as having chicken pox and the other ten families need to be informed; that there is no red paint for the planned art activity this morning and the child who is painting at the easel is demanding a substitute for the blue paint provided; that the puzzle table that is usually quite attractive to her group of children draws only uninterested glances this morning; that the birthday party scheduled for lunchtime will have to be moved to morning snack time to accommodate working parents' schedules; and that the child who usually separates from her grandmother easily has chosen today to run after her with heartbroken screams. While, after order is restored, it may build teacher confidence to realize that she has coped with these and other impromptu decisions and situations, at the time this teacher undoubtedly experienced a good deal of the stress that comes with having to adapt quickly.

Let's analyze the reasons behind the stress in such a scenario. One is that teachers of young children are inextricably bound to a variety of other adults, both coworkers and the parents of the children. Their schedules, needs, and wishes, to say nothing of values, all have to be acknowledged and do have an effect on the teacher's individual actions and schedule. A second reason is that teachers of young children have so many roles to play, and play simultaneously. Concurrently, this teacher is concerned with the health and safety of children, communicating with parents, planning and providing appropriate learn-

1960s

There is a resurgence of interest in Montessori schools in America, following the post-Sputnik discussions about the need for more structured programs for early education.

ing resources and daily schedule, and providing emotional support. Small wonder that there is room for stress. Another reason is the fact that young children are "predictably unpredictable" (Hyson, 1982, p. 26).

Fast-changing interests, emotions, and behavior mean that teachers are never quite sure how children will react to activities or situations, as in the case of the unexpected **separation** distress (see Fig. 7-2). With emphasis in the early childhood curriculum on children's choice and independent exploratory play, teachers regularly have to adapt to the decisions that children make about their preferences for use of materials. The unpredictable process of responding to children's choices means that teachers face stress in trying to provide appropriate curriculum activities and materials that can often not be planned long in advance. Teachers of older children usually follow a mandated curriculum that is designed with specific objectives, and criteria for assessment. While early childhood teachers are more likely to be free of such constraints on their decisions about appropriate classroom materials and methods, this freedom is itself

Separation: The process of learning to be apart from the attachment partner. A developmental task of toddlerhood.

THEORY INTO PRACTICE

This is Kim Brandon. She has been in the field of early education for about fifteen years. Recently she has completed an associate degree in early childhood education. She teaches in a mixed-age group of preschoolers in a church-sponsored NAEYC accredited child care center.

What has been a significant frustration for you in early education? How do you deal with it?

A significant frustration for me has been the low wages and the unprofessional image cast upon this field. I have dealt with this by participating in the 'Worthy Wage' campaign and by joining professional organizations, such as NAEYC.

What is one thing you learned in classes that you really discovered to be true when you started working with children?

One thing that I have discovered to be true is that children are naturally curious and eager to learn, whether it is a child experimenting with his/her lunch or a child using "invented" spelling. No matter what, a child is constantly learning. I observe this every day.

What is an area you are working on now to learn more about?

Soon I will be learning to be a Model/Mentor teacher, so I can help others in this field. I also want to learn more about inclusion and how it can work in my classroom.

Why have you stayed in early education?

I have stayed in early education because I love working with children and watching them grow. I love seeing the sparkle in a child's eye when he/she has discovered something new about life and the world around us.

What is a comment or piece of advice you would give to those beginning to work in early childhood education?

I would like to tell all who are entering education to keep one thing in mind: all children are different and unique and should be respected as individuals.

| Figure 7-2 | **Some stress is a result of never being quite sure how children will react in situations.** |

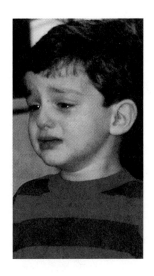

somewhat stressful, since it puts the burden for planning squarely on the individual teacher, rather than giving teachers the security of knowing some decisions have already been made for them.

> Teaching as the direct delivery of some preplanned curriculum, teaching as the orderly and scripted conveyance of information, teaching as clerking, is simply a myth. Teaching is much larger and much more alive that that; it contains more pain and conflict, more joy and intelligence, more uncertainty and ambiguity. It requires more judgement and energy and intensity than, on some days, seems humanly possible. Teaching is spectacularly unlimited (Ayers, 1993, p. 5).

For many teachers, this spectacular lack of limits, the variety, freedom, open-ended unpredictable nature of the early childhood classroom is an attractive feature. For others, this same variety and freedom may create anxiety and stress. What about you? Are you the kind of person who enjoys the opportunity to see your capacities challenged, and feels energized when you are stretched into new territory and decisions? Or are you continually anxious when you move into unfamiliar territory? You should realize that you will be frequently in the position of having to make decisions about whose outcome you may be uncertain, and that your days may often not have the security of sameness.

Lack of Definitive Answers

As any new parent can tell you, there are very few people in this world who don't seem to have quite definite ideas about childrearing and how it ought to be done. And since early childhood teachers seem to most laypeople to be closer to childrearer than teacher, they are thus fair game to hear the opinions of everyone–parents, grandparents, ordinary citizens, and policymakers– about just what should be done with young children and their programs. While most untrained people would be reluctant to tell their doctors just how their illnesses should be treated or their dentists how to drill and fill teeth, very few hesitate to tell early childhood teachers what they should be doing, and how they should be doing it. Early childhood teachers often find that it is difficult to persuade laypeople of the value of developmentally appropriate practices for young children: the practices often are so very different from most adults' memories of what school is supposed to look like (see Fig. 7-3). Many early education teachers feel as though they are caught up in cycles of continually defending what they do to people who do not understand.

And the tension is not only with laypeople who do not understand: there is not a clear-cut understanding and agreement among early childhood practitioners (Jones, 1991). There are not many longitudinal research studies that

Teaching is a complex task with hard-to-predict outcomes
—Elizabeth Jones and John Nimmo

1964
Benjamin Bloom publishes *Stability and Change in Human Characteristics.*

Figure 7-3   **Developmentally appropriate practice can look very different from other ideas of what school is supposed to look like. (Courtesy of Connie Glass)**

indicate definitive evidence about the best ways to teach young children. Part of the problem is that there is often conflicting research data that conclusively prove diametrically opposite ideas. For example, in a new book on issues in early childhood education (DelCampo and DelCampo, 1995), respected researchers and academics offer evidence and arguments that support absolute "yes" and "no" arguments to hotly debated topics such as "Should formal schooling begin at an early age?" and "Does spanking lead to child abuse and later violence?" (This would likely be an interesting resource for you to read as you familiarize yourself not only with controversial issues in early childhood education, but also the spectrum of opinion and research data that exists.) In the face of such conflicting evidence, it is difficult for teachers to make definitive statements about the best methods for early education.

Teaching has been said to be more art than science, and is partly a matter of personal judgement and opinion–although that judgement and opinion is hopefully based on accumulation of knowledge and fact. Nevertheless, teacher confidence can suffer when there is uncertainty that arises from not being able to point to definitive fact, and when everyone who has ever been a child or attended school feels equally qualified to state opinions about best practices.

Thus much of the security that teachers have is derived only from the strength of their personal convictions, rather than from the unanimous support of a professional body of knowledge. And much of the approval that humans look for regarding their accomplishments is lacking, often because others do not understand, or have different opinions. Teachers who realize that this approval is often not forthcoming have to find their own ways of finding approbation for their actions. Too often in the face of these differences, teachers "retreat into something certain and solid, something reliable, something we can see and get our hands around–lesson plans, say, or assertive discipline workshops" (Ayers, 1993, p. 7). Other teachers find confidence in banding together with colleagues, and continuing the dialogue in the spirit of creative search, acknowledging the uncertainty.

What about you? Is it hard for you to accept questions about your competence or decisions? Can you deal with criticism? Do you feel that, after you have had opportunities to study much more about child development, you will have the confidence to articulate your positions and opinions, knowing that you will meet many "experts" who have conflicting views and opinions to yours? Or are you only secure when there is no opposition to your actions? Early childhood education will not offer you an opposition-free atmosphere.

Frustrations

Teachers often have chosen their profession because of their high ideals and the opportunity to influence children's development in important ways. "They impose upon themselves the responsibility for unlocking each child's

1964

National Association for Nursery Education becomes National Association for the Education of Young Children, and the *Journal of Nursery Education* becomes *Young Children.*

potential" (Hyson, 1982, p. 27). Each child comes to the classroom with a particular background and cultural context, with unique abilities, interests, needs, and a specific history. There are enormous differences in what each needs from the teacher, and in the teacher's ability to respond to the individual child and family. And teachers, good teachers, try their very best to rise to each specific challenge, and to find the resources to help when they find they are unable to do the job themselves. They spread themselves around as much as they can, often painfully aware that, while there are one or perhaps two teachers or caregivers in a classroom, there may be three, five, ten times or more as many children, all demanding and deserving of help. There is never enough time to do all that teachers feel should be done. It is frustrating to feel inadequate to the need. Many teachers feel that needs seem to be increasing today, as families under pressure are often less able to care for their own children's total needs; we'll discuss this more shortly. "After a while," says one former teacher, "I couldn't stand the pain of knowing how very much there was that I couldn't do for them." This is a fierce frustration, and a compelling reason why some teachers leave the classroom.

A mind stretched by new ideas never returns to its original dimensions
—Oliver Wendell Holmes

Yet for others, the only comfort and satisfaction lies in knowing that they have given it their best efforts, and that, in some cases, they *have* indeed made a difference. One teacher tells us of her discovery, when her director helped her through such frustration:

> She gave me some advice that I will never forget:
> "Patti, you enjoy helping children with their emotional needs. And you're very good at it. But you must remember that you aren't going to be able to help everyone. It's just not possible. Some of them are going to slip through your fingers. You can't get so upset over 'the ones that got away.'". . . This time I not only understood the words—I accepted them. It was enough to be the best teacher I could be. Because no matter what I did, no matter how hard I tried, I couldn't save all the children (Wollman, 1994, p. 211).

When teachers can bring themselves to the point of accepting this truth, they will avoid the overwhelming frustration that defeats them.

Frustration also comes from the complexities of the teachers' tasks. The children are the main focus, of course, but every teacher would like to have more time to find ways to talk with parents, to share more ideas with colleagues, to prepare new teacher-made classroom materials, to reach out more to educate the community about young children's needs. The multiplicity of aims and goals may be daunting. Time just does not permit a sense of completion in all these activities, in many cases, and teachers feel frustrated, feeling that they could do their jobs better, "if only . . ." Teachers in the early elementary years cope with increasing amounts of paperwork, and feel frustrated because this task seems to detract from their main job with the children.

Another source of frustration for early childhood teachers may be that, although they are granted a large measure of freedom within their own classrooms, that freedom is still constrained by situational factors that are completely out of the teacher's control. For example, the quality of materials the teacher is

1965

Chapter One is funded under Title One, the Elementary and Secondary Education Act of 1965, to offer remedial education services to children needing extra assistance.

Figure 7-4 | **The quality of materials the teacher can provide for children is constrained by the program's budget.**

Licensing: Regulations whereby each state sets standards for child care programs to be eligible to be licensed. Include protections for health and safety of the facility, group size and adult-child ratios, and staff qualifications.

able to provide for children is constrained by the program's budget; the number of children a teacher is asked to care for is decided by the state's particular **licensing** requirements, or by the local school system decisions. Many teachers know what they should do with children, know what they would like to do were they free to do so, but are unable to do so because of situational constraints. This makes it seem as if teachers are expected to do their jobs in spite of "the endless and arbitrary demands of bureaucracies and distant state legislatures" (Ayers, 1993, p. 6). Frustration comes not only from being unable to accomplish everything one would like to accomplish with particular children or families. It comes also from the fact that often there are inadequate resources to support the work of schools and centers. In times of tight budgets, it is extremely rare to work in settings that provide all the materials and equipment that teachers feel are essential to their task (see Fig. 7-4). Indeed, the programs that serve the needs of children and families often seem to be the first items that feel the sting of the budget cuts.

These inadequacies translate into teacher perceptions that the needs of early childhood programs are not respected and therefore that the work is not valued. This lack of respect is, in fact, another whole challenge to the profession

1965
Forty-seven percent of all American children attend kindergarten.

that we will discuss. But on a day-to-day basis, limited resources mean constant efforts to stretch inadequate supplies of staff, materials, and supplies, in ways that are frustrating and sometimes downright humiliating. "I'm sorry," apologizes the infant caregiver, "we've run out of diapers so I'll have to ask you to bring some in for your child." "Only one cup of juice; we'll get seconds of water." "Just one dot of glue."

Frustration is a part of many occupations today, that are stretched to do complex jobs with inadequate supports or resources. If teachers are to avoid the burnout that comes with ever-mounting frustration, they will need to find the satisfaction that outweighs the frustrations in their work. What about your own response to frustration? Can you learn to live with the idea that your best efforts may never be quite enough to meet all needs? Understanding that there will be inevitable frustrations is important to your future well-being as a teacher. Your ability to focus on accomplishments instead of uncompleted tasks is a factor of a positive outlook, related to the old question: "Is this glass half-full or half-empty?" What is your answer?

> *It is the greatest of all mistakes to do nothing because you can only do a little. Do what you can*
> —Sydney Smith

Changing Times

One challenge for early childhood teachers is that their roles—always somewhat loosely defined—are even more nebulous and amorphous as society's demands and needs for the care and education of young children continue to grow and multiply. Earlier in this century and until a couple of decades ago, early childhood educators could focus purely on their educative roles, inasmuch as the primary care of young children for most of their waking hours rested within the family. Now that a majority of parents of young children are in the work force, the roles of early educators have expanded to include many other functions besides the purely educational. And some of these roles are in a *gray* area, neither teacher, nor parent, but somewhere in between. There are invisible boundaries over which teachers feel they ought not cross, but feel they are sometimes being pushed or pulled. For example, the infant caregiver knows that she is not a substitute for a parent, but is supplementing the parents' needs for care. Yet, since the parent isn't with the baby for so many hours, she wonders if she is becoming a substitute or **surrogate** mother. She knows the parent wouldn't like to hear those words, but secretly feels that they reflect her true feelings and position. And in that ambiguity there is confusion, sometimes resentment, sometimes concern about her perception regarding inadequate parenting. More than one preschool or elementary teacher has been heard to sigh that today's parents do not seem to have either the confidence or skills, and certainly not the necessary time or even inclination, to give their children what the children need. And so teachers feel drawn to make an even greater contribution to the children's upbringing in these changing times.

Surrogate: Substitute, as in surrogate mother.

Sometimes teachers feel they are asked to become counselors, psychologists, and social workers, tending to the stresses of both children and parents, while smarting with the impression that the parents themselves seem to pay less attention to their children's needs than do the teachers. Many teachers are unsure whether they even ought to be taking on some parental roles, although some educators argue for acting **in loco parentis**. One educator expresses that posi-

In Loco Parentis: Serving in the place of parent or guardian.

1965
Project Head Start is established by President Lyndon B. Johnson, as part of the War on Poverty, on May 18, and administered under the Office of Economic Opportunity.

Figure 7-5   **There may be ambiguity between the roles and feelings of teachers and parents.**

tion: "the institution of the school needs to orient itself increasingly to the norms of parenting that parents themselves seem to have forgotten" (van Manen, 1991, p. 6) (see Fig. 7-5.). And at the very same time that teachers perceive that families, and society in general, are expecting them to play far more roles than the teachers felt they had agreed to, child care programs and schools come under attack. Studies, books, articles–all claim that many of the difficulties with children's development and learning are the results of inadequate programs or education systems. No wonder that many early educators feel that they are not being appreciated. As one said, "They ask us to do more than is humanly possible, filling in all the gaps that the changes in families and society have created, and then they blame us for everything that is going wrong with children and schools. It's like they want it both ways: we're to be both the saviors and the scapegoats" (personal communication).

> "So what's the answer?"
> "I'm not sure," Marla responds. "With all children, I think we're less sure of what we should be teaching, and the children, in general, seem less able to sit still and learn" (Paley, 1995, p. 62).

This is likely one of those dilemmas that there is no way out of for teachers, but one that will require continuing recognition and dialogue among the segments of the community that work with today's families.

What about you? How do you feel about the idea that the changes in contemporary society expand general perceptions about what teachers should be

1965
A summer program of Head Start is held, serving 536,108 children in programs that ran two to six weeks.

doing? Can you be realistic about your contribution to society without placing impossible demands upon yourself, or allowing others to impose them on you? Can you work productively and non-judgmentally with parents whose parenting skills may concern you?

Attachment and Loss

In most classrooms, children leave and move on to new relationships with other teachers at least once a year. Early childhood teachers work by creating warm and nurturing relationships with the children in their care, and their families. Especially in child care situations with very young children, teachers are intimately involved with the daily care that leads to closeness, and with the momentous events that bring satisfaction to both child and adult. Those mutual relationships often lead to strong attachments, that are also fulfilling some of the teachers' emotional needs. To say goodbye on a regular, cyclical basis is difficult. Teachers often discover that the severing of ties with children and families is sad–although it must be said that there are inevitably those situations where teachers also breathe deep sighs of relief!

Some teachers protect themselves from the pain of loss by not forming meaningful attachments to the children under their care; but many of these teachers are then unable to be truly effective with children when they have not created reciprocal relationships. Instead, teachers have to learn to recognize the temporary, though briefly important, nature of their work with children. The inevitable sense of loss will be tempered by the realization of what has been accomplished through the relationship. Teachers also must learn to have most of their emotional needs met outside of classroom relationships, lest they become too dependent on those relationships.

> It was all connected, I realized, to a feeling of loss. Cathy and I were not only leaving the children, we were losing the ability to influence their lives. Who would these children talk to when they left us? Would their parents continue our work? Would their next teachers love them as much as we did? There were no answers to these questions. In the end, we told ourselves that it didn't really matter. We had done our best: we had given the kids a good beginning. No one could take that away from them–or from us, either (Wollman, 1994, p. 269).

What about you? Are you able to get most of your emotional needs met by the relationships in your personal life, so that you will not become too dependent on the relationships with the children you teach? Can you balance the sadness of leaving relationships with children with the realization of your indelible effect on their lives?

Adult Isolation

The fact of the matter is that most of your time as an early educator will be spent in the company of young children from infancy through the early ele-

There are people who put their dreams in a little box and say, "Yes, I've got dreams, of course, I've got dreams." Then they put the box away and bring it out once in a while to look in it, and yep, they're still there. These are great dreams, but they never even get out of the box. It takes an uncommon amount of guts to put your dreams on the line, to hold them up and say "How good or how bad am I?" That's where courage comes in

—Erma Bombeck

1966
Head Start expands to a year-long program.

Figure 7-6   **Most teachers spend the majority of their time alone with young children, never free from the responsibilities for their care.**

In the middle of every difficulty lies opportunity
–Albert Einstein

mentary years (see Fig. 7-6). Even when teachers have a coteacher who also works in the same classroom, most of the conversation and contacts in the classroom will be with the children. Even when parents are welcomed to spend time in the classroom, the actual amounts of time they spend there will be a small fraction of the work day. And delightful as teachers may find young children, the attention they focus on them is quite one-directional: that is to say, teachers share children's world, but children make no real attempt to share teachers' worlds.

Many administrators complain that their staff congregate together on the playground. Rather than being a sign of indifference to the need for supervising children, this congregating probably speaks of adults' needs for adult communication. Infrequent staff meetings or quick breaks are often the only opportunity for teachers to speak with other adults for any period. And the isolation of adults in their own classrooms means not only that they are often hungry to talk and share ideas with other adults; it also means that the total responsibility for the care of the children rests on them. It is not unusual to hear teachers complain that they never even have anyone to leave the children with so they can use the bathroom or make a telephone call. Such continual on-duty time and lack of privacy can be both physically and emotionally exhausting, and teachers have to find their own methods of self-renewal, without much benefit of encounters with or support from other adults.

What about you? How would you respond to spending most of your time in the company of young children, rather than with other adults? And would the feeling of complete responsibility for a group during the day wear on you to the point of severe stress? You will need to find ways to renew yourself. Has this

1966
A direct instruction program is developed by Bereiter and Engelmann, marketed under the trademark DISTAR.

been something you've been able to do in past situations where you have borne lots of responsibility?

Process Rather Than Product

Perhaps one of the most difficult parts about being a teacher is that there is not necessarily a finished product to show for all the effort. What results there are may be intangible and virtually unobservable. Human development is a process of becoming. Parents get both the rewards, as well as the headaches, of being able to watch the unfolding results of their efforts over long periods of time. The child they had in the womb, eventually becomes a responsible, caring adult in the best scenarios, and parents are eventually able to see the pay-off of their efforts and worries. Teachers, on the other hand, function for a relatively brief period in children's lives. While they may see progress during the time they work with children, they usually have no way of knowing what the final outcomes will be. Only occasionally do children come back, years later, to apprise the teacher of their progress. This makes teaching quite unlike a number of other professions or occupations, where the work that is done yields concrete and obvious immediate results. The doctor knows when the medicine that was prescribed cures the symptoms; the TV repairman knows when the correct wire has been connected to fix the problem; the painter sees the improved appearance of the house with a new coat of paint. Much of what teachers do is based on hope and belief in the future benefits of their present efforts. William Ayers said, "I teach in the hope of making the world a better place" (Ayers, 1993, p. 8). Truly this is the reward and satisfaction for teaching, but it requires an optimistic and progressive orientation, rather than the evidence of immediate rewards.

What about you? Are you the kind of person who needs immediate feedback and evidence that your work is productive? If so, teaching may be difficult for you, since so much of it is based on a concept of promise of future results. Can you happily live with the concept that your efforts may bear fruit long after you are around to see it?

When things "go right" in the classroom, teachers have no one to share these successful moments with, other than the children, who may or may not appreciate the brilliance of what was done
—Selma Wasserman

Ideals versus Realities

Few teachers enter the profession without some images of what it will be like, and ideals that drive their efforts. While you may have imagined working with always delightfully smiling and responsive children, your studies and practical experience will likely replace this image with a more realistic one before you have finished your program. But this is not to suggest that your ideals also need replacing. One of the most disillusioning things that teachers often encounter early on is people and institutions that try to strip them of their ideals. While it is certainly true that beginning teachers, and indeed all teachers, have to adapt to the real situations in which they find themselves, this by no means implies that they must discard the ideals and goals that drive them. In fact those ideals will allow teachers to continue to grow, to develop, to demand the best of themselves, their colleagues, and their schools. "It is important to be

1966
NAEYC has 48 affiliate groups.

At the time of the last census, NAEYC launched an educational effort to ensure that members of the profession were using uniform nomenclature to describe their work responsibilities. They felt this was important because national data could make the field look smaller than it really is if people used different terms to describe their occupations, and thus were classified in a variety of categories. Since public policy and private marketing decisions are made on the basis of census data, it was deemed important to convey the full sense of the profession.

IF THIS IS WHAT YOU DO	THIS IS WHAT YOU SHOULD SAY
You are primarily responsible for the care and education of a group of children in a child care center, preschool, Head Start, or other type of group program *or* if you equally share such responsibility with one or more coteachers.	Prekindergarten teacher
You assist in the care and education of a group of children in a child care program, preschool, Head Start, or other type of group program *or* you assist a family child care provider.	Child care assistant
You provide care and education for a small group of young children in your home.	Family child care provider
You assist a kindergarten or elementary school teacher	Elementary school teacher assistant
You care for someone else's child in the child's home.	Child care worker, private home
You are a director or educational coordinator, or fulfill another administrative function in a full- or part-day program serving young children.	Early childhood administrator

Figure 7-7 **Terminology that conveys respect for early childhood professionals. (Adapted from NAEYC)**

both a dreamer and a doer, to hold onto ideals but also to struggle continually to enact those ideals in concrete situations" (Ayers, 1993, p. 131).

What about you? Can you maintain your ideals even when people try to convince you that the "real world" demands giving them up? Can you be realistic enough to accept the things that cannot be changed, and to work with others to change things that can and should be changed?

These challenges that we have discussed so far are fairly inevitable and unchangeable realities that will affect teacher satisfaction. The next factors that we will discuss are those that can instead be changed by the efforts of those in the profession, and indeed are slowly changing, as we will discuss in later chapters.

Lack of Respect

"Playing with kids all day' has never been considered a high-status profession" (Hyson, 1982, p. 27). Indeed, there is enormous discussion both

1968
ERIC clearinghouse on early childhood education is established at the University of Illinois.

Figure 7-8 | **Teaching the youngest children and children in the primary grades has always been primarily women's work.**

within and outside of the world of early childhood education whether teaching young children is in fact a profession (see Spodek et al., 1988, and Chapter Nine), to say nothing of the public perception that it can hardly be considered real teaching! Some terminology alone that is frequently used implies that the work is not very important: who wants to be called a "baby-sitter" when to most of us that implies a temporary, and purely custodial, function? (See Fig. 7-7 for terminology that more accurately describes early education positions.) The legislative bodies that set training requirements in the states for child care suggest that care of the youngest children especially can be undertaken by just about anybody, with no special training required. Part of this attitude is no doubt a side-effect of the sexist orientation in society that implies that work that is associated with mothers, and other women primarily, is not very valuable. It is an interesting paradox that our culture pays vehement verbal respect to the importance of children and the power of mothering, yet finds few concrete ways to translate this rhetorical tribute into real support (Modligiani, 1988). "As a nation we historically have placed less value on any type of work done for or with young children. Pediatricians earn less than other types of physicians. Kindergarten and elementary school teachers earn less than secondary teachers" (NAEYC, 1990, p. 30). Teaching of the youngest children, even in the early grades in elementary schools, has always been primarily women's work, and is thus linked with a sense that it is somehow inferior and not requiring of much skill or knowledge (see Fig. 7-8).

This lack of respect is not a new state of affairs. Teaching as a profession at all levels has always been the "poor cousin" of the professions, requiring education, but less education than other recognized professions like law or medicine.

1969

Sesame Street begins on public television on Nov. 10.

> Teaching seems to have more than its share of status anomalies. It is honored and disdained, praised as "dedicated service" and lampooned as "easy work." It is permeated with the rhetoric of professionalism, yet features incomes below those earned by workers with considerably less education. . . . The real regard shown those who taught has never matched the professed regard (Lortie, 1975, p. 10).

The layers of bureaucracy and administration (typically male dominated) that blanket teachers suggest that this is a profession without many skills that can be managed. And the early childhood division of the schools has even more inferior status within teaching. Preschool teachers often note that they are treated with condescension by third or fourth grade teachers, as if their work is far inferior to the teachers of slightly older children, perhaps because they do not bear the stamp of teacher certification that distinguishes the elementary school teacher. The historical roots of the kindergarten and nursery school movements (see Chapter Eight) meant that these practitioners were trained separately in separate institutions, and in fact were usually housed in different buildings, and subject to different regulations than the teachers of the later years, thus not even subject to the small amount of respect accorded to teachers in traditional systems. And the early connections of child care systems with socially underprivileged families detracted even more from the status of child care workers.

One measure of respect and status in our society is the rate of pay, and, especially for teaching in the early childhood years, that rate has been called a national disgrace (Ayers, 1993). Again the historical roots of women involved in early education is a factor here, as women were presumed to be acting selflessly in children's best interests, and that selflessness implied economic disinterest. Especially in the early years, most teachers have been reluctant to form unions to lobby on their own behalf. In our competitive modern society, status and respect seem inextricably linked to concrete financial remuneration. The low salaries that are paid to early childhood teachers, and that also have enormous effects on issues of quality in early education (see Chapter Eleven), are important measures of the lack of society's respect for this crucial work. While there has been increasing recognition of the economic inequities between elementary teachers and other similarly educated workers in recent years, and some attempts to begin redressing the problem, preschool and child care teachers are still lagging far behind in salaries and benefits. Some of the highest paid child care workers nationally earn less than $16,000.00 annually (Whitebook et al., 1993), and the average **foregone annual wage**–what the worker could have earned in other female-dominated occupations–was $5,238.00 for teachers and $3,582.00 for assistants (NAEYC, 1995). Teachers are naturally demoralized by this message about their worth; it is hard to keep believing that one's work is important when surrounded by contrary messages that speak about status and worth. And the reality is that early childhood teachers have about the same kinds of daily living expenses as most other people, so the message of no respect is translated into financial woes. Many good teachers who not only love their work, but are also good at it, have found that they had to leave the field to find better remuneration elsewhere.

Foregone Annual Wages: Those additional amounts that practitioners could have earned annually in another occupation, with comparable education.

1969

The Office of Child Development is established, and now administers the Head Start program.

Fortunately, at this time, many early educators are realizing that their increased professionalism and efforts to garner respect for themselves and their work is a valid part of their jobs. As Katz has said, "My own concern about the social and occupational status of the early childhood practitioner is related to the assumption that we cannot have optimum environments for children unless the environments are also optimum for the adults who work with them" (Katz, 1995, p. 220).

The attempts to raise public consciousness about the need to respect early childhood professionals, is one and the same as the need to raise awareness about the importance of the early years in children's lives, and their need for nurturing environments. Working to gain respect and recognition as a professional is not an issue of self-interest, but rather a message of advocacy for the needs of children and families in the early years. What is good for teachers is good for children. In Chapter Eleven you will learn about the Worthy Wage Campaign that is working nationally to bring attention to issues of respect and remuneration (see Fig. 7-9). In this context it is important for you to recognize that the importance of teaching young children deserves far more respect and recognition than it presently receives.

What about you? Are you willing to join your efforts to those of other professionals in your community to continue to work for the respect you deserve? It is important that this lack of respect result in your being energized to educate, not demoralized. Do you know what the typical salaries are paid to early childhood teachers in various settings in your community? How does this information affect your plans? You should enter the profession realizing you will never get wealthy, but accepting the idea that other factors may be more important to you than financial compensation. As one Worthy Wage poster puts it: "I don't do this work for the money; I just need the money to keep doing this."

Men in Early Childhood

If you are a male entering the early childhood field, there are even different issues of respect for you to consider. At this time men constitute only a small part of all early childhood educators, probably about five percent (Seifert, 1988). Professional attitudes and practices may have been defined too narrowly as a result of the dominance of females in the field. But it is likely that men avoid the field for specific reasons that are related to status, economic conditions, and bias.

The culture has conveyed to most men the idea that they are to compete in the job field as a measure of their worth. We have already discussed the relatively low status accorded to early childhood teachers. Many men are reluctant to enter a field that is accorded so little recognition. Many men also report that family, friends, and even academic counselors strongly discourage working with young children as far beneath their talents. When considering long-term career opportunities, as most men have been socialized to do, the early childhood field appears to have relatively little opportunity for advancement.

The poor salaries in early childhood education probably encourage more men than women to look for other employment opportunities. Still today, many men are considering careers in the light of being a major contributor to the

Do you ever wonder if you've made a difference in this life? Whether any of those children who have come to your care have remembered anything you did for them— any ways you cared for them? I believe that by the time a child grows up, that child's first teacher and second teacher and all the important adults will have become incorporated into that child's development. That's the way it is with all children and, although they may not remember clearly, those of us who were the educators of their early lives will always be a part of who they are. Just like those who meant so much to us when we were children will always be a part of who we are

—Fred Rogers

1969

Parent Child Centers are funded in some Head Start programs.

Figure 7-9   **Teachers becoming involved in the Worthy Wage campaign are working to gain respect and recognition as full professionals. (Courtesy of Tracie O'Hara)**

financial support of a family, and it is difficult to imagine bearing the costs of raising a family on the limited salaries of most early childhood educators. The majority of men who work in the early childhood field are married, with at least one child (Robinson, 1988). Many find they can not afford to work many years with young children. Men certainly have more options than women do for employment even today, and would more likely opt for those that pay substantially more than early childhood education. And yet this contributes to a vicious cycle: it seems probable that if more men entered the field, the low salaries accorded to a mostly female profession might increase.

While it has become more prevalent in the decades since the women's movement for men to play a more active role in parenting, thus indicating their abilities and interest in nurturing young children, there is still widespread gender bias. This bias translates into both overt action and covert attitudes that prevent males from feeling acceptance in early childhood centers and schools, to say nothing of within preservice education programs (see Fig. 7-10). While early childhood education is associated with the roles of mothering, men who have no oppportunity to be mothers are seen as less capable of caring for young children. The teaching role is associated with a variety of characteristics generally classified as female characteristics, such as patience, gentle nurturing and emotional sensitivity, as opposed to aggressiveness and emotional control. Men who are willing to take on these roles are unfairly subjected to conjecture and suspicion about their masculinity.

A few widely publicized cases of sexual abuse in the past decade have added fuel to this discriminatory fire, to the point where men are often subjected

1969

The first Kinder-Care Learning Center opens in Montgomery, Alabama.

Figure 7-10   **Gender bias translates into covert attitudes that prevent males from feeling acceptance, even in preservice programs.**

to humiliating questions and restrictions. There have been instances where directors have refused to allow male students in rooms where diapers would be changed, or have refused employment to well-qualified candidates on the basis that "the parents would be uncomfortable." Men do report bias directed towards them by directors, parents, and even female coworkers. Small wonder that few choose to become uncomfortable minorities within the early childhood field.

And this is a pity. It would appear that men in early childhood classrooms would have much to offer. Seifert refers to "compensation hypotheses," meaning that male teachers could somehow compensate for the lack of male involvement in the lives of many young children, as well as offer children of both sexes a model of a caring, nurturant male. He also speaks of a "social equity hypotheses," meaning it would help society in general and children in particular, discover the many options available to men and women. So little research has been done on effective male early childhood teachers that only conjecture assumes what their style would be.

Hopefully men will not be discouraged by current questions of bias, or economic conditions, for their presence in the profession could add a stronger voice for the emergence of a true profession where colleagues are not restricted by current stereotypes of "women's work" (see Fig. 7-11).

What about you? As a male, are you willing to recognize the stereotypes and counter them with your own personality and ideals? As a female, are you able to support males as true colleagues who can work with you for the nurturing and care of young children, and for the growth of the profession?

I long to accomplish a great and noble task, but it is my chief duty to accept small tasks as if they were great and noble
—Helen Keller

CONDITIONS THAT HELP TEACHERS FACE CHALLENGES

One of the risks in discussing both the joys and the challenges of working with young children before you have actually had much opportunity to get

1969
Lamaze training is growing slowly. Forty-nine couples are prepared for childbirth in North Carolina.

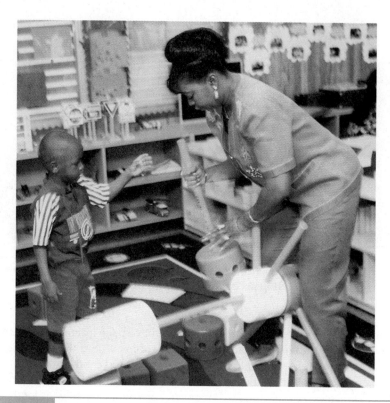

Figure 7-11   **What's wrong with this picture? Absolutely nothing–except it shows the typical classroom where bias and practice have excluded male teachers.**

involved in classroom situations is that the concepts may stay purely theoretical. You are encouraged to take every opportunity to discuss these ideas with experienced teachers, to hear about their real experiences and how they have made their choices to stay, and taken action to face the challenges. It is important that you be aware that passive acceptance of these conditions will probably cut short your classroom career; teachers who are able to avoid being overwhelmed take steps to avoid burnout. Let us consider some of the supports available.

Knowledge

Opportunities to learn and develop skills will help teachers deal with the pressure of decision-making and adaptation. The more you learn about current research and knowledge in early education, the more confident you will feel in the face of challenges and opposition. It is less frustrating when teachers can focus on what they can do with children, rather than what they cannot. Learning about current social conditions helps teachers see their positions within community efforts to support families. Understanding life span development will help teachers focus on the process of which they are a part. Continuing to learn and grow as a teacher allows teachers to face challenges with increasing degrees of confidence.

1969
Westinghouse Report declares that the cognitive gains made by children in Head Start programs is short term, not lasting through the elementary years.

You are now embarking on a program of preservice education. But it is important that you realize that it will be necessary to continue to acquire knowledge after you have completed that initial degree. The challenges will keep coming; it is important that your knowledge continues also.

Support

Challenges seem less overwhelming when teachers are not attempting to face them alone. Forming connections with colleagues allows teachers to release feelings and get emotional support, to generate more ideas for solutions to problems both large and small, and to decrease feelings of isolation. Teachers can obtain this collegial support from several sources. It is important to choose employment in a setting where collegiality is encouraged and facilitated by administrative support for teamwork and opportunities for collaboration. It is also important to realize that membership in local professional organizations can provide a sense of collective purpose and strength. A source of support often overlooked by many teachers is parents. Taking the time to form relationships and communicate with parents not only decreases many challenges, but increases insights and strength for meeting existing challenges (see Fig. 7-12).

Whenever I think about the children's differences, my sense of the excitement of teaching mounts. Without the uniqueness of each child, teaching would be a dull, repetitive exercise for me
—Vivian Paley

Alliances

The challenges that can be changed—those that are primarily related to social attitudes—require the work and effort of all early childhood professionals. The energy and sense of optimism that result from joining alliances and working together contribute to teachers' sense of professional well-being, as well as produces concrete results. The progress that has been made in the past decade in gaining political support for children's issues proves the efficacy of joint efforts when trying to educate the public or garner legislative or corporate support. Meeting and lessening challenges requires memberships in alliances; it is virtually impossible to go it alone.

Supervisor Support

Many teachers complain that the remoteness of their administrator is part of the challenge. It seems obvious that supervisors can either add to or ease teacher stress and frustration. It is important that teachers open communication with their supervisors, who can be a positive source of support for individuals and for developing team opportunities. Teachers need to avoid distancing themselves from their supervisors, and recognize that their supervisors have the same interests.

YOUR CHALLENGE

There is a somewhat cynical spirit in our society today, one that suggests that anyone who is motivated more by idealism, personal values, and morality and less by goals of personal gain and ambition is naive, that one must "look

1970
White House Conference on Children identifies child care as one of the major problems facing the American public.

Figure 7-12   **Collegial support is one protection against teacher burn-out.**

out for number one." There will be subtle and not-so-subtle pressures on you to give up the ideas of teaching young children, and leave it to someone else to "change the world," while you are urged to "grow up" and recognize harsh realities as unchangeable facts. You and you alone know how you feel now as you contemplate these challenges, and how you think about them as they will affect your future teaching. It was not intended that you become so discouraged that you decide early childhood education is not the career for you. But it was intended that you think long and hard about the difficulties involved with it. There is a long line of teachers past and present who hope that you too will decide this is worthy work, and that you will take the challenge.

How shall we respond to the dreams of youth?
–Jane Addams

> The work of a teacher–exhausting, complex, idiosyncratic, never twice the same–is, at its heart, an intellectual and ethical enterprise. Teaching is the vocation of vocations, a calling that shepherds a multitude of other callings. It is an activity that is intensely practical and yet transcendent, brutally matter-of-fact, and yet fundamentally a creative act. Teaching begins in challenge and is never far from mystery (Ayers, 1993, p. 127).

1970
High/Scope Educational Research Foundation is incorporated.

SUMMARY

There are numerous challenges that face those who enter early childhood education. Some of these include challenges that are inherent in the work, and that cannot be changed but must be adapted to. Others are challenges currently being worked on by others in the profession. The challenges include:

1. variety and unpredictability
2. lack of definitive answers
3. frustration
4. changing times
5. attachment and loss
6. adult isolation
7. process rather than product
8. ideals vs. realities
9. lack of respect
10. men in early childhood.

Teachers who expect to meet these challenges will benefit from knowledge, support systems, alliances, and supervisor support.

QUESTIONS FOR REVIEW

1. Identify at least six of the challenges discussed in this chapter, including at least one that is currently being slowly changed by the efforts of early childhood professionals.
2. Describe at least three of the conditions that help teachers face challenges.

ACTIVITIES FOR FURTHER STUDY

1. Review the answers you received from experienced teachers about their dissatisfactions with teaching. Which of the challenges discussed in this chapter do you find?
2. From your journal, think about any negative responses you recorded from others' reactions about your decision to become an early childhood teacher. How do you now feel about each?
3. Also in your journal, reflect on these various challenges. Are there any that seriously impact your ideas about becoming a teacher? Are there any that you don't feel will be a particular problem for you?
4. See if you can find a male early childhood teacher in your community. Have your instructor invite him to class to discuss his experiences, motivations, and any prejudice he has encountered.
5. Are there Worthy Wage efforts in your state or community? See what you can learn about their alliance and work. Keep this information to consider again in Chapter Eleven.

REFERENCES

Author. (1995, May). Cost, quality, and child outcomes in child care centers: Key findings and recommendations. *Young Children, 50,* (4) 40-44.

Ayers, William. (1993). *To teach: The journey of a teacher.* New York: Teachers College Press.

DelCampo, Robert L. & DelCampo, Diana S. (1995). *Taking sides: Clashing views on controversial issues in childhood and society.* Guilford, CT: The Dushkin Publishing Group, Inc.

Greenberg, P. (1994) *Behind the playdough curtain: A year in my life as a preschool teacher.* New York: Charles Scribner's Sons.

Wollman Greenberg, P. (1994). *Behind the playdough curtain: A year in my life as a preschool teacher.* New York: Charles Scribner's Sons.

Hyson, Marion C. (1982, January). Playing with kids all day: Job stress in early childhood education. *Young Children, 37,* (2), 25-31.

Jones, Elizabeth. (1991, May). Do ECE people really agree? Or are we just agreeable? *Young Children, 46,* (4), 59-61.

Katz, Lilian. (1995). *Talks with teachers of young children.* Norwood, NJ: Ablex Publishing Corp.

Lortie, Dan. (1975). *School teacher: A sociological study.* Chicago: University of Chicago Press.

Modligiani, Kathy. (1988, March). Twelve reasons for the low wages in child care. *Young Children, 43,* (3), 14-15.

Paley, Vivian Gussin. (1995). *Kwanzaa and me.* Cambridge, MA: Harvard University Press.

Robinson, Bryan. (1988, September). Vanishing breed: Men in child care programs. *Young Children, 43,* (6), 54-57.

Seifert, Kelvin. (1988). Men in early childhood education. In Spodek, Bernard, Saracho, Olivia N., & Peters, Donald L., (Eds.). *Professionalism and the early childhood practitioner.* New York: Teachers College Press.

Spodek, Bernard, Saracho, Olivia N., & Peters, Donald L., (Eds.). (1988). *Professionalism and the early childhood practitioner.* New York: Teachers College Press.

Whitebook, M., Howes, C., & Phillips, D. (1993). *Who cares? Child care teachers and the quality of care in America. The national child care staffing study.* Oakland, CA: Child Care Employee Project.

SUGGESTIONS FOR READING

Carter, Gloria. J. (1992, September). How can the teaching intern deal with the disparity between how she is taught to teach and how she is expected to teach in 'real world' primary grades? *Young Children, 47,* (6), 68-72.

Jorde-Bloom, Paula. (1988, September). Teachers need 'TLC' too. *Young Children, 43,* (6), 4-8.

Lay-Dopyera, Margaret & Dopyera, John. (1990). *Becoming a teacher of young children.* (4th ed.). New York: McGraw-Hill.

Nelson, Bryan G. & Sheppard, Bruce, (Eds.). (1992). *Men in child care and early education: A handbook for administrators and educators.* Minneapolis MN: Men in Child Care Project.

A SOCIAL EXPERIMENT
OF ENORMOUS SIGNIFICANCE

"We are embarking on a social experiment of enormous significance. Never before have so many of our infants and young children been cared for outside of the home on a regular basis. Such experiments have been carried out in other countries such as Russia, China, and Israel. But these countries are really not comparable to our own. Our values, culture, and attitudes toward children are all different. So child care programs abroad do not provide useful models for us.

Unfortunately, this experiment was unplanned. It is a side effect of the social revolution in our society that began in the 1960s and changed our attitudes and values toward minorities, women, sex, marriage, family, and childrearing. Although we know why the experiment is being conducted, there is bitter disagreement as to *how* it is to be carried out. Indeed, there are many who say it should not be carried out at all and that children should be cared for *at home* at least until the age of three. Others argue that out-of-home care should be an extension of the *school* and that even young children should be exposed to formal instruction. Still others believe that out-of-home care should be an extension of the *home* and should emphasize exploration, manipulation, and play.

We in early childhood education are caught in the middle. However the experiment came about, *we* are the ones who have to conduct it. And whatever the theoretical disagreements are, *we* are the ones who have to deal with a group of children on Monday morning. We are underpaid and overworked. We are expected to be teachers and nursemaids, therapists and educators, researchers and scholars. Our society has created a problem and somehow we are expected to provide a solution. If we do a good job it is taken for granted, but should we misstep, we are pilloried.

Ours is not an enviable position. . . . Yet I know that our strength lies in our commitment to young children, in our unswerving faith in their inherent decency and goodness, and in our conviction that what we do helps them realize the best of their humanness. However the experiment came about, whatever the controversy it entails, we are the ones who will see it through. And, God willing, we will make it a success.[2]

[2]From "From Our President" by David Elkind, 1986, *Young Children, 42*, (1), p. 2. National Association for the Education of Young Children. Reprinted with permission.

The Profession Comes of Age

Having considered the personal motivations towards teaching, as well as the challenges, it is time to consider the profession at large. In this section you will consider the profession of early education: what it has been, what it is now, and the directions for the future. Chapter Eight first looks backwards at the historical roots of work with young children, and the patterns that have developed into the present. Chapter Nine discusses the current work of the profession to create philosophical bases for discussion of common ideals, practices, and ethics. Chapter Ten outlines the educational patterns open to early childhood professional development, and career directions available within the field. Chapter Eleven raises the issues that receive current focus of interest within the profession. And Chapter Twelve leaves the students to embark on their personal professional journeys.

Again, you are challenged to see yourself taking a place within the ranks of this profession.

ROOTS OF EARLY EDUCATION

OBJECTIVES

After studying this chapter, students will be able to:

1. discuss several reasons for examining the history of early education.

2. identify the historical role of the federal government in early care and education.

3. differentiate the separate beginnings of child care systems and education systems.

4. discuss the separate kindergarten and nursery education traditions in Europe and America.

5. identify contributors from the male and female traditions in early education.

Many eyes glaze over when faced with a chapter on history. There may seem to be little relevance about learning what people did in past centuries or decades, to those who are beginning in a profession today. But in examining the history of early education, there are clear connections to conditions, patterns, and beliefs that you will encounter in your immediate experience. Some wise person once commented that unless people study history, they will be doomed to repeat the errors of the past. In the case of early education, we study history to understand the past that has created our present, and to better comprehend the work to be done in the future.

As you have been reading through the text, you have encountered the Timeline running across the bottom of each page, documenting events, sociological trends, and contributions of individual persons who have been of some importance in creating our present. This is meant to symbolize the idea that our current concerns and immediate issues are played against the backdrop of ideas and events that preceded this current time in our profession, and connects right to the present. As we examine contemporary conditions in early care and education, some of the reasons for why these conditions exist may become clear, in the light of past history.

This chapter is meant to be an overview of contributions of the past. That is, it will be left to later reading and coursework to describe fully the theories of the particular theorists or the description of particular philosophical approaches. Here you will see their place and influence in the overall development of the intricate mesh of early education that we see today.

Think about a bright, multicolored weaving, created of different strands brought together in an irregular and unpredictable pattern. Sometimes one strand is dominant, sometimes another takes its place. That is an appropriate metaphor to describe what we see when we look around us in early education today. The very fact that it took us all of Chapter Two to describe and define what early childhood education includes suggests the complexity of assembling the various sources and patterns that developed over time. The problem noted earlier in identifying appropriate terminology to designate early childhood practitioners derives from the diversity of experiences. Here we will examine each strand, to see what richness and experience it added to the pattern, and some of the reasons there is still work to be done in integrating that particular strand into the unified design.

REASONS FOR UNDERSTANDING THE HISTORY OF EARLY EDUCATION

As suggested in the introduction to this chapter, you should know that there are important reasons to understand the roots of the multiple traditions that have created the complex world of early education. First, it is important to recognize that the thinking and passionate efforts of many individuals live today in the daily practice of contemporary early educators. The importance of play in children's active learning, for example, is not an idea borne in the late twentieth century with the defining of developmentally appropriate practice. Nor is the concept of uniqueness in learning styles or the need for teaching practice to include families something that just developed, as we shall see. "The lack of historical perspective leads us to interpret too much of what passes for reform as new when, in fact, much of the reform had an earlier history" (Perrone, 1991, p. 120). There is a sense of continuity, of being in a long line of persons who have cared about young children, that is somewhat humbling as well as uplifting for today's professionals. So, on the Timeline and in this chapter, you will learn names of individuals who have contributed to the theory and practice of what we do.

Second, it is crucial to an appreciation of the importance of early education to understand that real events in history and sociological trends shape a profession and its practitioners, in response to particular events and needs in

1971
President Richard Nixon vetoes the Comprehensive Child Development Act.

the surrounding world. So as you have read the Timeline, you have noted statistics that suggest changes in family structure and resulting needs, as well as events that have focused national attention on children's education. These will be discussed in this chapter as well.

Third, it is important for developing professionals to be able to articulate the theoretical base for their practice–the *why* that undergirds the *what* that they do. The contributions of the various thinkers and researchers in the field of early education have been noted on the timeline, and will be discussed in this chapter in connection with the educational trends they influenced.

Fourth and last is the reason that understanding of our diversity in structure, professional preparation, social status, and attitudes comes with recogniz-

THEORY INTO PRACTICE

This is Lydia Ingram. Lydia has worked in the field of early childhood education for thirteen years. In contrast with the high rate of turnover in the field, she has worked in the same campus child care center where she did internships as a student while completing her associate's degree in early childhood. She teaches three-year-olds.

What has been a significant frustration for you in early education? How do you deal with it?

One of my frustrations has been the fact that we don't get the respect we deserve, and that we are not viewed as professional. I have joined organizations that promote professionalism. I try to carry myself in a professional way, and I get out and learn more about my career.

What is one thing you learned in classes that you really discovered to be true when you started working with children?

I learned that all children should be seen as individuals, and you can't really treat them all the same. What works with one may not work with another.

What is an area you are working on now to learn more about?

I'm working on ways to become a better observer of children in my care, on taking notes on what's going on in the classroom. All of this will help me make my room more developmentally appropriate.

Why have you stayed in early education?

I have stayed because I truly feel I have a lot to offer, not only to the children and families I work with, but also to other teachers and future teachers. I really do enjoy what I do, and I believe that if I can help one child or one family, I have done my job well.

What is a comment or piece of advice you would give to those beginning to work in early childhood education?

My advice is to be patient not only with your children, but with yourself. Don't expect yourself to know the answer to everything. Ask for help, learn where to go for answers, and most of all, learn to really listen and accept criticism. Just take things one step at a time. *Believe in yourself and what you are doing.*

ing the various and very separate forms of early care and education that developed in the United States in the last decades of the nineteenth century and on into the twentieth century. These forms are only recently coming together, not without difficulty. In fact, this last idea may be the most compelling reason to examine our historical roots–to help us see that the difficulties in getting professional consensus and public support result from our variant and separate strands, rather than from lack of will or ability to work together. Once we understand the original separations, it may be easier to remove them. It is this last idea that will focus our discussion in this chapter, as we identify questions and trends that have seemed to separate early education professionals, and separate professionals from policymakers.

WHO CARES FOR THE CHILDREN?

It is one of those puzzling issues that seems to make no sense: as the leading nation in the western industrial world, America lags far behind other countries in the care and services it provides for the nation's children and the families who raise them. "Although the United States ranks No. 2 worldwide in per capita income, this country does not even make it into the top ten on any significant indicator of child welfare" (Hewlett, 1991, p. 14). In her powerful book, *When the Bough Breaks: the Cost of Neglecting Our Children,* Hewlett goes on to document the facts of national failure to keep our children healthy, safe, and off to a good start educationally. Infant mortality in the United States ranks lower than 22 industrialized countries in the world, behind such countries as Spain and Singapore. "A black baby born in the shadow of the White House is now more likely to die in the first year of life than a baby born in Jamaica or Trinidad" (Hewlett, 1991, p. 15). And with the statistics on child abuse and violence in the streets, "a child is safer in Northern Ireland than in America" (Hewlett, 1991, p. 15). Educationally, children are also behind children almost everywhere: "American kids are at or near the bottom in most international surveys measuring educational achievement: seventh out of ten countries in physics; ninth out of ten countries in chemistry; and tenth–dead last–in average mathematical proficiency" (Hewlett, 1991, p. 16). Average SAT scores have fallen 70 points over the last 30 years; only 73 percent of American teenagers graduate from high school, compared with 90 percent of Japanese teenagers. In France, 98 percent of preschoolers are in tuition-free, state-run (and excellent) preschools; half of American children are getting some preschool education, much of it mediocre at best. And less than one-half of preschool children in this country are read to each day. America is almost the only industrialized western nation that does not support families at the time of transition of a new birth with paid family leave. Indeed, it was not until President Bill Clinton that legislation permitting an unpaid leave for parents was passed in 1993, after President George Bush's veto of it in 1990.

Why is it that so little of the nation's resources (5 percent in 1987) are directed towards programs that benefit children? How can it be, that in a country with such great resources, about one-quarter of its young children live in poverty, with family income below the level established by the federal government? And of those poor children, less than half are in preschool programs?

If you do not know your history, you lose essential memory. And you cannot know yourself. If you remain ignorant of history, you cannot hope to affect change in society or even in your life
                                              –Margaret Randall

1971
The National Center for Child Advocacy is established by the Office of Child Development.

How is it that there are hundreds of thousands of homeless children in the United States? How can nearly half of American children under the age of two not be fully immunized? Why are thousands of children in most states on waiting lists for child care? The answer has its roots back when the United States was first established. The colonists who came to America from Britain brought with them a social understanding that firmly separated family, church and state, "with the nuclear family (an idea transported from England) carrying *by far* the greatest burden" (Cremin, in Kagan, 1994, p. 4). Childrearing was assumed to be a family affair, separate from public life and policy. Beyond the family's near total responsibility for children, the church carried a diminished responsibility for moral teaching and ceremonies to solidify families. And the schools were merely responsible for teaching the reading and writing skills that were needed mainly for Bible study and other moral teachings.

> *The proper start in school subjects and activities common to all good curricula is a worthy function for the kindergartens, but it is not the most important. Of still greater importance are the foundations of physical and mental health*
>
> –Patty Smith Hill

An institutionalization of this division of responsibility was made in the Poor Laws of 1601, which indicated that families were the first source of assistance, with communities stepping in only when families failed, and then only for residents of the immediate community. This early precedent set the pattern for later developments: the attitude of failure and weakness when families needed assistance from the community; and the concept that the federal government would not involve itself in issues related to services for families, leaving those social services to local or state control (although education was seen as a necessity for all citizens). Both of these patterns remain with us today, and it is the stigma applied to families who need social assistance, and the benefit of local community assistance only in the case of failure that has kept federal legislation and budgets from reflecting any widespread commitment to children and families until very recently.

On the Timeline, you will find several notable exceptions to this generalized pattern of federal removal from policy or expenditures that supported families. In this century, when dollars were spent on early care and education, it was only when the United States was perceived to be in a time of crisis and overwhelming social emergency. The first such occasion was during the Great Depression of the 1930s. During this period, hundreds of thousands of workers were unemployed and dislocated. The government organized a variety of work projects under the Works Progress Administration (WPA) to find employment for the many who were forced to depend on public relief to support themselves and their families. Two million dollars was allocated in 1933, to establish about 2,000 **WPA nursery schools**. Their purpose was to provide employment for thousands of out-of-work teachers, nurses, nutritionists, and social workers.

WPA Nursery Schools: Nursery schools established during the Great Depression to provide work for unemployed teachers, nurses, and social workers.

Incidentally, although this was not the primary intent, many thousands of children from poor families (and in those troubled times, this included a large number of formerly middle-class families) received an excellent nursery school education. Leaders from the three main preschool organizations (National Association for Nursery Education [NANE], ACEI, and the National Council for Parent Education) organized the National Advisory Committee on Emergency Nursery Schools, with a system of regional supervisors (Beatty, 1995). By 1937, there were 1,900 programs established and approximately 40,000 children being served (Olmsted, 1992).

1971
The U.S. Office of Education reports that 40 percent of three-, four-, and five-year-olds are in school.

Unfortunately, with teachers generally trained to teach much older children and ratios as high as one to nineteen, many of the centers were not of the highest quality. One benefit of the WPA nursery schools was to focus public attention on the positive value of group education for young children, and to stimulate further research.

Just about the time that most WPA nursery schools were closing, the United States entered World War II. In the massive war effort, about one-third of American women began to work outside of their homes in occupations that had formerly been filled by the men who were now involved in the armed services. As never before in this country's history, there was a need for child care in many communities around the country. The **Lanham Act**, passed by Congress in 1941, made monies available by 1943 to establish child care centers near factories essential for the war effort during this time of need (and also mandated that the monies to support the centers be withdrawn within six months after the war ended).

The term "day care" was introduced by Lanham centers to refer to full-day programs for young children. Many of the centers operated for twelve hours, and some for eighteen. The basic materials and programs from nursery education were brought to the programs by teachers trained in child development, along with modifications for the longer day. In 1945, between 105,000 and 130,000 children were enrolled in over 3,000 centers (Olmsted, 1992).

Additional support for needed child care at this time came from private industry. The Kaiser shipyards of Portland, Oregon, established round-the-clock child care for mothers working in their industry. The centers were located at the entrance to the plants, and offered additional services beyond the nursery education: there was an infirmary for sick children, a rental library of children's books, and a "store where mothers could buy items like combs, shoelaces, and other children's items" (Beatty, 1995, p. 191), as well as hot meals for mothers to pick up when they took their children home. The Kaiser centers were under the direction of two people whose names later became prominent in early childhood thinking: Lois Stolz and James Hymes, Jr. Those who report about the centers tell of models of excellent education for young children (Hymes, 1978). For the first time, the country had a concrete example of how child care could work for middle-class as well as low-income families. But when the war ended, the funds were withdrawn, and the Lanham centers closed in every state except California.

Federal attention did not focus on children's care again until the mid-60s, and when attention returned, for the first time it was as a concern for children, rather than because of need for adult employment. The country was in a panic about the state of education. Since the launch of the Russian satellite Sputnik in 1957, serious questions were being raised about the effectiveness of the school systems. Hunt (1961) stated that deficits in early stimulation could be corrected by early intervention. Several model early intervention programs (see Timeline: Perry, 1962; Gray, 1962; and Deutsch, 1963) had suggested the positive gains that could be made with young children who were at-risk for school failure. Bloom's work (1964) was interpreted to mean that half of a child's intelligence is developed by age four, encouraging the concern to value this potential growth period.

Let us suppose the mind to be, as we say, white paper void of all characters, without ideas
—John Locke

Lanham Act: Federal legislation that provided funds for the development of child care centers for the mothers working in the war effort in World War II.

1971
The first modern corporate-sponsored child care center is opened in Boston by The Stride Rite Company.

This attention occurred at the same time as the civil rights struggles of the early 1960s, which sought equality for all people. In 1964, the federal government launched a War on Poverty under President Lyndon Johnson, with the passage of the Economic Opportunity Act. Under the Office of Economic Opportunity, Project Head Start was designed and administered as the educational thrust of the effort. Initially begun as a summer program in 1965, the intent was to give social and educational opportunities to young children from disadvantaged environments who would otherwise enter first grade already behind. With the provisions of educational, social, medical, dental, nutritional, and mental health services to children and the mandated involvement of their parents, Head Start's charter was to break the cycle of poverty.

Soon after the first demonstration programs, Head Start became a year-round program. Although there were early studies that suggested that the benefits to Head Start were only temporary (Westinghouse, 1969), later studies showed gains for children, and benefits for their entire family (Consortium, 1979; Schweinhart and Weikart, 1986). In the 70s, different formats for delivery of Head Start services were added (see Home Start and Parent Child Centers on the Timeline, and remember Annie's story), and children with disabilities were included after 1972. Head Start has precipitated much good research and dialogue about early childhood education, as well as the realization of the need for an abundance of trained early education professionals. This resulted in the development of the **Child Development Associate** credentialing system (1972).

Child Development Associate (CDA): A system for credentialing of early childhood teachers, based on proving competency in six areas and thirteen functional areas.

Head Start has continued to receive legislative support, including an expansion on support in 1993, that now allows funds to serve about 40 percent of eligible children nationwide. Currently about three-quarters of a million children are served annually, including homeless and migrant children, and the annual budget is over 3.5 billion dollars. Many programs now offer full-day services, recognizing that parents will never break the poverty cycle until they are fully employed. What Head Start has done as well is continue to focus public attention on the need for providing young children with services to help develop the whole child. Even in fiscally conservative times, Congress has continued to support Head Start.

Other federally supported efforts have all been for families that were unable to provide full financial support for their children's needs, rather than as any recognition that all families need various kinds of education and support from time to time. Even Start, the federally funded literacy program, was authorized in 1988 to help break family patterns of illiteracy. Operated through the public school system, and funded by Chapter One, Even Start involves children in early education activities, and parents in adult literacy programs, including activities which parents and children share together.

It is the nature of everything that comes into being, that while tender it is easily bent and formed, but that, when it has grown hard, it is not easy to alter

–John Comenius

Federal support to child care comes through various avenues. Title XX of the Social Security Act provides money for child care for certain eligible families, such as families that receive AFDC (Aid for Families with Dependent Children) funds, or other eligibility standards established by the states. The USDA (U.S. Department of Agriculture) Child Care Food Program gives monies to child care centers and homes to support their nutritional programs. More

1972
There are 110 employer-sponsored child care programs nationwide.

recently, child care credits for federal income taxes have assisted all families paying for child care.

The other social development of the 1960s that pressured the federal government to consider the care of children at all social levels was the women's movement. Increasingly, women entered the work force, beginning in the 60s, and increasing in numbers until the present (see Timeline). Both the breakdown of traditional marriage patterns and the increase in births to never-married women contributed to the phenomenon of greater numbers of households being headed by women. Even when there are two parents present in the home, economic pressures and personal desires have taken women of all social classes into the workplace. The resulting increase in demand for various kinds of child care has made the cry louder for the federal government to address issues of quality, affordability, and availability.

Although for two decades, the nation was not yet ready to answer the question of who would care for all families; they would still assume that public commitment would be largely limited to poor and minority families. The Comprehensive Child Development Bill of 1971 was passed by both houses of Congress, and would have established a national child care program for the first time in the United States. However, under strong pressure from right-wing activists, President Richard Nixon vetoed the bill, with a strong statement that it was not desirable to alter the family relationship and commit the "vast moral authority of the national government to the side of communal approaches in child rearing over and against the family-centered approach" (Olmsted, 1992, p. 6). This veto ignored the very real needs of working parents in favor of the traditional national image of strong families being sufficient to provide for all their own needs. "Government policy since this watershed event has indeed steered a course far shy of any national child care program" (Olmsted, 1992, p. 6). The major principles in federal child care policy in the 1980s were "decentralization, privatization, and deregulation" (Olmsted, 1992, p. 6).

Decentralization included a combination of federal funding cutbacks, and the conversion of federal funds for child care services into Social Services Block Grant funds in 1981, that allowed policy and program decisions to be made by individual states. Privatization included offering incentives to employers for child care subsidies for employees, providing tax benefits to families, and easing requirements for non-profit providers. Deregulation included the failure to enact the Federal Interagency Day Care Requirements, developed by child development experts in the late 1970s. These would have established minimum standards for child care services–at least for those programs that received federal funding–and would have provided general guidelines for quality care in all child care services. But, since Congress did not accept these standards, it was left to individual state policy to set the widely varying standards that exist today.

The demographic changes were gradually influencing social policy, though. In 1988, more than 100 child care bills were introduced in Congress (Zigler and Lang, 1991). But it was not until 1990, after years of lobbying by a strong coalition of early childhood organizations and advocates, that the federal government was finally drawn into providing funds in child development block grants to the states to improve and monitor the quality of child care available to

When we come to the stage where we build curricula based upon the right of the younger child to learn healthy habits of food, sleep, rest, open air play and work, emotional sanity, and social poise, we can hope for the nursery schools, kindergartens, and the lower grades to unite in contributing a most highly honored function in our public school systems of America

–Patty Smith Hill

1972

Home Start programs are established to provide Head Start's comprehensive services to children and families at home.

families. With this final positive step, the federal government has moved in a new direction to answer the question, "Who cares for the children?" by recognizing that all of society is affected by the quality of care its children receive. Perhaps this move suggests that "the once-prevalent refrain, 'Parents first; government when they fail' is slowly being replaced by 'Parents are primary; society is willingly supportive'" (Kagan, 1994, p. 8). You will be able to follow the nation's progress in exploring this question further from your own vantage point as an informed professional and citizen.

WHY ARE EARLY CARE AND EDUCATION SEEN AS SEPARATE?

The dual developmental origins of the care and education of young children by others beyond their families haunt us today, with real impact on the education and social status of the adults involved in this care, and therefore on quality care, and on separate availability of funding streams. Early education professionals themselves are not immune from the subtle effects of considering these two aspects as separate. It is not unusual for sponsoring agencies such as churches to maintain two entirely separate programs, such a nursery school program with higher standards (and salaries) for their staff than those for the staff of the full-day child care program, and the resultant rivalry, discord, and distance that you can imagine. What are the roots for such a division?

The time is drawing near when methods of teaching will be so simplified that each mother will be able not only to teach her children without help, but continue her own education at the same time
—Johann Pestalozzi

Thinking back to the discussion in the last section, you will recall that family self-sufficiency was seen as a virtue in early American society, and in the European cultures from which that society is derived. "Historically, child care workers have been those <u>who have looked after children when nobody else could provide care</u>" (Vander Ven, 1986, p. 3). When families were in some kind of crisis, such as death, illness, unfitness, or desertion of parents, or when parents had to work outside of the home for such hours that they were unable to provide for their children's care, some custodial agency had to step in to look after children. The original intention of such care was to keep children safe and reasonably occupied "while waiting for someone else to come, either to take the children home or to provide them with an activity regarded as more important" (Vander Ven, p. 8). Small wonder that little respect was tied to so minimal a function. Even the most enlightened of the first child care situations, that were established for children of mill workers in Lancaster, England, in 1816 by Robert Owen, were primarily to protect children from the rigors of employment in the mill rather than to educate. The name for the first recognized group child care in America—the Nursery for the Children of Poor Women in New York City, 1854—suggests the stigma attached to this care. The first day nurseries in this country appeared soon after the flood of immigration that "brought more than five million foreign families to the United States between 1815 and 1860 (Olmsted, 1992). The **philanthropic** agencies and settlement houses began sponsoring day nurseries, and considered this child care service to be a means of family preservation. "Based on the French model of the crèche, day nurseries had as their main purpose the physical care of children (feeding, bathing, keeping them safe from the dangers of the street) 6 days a week, 12 hours a day" (Olmsted, 1992, p. 5).

Philanthropy: Organization established for the provision of social services to clients, to better their lives.

1972
Work is begun on the CDA credentialing system, following a proposal by Dr. Edward Zigler, head of the Office of Child Development.

In addition to caring for children while their mothers worked, settlement houses also provided drop-off care, care for sick children, and 24-hour care when necessary (Youcha, 1995). Children were provided with nutritious hot meals, but frequently little to occupy their minds or attention. Child care operated within the social service framework; the mother was the client, and the care of the child was the service provided for her. What actually happened to the child was of little primary importance.

Because of that orientation, there were stark contrasts between child care situations for poor and disadvantaged children, and the nursery schools and kindergarten classrooms of America in the early decades of this century. Osborn (1991) compares the two experiences in 1920, describing the day care setting as drab in appearance, with poor equipment. Children were largely inactive in large groups, kept quiet by untrained staff who organized no program, or by nurses most concerned with cleanliness. Abigail Eliot, one of the leaders of the nursery school movement, remembered "dull green walls, no light colors, nothing pretty–spotlessly clean places, with rows of white-faced listless little children sitting, doing nothing. There was a drabness, an emptiness, a nothingness" (Eliot in Gordon and Browne, 1993, p. 20). **Custodial care** was the only purpose, and it was a service for parents who absolutely *had* to send their children. But they did not participate in the program in any way.

In contrast, the nursery school traditions that were exported from Europe to America found their first support from middle-class families. The nursery schools were attractive and colorful, offering planned programs, where children played with well-designed and child-oriented equipment. Eliot said, "In the new nursery school, the children were active, alive, choosing. . . gay, busy, happy" (Gordon and Browne, 1993, p. 20). Staff specially trained to work with children taught the small groups of children enrolled by parents who chose to send their children for this educational experience, and were themselves actively involved in the education process (Osborn, 1991, p. 119). The services focused on the child as client. The clear contrast made child care a social service provided for poor working class and often dysfunctional families, and nursery schools an opportunity for middle-class children.

As more public assistance became available for mothers, the number of day care centers actually declined until the 1960s, with the notable exception of the Lanham Act centers discussed in the previous section that offered such an excellent example of combining the two traditions. Despite the change in women's work patterns in the 60s, and even when day care services began to be used by middle-class families as a necessary supplement for care at home, the negative attitude remained. Much of the early research was done from a perspective that children's development was likely at risk when placed in day care programs, most of which were assumed to be of poor quality (Caldwell, 1985). Part of the discomfort of using child care stemmed from the tension associated with the national attitude about the primacy of the family for childrearing and the belief that childrearing should be a private undertaking. And unfortunately, the long-held attitude that child care was purely custodial care and not intended to be anything beyond that, likely influenced the failure of many state legislative bodies to mandate standards in group size, staff qualifications, or for

> **Custodial Care:** Caring for basic needs, primarily physical, and protecting from danger.

> *All my life I have fought against formula. Once you have set down a formula, you are imprisoned by it as surely as the primitive tribesman is imprisoned by the witch doctor's magic circle*
> —Caroline Pratt

1972
Head Start establishes a requirement that 10 percent of enrollment should be reserved for children with disabilities.

| Figure 8-1 | **Rousseau's thinking about young children has influenced early educators for nearly three hundred years.** |

child care that contributed to overall educational quality. The most recent evidence of the effects of this long-standing attitude is in the study on child care (1995) that you will read more about in Chapter Eleven.

The negative attitudes towards child care notwithstanding, it should be noted that modern demographics have brought the two traditions of early childhood education and child care together. They were on converging tracks, says Caldwell (1986) and "have now merged. The resulting service is both educational and protective, and the client is the family unit" (p. 8).

> The child care and early education model currently seen in well-thought-of employer-sponsored programs, the best of the child care chains and church-related schools, and the "developmentally appropriate" programs for 2s, 3s, 4s, and 5s accredited by NAEYC, most typically are, with a few amendments or appendages here or there, the "traditional" nursery school/kindergarten model created by the creative progressive educators from the early 1900's on through the 1930's (Greenberg, 1987, p. 77).

The standards for accreditation that you will read more about in Chapter Nine, parent recognition of and demand for quality, and the entrance of the business community into awareness of the need for quality child care for their employees are surely trends that will help with overall quality. Now what remains to be changed is the old uncomfortable attitude that child care is both a relatively unimportant institution, and its use is indicative of family dysfunction.

WHAT ARE THE DIFFERENCES BETWEEN THE NURSERY SCHOOL AND KINDERGARTEN TRADITIONS?

Both the nursery school and kindergarten traditions are now united within the definition of early childhood education, but the different heritages have left behind some practices and institutionalized policies that sometimes cause confusion and conflict. Here we will trace the separate paths of the development of the two traditions.

Kindergartens

The establishment of the first kindergarten extends back further through the lines of philosophical thinking about children and education. The English philosopher John Locke (1632-1704) wrote of the importance of early experiences, and was one of the first to point out individual differences in children. He pointed out the importance of children learning through play, and emphasized "natural" education, rather than the harsh discipline more common to his time. Yet another who wrote of the importance of natural methods of childrearing was the French philosopher Jean Jacques Rousseau (1712-1778) (see Fig. 8-1). In *Emile,* the fic-

All that we lack at birth and need when grown up is given us by education. This education comes to us from nature, from men, or from things
—Jean Jacques Rousseau

> Figure 8-2 **Pestalozzi is considered to have been the first early childhood educator.**

tional account of raising a child, he discussed the need to protect children from the evils of society, and the importance of planning educational experiences that were directly related to children's interests. Both of these authors influenced the thinking of Johann Pestalozzi (1746-1827), who is actually known as the first early childhood educator, since he opened a school for young children in Yverdon, Switzerland, in 1801 (see Fig. 8-2). He believed that children are capable of making their own discoveries, and encouraged his teachers to respect each child's individuality. His school was influential in allowing others to observe his theories in practice: Robert Owen, who opened the first infant school referred to in the last section, visited his school, and Friedrich Froebel taught there.

It is Froebel (1782-1852) who is in fact known as the originator of the kindergarten as it was known in his German language, or *children's garden,* It was his belief that children could grow and flourish like plants in the right environment, developing internal impulses that would unfold naturally. The kindergarten was designed for children between the ages of three and six years. His curriculum was designed to emphasize language, numbers, forms, eye-hand coordination, and to train children in ways that would establish courtesy, punctuality, neatness and cleanliness, as well as respect for others.

The most notable elements of his tradition were the curriculum materials that he called *gifts* and *occupations.* The gifts were a series of ten concrete kinds of manipulative materials, such as woolen balls, wooden shapes and cubes of various sizes, tablets, wooden sticks, and a variety of natural objects, all presented to children at defined intervals, with specific skills and symbolic concepts to learn. The occupations included sewing, perforating paper, weaving, clay work, and paper cutting. As Froebel said, "What the child tries to represent, he begins to understand" (Olmsted, 1992, p. 4). While this idea seems very familiar to us, it was considered quite revolutionary to educate children in a group, outside the home, and using play materials (see Fig. 8-3).

His ideas and model of the kindergarten were imported to the United States primarily by German immigrants who had been trained in Froebelian principles in Germany. Margarethe Schurz opened the first German language kindergarten in her home in Wisconsin in 1856, and was the person who explained the Froebelian principles to Elizabeth Peabody. Elizabeth Peabody (1804-1894) opened the first English language kindergarten in Boston in 1860, and is generally credited with gaining acceptance for the kindergarten movement in the United States. It was Peabody who influenced the superintendent of the St. Louis Schools to sponsor the first public kindergarten in the United States in 1873. It was at one of her lectures that Milton Bradley, the toy manufacturer, first learned of Froebelian methods, and began to manufacture the gifts and occupations for sale to American kindergartens. Kindergarten normal schools opened: the Oshkosh Normal School in 1880, the Chicago Kindergarten College in 1886, and the Wheelock School in Boston in 1888. Peabody founded the American Froebel Association in 1878 for interested **kindergartners**, as the first teachers were known.

Kindergartners: Term used for the first, Froebelian-trained kindergarten teachers in the 1800s and early 20th century.

1972

The Report of the Surgeon General's Advisory Committee on Television and Social Behavior spotlights the causal link between television violence and subsequent aggressive child behavior.

| Figure 8-3 | **Froebel is the father of the modern kindergarten.** |

Public school sponsorship of kindergartens came slowly, and for a time during the later years of the last century and the first years of this century, many were sponsored by churches, charitable organizations, and settlement houses. Patty Smith Hill, writing in 1926, said, "When the kindergarten was introduced into this country more than a century ago, it survived as a philanthropy long before it was accepted as an organic member of the educational system" (Hill, 1987, p. 12). This was the time of heavy emigration, when slums were being developed in the major cities, with the social problems of crime, delinquency and other difficulties associated with rapid increases in foreign population. The settlement houses were created in major cities to combat the problems and to help new citizens assimilate new standards of living. The philanthropists adopted kindergartens as the hope of beginning with the young children. The first president of the New York Kindergarten Association is quoted as saying, "The kindergarten age marks our earliest opportunities to catch the little Russian, the little Italian. . . and begin to make good American citizens of them. The children are brought into a new social order" (Youcha, 1995, p. 148).

The standard kindergarten schedule of morning classroom programs left the kindergarten teachers free to visit in the afternoons, basically functioning as a social welfare worker, "seeking work for the unemployed; space in hospitals for ill mothers, sisters, and brothers; physicians who would remove adenoids and tonsils; or dentists who would extract diseased teeth" (Hill, 1987, p. 13). Gradually, according to Hill's account, the philanthropies turned to the schools to ask them to accept the kindergarten "as a member in good and regular standing." They usually asked to be able to use an empty room in the school, and the philanthropic agencies still paid for the teacher's salary and the program expenses. Then, gradually, the boards of education were persuaded to take full responsibility for the kindergartens, and so the kindergartens became part of the public school systems.

But there were problems in their acceptance within the school systems. Kindergarten teachers had been trained in normal schools that were separate from those that trained the other teachers in the system, and used curriculum, materials, and methods—encouraging children to "talk, sing, dance, dramatize, model, paint, draw, build, and construct"—that seemed quite foreign to teachers who used a curriculum "based upon the acquirement of the three Rs in their baldest and most barren form" (Hill, 1987, p. 14). The kindergarten method of handling behavior problems was considered soft and sentimental, and certainly did not prepare the children to enter first grade. Hill comments that kindergarten children were not welcomed by first grade teachers, through no fault of either kindergarten or first grade teachers. "It was due to the fact that children were supposed to pass on from one teacher to another with continuity of work when the two teachers were trained in diametrically opposed philosophies, curricula, and methods" (Hill, 1987, p. 14). Does not this comment sound like it was written today, instead of about an era seventy years ago?

1973

Standards for child care licensing are prepared by the U.S. Office of Child Development, as nonbinding models to help states and cities improve their regulatory function.

But, besides the difficulties with acceptance in the schools, kindergartners were having their own difficulties with each other. The original Froebelian methods were perceived to be too rigid and abstract, centered around prescribed methods and symbols with the order of the activities precisely sequenced, and unresponsive to new learning about children that was evolving from the **child study movement**. These "progressives" felt that the kindergarten curriculum should be based on scientific knowledge rather than the mystic religious tenets of Froebelian philosophy.

Two important Americans were influencing these ideas about appropriate education for young children. The first to note is John Dewey (1859-1952). With his progressive philosophy, Dewey believed that education was a method of social reform, that information and knowledge would enable individuals to improve the quality of their lives, and that schools must represent life. He opposed the idealistic, religious philosophy of Froebel and his concept of "unfolding," and wanted to base the education of young children on scientific knowledge about their abilities. He was opposed to the traditional method of teaching children by **rote learning**, and wanted the active involvement of the "whole child" and interaction, as described in *My Pedagogic Creed,* published in 1897. In 1896, he and his wife opened a laboratory school at the University of Chicago for four- and five-year-olds, which he called "subprimary" rather than a kindergarten, possibly to distinguish it from the Froebelian model. Dewey's influence on the growing kindergarten movement was profound, as was his influence on the whole scope of **"progressive education"** in America. (You will see a reference to how he influenced the practice of the pioneer women nursery educators in the next section.)

The other name associated with new thinking about kindergartens is G. Stanley Hall (1844-1924). Hall is credited with being the first to begin scientific study of children. His *The Content of Children's Minds* (1883) focused on descriptions of children's concepts, and the educational implications of these findings for teachers. "Hall criticized Froebelian kindergarten theory as being superficial and fantastic–he considered that young children needed large, bold movements rather than the sedentary activities of gifts and occupations and asserted that free play could serve their developmental needs" (Spodek, in Osborn, 1991, p. 76). Hall's influence on the movement away from the Froebelian kindergarten was eventually profound, although at a seminar in 1895, most of the kindergartners he had assembled to share his child development research with, left infuriated.

The controversies were beginning to split the Froebelian kindergartners. They had begun the International Kindergarten Union in 1892, to promote the establishment of kindergartens and elevate the standards of professional training for kindergartners. By 1896, Teachers College had two women on faculty representing the opposite viewpoints: Susan Blow represented the traditional Froebelian kindergarten thought, and Patty Smith Hill, who had spent the previous summer with Dr. Hall learning techniques for scientific study of children that represented the more developmental perspective. By the meeting of the IKU in 1903, conflict was so disruptive that the Committee of Nineteen was established to "formulate contemporary kindergarten thought" (Osborn, 1995, p. 78).

Child Study Movement: The university-based scientific research on child development that began to be widespread in the 1920s, and facilitated the development of early childhood education.

Rote Learning: Form of learning by repetition, memory, and habit, rather than from firsthand understanding.

Progressive Education: Term that applies to educational philosophy based on the tenets of John Dewey, promoting active involvement of the individual in learning.

1973

The Children's Defense Fund of the Washington Research Project is established by Marian Wright Edelman, later to become the Children's Defense Fund.

We sought to give our children from the youngest up, a full life of rich experiences and an opportunity to function in and through these experiences
–Lucy Sprague Mitchell

When they finally published their report in 1913, the group had so splintered that three reports were given: the conservative (Froebelian) position; the Liberal (Progressive-Dewey) position; and the Liberal-Conservative (a combination of the two). Patty Smith Hill (1868-1946) of Columbia Teachers College was the leader of the movement that incorporated the ideas of the new child psychology and the ideas of Dewey and the Progressive school of thought. The face of kindergartens changed, discarding the formal teacher-directed Froebelian methods in favor of child-centered, more informal learning. "Large blocks replaced the tiny gift blocks. Toys, large crayons, paint brushes, hammers, and saws took the place of sewing cards, paper-folding and weaving mats " (Osborn, 1991, p. 104). The International Kindergarten Union remained as the official organization of those interested in principles of kindergarten education, changing its name in 1930 to Association of Childhood Education International (see Chapter Nine), and gradually including elementary teachers in the membership.

Nursery Schools

Meanwhile, in England, another form of early education was evolving for even younger children. A 1908 British government report had pointed out that, while most children were born healthy, about 80 percent arrived at school age in poor health. In response, that same year Rachel and Margaret McMillan established the London School Clinic for children under five years. Then in 1911, in Deptford, they established the Deptford School–later renamed the Rachel McMillan School–as an open air **nursery school**. This was the first time that the term "nursery school" was used. There was an emphasis on healthy living for children, as well as nurturing for the whole child.

Nursery Schools: Programs modeled after the McMillan philosophy of physical, emotional, and social development, usually for three- and four-year-olds, usually operated for a part-day.

Other tenets of the nursery school philosophy was that schools should develop close links with children's families and communities, and that teachers of young children should be well-trained. Thus the nursery school also functioned for many years as a teacher training laboratory. Although Rachel McMillan died in 1917, Margaret continued her influential work in nursery education. She published *The Nursery School* in 1919, and advocated for government support for nursery schools, which led to the establishment of public nursery schools in England as part of the national education system.

American interest in nursery schools developed rapidly around 1920. The first mention of a nursery school is actually the establishing of a parent cooperative nursery school by a group of faculty wives at the University of Chicago in 1915. (**Parent Cooperative Nursery Schools** continued to develop in middle-class communities, becoming even more numerous after World War II, with about 1,000 nationwide by 1960.) In 1919 Harriet Johnson, whose name we will hear again in connection with the beginnings of the later Bank Street School, began a nursery school at the Bureau of Educational Experiments. Patty Smith Hill began a lab nursery school at Columbia Teachers College in 1921, and encouraged Abigail Adams Eliot to visit the McMillan program in England to learn nursery education firsthand. After being trained in the Deptford School, Eliot returned to the United States and began the Ruggles Street Nursery School and Training Center in Boston in 1922, one of the first centers where American

Parent Cooperative Nursery School: The form of nursery school that involves parents in the classroom and administration of the school.

teachers could be trained in nursery education. About the same time, Edna White began a nursery school at the Merrill-Palmer School, that had originally been established to teach young women how to be mothers. Abigail Eliot (1892-1992) is generally believed to be responsible for bringing the nursery school movement to America, although you can see that there were several women who were involved from the beginning. However, since Eliot had trained at the McMillan School, her center was believed to be most consistent with the philosophy and practice of the McMillan principles.

The time was right for the nursery schools, because of the widespread interest in the development of young children generated by the child study movement. Nursery schools were established in laboratory settings as part of the child study programs. Funds were provided by the will of Laura Spelman Rockefeller in 1923 to establish child study centers in major research universities, such as Yale, the University of California, the University of Minnesota, the University of Iowa, and Columbia University. Interestingly enough, the method of distribution of these funds required the child study centers to be outside of the college of education. For example, at the University of Minnesota, the funds were withheld until the Institute of Child Development withdrew from the college of education and was established as a separate unit in the university. This pattern likely contributed to the further separation of nursery school and kindergarten education seen today in universities, of departments of education that are concerned with the education of children age five and over, and other units, sometimes under the auspices of child and family development or home economics, that are concerned with the education of under five's.

One name associated with the child study movement that was to influence the development of nursery education was Arnold Gesell (1880-1961). A medical doctor, he established the Clinic of Child Development at Yale University. With recorded observations of children in natural settings, he collected data on norms of development of young children. He supported nursery schools as part of the total educational system, writing *The Significance of the Nursery School* in 1924.

The nursery school and child study movements were amazingly **multidisciplinary**, in contrast to the kindergarten movement whose leaders were all from a background of education, with the only exception of G. Stanley Hall, who came from the field of psychology. Nursery school leaders included professionals with backgrounds from nursing, social work, medicine, home economics and education (Osborn, 1991, p. 122). Lawrence Frank was the administrator of the Rockefeller grants to establish the child study centers in the universities, and is credited with the support of an interdisciplinary approach to studying children, incorporating the findings of various disciplines, such as biology, education, medicine, and psychology to develop understandings of the whole child. It was Frank's belief that nursery schools should be a part of home economics because they were a supplement to the family. We have already noted how this began the separation in thinking about education for kindergarten and older from education of preschoolers. "Colleges of education discussed educational foundations and curriculum methods; home economics training programs emphasized child development, child psychology, psychological learning theories, Freudian and neo-Freudian theory, and family life" (Osborn, 1991, p. 125).

All of the schools. . . (Dewey's) [exhibit] a common emphasis upon respect for individuality and for increased freedom; a common disposition to build upon the nature and experience of the boys and girls that come to them, instead of imposing from without external subject-matter standards
—John Dewey

Multidisciplinary: Using the knowledge from several different disciplines, such as medicine, psychology, and education.

1975
The first CDA credential is awarded—actually, twelve of them.

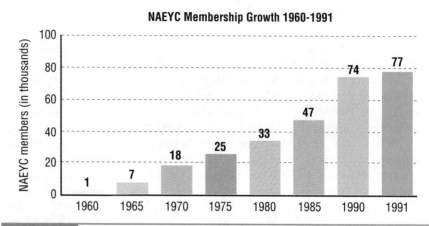

NAEYC Membership Growth 1960-1991

Figure 8-4 NAEYC, started with a handful of early childhood educators in 1925, has continued to grow over the years and is now the nation's largest early education professional organization.

Pediatrician: A medical specialist in the branch of medicine related to children's diseases and health.

The child development approach born in interdisciplinary studies was expansive and inclusive, considering children in the complete contexts of their families and communities, rather than more narrowly focused on early childhood education alone. This interdisciplinary inclusiveness was apparent when Patty Smith Hill called a conference of 25 people interested in nursery education in 1925. (It is interesting to note that Patty Smith Hill is the one name that is influential in both nursery school and kindergarten movements. Her name is also famous as the author of the song "Happy Birthday"!) The meeting, and succeeding conferences in 1926, 1927, and 1929–at which the organization was more formally structured and named the National Association for Nursery Education (NANE)–was attended by nursery school teachers, home economists, psychologists, **pediatricians**, nurses, and social workers. This organization, renamed the National Association for the Education of Young Children (NAEYC) in 1964, is the largest and most influential of professional organizations for early educators, and is still inclusive of various disciplines and educational models (see Fig. 8-4). You will read much more about the organization's present efforts in Chapter Nine.

And so kindergarten and nursery school programs came from very different traditions to be included within the early education profession today. Understanding the traditions, and the reasons behind the very different professional preparation patterns and organizations, may help today's early educators find new ways to find common ground (see also Granucci, 1990).

WHERE HAVE ALL THESE WOMEN GONE?

When Polly Greenberg asked this question (1987), she was wondering why so few in our field recognize the names of some very important contributors to the profession who are female, while the names of male theorists are prominent in most texts. Silin (1985) wondered something similar:

1975

The Education of All Handicapped Children Act PL 94-142 is passed, mandating free public educational services in the "least restrictive environment" for children ages three to six with special needs.

Figure 8-5	**Freud revolutionized modern understanding of personality development.**

When Ade (1982) talks about the systematization of knowledge in early childhood, he mentions Sigmund Freud, Arnold Gesell, Erik Erikson, Jean Piaget, E.L. Thorndike, and B.F. Skinner. But, one must ask, what happened to Abigail Eliot, Patty Smith Hill, Susan Isaacs, and Caroline Pratt, among others? The division along gender lines of these two lists signals the complex ramifications of the professionalization issue (Silin, 1985, p. 43).

In this section of our consideration of history, we will rectify this situation of missing links in understanding our heritage by briefly identifying the male theorists, and then describing the contributions of those women who are often absent from such accounts.

Theorists

Sigmund Freud (1856-1939) was the founder of psychoanalytic theory (see Fig. 8-5). His work with adults with psychological problems led him to believe that childhood was the source of difficulties in personality formation. His work describing the stages of emotional development in childhood forever changed the thinking about the nature of the child. Freud's ideas were more readily adopted by the nursery school movement than by those in kindergarten education, partly because of the work of Susan Isaacs (1885-1948). In 1929, her book *The Nursery Years* interpreted Freudian theory for teachers, and suggested how early education schools should apply this new insight about the unconscious to their work with children.

Erik Erikson (1902-1994) further developed Freud's thought into a **psychosocial** theory of personality development, extending through the life span (see Fig. 8-6). He theorized that each stage of life offered a specific psychological struggle that contributes to a major aspect of personality. Erikson was one of the first to suggest the idea that children develop in the context of their societies' expectations and prohibitions. His theory continues to influence our understanding of the environmental responses and supports that help children achieve healthy development.

Jean Piaget's (1896-1980) substantial body of work has greatly influenced early childhood education today, with his focus on the cognitive development of children. His theory explained how children's understanding of the world continues to grow through adaptations made as a result of interaction between the individual and the physical and social environment. Piaget has influenced the way we believe that children think and learn, with implications for our educational settings that allow children to explore, experiment, and manipulate materials (see Fig. 8-7).

Lev Vygotsky (1896-1934), a contemporary of Piaget whose work has been translated into English more recently, also believed that children construct their own understandings of the world. He differs from Piaget in emphasizing

Psychosocial: Psychological issues related to relations of the individual with others in the environment. Generally used to describe Erikson's theory of personality development, in which the individual must resolve conflict with the environment, including other persons.

1976
Lawrence Kohlberg describes his view of the stages of moral reasoning in "Moral Stages and Moralization."

Figure 8-6	**Expanding on Freud's ideas, Erikson's theory of psychosocial development influences our practices with young children.**

Figure 8-7	**Piaget's ideas about children's cognitive development include the need for active involvement with materials and people.**

that social interaction and experience with others is the major learning process for children. For Vygotsky, the development of language is a primary task of learning. There are important implications for early educators in Vygotsky's theory because he stresses the adult's role in assisting children with collaborative learning (see Fig. 8-8).

Lawrence Kohlberg (1927-87), influenced by the work of Piaget, developed his own theory of moral reasoning based on cognitive development. Both Piaget and Kohlberg believed that children form their own moral views based on their development of reasoning. Unlike Piaget, Kohlberg differentiated between the moral reasoning of children and adults. Kohlberg believed that children's moral development occurs in three fixed and invariable developmental levels of moral thinking through which all children pass, though perhaps at different rates.

B. F. Skinner (1904-1990) is the most prominent theorist of **behavioral theory**; other work was done before him by Thorndike and Watson. Behaviorists, unlike that of the previous theorists, believe that children are shaped by external forces in the environment, and that almost all behavior can be learned through experience. Specific behaviors, according to learning theory, can be strengthened or weakened by the responses children are given following the behavior (see Fig. 8-9).

The theorist who has received recent attention related to educational issues is Howard Gardner (1943-), with his theory of **multiple intelligences**. He identifies seven intelligences: linguistic, musical, logical-mathematical, spatial, bodily-kinesthetic, interpersonal, and intrapersonal, rather than measuring intelligence from one perspective. This theory has interesting implications for individualizing of learning experiences and expectations.

You will become more familiar with the details and exact terminology related to each individual's theory in your coursework on child development. But you are unlikely to read detailed study of the names of the women that fol-

Behavioral Theory: (Also learning theory) A psychological theory developed in the United States that believes that behavior is learned, and can be modified by changing environmental responses of reward and punishment.

Multiple Intelligences: Theory described by Howard Gardner, suggesting that intelligence may be organized into seven different kinds of abilities.

1976
Almost half the babies in the United States are wearing Pampers.

Figure 8-8	**Vygotsky's ideas impact our contemporary concept of teachers as facilitators.**

Figure 8-9	**Skinner's work on learning theory has implications for class-room teachers considering the effects of reinforcement and punishment.**

low (with the possible exception of Montessori), all of whom have made important contributions to the world of early education that we know today.

Important Female Contributors

Maria Montessori (1870-1952) was the first Italian woman to earn a medical degree. From her observations of children, Montessori recognized the uniqueness of each child. Her phrase the *absorbent mind* captures her philosophy of children educating themselves, actively, in a prepared environment, using carefully selected didactic materials. (You will recall the earlier discussion of Montessori in Chapter Two.) From the time her *Casa dei Bambini* (Children's House) was opened to work with children in the tenements of Rome in 1907 until the present, Montessori's philosophy has had an impact on early childhood education, although not universal acceptance. There were Montessori schools in America within the next decade, but the real popularity of Montessori education in the United States did not happen until the resurgence of interest in early childhood education in the mid-60s. Again within the last decade, as concerns have risen about public school systems and social breakdowns, Montessori schools have increased in popularity, including as choices of magnet schools within large cities.

The lasting contributions of Montessori philosophy include: an attitude of respect for children; the idea that young children are essentially self-didactic, or learn through their own activities and adaptations; the concept that teachers learn through their interaction with children; the prepared, attractive environment, with child-sized furniture; the quality of manipulative materials (adapted from Elkind, 1983). Contemporary questions that suggest much Montessori practice may not fall within the guidelines for developmentally appropriate practice include: the emphasis on work and absence of fantasy from traditional Montessori education; children's lack of freedom to experiment with materials, once they have been introduced to their appropriate use; the discouragement of cooperative and col-

1976
Percentage of infants under one year who have mothers in the work force is 11 percent.

Figure 8-10   **Montessori's ideas are embodied today in Montessori schools all over the world.**

legial planning and conversation; and the strictly sequenced series of activities, and tight teacher control of how space, time, and materials are used (Greenberg, 1990). Because Montessori philosophy and training have been maintained so separately from other institutions within early education, Montessori and her schools maintain a separate and unique place in our history (see Fig. 8-10).

But right in the mainstream of early education history are several names of women whose lives and work were closely intertwined. Caroline Pratt, frustrated with the Froebelian-based teacher preparation she had received at Teachers College, began an experimental school for six five-year-olds in New York City in 1913. The following year, she opened a larger school–the Play School, now City and Country School still in New York City–one of the nation's first truly progressive schools. Another accomplishment that lasts until today is her creation of the first set of **unit blocks**, under the inspiration of having seen blocks created by Patty Smith Hill at the Teachers College kindergarten (see fig. 8-11). In her interesting book (Pratt, 1948, 1970), she notes her reliance on the ideas of John Dewey, and describes the children's active involvement in exploring their neighborhood as well as the play materials of the school. She also documents the beginnings of the working relationships with herself, Harriet Johnson, and Lucy Sprague Mitchell (1878-1967).

Unit Blocks: Set of wooden blocks, as developed by Caroline Pratt, in precise mathematical shapes.

> Harriet Johnson, then a Visiting Teacher in the service set up by the Public Education Association for the public schools, brought Lucy Sprague Mitchell to visit, and Mrs. Mitchell brought with her a fresh tide of plans for expansion empowered by her characteristic enthusiasm.
>
> She offered us financial support. She offered us a new home, a converted garage in MacDougal Alley, behind her own Washington Square home. Best of all, she offered her own services as a teacher, and this was the beginning of a long and rich association (Pratt, 1970, p. 54).

For 15 years, Pratt's Play School was housed in the Mitchell's homes and backyards, and Mitchell was the teacher of the five-year-olds, with her own four children entering the school, one by one, and the school soon extended down to include three-year-olds. According to Pratt, the Play School differed from the usual experimental school in which teachers were the experimenters.

Individuals come to a task, problem, or conversation with their own subjective ways of making sense of it
—Lev Vygotsky

> In the Play School, children worked in an open, free environment and were themselves the experimenters (p. 241). . . . In fact all aspects of traditional pedagogy had been discarded. The Play School, whose title itself might be seen as a contradiction in terms, had no set curriculum or formal classroom goals. Even for older children, there were no periods devoted to reading, writing, or arithmetic. Instead, students played with toys and blocks, did shop work, painted, told stories, made music, did pantomime, or occupied themselves in freely chosen ways (Antler, 1987, p. 239).

1977
Staff turnover in childcare centers is 15 percent.

Figure 8-11 **The unit blocks used in most early childhood classrooms are a direct legacy from Caroline Pratt. (Courtesy of Barbara Rawlins)**

The Play School and the Children's School (now Walden School, founded by Margaret Naumburg, another Dewey supporter, also in 1914) "were probably the first two nursery schools in the United States of the kind we now define as 'developmentally appropriate', learning-through-play schools for 2s, 3s, and 4s" (Greenberg, 1987, p. 77).

Lucy Sprague Mitchell had studied with both John Dewey and Edward Thorndike, and had early experience in the settlement houses in Chicago and New York. She believed in the power of early education, and was fascinated with how young children learn. Besides teaching in and supporting the Play School, she is known for other lasting contributions to the field of early education. Together with Harriet Johnson, who had been a nurse, teacher, and settlement house worker, she founded in 1916 in New York City, the Bureau of Educational Experiments. At the time, as Mitchell noted, there were two different kinds of work with children just beginning: experimental schools and research organizations studying child development. The unique idea of the plan for the Bureau of Educational Experiments was to "combine these two kinds of thinking and work within one organization in a functional relationship" (Mitchell, 1953, p. 24).

Mitchell and Johnson pioneered this union of research theory and practice. The staff included doctors, psychologists, social workers, and teachers to record and analyze data. In 1919, Harriet Johnson established and directed a nursery school as part of the Bureau for children from fifteen months to three years, joining it to Pratt's Play School for three- to seven-year-olds, and adding an eight-year-old class. This was also what later became the Bank Street School. In 1930 Mitchell began a cooperative school for experienced teachers at the Bureau. Her efforts to create a "whole teacher" in teacher education was almost as much a pio-

I differed from my colleagues in that I instinctively felt that mental deficiency was more of an educational than medical problem

—Maria Montessori

1977
For the first time in this nation's history, almost half of the mothers of children under 18–49 percent–are in the labor force.

I believe, finally, that the teacher is engaged, not simply in the training of individuals, but in the formation of a proper social life. I believe that every teacher should realize the dignity of his calling

–John Dewey

neer front at that time as the study of children and experimental schools had been in 1916 (Antler, 1987); Bank Street College is world renowned in early education today. Mitchell, who stated the principle that all their work was in relation to public education, also began the Bank Street Public School Workshops in 1943.

The enduring legacy of Mitchell, Johnson, and Pratt is that the words "Bank Street philosophy" are meaningful today in describing what is now known as the traditional nursery school, although far removed from the original nursery schools with their strong emphasis on health care and social services. Greenberg points out that in the earliest staff-written concept document from the team designing the educational component of Head Start appear the words: "The basic Head Start classroom should work like a Bank Street College elementary classroom for nursery/kindergarten" (Greenberg, 1987, p. 76). So our heritages are linked together over time.

Lucy Sprague Mitchell also contributed to the world of children's literature that we know today. In 1921, after noting that there were no stories for children under age six that dealt with the modern world, Lucy wrote the *Here and Now Stories*. Later, in 1938, she established the Writers' Laboratory to influence the kinds of juvenile books being written. With such a body of accomplishments, we wonder, along with Greenberg, why these are not names as well known as the theorists whose ideas these women integrated into their practice? Greenberg suggests that it may have been because they chose to work collectively and cooperatively, and also because they dared to step out of the world of the home where they "belonged" and

> into the public sector, the world of higher education, research, publication, thought–all by tradition exclusively male terrain. Moreover, these social revolutionaries stepped smack into the sensitive, always-near-meltdown core of the nations' reactor–caring for and educating young children *outside the family* [italics added]. The progressives promoted radically different childrearing and educational practices, always a dangerous thing to do. Indeed they rocked the nations' cradle! (Greenberg, 1987, p. 84).

Now you, as beginning professionals, can help keep alive the names of the foremothers of early education.

1977

The Consumer Product Safety Commission issues a regulation setting the minimum size for a baby's rattle, after eight children had died in 1976 from swallowing or choking on their rattles.

QUESTIONS FOR REVIEW

1. List several reasons for a study of the history of early education.
2. Identify the different occasions when the federal government has taken a role in supporting early care and education.
3. Explain why early care and education were originally thought of as two separate entities.
4. Discuss the separate developments of kindergartens and nursery schools in Europe and in America, identifying key names in each tradition.
5. Order the following names chronologically, stating for each the importance in early education: Erik Erikson; Sigmund Freud; Howard Gardner; Harriet Johnson; Lawrence Kohlberg; Lucy Sprague Mitchell; Maria Montessori; Jean Piaget; Caroline Pratt; B. F. Skinner.

ACTIVITIES FOR FURTHER LEARNING

1. Read one of the articles or books listed in "References" or "Suggestions for Reading," to learn more about one of the individuals you have learned about in this chapter.

REFERENCES

Antler, Joyce. (1987). *Lucy Sprague Mitchell: The making of a modern woman*. New Haven CT: Yale University Press.

Beatty, Barbara. (1995). *Preschool education in America: The culture of young children from the colonial era to the present*. New Haven, CT: Yale University Press.

Bloom, Benjamin. (1964). *Stability and Change in Human Behavior*. New York: Wiley.

Caldwell, Bettye. (1985). *What is quality child care?* Washington, DC: NAEYC.

Caldwell, Bettye. (1986). Professional child care: A supplement to parental care. In Caldwell, Bettye, & Gunzenhouser, N., (Eds.). *Group care for young children: Considerations for child care and health professionals, public policy makers and parents*. Skillman, NJ: Johnson and Johnson Baby Products.

Cicerelli, V. et al. (1969). *The impact of head start. An evaluation of the effects of head start on children's cognitive and affective development*. Westinghouse Learning Corporation and Ohio University. Washington DC: Government Printing Office.

Elkind, David. (1983, January). Montessori education: Abiding contributions and contemporary challenges. *Young Children, 38,* (2), 3-10.

Gordon, Ann, & Browne, Kathryn Williams. (1996). *Beginnings and beyond*. 3d ed. Albany, NY: Delmar Publishers Inc.

Granucci, Pamela Lesiak. (1990, March). Kindergarten teachers: Working through our identity crisis. *Young Children, 45,* (3), 6-11.

Greenberg, Polly. (1987, July). Lucy Sprague Mitchell: A major missing link between early childhood education in the 1980's and progressive education in the 1890s-1930s. *Young Children, 42,* (5), 70-84.

It is important to understand the traditions that comprise the various components of the heritage of early education, to recognize the continuity with earlier practitioners and theorists, to realize how real life events and trends influence the responses of the profession, and to answer questions that separate early education today. These questions include: Who cares for the children? What role will the federal government play in early care and education?; Why are care and education seen as separate? What are the separate traditions of kindergarten and nursery education in Europe and America? Who are the forgotten and familiar names in early education?

Greenberg, Polly. (1990, January). Why not academic preschool? (Part 1) *Young Children, 45,* (2), 70-80.

Hewlett, Sylvia Ann. (1991). *When the bough breaks: The cost of neglecting our children.* New York: Harper Collins Publishers.

Hill, Patty Smith. (1987, July). The function of the kindergarten. *Young Children, 42,* (5), 12-19.

Hunt, J. McVicker. (1961). *Intelligence and experience.* New York: Ronald.

Hymes, James, Jr. (1978-79). *Living history interviews. Books 1-3.* Carmel CA: Hacienda Press.

Kagan, Sharon L. (1994, Fall). Families and children: Who is responsible? *Childhood Education. 71,* (1), 4-8.

Lazar, I., & Darlington, N. (1979). Consortium for longitudinal studies. *Lasting effects after preschool: Summary report.* Washington DC: U.S. Dept. of Health, Education, and Welfare.

Mitchell, Lucy Sprague. (1953). *Two lives.* New York: Simon and Schuster.

Olmsted, Patricia P. (1992, Fall). Where did our diversity come from? *High/Scope Resource.* 4-9.

Osborn, D. Keith. (1991). *Early childhood education in historical perspective.* 3rd ed. Athens GA: Education Associates, Div. of The Daye Press, Inc.

Perrone, Vito. (1991). *A letter to teachers: Reflections of schooling and the art of teaching.* San Francisco: Jossey-Bass Publishers.

Pratt, Caroline. (1970). *I learn from children.* New York: Harper and Row.

Schweinhart, Lawrence J., & Weikart, David P. (1986, January). What do we know so far? A review of the Head Start Synthesis Project. *Young Children, 41,* (2), 49-55.

Silin, Jonathan G. (1985, March). Authority as knowledge: A problem of professionalization. *Young Children, 40,* (3), 41-46.

Spodek, Bernard, Saracho, Olivia N., & Peters, Donald L., (Eds.). (1988). *Professionalism and the early childhood practitioner.* New York: Teachers College Press.

Vander Ven, Karen. (1986). You've come a long way baby: The evolution and significance of caregiving. In Karen Vander Ven & Ethel Tittnich (Eds.). *Competent caregivers-competent children: Training and education for child care practice.* New York: The Haworth Press.

Youcha, Geraldine. (1995). *Minding the children: Child care in America from colonial times to the present.* New York: Scribner.

Zigler, Edward F., & Lang, Mary E. (1991). *Child care choices: Balancing the needs of children, families, and society.* New York: The Free Press.

SUGGESTIONS FOR READING

Baylor, R. (1965). *Elizabeth Peabody: Kindergarten pioneer.* Philadelphia: University of Pennsylvania Press.

Bradburn, E. (1989). *Margaret McMillan: Portrait of a pioneer.* London: Routledge.

Froebel, Friedrich. (1896). *The education of man.* New York: Appleton.

Gardner, Howard. (1985). *Frames of mind: The theory of multiple intelligence.* New York: Basic Books.

Gesell, Arnold. The significance of the nursery school. *Childhood Education, 1,* (1), 11-20.

Greenberg, Polly. (1990, September). Head Start–Part of a multi-pronged anti-poverty effort for children and their families. . .Before the beginning: A participant's view. *Young Children, 45,* (6), 41-52.

Isaacs, Susan. (1968). *The nursery years.* New York: Schocken Books.

Johnson, Harriet. (1928). *Children in the nursery school.* New York: John Day.

Kohlberg, Lawrence, & Lickona, Thomas. (1986). *The stages of ethical development: From childhood through old age*. New York: Harper Books.

McMillan, Margaret. (1919). *The nursery school*. New York: E.P. Dutton.

Montessori, Maria. (1967). *The Montessori method*. (Anne E. George, trans.) Cambridge, MA.

Paciorek, Karen, & Munro, Joyce. (Eds.). (1996). Sources: *Notable selections in early childhood education*. Guilford, CT: Dushkin Publishing Group. (Selections from writings by many of the early theorists and practitioners, such as Abigail Eliot, Katherine Read, Elizabeth Peabody, Patty Smith Hill, Friedrich Froebel, Lucy Sprague Mitchell, Maria Montessori, Harriet Johnson, John Dewey, Susan Blow, Margaret McMillan, Arnold Gesell, Robert Owen, G. Stanley Hall.)

Reeves, Carolyn, Howard, Esther, & Grace, Cathy. (1990, Fall). A model preschool: London's Rachel McMillan Nursery School. *Dimensions, 19,* (1), 10-13.

Zinsser, C. (1988). The best day care there ever was. In *Early Childhood Education 88/89*. Guilford, CT: Dushkin Publishing Group.

THE MODERN PROFESSION

As we consider the modern emergence of the early childhood profession, it is both surprising and exciting to realize that you are entering this field only about thirty years into the modern era. That era began with the establishment of Head Start, an event that signaled a new period of interest in the importance of early childhood education. Head Start was also a reflection of the social currents that demanded equality for racial minorities and women, and that emphasized the need to expand the field of child care and early education.

Thirty years is a relatively brief period when the development of a profession is considered. As we shall see, it took some time before early childhood leaders questioned how teaching young children compared with other professions, and how unity could strengthen the efforts of the field: the discussions that guided some of the developments that will be described in this chapter. And it is really only in the past decade that dialogues, institutes, position statements, and other pronouncements by professional groups have given early childhood practitioners substantive evidence that there are indeed unifying ideas and issues that help the profession continue to evolve.

The concept of a profession suggests that there is already unity and consensus. However, as you have already realized, early childhood practitioners have likely come to their work via different entry points and varied training, traditions, and preparation. And the work they do is itself very different. This diversity is atypical of many other professions. This chapter will continue to demonstrate this diversity to you, as we trace the various steps that have been taken to define cohesive knowledge and practices in an evolving profession.

IS EARLY CHILDHOOD EDUCATION A PROFESSION?

Sarah C. works as an assistant in a classroom for toddlers. She took the job because it was advertised in her local newspaper, and she thought it might be fun for a while. She has no training beyond the orientation given by her director for new staff, and no plans to get anything beyond the sixteen hours of workshops she is required to attend each year by her state child care licensing requirements. Eventually she'd like to study interior design.

Tom B. is a Head Start teacher. He took the job of assistant several years ago, after volunteering when his daughter attended a Head Start program. He liked the teaching, and decided to stay and take advantage of the CDA training offered. He has recently earned the CDA credential, and is considering beginning work on a four-year degree, so that he will be certified to teach in his state's elementary schools. This would offer him better salary and benefits.

Mary A. is the lead teacher in a multi-age preschool classroom. She completed an associate of arts degree in early childhood education at her local community college, which she attended immediately after graduating from high school.

Rachel F. is a family child care provider. Originally trained as a data entry operator, she began her center so that she could be at home while her own children were young. While she is currently active in her local family child care provider organization and has completed a short training program for home care providers, she plans eventually to return to data entry.

Martha H. has almost completed a master's degree in early childhood education. After five years in preschool classrooms, she has just accepted a promotion that includes doing some administration as well as staff training at her center.

Towanya B. is a teacher aide in a second grade classroom. Her major duties include individual tutoring in reading and checking the children's work. She is a high school graduate with one semester of college general education courses.

Susanne S. teaches a K-2 mixed-age grouping in a private school.

Are these all early childhood professionals? What criteria did you use to decide whether they were professionals? Keep these criteria in mind as we continue our discussion of professionalism.

All of these individuals represent the complexity of discussing early childhood education as a profession. Working in different strands of the field, with varying educational and training backgrounds, and quite separate goals, these stories illustrate the breadth that must be included in any discussion about early childhood as a profession.

Throughout this book, we have been using the term "profession" to refer to those who are involved in teaching in the early years. This is, in fact, the terminology being used by leaders in the field during the current discussions. For example, Sue Bredekamp, Director of Professional Development for NAEYC, clarifies her use of the term "early childhood professional": "The term early childhood professional or early childhood educator is used here to refer to individuals who are responsible for the care and education of children, birth through age eight, in centers, homes, and schools, and others who support that delivery of service" (Bredekamp, 1992, p. 52) (see Fig. 9-1). Whether or not

1978
The world's first test-tube baby–Baby Louise–is born in England.

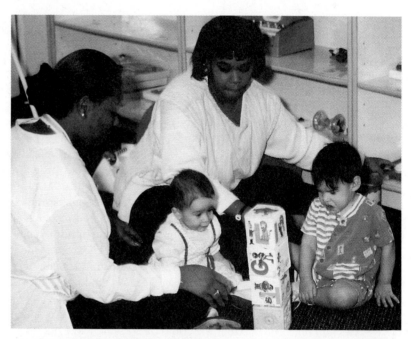

Figure 9-1 | **Early childhood professionals are those who are responsible for the care of education of children birth through age 8, in centers, homes, and schools.**

early childhood education is truly a profession is something that has been debated in recent years.

Milly Almy (1988) has stated flatly that, although the early educator role requires professional attitudes and behaviors, it does not meet the standards for a profession. "With its shaky knowledge base, its ambiguous clientele, and its lack of a code of ethics, early childhood education qualifies only as an occupation or, at best, a semiprofession" (Almy, 1988, p. 50). (Note: We shall see that the lack of a code of ethics has been remedied since her statement.) Almy describes early childhood educators as "double specialists"; these double specialities include both teaching young children and assessing their development,

THEORY INTO PRACTICE

This is Debbie Wolfe. Debbie has been in the field of early education for ten years, including several years when she operated a registered family child care home while working on courses at a community college, and doing clinical work. She has also been a director of a small half-day program at her church, has completed an associate's degree in early childhood education, has nearly completed the course work for her bachelor's and licensure in Birth-Kindergarten in her state. Currently she is the director of a well-established program that includes both half- and full-day children.

What has been a significant frustration for you in early education? How do you deal with it?

A great frustration is the constant interruptions in the course of my work, things like mopping up from a backed up toilet and every other horror story you hear. What I sometimes wonder is what does this have to do with caring for children? Luckily, I work with a great bunch of people, so I can blow off steam jokingly with them, and know that those logistical things have to be done for children to be cared for in any program.

What is one thing you learned in classes that you really discovered to be true when you started working with children?

I truly believe that it is very important to give children choices. Choices empower people of all ages. Everybody wants to have choices and not be told what they have to do.

What is an area you are working on now to learn more about?

I keep learning more about working with families, to be able to remember that I cannot work independently without considering the other environments of children, in the family and the community. I have to learn to work with families, not isolated with children only.

Why have you stayed in early education?

I stay in early education because I think families need to be such a priority in our culture and our society. In order for that to happen, people need to be in this field. We can't just talk about it. We can't just be wanting the best for our family, without recognizing it has to be the best for all families. Also for selfish reasons—it works really well for me.

What is a comment or piece of advice you would give to those beginning to work in early childhood education?

I would strongly suggest that people entering the field do all the work they can, volunteering to get experience with children, going beyond just what they have to do in practicums. In every way explore the work deeply, find all the frustrations. If this is what you want and what you are able to do, go for it. You won't really know fully what the work involves until you do it.

working with children and with adults, and thinking concretely in practice, and formally, in theory. This certainly sounds like demanding work for something she claims is not a profession.

Ade (1982) agreed that the unique characteristics associated with professional status included "specialized knowledge, a desirable service, and an assurance of quality, dependability, and effectiveness" (p. 25) were lacking in early childhood, but that certain changes in the field could help move it closer to professionalization. The changes he identified are: to require a greater familiarity with the field's knowledge base, thus increasing the specialized knowledge needed to practice and extending the length of the training period; to identify and establish uniform criteria for admitting new members, including entry criteria for training and content of training; to develop the kind of practitioner licensing system that would ensure meeting of criteria and exclusion of those who do not meet the criteria; to gain internal control of the licensing system to allow members to have input for requirements and thus greater self-regulation; and to obtain stronger voices with parents and other decision-makers to determine needs and the provision of appropriate services to meet those needs. These are all steps in which NAEYC discussions on professionalism are focused.

Spodek et al. (1988) suggest that professional is a term used in a variety of ways, including: (1) individuals who are paid to do a certain work without implication of level of skill, (2) those "with a high degree of skill and competence," (p. 7), but more often implying, (3) one of the "learned professions" in which there is a high degree of training involved, and that usually involves mental rather than physical work. The fields that require less preparation, and therefore often have lower levels of status, include teaching, social work, and counseling, might be called semiprofessions, having some but not all of the attributes of true professions.

Lilian Katz (1995) suggests that eight criteria must be met before an occupation can be classifed as a profession, and that those in the early childhood community must work to gain consensus and take needed steps in the following areas:

1. Social Necessity

   The work of a profession is essential to the well-being of a society, and society would be weakened if the profession did not function. There are few in the early childhood field who do not believe in the absolute importance of the nurturance and development of children in the first eight years of life. Increasingly, public attention and support has been drawn to this truth by the advocacy efforts of practitioners (see Fig. 9-2). The longitudinal studies on effects of early education (Lazar et al., 1977) offer empirical evidence about these previously more subjective ideas. But the lack of public respect and fiscal support for early childhood programs suggests that the full necessity of these supports for children and families is imperfectly understood by society.

2. Altruism

   The purpose of a profession is said to be altruistic when it is directed towards service instead of profits, and performed unselfishly with an

Conservationists have their societies: Friends of the Sea Otter... Friends of the Earth. Childhood also is in some danger of extinction. Young children are an endangered species. A good program will make a bold, defiant claim:
We are friends of little children
–James Hymes

1979
The "Year of the Child" is officially named by the United Nations.

| Figure 9-2 | **Increasingly, public attention has been drawn to the social necessity of nurturing young children's development.** |

emphasis on social goals. From the beginning, early childhood education has been grounded in principles of social improvement of the lives of children and families. Early childhood teachers certainly rank highly in this characteristic of professionalism, since their salaries could be said to be truly sacrificial, and their concerns are with children and families.

3. Autonomy

Professionals are said to be autonomous when clients do not dictate what services are to be delivered, or how they are to be delivered. Early childhood teachers are in the somewhat complex position of defining children, parents, and society as clients, and are challenged by trying to respond to various opposing ideas about goals and methods for practice. For example, what about the situation when parental demands suggest curriculum that teachers feel is not in children's developmental interests? Or when the community defines family support systems that seem to usurp parental roles? Early childhood teachers are often caught in the middle, forced to respond to ideas that limit their autonomy. Often under the direction of school boards that argue for standards that teachers feel may not be in children's best interests, or licensing requirements dictated by laypeople in the legislature, early childhood teachers are a long way from having the kind of autonomy that allows them to decide independently on optimum educational directions.

4. Distance from Client

Since the practice of a profession requires applying knowledge to particular situations involving individuals, the relationship between professionals and those served is expected to be distinguished by emotional distance that would prevent clouded judgement. In this tradition, for example, doctors are not expected to treat members of their own

1979
Kinder-Care Centers in the United States and Canada number 459, making it the largest child care program.

| Figure 9-3 | An "optimum distance" allows teachers to be compassionate and caring as well as to exercise professional judgement. |

families. Many teachers in early education question this aspect of professionalism, noting that it is more important to meet children's needs for closeness and affection than to create professional distance. Early childhood teachers struggle with the idea of creating caring relationships with children and families while maintaining some distance that is helpful to all parties. Katz notes that maintaining an "optimum distance" allows teachers to be compassionate and caring as well as to exercise professional judgement, while protecting teachers from the dangers of emotional overinvolvement and burnout (see Fig. 9-3).

5. Code of Ethics

A profession requires conformity to standards that are defined by a **code of ethics**. This code is adopted by all members of the profession to ensure that there will be uniformly high standards of acceptable conduct. In addition, there is a professional body that institutes procedures for ensuring that members do not violate this code. NAEYC, after working through through various stages to gain consensus, adopted and published a Code of Ethics in 1989. The fact is that many practitioners are still likely unaware of the Code's existence, and there is no means

Code of Ethics: Statements of a profession that govern moral behavior and ethical decisions. NAEYC published the early childhood Code of Ethics in 1989.

1980
United States has the highest percentage of children living in poverty of all western nations, a figure which continues to rise throughout the 80s and 90s.

of enforcing or disciplining those who violate its precepts. Nevertheless, the discussions that have ensued among professionals during the development of the Code and since, are a part of the process towards defining the issues that unite the profession. A little later in this chapter we will examine the Code and its meaning for early childhood teachers.

6. Standards of Practice

Professions adopt standards of practice to insure that professionals apply uniform procedures and principles in response to typical situations using their best professional judgement, and that no professional's behavior will fall below the standards. One area that is as yet lacking in professionalization of the early childhood field is the identification of a collection of typical situations, as Lilian Katz points out in her classic discussion about how a professional early childhood teacher would teach in the situation where children are in a conflict over a tricycle (Katz, 1984). But a step towards standards of practice was taken when NAEYC adopted the position statements on developmentally appropriate practice in 1987, and on curriculum and assessment in 1992. The continuing discussions and debate, and the refining of these position statements, will continue to move practitioners towards a profession with clear standards, as well as towards fuller understanding about the nature of their work. The position statements will be explored further in this chapter.

Zeal without knowledge is fire without light
—Thomas Fuller

7. Prolonged Training

A major characteristic of a profession is that entrants are required to undergo extensive training, with requirements for entry that screen out individuals. The training is specialized and contains a common core of knowledge. The training is also expected to be difficult. By stretching cognitive abilities, it is more extensive than daily practice requires, and it is offered by accredited training institutions. In addition, regular continuing education is systematically required of the profession's practitioners.

As you will recall from our examples at the beginning of this chapter, there are enormous variations in the amounts and types of pre-service and in-service training required of early childhood teachers, ranging from almost nothing at all to advanced degrees. Further, because of the shortages of caregivers, trained or otherwise, there are virtually no entry requirements for practitioners, other than age and minimal literacy, in many settings. In too many cases, quality of programs is compromised by the lack of training and the acceptance of unprepared and unqualified workers. This is a complex dilemma that relates to some of the challenges regarding wages and status of the work that were discussed in Chapter Seven. As we consider the early childhood profession's career lattice plan later in Chapter Ten, we will see the attempt to respond to the varying entry points and training

1980
Of the 12.6 million children living with only one parent, 92 percent of them live with their mothers.

options that presently exist in the field, while facilitating professional-ization for all employed in programs for young children.

8. Specialized Knowledge

There is fairly universal agreement that a profession is work that involves specialized knowledge, and skills that are based on a system-atic body of principles. The knowledge is abstract, relevant to practice and expressed in very technical terminology; and exclusive, known only to those who have been trained in the profession, and unknown to laypersons. Inasmuch as developmentally appropriate practice is an attempt to base decisions on best practices for young children on child development research and current knowledge about learning, this offers a body of specialized knowledge to trained early childhood teachers. When, however, untrained teachers base their actions on good will and "what comes naturally," they are likely using the best intuitions about childrearing that parents and laypeople have used for generations.

. . . the problem for childcare workers is that the care of normal pre-schoolers is very "familiar to everyone," and especially to their parent-clients. Thus for early childhood education, the main struggle with clients is . . . to be acknowledged as "professional". . . — to make the status leap from "babysitter" to "educator" (Joffe, 1977, p. 22).

It is not surprising, therefore, that when these teachers base their actions on intuition, they do not garner the professional respect that they deserve.

In considering these eight characteristics of being a profession, you can see that the idea of a semiprofession, or not quite achieving full professional status, has some validity. It is hopeful that impressive progress has been made in the past decade or so, and this progress has brought early childhood education closer to becoming a true profession (see Fig. 9-4).

Professional rather than personal responsibility provides the continuity in children's experience in early childhood programs
—Elizabeth Jones and Gretchen Reynolds

As someone has said, "Saying that you are a professional doesn't make it so; others have to perceive you as professional." Vander Ven (1988) suggests that professionalization refers to the public recognition of and demand for a specialized service that can only be provided by people prepared to do it. It will require the joint efforts of us all to make this kind of professionalism a reality. And it is this movement towards professionalism that will overcome some of the challenges discussed in Chapter Seven.

Spodek et al. (1988) define seven questions that need to be the focus of efforts towards professionalism. These are questions that we will find partial answers to in this and the following chapters.

1. How do we establish standards of quality for practitioners in the field?

2. What standards of early childhood professionalism are reasonable in our field?

3. How should entry to the field be determined?

1982
Mary Ainsworth continues the discussion of attachment in infancy, in "Early Caregiving and Later Patterns of Attachment."

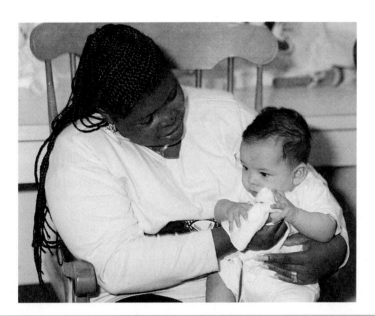

| Figure 9-4 | **As early educators perceive themselves as being part of a profession, they will help increase public recognition of the worth of their work.** |

4. Should the field of early childhood education become more inclusive or more exclusive?

5. How should standards be applied and by whom?

6. How should gender and economic issues be dealt with?

7. How do we define professional knowledge and values?

Silin (1985) injects a cautionary note into these discussions about professionalism, noting that "early childhood education has a unique history that needs to be taken into account when exploring these issues" (p. 42). He suggests that our authority as professionals is not based on knowledge of child development alone, but is also based on moral, ethical, and esthetic notions about what is right and true, knowledge that is not highly valued in our society. Thus too much emphasis on a search for professional status through emphasizing "pedagogic reforms or technical knowledge" (p. 45) might deflect attention from relevant questions about the need for socioeconomic and philosophical changes in society at large.

While the discussion about professionalism is ongoing, it is worth noting that even some leaders in the field recognize both these kinds of concerns, as well as the benefits inherent in the idea of professionalizing. Concerns include: the possibility of becoming separated from contact with children, as happens when increased qualifications and status are associated with positions that remove early childhood professionals from the classroom; parents' concern that increasing training and professionalism of early childhood teachers will mean increasing institutionalization and uncaring environments for children; a wish

1982
The House Select Committee on Children, Youth, and Families is established.

1 – Specialized knowledge
2 – General knowledge
3 – Type of supervision

No specialized knowledge. Requires direct supervision for effective practice.

Has knowledge and skills needed for effective practice. Requires occasional supervision, although may supervise others.

Increasing breadth and depth of specialized and general knowledge. Takes opportunities to generate new knowledge and skills. Supervises others.

Adapted from A "New" Paradigm of Early Childhood Professional Development by B. Willer & S. Bredekamp, 1993, May, *Young Children, 48* (4), 63-66.

Figure 9-5   Continuum of professionalization.

to avoid the hierarchical systems that result when distinctions are made between nonprofessionals, paraprofessionals and more highly trained professionals; the increased cost of services that comes with improved compensation and that is necessary for raising the level of professionalism; and the possiblity of excluding individuals who typically are denied access to higher education because of economic factors, yet who are needed in early childhood education to represent the cultural diversity of our society.

But the advantages of enhancing professionalism are unmistakable. They include: better care and education for children resulting from a shared knowledge base; consistency across the settings, and developmental continuity between programs; ethical behavior; shared meanings and expanded knowledge; and improved compensation (Bredekamp and Willer, 1993).

An interesting thought related to professionalism is provided by Willer and Bredekamp (1993) that is inclusive of the variety of configurations of experience, training, and entry into the early childhood field. Drawing particular lines to show acceptable criteria for entry into the field will "always be too high for some and too low for others, and as the field changes over time, it will likely become obsolete" (Willer and Bredekamp, 1993, p. 64). So it may be more useful to focus on the process of "professionalizing" rather than defining the product "professional"; this assumes that everyone who works with young children is involved in a process of professional development. They offer us a diagrammatic model (see Fig. 9-5) with three interrelated dimensions of professionalizing–specialized knowledge, general knowledge, and professional supervision–and suggest that every early childhood educator be able to locate themselves and their efforts at professionalization somewhere on the continuum.

As a beginning teacher, it is probably important that, at the same time that you recognize there is work to be done in the profession as a whole, you begin to think of yourself as a member of a profession that has made–and continues to make–major contributions to American families and society. This will allow you to begin with a personal sense of self-respect, enable you to represent the educated and articulate practitioners who work to gain public recognition of the value of early childhood education. Your program of training will help you see how your own competence and knowledge is developing as you progress through courses and practicums. You will see your own movement on the continuum towards increasingly professional behavior and attitudes. Where do you think you are on the continuum at this point? Thus you can work more effectively with children and families as time goes by, truly representing the best of professional practice, and also contribute to this growing profession. What an exciting time to join us!

PROFESSIONAL ORGANIZATIONS

As you know from reading the last chapter, professional organizations appeared early in the kindergarten and nursery school traditions in the United States. The American Froebel Union established in 1878 was probably the first national professional early childhood organization, followed in 1892 by the International Kindergarten Union, later to become the Association of Childhood Education International (ACEI). With the advent of the nursery school and nursery education, a separate organization was formed, The National Association of Nursery Education, the precursor of the modern National Association for the Education of Young Children (NAEYC). As a growing professional, you will want to become familiar with the various professional early childhood organizations that exist today nationally and regionally, to learn how they can support your development as an early educator, and how you can contribute to their efforts. Because of the leadership that is being exercised on many fronts by NAEYC, you will find that organization's current work discussed here to a great extent. Nevertheless, all of the professional organizations have important roles in increasing professionalism and quality practice. In addition to the organizations listed here, there are organizations for various regions and special interest groups, such as church-sponsored child care, those interested in home schooling, for-profit child care, and so on, that you may want to find out more about.

Association for Childhood Education International

The professional early childhood organization with the oldest roots, ACEI, has membership that includes professionals who work with ages ranging from infancy through early adolescence. Current national membership is about 11,000, and is largely drawn from kindergarten and elementary school teachers. An annual national study conference is held, in addition to regional workshops and a summer world conference. ACEI has a number of state associations and local branches, as well as more than 150 branches around the world. ACEI has published a number of position statements, and maintains a library of publications. ACEI also has a representative at the United Nations supporting their policies and missions. The journal *Childhood Education,* available to members only, is published five times a year, and includes articles that relate to interna-

1983

Publication of *A Nation at Risk,* a report on American schools that precipitated discussion about needed reforms.

tional and intercultural issues and practice with a wide range of ages. The *Journal of Research in Childhood Education* is research-oriented. See if your college library has these journals. For more information contact: ACEI, 11501 Georgia Avenue, Suite 315, Wheaton, Maryland, 20902, (800) 423-3563.

World Organization for Early Education

The World Organization for Early Education, established in 1948, is known by the French title of Organisation Modial pour l'Education Prescolaire (OMEP). Its goals are to encourage the study and education of young children, and to assist those working with young children to learn of their needs, by sharing information among educators throughout the world. OMEP focuses on elements of education, development, health and nutrition, materials, and environments. An international assembly is held every two years. OMEP also works with UNESCO on projects of joint concern. Biennial conferences are held in various sites throughout the world. The organization's journal is the *International Journal of Early Childhood Education.*

National Association for the Education of Young Children

For those of us who have been trained to believe in teaching as "direct instruction" only, the idea of teaching as reflection-on-action may be hard to swallow; yet it is a significant aspect of a teacher's professional functioning. It is the level at which experts operate in all professions
—Selma Wasserman

The largest of the early childhood organizations, the National Association for the Education of Young Children (NAEYC), functions in a number of distinct ways. It offers professional development opportunities to early childhood educators, all designed to improve the quality of services to children from birth through age eight. The organization has two major goals: to facilitate improvements in the professional practice of early childhood education; and to increase public understanding and support for high quality programs for young children and their families (Smith, 1987). From the very beginning, the association has been committed to a multidisciplinary association: "the founders included nursery school people, pediatricians, home economists, social workers, nurses, and child development researchers" (Smith, 1987, p. 33). Current membership includes child care workers, Head Start teachers, family child care providers, elementary school teachers, academic researchers and college teachers from the United States and other countries as well, with membership numbering about 90,000. In past decades, NAEYC has offered an increasingly strong voice on behalf of children's issues and the adults who support children. The organization has become such a visible lobbyist that, during the efforts to pass the Child Development Block Grant (then called ABC) legislation in 1990, one senator asked that NAEYC "call off their troops," claiming that their membership was swamping his phone lines!

The following list includes some of NAEYC's services, for members and the profession at large.

Young Children. NAEYC's journal, begun over fifty years ago, is published bimonthly, and presents current research, theory, and up-to-date information on superior classroom practice. Issues for advocacy and updates on legislative action are presented. You will likely find that your college library has issues of

1984
FCC removes all guidelines for general program content and abolishes limits on advertising on television programs for young people.

Young Children, which you will find very helpful in doing research for classroom assignments. Begin the habit now of keeping up-to-date by regularly reading *Young Children.* The *Early Childhood Research Quarterly* is the research publication of NAEYC.

Publications. Over 100 books are published by NAEYC, on a variety of topics of current interest. The books include curriculum ideas and resources as well as current research. Those who choose NAEYC's comprehensive membership automatically receive major new publications each year. In addition, NAEYC publishes a variety of educational brochures useful for distribution to parents, policymakers, and beginning professionals, posters, and instructional videos. A catalog detailing these materials is issued twice a year. You will most likely want to take advantage of these resources as you study and move into your own classroom.

Information Services. In addition to the journal and other publications, NAEYC maintains a public policy information service as well as a centralized source of information sharing, distribution, and collaboration, available also by electronic delivery system.

Affiliate Groups. Over 450 **affiliate groups** exist in regions, states, cities, and colleges all over the country. Often the membership fee you pay will include membership in both state and national groups. The local affiliates provide opportunities for networking and in-service training, as well as create working groups to tackle local issues and advocacy efforts. Many affiliates sponsor their own annual study conferences–check the Calendar of Conferences in each issue of *Young Children.* One of the activities sponsored by many affiliate groups includes a Week of the Young Child, designated in April each year for over 25 years, to call public attention to the needs and importance of the early childhood years (see Fig. 9-6). Investigate where your nearest local affiliate AEYC group is, and what their current activities are.

> **Affiliate Groups:** Local, state or regional branches of professional organizations, such as ACEI and NAEYC.

Annual Conference. An annual conference is held in a major American city each year, usually in late November. This conference offers opportunities to choose among hundreds of workshops, seminars and keynote speeches by leaders in the early childhood field. Attended by over 20,000, this conference offers an image of the complexity of the work done by the thousands of professionals who work with young children. It also demonstrates the full power possible in the collective efforts when early childhood practitioners work together to improve policies and programs. Make it a goal to try to attend an annual conference. You will find the variety of opportunities for learning, interaction, and networking to be truly inspiring for your professional growth.

Position Statements. Beginning in the 1980s, NAEYC has sought to support and unify early childhood professionals by issuing a number of position state-

1984
Mister Rogers' Neighborhood celebrates its 21st year.

| Figure 9-6 | **Many communities hold special events during the Week of the Young Child, such as this Family Fun Fair, to draw community attention to children's issues and the importance of good early childhood education.** |

ments. These philosophical papers offer guidance to those who design programs and policies of the highest quality to benefit young children. The position statements include: Developmentally appropriate practice (DAP) in early childhood programs serving children from birth through age eight (1987); Standardized Testing of Young Children Three through Eight Years of Age (1987); Code of Ethics and Statement of Commitment (1989; 1992); School Readiness (1990); Guidelines for Compensation of Early Childhood Professionals (1990; 1993); Guidelines for Appropriate Curriculum Content and Assessment in Programs Serving Children Ages Three through Eight (1990); Conceptual Framework for Early Childhood Professional Development (1993); Violence in the Lives of Children (1993); and numerous others. A full listing of all position statements is available entitled *NAEYC Position Statements* (1994). As you become familiar with these position statements, you will see how much information, assistance, and support is available from NAEYC for individual early childhood practitioners.

In addition to the position statements, NAEYC has two ongoing initiatives that will impact professional growth and development. These are the **Quality, Compensation, and Affordability** initiatives, and the National Institute for Professional Development. We will hear more about these programs in coming chapters.

Quality, Compensation, and Affordability: An initiative sponsored by NAEYC, to draw attention to correlations between staff compensation and the factors that produce quality in programs.

Membership Action Grants. NAEYC uses available contributions and funding sources to fund small grants to members annually. These members apply

1984

The Ecumenical Child Care Network is established as an outcome of a study of churches affiliated with the National Council of Churches, revealing the great extent to which churches had become the country's providers of child care.

| Figure 9-7 | **A certificate of accreditation is a recognized symbol of quality in a program. (Courtesy of Open Door School, Charlotte, NC)** |

for funds to stimulate projects within their local communities that can benefit children and the quality of programs available to them and their families.

NATIONAL ACADEMY OF EARLY CHILDHOOD PROGRAMS

Since 1985, NAEYC has administered a national, voluntary **accreditation** system for early childhood programs and schools. The accreditation system was designed to meet two major goals: to help early childhood professionals make real and lasting improvements in the quality of the programs serving young children; and to evaluate the quality of the program for the purpose of accrediting the programs that substantially comply with the criteria for high-quality programs (Bredekamp, 1991). The familiar position statement on DAP (1987) was developed in order to make even more explicit some of the desired criteria in the self-study and validation visit. It was found that the accreditation documents used terminology like "developmentally appropriate activities" which were open to a variety of interpretations until the position statement clarified more precise meanings.

Through a process of self-study, guided by the NAEYC publication *Accreditation Criteria and Procedures* for the **National Academy of Early Childhood Programs** (Bredekamp, 1991), administrators, staff, and parents work on constructive improvements to create high-quality programs, whose excellence is then verified by NAEYC (see Fig. 9-7). The process of self-study involves taking an in-depth, honest, and critical look at a program, using an Early Childhood Observation booklet developed by NAEYC, parent surveys, staff surveys, and discussion about the findings of all of these. The criteria for accreditation of the program examine:

Accreditation: A system of voluntary evaluation of excellence in early childhood centers, administered by the National Academy for Early Childhood Education, and established by NAEYC.

Bredekamp, 1987

National Academy of Early Childhood Programs: The body within NAEYC that administers the voluntary accreditation system for child care programs.

1985

Parents as Teachers program operates through the Missouri state school systems, offering parental information and support in a program designed by Dr. Burton White.

▶ interaction among staff and children;

▶ curriculum;

▶ staff-parent interaction;

▶ staff qualifications and development;

▶ administrative procedures;

▶ staffing patterns;

▶ physical environment;

▶ provision for health and safety;

▶ provision of nutrition and food services; and

▶ assessment of program effectiveness.

Most staff who have participated in this self-study process find that it gives them the vehicle they need to facilitate discussion of philosophical similarities and differences (Norris, 1994). Then needed improvements are implemented. The self-study process and improvement of practices often takes up to a year or longer. The center completes a written program description to send to the Academy. When the Academy determines that the standards have been met, a validation visit is scheduled. Validators are volunteer early childhood professionals who have been trained to visit classrooms and examine programs. When, after spending time observing in the classrooms and asking questions of staff, the validators agree that most of the criteria on which the center has rated itself have been validated, their recommendation to the Academy is that the program should be accredited. Accreditation is valid for three years, after which centers go through substantially the same process for reaccreditation (National Academy, 1990).

Currently, well over 4,000 programs nationwide are accredited, and thousands more are involved in self-study. Look at the map in Fig. 9-8 to see how many accredited centers there are in your state. Whatever the number, it is still only a small percentage of the programs that need to become involved in improving the quality of their offerings for children and families. Hopefully, you will have opportunities to observe and work in accredited programs, or to influence programs to consider using the self-study process as a means to improvement.

Why should centers go through the accreditation process? Those who have, point to the personal and professional growth of staff, as they have the opportunity to learn about the real meaning of standards for a developmentally appropriate program. The process is invaluable to a quality program that is recognized for having the highest standards, and for being one of a minority nationally. As one director said, "We knew we were good, but comparing oneself positively to nationally accepted standards of quality is a real ego boost. . . . Our quality has been verified and our excellence recognized" (Norris, 1994, pp. 72-73). The teachers in the program go on record for excellence, and know they are making an excellent offering to parents, children, and the community. Having excellent programs within the community gives the public a model of what early childhood education should look like.

As you have read about the work of professional organizations, it should be obvious that there are many resources and a varied number of

There is more to teaching than meets the senses, and this includes the feelings, ideas, values, beliefs, and intentions and other unseen but present territory of the minds of children and teachers
—Margaret Yonemura

1985
NAEYC establishes a voluntary accreditation system for centers.

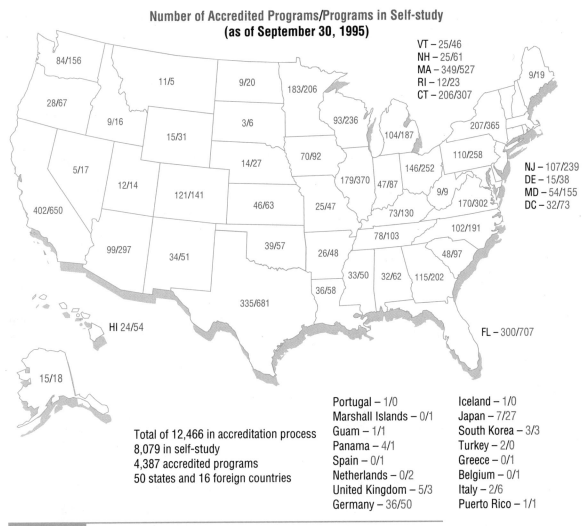

Number of Accredited Programs/Programs in Self-study
(as of September 30, 1995)

VT – 25/46
NH – 25/61
MA – 349/527
RI – 12/23
CT – 206/307

9/19

84/156

11/5   9/20   183/206

207/365

28/67

9/16   3/6   93/236

110/258

15/31   104/187

NJ – 107/239
DE – 15/38
MD – 54/155
DC – 32/73

14/27   70/92   146/252

5/17   179/370   47/87

12/14   121/141   9/9   170/302

402/650   46/63   25/47   73/130

102/191

99/297   39/57   78/103

34/51   26/48   48/97

33/50   32/62   115/202

36/58

335/681

HI 24/54

FL – 300/707

15/18

Portugal – 1/0   Iceland – 1/0
Marshall Islands – 0/1   Japan – 7/27
Guam – 1/1   South Korea – 3/3
Panama – 4/1   Turkey – 2/0
Spain – 0/1   Greece – 0/1
Netherlands – 0/2   Belgium – 0/1
United Kingdom – 5/3   Italy – 2/6
Germany – 36/50   Puerto Rico – 1/1

Total of 12,466 in accreditation process
8,079 in self-study
4,387 accredited programs
50 states and 16 foreign countries

Figure 9-8   **How many accredited centers are there in your state? (NAEYC October 1992–September 1993. Numbers of accredited programs/programs in self-study. NAEYC Annual Report)**

vehicles for early childhood educators to achieve professionalization, both as individuals and with colleagues. Keeping aware of what the professional organizations are doing is critical for this growth. Make sure that one of the first things you do, as a student or new teacher, is to join a professional organization.

OTHER PROFESSIONAL ORGANIZATIONS

Other professional organizations you may contact to learn more about their particular focus and membership benefits include:

1985
Of mothers of children under age six, 52.1 percent are in the work force.

Southern Association on Children Under Six, Box 5403 Brady Station, Little Rock, AR 72205 (annual conference, journal *Dimensions);*

National Head Start Association, 201 N. Union Street, Suite 320, Alexandria, VA 22314 (annual and regional conferences);

Society for Research in Child Development, 100 North Carolina Avenue SE, Suite 1, Washington, DC 20003;

The Children's Defense Fund, 122 C Street NW, Washington DC 20001;

National Council of Churches Ecumenical Child Care Network, 475 Riverside Drive, Room 572, New York, NY;

School-Age Child Care Project, Wellesley College, Center for Research on Women, Wellesley, MA 02181;

The American Montessori Society, 150 Fifth Avenue, #203, New York, NY 10011 (212)924-3209;

Association Montessori International, 170 Scholfield Road, Rochester, NY 14617 (716)544-6708;

North American Montessori Teachers' Association, 11424 Bellflower Road, NE, Cleveland, OH 44106 (216)421-1905;

National Black Child Development Institute, 1463 Rhode Island Avenue NW, Washington, DC 20005 (annual conference);

National Association for Family Child Care, 1331A Pennsylvania Avenue NW, Washington, DC 20004, 800-359-3817 (accreditation system, annual conference);

National Education Association, 1201 16th Street NW, Washington, DC 20009;

Parent Cooperative Preschool International, 9111 Alton Parkway, Silver Spring, MD 20910;

Council for Exceptional Children, 1920 Association Drive, Reston, VA 22091. (journal *Teaching Exceptional Children*).

CODE OF ETHICS

In the discussion earlier in this chapter about the characteristics of a profession, it was noted that a profession has a code of ethics. NAEYC has given the early childhood profession such a code; we will examine that code and its importance here. Early childhood teachers are frequently faced with dilemmas about their actions.

What would you do when a parent demands to know who bit their child?

What would you do when a coworker complains to you about another coworker's treatment of a child?

What would you do when a neighbor tells you she's heard bad things about the last center you worked in?

What is your responsibility when another teacher tells you of symptoms she's seen that make her suspicious of child abuse, but that she is afraid to report?

When you work in early childhood classrooms, you will be asked to make many decisions about appropriate behavior. Some of these decisions will be not answerable only on the basis of your accumulated knowedge of child development or educational practice. Some of them pose genuine moral dilemmas,

The teacher who wishes to be more than a functionary cannot escape the value problem or the difficult matter of moral choice

—Maxine Greene

1985
According to Census Bureau statistics, one out of every four children live with only one parent.

where you have to weigh your actions carefully in considering the various parties involved. The issues raised above, and others like them, are answered only by considering professional ethics, or the system of morals that defines a profession's proper work practices. A code of ethics is "a set of statements that helps us to deal with the temptations inherent in our occupations, . . . helps us to act in terms of that which we believe to be right rather than what is expedient–especially when doing what we believe is right carries risks" (Katz, 1991, p. 3). Such risks could be losing a job or alienating others with whom one must work. A code expresses the profession's belief about correct, rather than expedient, behavior; about good, rather than merely practical, actions; about what professionals must never do or condone, for the good and protection of those they serve.

The value in having an explicit code is that members have a document that helps them go past their individual intuitions and beliefs to focus on core professional values; "it is not so much what 'I' care about but rather what the good early childhood educator should care about" (Kipnis, 1987, p. 28). The code can remind teachers of their priorities and responsibilities, and can provide solid guidance and professional support for the decisions and behavior of an individual teacher.

NAEYC developed the Code of Ethical Conduct over a period of time, as they gained insights from many professionals and practitioners. An Ethics Commission was appointed by the NAEYC Board to explore and clarify the early childhood profession's understanding of its ethics. Members were surveyed to learn concerns, workshops were held to identify and explore issues, and were followed by another survey of members to help formulate principles of ethical action. A draft code was further refined, and the final document was approved by NAEYC's Governing Board in July 1989. (You may be interested to know that the National Education Association has had a code of ethics since 1929, for teachers in school systems; however, there is nothing in the current code about parent-teacher relationships, so the NAEYC Code is likely more relevant to your practice in early education.) The preamble states that the focus of the guidelines in the Code is on daily practice with children and their families in programs and classrooms, although many of the provisions also apply to specialists who do not work directly with children (see Fig. 9-9).

In general I have found that regardless of the label–Montessori, Waldorf, Play, Behavioral, or what not–teachers who know young children are much more alike in practice than those who do not
—David Elkind

The National Association for the Education of Young Children Code of Ethical Conduct

NAEYC recognizes that many daily decisions required of those who work with young children are of a moral and ethical nature. The NAEYC Code of Ethical Conduct offers guidelines for responsible behavior and sets forth a common basis for resolving the principal ethical dilemmas encountered in early childhood education. The primary focus is on daily practice with children and their families in programs for children from birth to eight years of age: preschools, child care centers, family day care homes, kindergartens, and primary classrooms. Many of the provisions also apply to specialists who do not work directly with children, including program

1985
A new CDA credential for family child care providers is offered.

Figure 9-9   **The focus on the Code of Ethics is on guidelines for situations that may arise in daily practice with children, families, and colleagues in programs.**

administrators, parent educators, college professors, and child care licensing specialists.

Standards of ethical behavior in early childhood education are based on commitment to core values that are deeply rooted in the history of our field. We have committed ourselves to:

–appreciating childhood as a unique and valuable stage of the human life cycle

–basing our work with children on knowledge of child development

–appreciating and supporting the close ties between the child and family

–recognizing that children are best understood in the context of family, culture, and society

–respecting the dignity, worth, and uniqueness of each individual (child, family member, and colleague)

–helping children and adults achieve their full potential in the context of relationships that are based on trust, respect, and positive regard

The Code sets forth a conception of our professional responsibilities in four sections, each addressing an arena of professional relationships: (1) children, (2) families, (3) colleagues, and (4) community and society. Each section includes an introduction to the primary responsibilities of the early childhood practitioner in that arena, a set of ideals pointing in the direction of exemplary professional practice, and a set of principles defining practices that are required, prohibited, and permitted.

1986

All fifty states are providing financial support for public kindergartens.

The ideals reflect the aspirations of practitioners. The principles are intended to guide conduct and assist practitioners in resolving ethical dilemmas encountered in the field. There is not necessarily a corresponding principle for each ideal. Both ideals and principles are intended to direct practitioners to those questions which, when responsibly answered, will provide the basis for conscientious decision making. While the Code provides specific direction for addressing some ethical dilemmas, many others will require the practitioner to combine the guidance of the Code with sound professional judgment.

The ideals and principles in this Code present a shared conception of professional responsibility that affirms our commitment to the core values of our field. The Code publicly acknowledges the responsibilities that we in the field have assumed and in so doing supports ethical behavior in our work. Practitioners who face ethical dilemmas are urged to seek guidance in the applicable parts of this Code and in the spirit that informs the whole.

SECTION I: ETHICAL RESPONSIBILITIES TO CHILDREN

Childhood is a unique and valuable stage in the life cycle. Our paramount responsibility is to provide safe, healthy, nurturing, and responsive settings for children. We are committed to supporting children's development by cherishing individual differences, by helping them learn to live and work cooperatively, and by promoting their self-esteem.

IDEALS

I-1.1 To be familiar with the knowledge base of early childhood education and to keep current through continuing education and in-service training.

I-1.2 To base program practices upon current knowledge in the field of child development and related disciplines and upon particular knowledge of each child.

I-1.3 To recognize and respect the uniqueness and the potential of each child.

I-1.4 To appreciate the special vulnerability of children.

I-1.5 To create and maintain safe and healthy settings that foster children's social, emotional, intellectual, and physical development and that respect their dignity and their contributions.

I-1.6 To support the right of children with special needs to partic-pate, consistent with their ability, in regular childhood programs.

PRINCIPLES

P-1.1 Above all, we shall not harm children. We shall not participate in practices that are disrespectful, degrading, dangerous, exploitative, intimidating, psychologically damaging, or physically harmful to children. **This principle has precedence over all others in this Code.**

P-1.2 We shall not participate in practices that discriminate against children by denying benefits, giving special advantages, or excluding them from programs or activities on the basis of their race, religion, sex, national origin, or the status, behavior, or beliefs of their parents.

1986
One-third of all five-year-olds now attend full-day kindergartens.

(This principle does not apply to programs that have a lawful mandate to provide services to a particular population of children.)

P-1.3 We shall involve all of those with relevant knowledge (including staff and parents) in decisions concerning a child.

P-1.4 When, after appropriate efforts have been made with a child and the family, the child still does not appear to be benefitting from a program, we shall communicate our concern to the family in a positive way and offer them assistance in finding a more suitable setting.

P-1.5 We shall be familiar with the symptoms of child abuse and neglect and know and follow community procedures and state laws that protect children against abuse and neglect.

P-1.6 When we have evidence of child abuse or neglect, we shall report the evidence to the appropriate community agency and follow up to ensure that appropriate action has been taken. When possible, parents will be informed that the referral has been made.

P-1.7 When another person tells us of their suspicion that a child is being abused or neglected but we lack evidence, we shall assist that person in taking appropriate action to protect the child.

P-1.8 When a child protective agency fails to provide adequate protection for abused or neglected children, we acknowledge a collective ethical responsibility to work toward improvement of these services.

P-1.9 When we become aware of a practice or situation that endangers the health or safety of children, but has not been previously known to do so, we have an ethical responsibility to inform those who can remedy the situation and who can keep other children from being similarly endangered.

SECTION II: ETHICAL RESPONSIBILITIES TO FAMILIES

Families are of primary importance in children's development. (The term *family* may include others, besides parents, who are responsibly involved with the child.) Because the family and the early childhood educator have a common interest in the child's welfare, we acknowledge a primary responsibility to bring about collaboration between the home and school in ways that enhance the child's development.

IDEALS

I-2.1 To develop relationships of mutual trust with the families we serve.

I-2.2 To acknowledge and build upon strengths and competencies as we support families in their task of nurturing children.

I-2.3 To respect the dignity of each family and its culture, customs, and beliefs.

I-2.4 To respect families' childrearing values and their right to make decisions for their children.

I-2.5 To interpret each child's progress to parents within the framework of a developmental perspective and to help families understand and appreciate the value of developmentally appropriate early childhood programs.

1986
NAEYC accredits its first center-based early childhood programs—in fact, 137 of them, with 1,000 more preparing for accreditation.

I-2.6 To help family members improve their understanding of their children and to enhance their skills as parents.

I-2.7 To participate in building support networks for families by providing them with opportunities to interact with program staff and families.

PRINCIPLES

P-2.1 We shall not deny family members access to their child's classroom or program setting.

P-2.2 We shall inform families of program philosophy, policies, and personnel qualifications and explain why we teach as we do.

P-2.3 We shall inform families of and, when appropriate, involve them in policy decisions.

P-2.4 We shall inform families of and, when appropriate, involve them in significant decisions affecting their child.

P-2.5 We shall inform the family of accidents involving their child, of risks such as exposures to contagious disease that may result in infection, and of events that might result in psychological damage.

P-2.6 We shall not permit or participate in research that could in any way hinder the education or development of the children in our programs. Families shall be fully informed of any proposed research projects involving their children and shall have the opportunity to give or withhold consent.

P-2.7 We shall not engage in or support exploitation of families. We shall not use our relationship with a family for private advantage or personal gain, or enter into relationships with family members that might impair our effectiveness in working with children.

P-2.8 We shall develop written policies for the protection of confidentiality and the disclosure of children's records. The policy documents shall be made available to all program personnel and families. Disclosure of children's records beyond family members, program personnel, and consultants having an obligation of confidentiality shall require familial consent (except in cases of abuse or neglect).

P-2.9 We shall maintain confidentiality and shall respect the family's right to privacy, refraining from disclosure of confidential information and intrusion into family life. However, when we are concerned about a child's welfare, it is permissible to reveal confidential information to agencies and individuals who may be able to act in the child's interest.

P-2.10 In cases where family members are in conflict we shall work openly, sharing our observations of the child, to help all parties involved make informed decisions. We shall refrain from becoming an advocate for one party.

P-2.11 We shall be familiar with and appropriately use community resources and professional services that support families. After a referral has been made, we shall follow up to ensure that services have been adequately provided.

SECTION III: ETHICAL RESPONSIBILITIES TO COLLEAGUES

In a caring, cooperative workplace human dignity is respected, professional satisfaction is promoted, and positive relationships are modeled.

1986
PL 99-457 The Education of the Handicapped Act Amendments extends educational services to infants and toddlers with special needs, and requires a focus on the family for delivery of services.

Our primary responsibility in this arena is to establish and maintain settings and relationships that support productive work and meet professional needs.

A—RESPONSIBILITIES TO CO-WORKERS: IDEALS

I-3A.1 To establish and maintain relationships of trust and cooperation with co-workers.

I-3A.2 To share resources and information with co-workers.

I-3A.3 To support co-workers in meeting their professional needs and in their professional development.

I-3A.4 To accord co-workers due recognition of professional achievement.

PRINCIPLES

P-3A.1 When we have concern about the professional behavior of a co-worker, we shall first let that person know of our concern and attempt to resolve the matter collegially.

P-3A.2 We shall exercise care in expressing views regarding the personal attributes or professional conduct of co-workers. Statements should be based on firsthand knowledge and relevant to the interests of children and programs.

B—RESPONSIBILITIES TO EMPLOYERS: IDEALS

I-3B.1 To assist the program in providing the highest quality of service.

I-3B.2 To maintain loyalty to the program and uphold its reputation.

PRINCIPLES

P-3B.1 When we do not agree with program policies, we shall first attempt to affect change through constructive action within the organization.

P-3B.2 We shall speak or act on behalf of the organization only when authorized. We shall take care to note when we are speaking for the organization and when we are expressing a personal judgment.

C—RESPONSIBILITIES TO EMPLOYEES: IDEALS

I-3C.1 To promote policies and working conditions that foster competence, well-being, and self-esteem in staff members.

I-3C.2 To create a climate of trust and candor that will enable staff to speak and act in the best interests of children, families, and the field of early childhood education.

I-3C.3 To strive to secure an adequate livelihood for those who work with or on behalf of young children.

PRINCIPLES

P-3C.1 In decisions concerning children and programs, we shall appropriately utilize the training, experience, and expertise of staff members.

P-3C.2 We shall provide staff members with working conditions that permit them to carry out their responsibilities, timely and nonthreatening evaluation procedures, written grievance procedures, constructive feedback, and opportunities for continuing professional development and advancement.

1987
Congress creates National Commission to Prevent Infant Mortality.

P-3C.3 We shall develop and maintain comprehensive written personnel policies that define program standards and, when applicable, that specify the extent to which employees are accountable for their conduct outside the workplace. These policies shall be given to new staff members and shall be available for review by all staff members.

P-3C.4 Employees who do not meet program standards shall be informed of areas of concern and, when possible, assisted in improving their performance.

P-3C.5 Employees who are dismissed shall be informed of the reasons for the termination. When a dismissal is for cause, justification must be based on evidence of inadequate or inappropriate behavior that is accurately documented, current, and available for the employee to review.

P-3C.6 In making evaluations and recommendations, judgments shall be based on fact and relevant to the interests of children and programs.

P-3C.7 Hiring and promotion shall be based solely on a person's record of accomplishment and ability to carry out the responsibilities of the position.

P-3C.8 In hiring, promotion, and provision of training, we shall not participate in any form of discrimination based on race, religion, sex, national origin, handicap, age, or sexual preference. We shall be familiar with laws and regulations that pertain to employment discrimination.

SECTION IV: ETHICAL RESPONSIBILITES TO COMMUNITY AND SOCIETY

Early childhood programs operate within a context of an immediate community made up of families and other institutions concerned with children's welfare. Our responsibilities to the community are to provide programs that meet its needs and to cooperate with agencies and professions that share responsibility for children. Because the larger society has a measure of responsibility for the welfare and protection of children, and because of our specialized expertise in child development, we acknowledge an obligation to serve as a voice of children everywhere.

IDEALS

I-4.1 To provide the community with high-quality, culturally sensitive programs and services.

I-4.2 To promote cooperation among agencies and professions concerned with the welfare of young children, their families, and their teachers.

I-4.3 To work, through education, research, and advocacy, toward an environmentally safe world in which all children are adequately fed, sheltered, and nurtured.

I-4.4 To work, through education, research, and advocacy, toward a society in which all young children have access to quality programs.

I-4.5 To promote knowledge and understanding of young children and their needs. To work toward greater social acknowledgement of children's rights and greater social acceptance of responsibility for their well-being.

1987
Less than 5 percent of the Federal budget is devoted to programs that benefit children.

I-4.6 To support policies and laws that promote the well-being of children and families. To oppose those that impair their well-being. To cooperate with other individuals and groups in these efforts.

I-4.7 To further the professional development of the field of early childhood education and to strengthen its commitment to realizing its core values as reflected in this Code.

PRINCIPLES

P-4.1 We shall communicate openly and truthfully about the nature and extent of services that we provide.

P-4.2 We shall not accept or continue to work in positions for which we are personally unsuited or professionally unqualified. We shall not offer services that we do not have the competence, qualifications, or resources to provide.

P-4.3 We shall be objective and accurate in reporting the knowledge upon which we base our program practices.

P-4.4 We shall cooperate with other professionals who work with children and their families.

P-4.5 We shall not hire or recommend for employment any person who is unsuited for a position with respect to competence, qualifications, or character.

P-4.6 We shall report the unethical or incompetent behavior of a colleague to a supervisor when informal resolution is not effective.

P-4.7 We shall be familiar with laws and regulations that serve to protect the children in our programs.

P-4.8 We shall not participate in practices which are in violation of laws and regulations that protect the children in our programs.

P-4.9 When we have evidence that an early childhood program is violating laws or regulations protecting children, we shall report it to persons responsible for the programs. If compliance is not accomplished within a reasonable time, we will report the violation to appropriate authorities who can be expected to remedy the situation.

P-4.10 When we have evidence that an agency or a professional charged with providing services to children, families, or teachers is failing to meet its obligations, we acknowledge a collective ethical responsibility to report the problem to appropriate authorities or to the public.

P-4.11 When a program violates or requires its employees to violate this Code, it is permissible, after fair assessment of the evidence, to disclose the identity of that program.

(Reprinted with permission from NAEYC)

As you can see, the Code offers abundant direction for deciding some ethical issues, although often teachers will have to use the Code as a tool to help sort out conflict between established beliefs. For example, in considering the first question posed earlier, good teachers likely believe in the importance of informing parents of issues involving their children, and in maintaining lines of communication. But at the same time, they believe in protecting children's rights to privacy while they are in a center. Teachers have to carefully sort out the issues that must be addressed by different people–teachers, parents, directors. By carefully reading the various segments of the Code, teachers will be able to find the relevant ideals and principles, and decide which have priority and precedent to help teachers make the most ethical choices for determining a plan of action. Principle P-1.1 is an important principle to note as you read through the Code, giving precedence over any other considerations to protecting children.

Let's go back to the example in the introduction to this section. Because this dilemma involves children's rights as well as the parents' desire for information, the practitioner would need to safeguard the child's privacy, while working empathetically with parents to help them get all the relevant information about biting, and about the precautions taken to protect their own child.

After a thorough reading of all parts of the Code, go back to the other ethical dilemmas posed at the beginning of this section. Choose the relevant parts of the Code that would help a teacher to decide on ethical responses. Because each of these situations involves making decisions about the best interests of more than one of the groups that teachers work with, you will find that you need to decide which groups are involved, and read those sections completely to make your decisions. You will also find other situations in the *"Activities for Further Study"* at chapter end to help you become knowledgeable of the content and use of the Code.

It is important that you understand professional ethics before you begin your practicum experiences. Be sure that you keep your copy of the Code handy when you enter an early childhood classroom. It will be comforting to you and useful to your colleagues to be able to refer to this professional standard for behavior, because it gives you professional permission to approach others and work through solutions that are based on right actions, not status, hierarchy, or the easiest way out. Know also that "the Code is not set in concrete. It should respond to changes in the Associations, the memberships, the moral climate, and to new changes in the profession" (Feeney, 1990, p. 20). The Ethics Commission will revise it at regular intervals, and they want to help early childhood teachers with troubling ethical dilemmas. They suggest that teachers who need assistance with difficulties write to the Ethics Commission, care of NAEYC.

The development of the Code of Ethics and the Statement of Commitment (which you will see in Chapter Twelve) was an important step in the increasing professionalization of early childhood teachers. You should not only be proud of this step, but also do everything in your ability to encourage others to become familiar with its principles and use.

Teachers are interactive professionals... who draw on training, skill, a growing body of experience, habit, personal values, art, science, and native wit to do their work
—William Ayers

POSITION STATEMENT ON DEVELOPMENTALLY APPROPRIATE PRACTICE

Earlier you read about NAEYC's publication of the position statement on developmentally appropriate practice for programs serving children birth through age eight. In this discussion of professionalization, it is important to note that enormous progress has been made in both attitudes of professionalism and more unified thinking about teaching practices as a result of this document.

1987
NAEYC publishes its position statement on Developmentally Appropriate Practice, revised from a preliminary statement in 1984.

Figure 9-10   **It is reassuring for individual teachers to know their practices have the support of the position statement on developmentally appropriate practices.**

Consider the teacher who is faced with parents who are asking for more structured academic curriculum for their preschooler, or with an untrained assistant teacher who sees no difficulty in using fairly negative and punitive discipline techniques. If the teacher responds with ideas from her own child development education background, she may meet with the resistance that comes when others interpret the response as a personal opinion. What the position statement gives is the strength of professional consensus, based on knowledge. The teacher may present the information with the confidence that this has the support of the entire professional organization. The position statement expresses clearly and succinctly the kind of information that many teachers struggle to articulate to others. Indeed,this gives teachers power and assurance to know that their practices have the support of the best, most current thinking in the profession (see Fig. 9-10).

The position statement has also made it possible for teachers to discuss issues with colleagues in a nonthreatening environment, and by focusing their discussion on interpreting their practices in light of the position statement. Thus discussion is less likely to be interpreted as personal challenge, and more likely to create genuine dialogue focused on objective issues that produce real changes in programs for children. It will be important that you become familiar enough with both the Code of Ethics and the position statement on developmentally appropriate practice that you can use them to support positive environments for children. This is what is increasing the professionalization of individual teachers today.

When all is said and done, the debates about whether or not early childhood teachers are part of a profession come down to individual attitudes, knowledge, and actions. Saying that we are professionals does not, in fact, make others treat us as if we are professionals. But when we believe that we are professionals and act accordingly, we are more likely to garner the respect of others. Professional teachers make informed decisions and judgements based on the accumulation of knowledge and experience, and with increasing confidence as they understand how their decisions match common standards of others within the profession (Katz, 1995).

We as teachers can believe in our professional status when we realize that our place is in a long line of those who have applied the available knowledge to serve the best interests of children and families. Therefore we must continue to seek the best knowledge in our training, and the supports and standards offered by our modern professional organizations. Most of all, it is easier to see oneself as a professional when we are within the company of others of like interest and intent. This is what you are encouraged to do. Professional pride and self-esteem is enhanced when we engage in lifelong learning to advance our knowledge and practice, when we inform the public and policy-makers with the authority of our knowledge, and when we work collectively to support our colleagues and profession.

This discussion on professionalism will conclude with a commentary from one individual teacher, who traces her individual growth as a professional. Notice what steps she saw as important in her development, and how her knowledge and actions were supported by the standards of the profession at large.

Reflection enables us to know what we are about when we act

—John Dewey

MY PERSONAL JOURNEY TOWARD PROFESSIONALISM

This short, personal article is about my own growth. It is about the process I experienced at coming to identify myself as a professional.

I first began to consider myself a professional while I was teaching at a preschool in Utah. When I had left New York City after three years of training and teaching, I knew that I had learned to teach effectively, and I felt good about what I had learned and done. . . . I did not consider myself a professional. I had only two years of college and no education courses. I just had some skills and an opportunity to share them.

To be a professional implies that I have a certain body of assimilated knowledge in my field and the skill to use it effectively. To me a profession is a vocation rather than a job. A vocation is a calling: calling me out to a specific kind of work in the world; calling forth from me not only my skills but also my growing self in a broader context than just that specific, current work. As a professional I assume that I need to keep growing, improving, learning, discovering, studying, expanding into a fuller expression of that vocation. These activities occur away from my work site as well as on the site. As I observe and assess my involvement there, I try to look behind the immediate "what" to see the issues of "how" and "why". As I participate in professional organizations, I expect to be both learner and teacher. Dialogue helps me to keep flowing out toward new possibilities.

I am partially defined by my profession. . . . However, I also partially define that profession by my own interaction with it. Who I am, what values I hold, what theories I advocate, and the manner of sharing my own

1988
Percentage of infants under one year who have mothers in the work force increased to 51 percent.

self in my work are all interrelated with the work itself. I am now a preschool teacher in the broader field of human development. As I work in other ways with children and adults, my professionalism expands.

What happened that slowly made me feel professional? In 1966, without seeking it, I was invited to work at a preschool. The director had participated in workshops with me and wanted me to co-teach a class of 3-year-olds with a solidly established teacher. I struggled that year with reestablishing my own style of team teaching with a woman whose style was significantly different from mine. It was *her* room and *her* program by virtue of her tenure there. I was uncomfortable with many of her rules and controls. The program was restrictive for me and for the children. . . .

During that year the entire staff had several inservice workshops and study days. I found myself preparing for and participating in those days with an intensity new to me. I was able to raise issues at the theoretical level with the whole staff–issues that my co-teacher had avoided or refused to discuss in our own planning meetings. In response to these discussions, the staff made several significant changes in our style of relating with the children. Over time we experimented with new activities and with removing some of the rules. In many cases, after evaluating these changes, we found our teaching energy less consumed by controlling. The children appeared more joyful and became more responsible for their own behavior.

I want to share an example of this process. The two swings on our playground were a constant source of conflict and tension for both children and teachers. The teachers monitored a "line-up" and kept roughly aware of time to tell the swinger to "get off now, it's ——'s turn." A constant hassle of "she's had too long a turn" and "just a little bit more" and "he's cutting in line" ensued regularly. I hated being on the playground. When I mentioned how I felt to my coteacher, she dismissed my feelings with an "Oh, you'll get used to it!"

At a staff meeting later, I took advantage of an opening to share frustrations and raised the swing issue as a difficult one for me. The staff discussed the situation, sharing our mutual frustrations and what we were actually teaching the children. We explored alternative approaches and agreed to try another way for two weeks. We simply told the children who came to line up that there would be no line, that they could find other things to do (there were *many,* and we suggested some). Later, when the swing was free, they could use it if they chose. My coteacher was convinced that a certain few children would monopolize the swings, and she did not want to allow that by assuming a laissez-faire attitude. Initially she was right. The first few days most children had no turn to use the swings. We told them, as we had agreed, that they would be able to use the swing some other day. It was *hard* for us teachers to live with that, but we did. At the end of the first week, the same few children ran to get the swings when the class went outside, but they lost interest when the other children were no longer pestering them for a turn. The others had given up using the swings and had begun a fascinating new project in another part of the yard: digging a huge hole together. By the end of the second week, the swings had lost their magic as a source of tension for

The future belongs to those who believe in the beauty of their dreams
—Eleanor Roosevelt

1988
Staff turnover in child care centers averages 41 percent, including a 74 percent rate in for-profit centers and 30 percent in non-profit programs.

us all. A child who wanted to swing for a long time could do so, and another could learn to negotiate for a turn as she wished.

The staff evaluated what had happened and what we had learned. We made some minor modifications and adopted this procedure with other activities also. As a spin-off from our experience, we embarked on an extended study of the whole issue of sharing.

I learned much from the swings experience about process, about children, about colleagueship, and about myself. I was frustrated by my inability to change the method with my co-teacher, and I did not have the power to change it alone. By raising the issue in the larger staff group, tapping into others' frustrations about the swings, facilitating discussion from a more theoretical perspective of *what* we were teaching as well as how, I was able to help effect the change as a process of the group. Had there not been other thoughtful, open people on the staff, a different decision might have been made. I know that. I'm also certain that several other ways of experimenting with the problem could have worked. Either way it was exciting for me to discover the power of the group process to deal with the issue effectively. In a one-to-one confrontation with my coteacher, both the children and I would have lost. Yet as the change did occur, she did not lose face. In subsequent staff decision making, I was usually pleased and occasionally not, but the more open process allowed for the possibility of differing without alienation.

Is there anything bad about professionalism? I believe that the most negative aspect of professionalism occurs when the perceived differences between a professional and a lay person alienate them from each other. Sometimes the lay person puts the professional on a pedestal; sometimes the professional looks down on the lay person. Either attitude prevents them from seeing face-to-face. It is important to me to try to see people in their own contexts. . . .

I am no longer just a person who teaches preschool; I am a preschool teacher. At the end of that year at the Utah preschool, as I prepared to move to a different class and co-worker, I no longer thought of myself as a person who, along with many other activities, happened to teach preschool. I was a preschool teacher, just as I was a wife and mother. The change had been subtle yet basic and permanent. I no longer did teaching things with young children in a preschool space. I was a person who used all of myself–intelligence and reflection as well as energy and skills and knowledge–to create an atmosphere of discovery and learning for all of us who shared in that setting. I know now, 25 years and two schools later, that when I no longer work in a preschool setting, I will continue to be a preschool teacher, along with all the other things I am. In the varied settings of my life, I use what I have become, even as I am developing other professional abilities within and outside of the preschool world.[1]

Obstacles are things a person sees when he takes his eyes off his goal
–E. Joseph Cossman

---

[1]Used with permission, from G. Brooke, "My Personal Journey Toward Professionalism," *Young Children* (Washington, DC: National Association for the Education of Young Children, September 1994) pp. 69-71 © by NAEYC.

1988
Jay Belsky raises questions about the effects of infant day care.

SUMMARY

There is a debate about the extent to which early childhood teachers are part of a true profession. When compared with the generally accepted characteristics of a profession, early childhood education does show mixed results. Recent accomplishments of NAEYC and other professional organizations have produced position statements that work to set standards of practice, an accreditation system to recognize developmentally appropriate programs, and a Code of Ethics that help guide practitioners in decisions about ethical dilemmas. It is important that teachers work on improving their attitudes and increasing their own knowledge to move towards personal standards of professionalism.

QUESTIONS FOR REVIEW

1. Describe several of the characteristics of a profession, and discuss how early childhood education matches the standard.
2. Name two major early childhood professional organizations, discussing services of each.
3. Describe the process of voluntary accreditation by NAEYC's National Academy, and discuss benefits of the accreditation process.
4. Discuss the Code of Ethics, its component parts, and its uses for early childhood practitioners.
5. Discuss the importance of the position statement on developmentally appropriate practice.

ACTIVITIES FOR FURTHER STUDY

1. Visit your college library to learn what journals from professional early childhood organizations are available. Read several articles from a representative issue, and write brief reports that indicate the kinds of knowledge you obtain. Examine the issues for regular features that would be helpful to early childhood teachers in their practice, and in learning about policy and wider issues of the profession.
2. Using your community resource guide and/or contacts with early childhood teachers, learn what professional organizations are available and used by teachers in your area. If possible, attend a local meeting. Talk with local teachers who are members of the organization to learn how they have benefited by their membership. If there are no local groups, call or write the nearest affiliate to get a listing of their current activities and get on their mailing list, if possible.
3. Find out if there is a Week of the Young Child activity held in your community. If there is, find out how you and other students can be involved. If there is not, what could you do to initiate one?
4. With classmates, use the Code of Ethics to discuss the following issues that could occur in a classroom. Some of these are adapted from articles published in *Young Children* to encourage practitioners to see the practical applications of the Code.
   a. A parent asks an infant caregiver to please not feed the baby in the late afternoon, so that she can feed her at home and put her to sleep. The baby cries each day until her mother comes.
   b. A coworker has discussed a family at your child care center with her boyfriend's family, who ask you about the situation.
   c. A four-year-old is angry when his mother leaves him each morning and treats other children aggressively. The assistant teacher is bothered by the lead teacher's response, which is to put him in time-out for long periods.

     d. A teacher is told by her supervisor that a child has contagious diarrhea, so that teachers should wash hands carefully. The teacher is surprised that a notice is not posted to inform parents.

     e. A teacher of three-year-olds is unaware when first employed that the number of children in her room exceeds the staff-child ratio standards of the state day care regulations. When the licensing worker comes to inspect, the director tells her that the cook is also a teacher who works regularly in the classroom.

     f. A mother asks you not to let her four-year-old son nap in the afternoon, since he then wants to stay up late at night and she has to get up early to go to work. The child seems to need his nap to play happily in the afternoon.

5. Find out if there is an NAEYC accredited program in your community. If there is, visit; talk with the director and staff about their learning process during the self-study, and what accreditation has meant to the parents and community.

6. Read carefully through NAEYC's position statement on Developmentally Appropriate Practice for Early Childhood Programs Serving Children Birth through Age 8 (1987). Then create with your classmates statements that you might make, or newsletters to parents or letters to the editor that you might create, to address the following situations with ideas from the position statement.

     a. The school board is holding a public hearing on adopting a fairly stringent academic curriculum for kindergarten, recommending that children whose parents do not think they are ready for this level of work keep them out of school for an additional year.

     b. Outdoor play time for the preschoolers is being cut, to allow for more indoor curriculum.

     c. Parents are requesting that children bring home art projects each day, so they can see the evidence of their work.

     d. A newspaper editorial complains that the current problems in the schools are directly attibutable to the absence of corporal punishment.

     e. A policy in a child care program allows teachers only to decide whether children should remain in classrooms, or move on.

REFERENCES

Ade, William. (1982, March). Professionalization and its implications for the field of early childhood education. *Young Children, 37,* (3), 25-32.

Almy, Millie. (1988). The early childhood educator revisited. In Spodek, Bernard, Saracho, Olivia N., & Peters, Donald L., (Eds.). *Professionalism and the early childhood practitioner.* New York: Teachers College Press.

Bredekamp, Sue. (1992, January). Composing a profession. *Young Children, 47,* (2), 52-54.

Bredekamp, Sue. (Ed.). (1987). *Developmentally appropriate practice in early childhood programs serving children from birth through age 8.* Washington, DC: NAEYC.

Bredekamp, Sue. (1991) *Accreditation criteria and procedures of the National Academy of Early Childhood Programs.* (Rev. Ed.). Washington, DC: NAEYC.

Bredekamp, Sue, & Willer, Barbara. (1993, March) Professionalizing the field of early childhood education: Pros and cons. *Young Children, 48,* (3), 82-84.

Brooke, Gretchen E. (1994, September). My personal journey toward professionalism. *Young Children. 49,* (6), 69-71.

Feeney, Stephanie. (1990, May). Update on the NAEYC Code of Ethical Conduct. *Young Children, 45,* (4), 20-21.

Joffe, C. (1977). *Friendly intruders.* Berkeley, CA: University of California Press.

Katz, Lilian. (1984, July). The professional early childhood teacher. *Young Children. 39,* (5), 3-10.

Katz, Lilian. (1991). Ethical issues in working with young children. In *Ethical behavior in early childhood education, expanded edition.* In Lillian Katz & Evangeline Ward (Eds.), Washington, DC: NAEYC.

Katz, Lilian. (1995). The nature of professions: Where is early childhood education? In *Talks with teachers of young children.* Norwood, NJ: Ablex Publishing Corp.

Kipnis, Kenneth. (1987, May). How to discuss professional ethics. *Young Children, 42,* (40), 26-30.

Lazar, I., Hubbell, V. R., Murray, H., Rosthe, M., & Royce, J. (1977). *Summary Report: The persistence of preschool effects: A long-term follow-up of fourteen infant and preschool experiments.* Washington, DC: U.S. Dept. of Health, Education, and Welfare. OHDS #78-30129.

NAEYC. (1994). *Position statements.* Washington, DC: Author.

National Academy. (1990, January). Reaccreditation: A snapshot of growth and change in high-quality early childhood programs. *Young Children, 45,* (2), 58-61.

Norris, N. Catherine. (1994, September). The NAEYC accreditation process isn't really so scary–Why not try it? *Young Children, 49,* (6), 72-74.

Silin, Jonathan G. (1985, March). Authority as knowledge: A problem of professionalization. *Young Children, 40,* (3), 41-45.

Smith, Marilyn. (1987, March). NAEYC at 60: Visions for the year 2000. *Young Children, 42,* (3), 33-39.

Spodek, Bernard, Saracho, Olivia N., & Peters, Donald L. (1988). Professionalism, semi-professionalism, and craftsmanship. In Bernard Spodek, Olivia N. Saracho, & Donald L. Peters (Eds.), *Professionalism and the early childhood practitioner.* New York: Teachers College Press.

Spodek, Bernard. (1988). Professionalizing the tasks ahead. In Bernard Spodek, Olivia N. Saracho, & Donald L. Peters (Eds.), *Professionalism and the early childhood practitioner.* New York: Teachers College Press.

Vander Ven, Karen. (1988). Pathways to professional effectiveness for early childhood educators. In Bernard Spodek, Olivia N. Saracho, & Donald L. Peters (Eds.), *Professionalism and the early childhood practitioner.* New York: Teachers College Press.

Willer, Barbara, & Bredekamp, Sue. (1993, May). A 'new' paradigm of early childhood professional development." *Young Children, 48,* (4), 63-66.

SUGGESTIONS FOR READING

Boyer, Ernest. (1990). *Ready to learn: A mandate for the nation.* Carnegie Fund for the Advancement of Teaching.

Buck, Linda. (1987, Janauary). Directors: How to sell accreditation to staff, board, and parents. *Young Children, 42,* (2), 46-49.

Bundy, Blakely Fetridge. Achieving accreditation: A journal of one program's experience. *Young Children, 43,* (6), 27-34.

Radomski, Mary Ann. (1986, July). Professionalization of early childhood educators: How far have we progressed? *Young Children, 41,* (5), 20-23.

Swanson, Lou. Changes–How our nursery school replaced adult-directed art projects with child-directed experiences and changed to an accredited, child-sensitive, developmentally appropriate school. *Young Children, 49,* (4), 69-73.

10

PROFESSIONAL EDUCATION AND CAREER DIRECTIONS

As you consider joining the early childhood profession, you will want to know what educational training and professional experience you will need to prepare you to begin teaching. Many of you will also want to know about other career directions that are possible for those who enter the early childhood field, in addition to classroom teaching. As you can imagine from what you have already learned about early education, the answers to these questions are not simple. Because of the different regulatory systems that govern the functioning of the various kinds of programs for young children, quite different educational requirements are required for different areas of teaching. Because of the diversity of entry path and job requirements for teachers in the field, the profession itself is struggling with issues of common knowledge that is needed and vehicles for providing it. And because of the varied educational backgrounds of early childhood practitioners, particular career directions may be open or closed.

The dilemma for the profession has been to define educational standards that will enhance the quality of programs for children without excluding those who represent and enrich the diversity of culture and experience typical of American society in general. This chapter will explore issues of necessary core knowledge for early childhood teachers, types of training programs and institutions, and possible career directions. This will be helpful knowledge for you as you chart your own particular course of professional preparation and career planning.

OBJECTIVES

After studying this chapter, students will be able to:

1. differentiate between licensing and certification requirements.

2. discuss the reasons why differing types of educational preparation for early childhood educators exist.

3. identify and describe NAEYC's National Institute for Early Childhood Professional Development.

4. identify and describe what is meant by the term "career lattice."

5. describe the Child Development Associate Credential, and identify the reason for developing this credential.

OBJECTIVES

6. discuss the concept of "mentoring" as it is currently being used in professional development of early educators.

7. discuss various career options in the early childhood field.

DIVERSITY IN EARLY CHILDHOOD PROFESSIONAL PREPARATION

Cheryl W. is currently a student in a community college early childhood education progam, where she will earn an Associate in Applied Science degree in early childhood. She plans to teach in a child care program with preschool children. The center where she hopes to teach has two teachers with four-year degrees in elementary education and teacher certification credentials, one who has a bachelor's degree with a major in abnormal psychology, two who have earned a certificate in early childhood education offered by the local technical college after completion of twenty credit hours of early childhood courses, and four who have no more than the twenty clock hours of training related to children that is mandated by the state licensing requirements. Cheryl's parents have wondered why she feels she must complete her two-year degree, since several of the staff at the center evidently have fewer qualifications than that.

Christy S. is a student in a university, completing a bachelor's degree, with a major in Child and Family Development. She has taken a number of additional courses to earn a license to teach children from birth through kindergarten (B-K) in her state. She hopes to be a kindergarten teacher. Daryl Ann E. is also preparing to gain certification that will enable her to teach kindergarten in another state. In her case, she must complete coursework in her college's school of education that will earn her a certification to teach children from kindergarten through sixth grade (K-6). Most of her classmates are completing the requirements in order to become qualified to teach in the early elementary grades, several hoping for mixed-age K-2 classes. One of her classmates has recently decided, after visiting a local Head Start center, that he will apply for a position as a lead teacher with Head Start after he finishes his certification requirements. When he talked with several current Head Start teachers, he learned that one of them had earned a Child Development Associate (CDA) credential, and two others hoped to be assessed for the credential soon. All of these practitioners had the same goal of becoming lead teachers in the Head Start program.

Why are there such differences in the educational paths taken by all these individuals, many of whom have similar career goals? What do these differences in education and training mean to their performance in classrooms, and ultimately to the question of quality in programs for young children? Today you will find such differences in every program for children, in every state and location you visit. What do you already know about the state requirements where you hope to teach?

One of the reasons for the multiplicity of forms of educational paths is that there are also several typical routes by which people become early childhood professionals: the traditional route, the parent route, and the "serendipitous" route (Bredekamp, 1992). If you recall the three teachers you met earlier, they exemplify these three routes. Martha knew very early on that she wanted to enter early childhood education, so she enrolled in a college program that would prepare her for that goal. Annie, however, assumed she would be involved in the world of business until she became a parent of a child with spe-

1988

The National Association of State Boards of Education publishes *Right from the Start,* calling for a "new vision of early childhood education," with establishment of separate public school early childhood units for children ages four to eight.

cial needs who was enrolled in a Head Start Parent-Child program that involved her in parent training and classroom volunteering. Connie, in looking for a part-time job, stumbled into an early childhood program and discovered this was something she loved. When teachers come into the profession via different routes, the profession must respond with different kinds of training, much of it not offered preservice.

Regulation and Certification

A major reason for the difference in requirements is a result of the fact that states have two separate processes to define and regulate the qualifications for those who work with young children. State licensing agencies give the state's permission to operate a child care center or home to facilities that meet the requirements decided on by the legislature (see Fig. 10-1). Licensing regulations

THEORY INTO PRACTICE

This is Sherry McIntyre. She has worked in the field of early education for 17 years–as a teacher, then director, then parent counselor in a resource and referral agency, and now in her current position as a trainer of other child care professionals.

What has been a significant frustration for you in early education? How do you deal with it?

A significant frustration is the disrespect that the public has, regarding the importance of the first five years. I work against this by early childhood advocacy, spreading the word through writing, calling, and talking on a local, state, and national level.

What is one thing you learned in classes that you really discovered to be true when you started working with children?

I really discovered how important flexibility is. Listen to what the child is saying or watch what he/she is doing. I've learned to take my cues from the child.

What is an area you are working on now to learn more about?

Right now I'm working to learn more about diversity, and how all our differences create a unique and wonderful world!

Why have you stayed in early education?

As a teacher, director, parent counselor, and trainer I have tried to plant many seeds and I am amazed at the growth that many have taken. I am convinced that if we work together, in my lifetime we are capable of experiencing even more remarkable changes in all the different facets of early childhood development. Perhaps some day we will see those seeds reach maturity!

What is a comment or piece of advice you would give to those beginning to work in early childhood education?

My advice is: cherish the opportunities you share with children and parents, for they are short-lived, but they will be remembered for a lifetime.

Figure 10-1 | **State legislatures mandate requirements for licensing standards, including size of classroom space and number of children permitted in groups.**

Developmentally appropriate practice in early childhood education is also a good model for effective practice in teacher education. Adult learners, like children, need to play–that is, they need to take initiative, make choices among possibilities, act and interact

—Elizabeth Jones

cover teachers who work with prekindergarten programs in child care centers, in private before- and after-school care programs. In some states they also cover family child care providers (although, according to Corsini et al. [1988] the majority of family child care providers do not register or comply with these regulations), and in about half the states they also cover half-day preschool programs. Licensing does not apply to public schools, even to prekindergarten children in programs administered by the public schools.

Licensing mandates many components of child care programs, including health, sanitation, safety, fire and building codes, size of space inside and out, group sizes, adult-child ratios, and appropriate guidance. One of the other requirements for licensing facilities includes meeting various qualifications set by the state for individuals employed in the program, as well as various training requirements for individuals filling various roles. For example, a state may require that: there are minimum age requirements for teachers, for assistants, and for directors; minimum education requirements, such as high school graduation or equivalency; minimum character requirements, such as no convictions for child abuse or neglect; and minimum training requirements that may include preservice training, orientation training, and annual ongoing training requirements.

Preservice training may be required for some roles only, such as completion of thirty-three hours of administrative training for directors. Also, there are often differences for training for other roles, such as annual in-service training requirements that may require more hours for lead teachers than for assistants. In some cases, experience is substituted as a training requirement.

It will be important for you to become familiar with the training requirements mandated by your state licensing regulator. There are still states that do not require early childhood educators to have any training at all to work in programs with young children. Even for those states that do require training, there are wide

1988
Over 100 child care bills were introduced in Congress.

| Figure 10-2 | **When licensing requirements do not mandate that teachers have specific training in positive guidance techniques, handling a situation like this one could be very difficult.** |

differences in the amount and type of necessary training. The existence of training requirements does not necessarily mean that practitioners have adequate knowledge to plan appropriate learning experiences for children, since the content of the training may not be specified, and there may be no distribution requirements (see Fig. 10-2). For example, the annual training requirement in some states may be met by taking a minicourse to meet recertification requirements for CPR and first aid training each year. While this is certainly important and necessary training, it would leave large gaps in the practitioner's knowledge if this were the only training received each year. In some cases, when teachers have certain numbers of years of experience, the training requirements are lifted or lightened.

Often licensing requirements do not cover all of the child care facilities in a state, as the definition of a center may vary from state to state. For example, family child care arrangements may be exempt from state regulation, as may programs run by religious institutions, part-day programs, or prekindergarten programs run by independent schools as part of their graded educational programs. In the case of programs where licensing regulations do not apply, there will usually be no training requirements at all. Thus you will likely find differences in the preparation for practitioners from state to state; the related differences to quality will also be apparent.

Certification, called licensure in some areas, is the process by which each state qualifies individuals for teaching positions in the public school system.

Since we believed in concrete experience as the essence of education for little children, it was natural to trust in the same principle for the education of teachers
—Caroline Pratt

Figure 10-3 | **Certification means that teachers have completed a prescribed education program at an accredited college or university and have a legal license to teach a certain grade level.**

Certification is usually issued to teachers who have at least four years of approved college education, consisting of professional study and general requirements. Certification is granted by the state's department of education on the basis of college transcripts proving the prescribed programs from accredited colleges and universities, and is a legal license to teach a certain grade level (see Fig. 10-3). Because most state certification systems were developed before the widespread availability and demand for early childhood education programs, their requirements usually do not reflect the need for understanding the distinctive knowledge base about the development and learning of the youngest children. State certification systems often prepare teachers to work with larger spans of grades (K-6, K-3, K-8), based on "school building organizational structures that are rapidly becoming obsolete" (NAEYC, 1991a, p. 17).

Thus, according to NAEYC position statements (1991, 1994, 1995), most states lack consistent standards for specialized early childhood education certification, and therefore also lack adequate preparation programs in early childhood education at the baccalaureate level. As of 1991, 15 states had certification programs that spanned prekindergarten and the lower elementary grades, 10 states had an add-on early childhood endorsement for elementary education certificates, 10 more had specialized pre-kindergarten certificates, while 16 states had no prekindergarten add-on or endorsement (Morgan et al., 1994), suggesting the relative importance assigned to early education by the state boards in these states. Because most four- and five-year teacher education programs are driven by state certification requirements, there is often little information and coursework about preschool children, especially infants and toddlers, other than purely theoretical or research-based knowledge. "In most states, a teacher could be certified to work with children under the age of five without any direct experience working with that age group" (Morgan et al., 1994, p. 40).

In those states that do require a practicum–an opportunity to put theory into practice under the supervision of an experienced teacher, sometimes called internship or student teaching–the practicum may only be for part of a semester, and may be in a kindergarten classroom, which may in no way prepare the early educator for later work with toddlers or three-year-olds (see Fig. 10-4).

The very definition of early childhood education varies widely from state to state, with 11 different definitions being noted (Goffin and Day, 1994). The different age-spans defined by the various states include: birth through age four; birth through age five; birth through age eight; three- to four-year-olds; three- to five-year-olds; three- to eight-year-olds; three- to nine-year-olds; five- to eight-year-olds; five- to nine-year-olds; and three- to twelve-year-olds! (Goffin and Day, p. 10). Small wonder that there is lack of uniformity. NAEYC has issued a call, along with the Association of Teacher Educators, for states to adopt certification standards that recognize the need for professional training for teachers of children from birth through age eight to acquire the unique information to work effectively with children of these ages (NAEYC, 1991a). Presently, you should recognize that vast differences in teacher certification programs and requirements exist, even when states use terminology indicating certification for early childhood teachers.

There is no bridge between the child care licensing and teacher certification process. While certified teachers may choose to work in child care, their training is often neither widely recognized as appropriate nor required, and indeed may be quite irrelevant to their work. Moreover, the experience and knowledge of early educators in the child care system are in no way able to meet the academic requirements of the certification system.

This two-tier system of considering early education needs of young children has contributed to the lack of coordination in defining common standards of quality or need for specialized training. But, perhaps even more importantly as you consider your future in working with young children, it has created separate career preparation paths that exist at this time. It is extremely important that you be quite aware of the licensing or certification requirements for any career goal you may set for yourself, in the present and in the future, so that you can find the most appropriate educational setting to assist you in furthering your plans.

Teachers can "know" something in a variety of ways: directly through lived classroom experience, vicariously through the observed or described experiences of other teachers, formally through professional reading and study, or intuitively through their value systems
—Mary Jalongo

NATIONAL INSTITUTE FOR EARLY CHILDHOOD PROFESSIONAL DEVELOPMENT

Because of the differences in training requirements, the training itself is generally offered by separate institutions. Education programs leading to certification for teaching in the public school systems is purely the province of the state's four- or five-year degree-granting institutions, with course offerings

1988
Association for the Accreditation of Montessori Teacher Education is established.

**Teachers Certification: Individual States' Early Childhood
Certification/Endorsement Requirements**

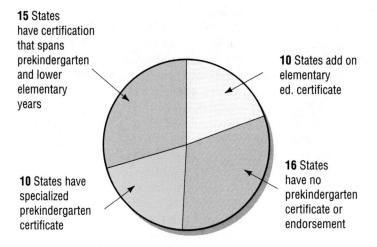

15 States
have certification
that spans
prekindergarten
and lower
elementary
years

10 States add on
elementary
ed. certificate

16 States
have no
prekindergarten
certificate or
endorsement

10 States have
specialized
prekindergarten
certificate

What About Your State?

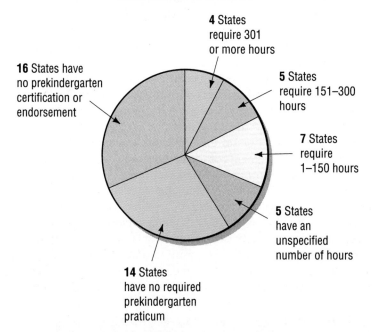

4 States
require 301
or more hours

5 States
require 151–300
hours

16 States have
no prekindergarten
certification or
endorsement

7 States
require
1–150 hours

5 States
have an
unspecified
number of hours

14 States
have no required
prekindergarten
praticum

**Teachers Certification: Practicum Requirements For
Individual States' Prekindergarten**

Figure 10-4 | **Uneven and non-existent requirements from state to state for
certification in early childhood education mean very different
performance abilities.**

driven by decisions made by state boards of education, and is only minimally influenced by the early childhood education profession (Spodek, 1994). There are recent attempts to establish criteria for accrediting teacher education programs–NAEYC is one of a coalition of 28 professional organizations that make up NCATE (National Council for Accreditation of Teacher Education)–but so far only 33 states are voluntarily coordinating their review processes with NCATE. However, this is an important step in developing common standards to improve the quality of early childhood professional preparation.

At the present time, there is enormous diversity in the kind of actual knowledge or practice for working with young children offered by baccalaureate institutions. The most recent NAEYC position statement on this topic–Guidelines for Preparation of Early Childhood Professionals: Associate, Baccalaureate, and Advanced Levels (1995)–outlines specifics for programs, to ensure a common core of professional knowledge.

Most training for teachers who work in the child care programs that fall under licensing requirements is offered by two-year technical or community college programs, offering associate degrees in education programs that typically stress working with children younger than traditional school entry age. While some of these programs may be designed to articulate with **baccalaureate** programs, many are not. NAEYC has established guidelines for associate-degree programs (1985, 1995), but there is no system for enforcing the guidelines, and only a beginning towards accrediting the institutions that comply with them.

But most of the training acquired by early childhood staff to meet their licensing requirements is in the form of shorter courses and workshops offered by continuing education divisions or training agencies that do not offer college credit for advancing to recognized degrees, or connecting with the larger system. Some early childhood teachers began their training with vocational programs in high school, that may or may not **articulate** with local two-year college programs. Thus, even for those early childhood teachers who are getting training to enhance their abilities to work effectively with young children, the content of their coursework may be quite uneven, with no clear standards for knowledge or practice, and the courses may not assist teachers to develop clear pathways for professional development and advancement in education.

NAEYC launched the **National Institute for Early Childhood Professional Development** in 1991, recognizing the fact that the current system for preparing early childhood teachers is

> not a system at all, but a hodgepodge of workshops, training to meet state licensing requirements (precredential training), vocational-technical, associate-degree, baccalaureate-degree, and in-service training that is not articulated and often not congruent in content or focus (NAEYC, 1991b, p. 37).

The Institute has been established to respond to the need to improve the preparation and stability of early childhood practitioners, in order to achieve the goal of ensuring high-quality and developmentally appropriate care and education for all of the nation's young children (see Fig. 10-5). A major effort will be to "improve the quality, consistency, and accessibility of professional

---

It is the individual teacher who makes teaching an art as well as a science—not the school principal, nor the superintendent, nor even the educational psychologist, but the person who lives the hours of the school day with the children themselves

—Caroline Pratt

Baccalaureate: A bachelor's degree (B.A), awarded by a college or university after completing four academic years of a prescribed course of study.

Articulate: Arrangements made between educational programs for students to transfer and continue on to higher educational levels, without loss of academic credit.

National Institute for Early Childhood Professional Development: Established by NAEYC to promote educational and professional advancement within the field.

1989
Thirty-one states appropriate funds for state-supported prekindergartens.

Figure 10-5   **High quality, developmentally appropriate education for all children depends on the preparation of early childhood practitioners. (Courtesy of Connie Glass)**

preparation programs, thus increasing the likelihood of obtaining a coordinated, articulated professional development system for the field of early childhood education" (NAEYC, 1991b, p. 38). Currently the Institute is reviewing existing standards for professional preparation at the various academic levels, and developing standards for state certification for teachers and in-service training, striving to influence the quality of training and the likelihood of articulation across teacher preparation programs. Another aspect of the Institute's work is to initiate a Leadership Development Program designed to train professionals in effective ways of advocating for the association's positions. This is all part of a dynamic view of professionalism that acknowledges many levels of professionalism, with various roles, responsibilities, and necessary qualifications.

The Institute recognizes that there is a long road ahead in attempting to implement this vision. The separations in the regulatory systems and the institutions constitute a barrier that must be made less rigid. But perhaps the largest barrier is in attitudes that still separate those involved in care from those involved in education, and that interpret discussions of professional qualifications as "a measure of an individual's worth" (NAEYC, 1991a, p. 36). The dilemma is in continuing to allow access to the profession by diverse groups, while still providing a variety of vehicles to improve their educational qualifications and professional development (see Fig. 10-6).

Career Lattice

A conceptual framework of early childhood professional development must achieve a balance between inclusivity and exclusivity. It must fully

1989

17 percent of American school districts offer some form of before- and after-school child care, or let others use their buildings to provide it.

Figure 10-6   **The dilemma is in continuing to allow access to the profession from diverse paths while still providing a variety of vehicles to enhance professional development.**

embrace the diversity of roles and levels of preparation required for professionals working with young children to provide high-quality services. It must also recognize that individuals enter the profession with diverse educational qualifications and experience and promote a system that encourages ongoing professional development for individuals at all levels and in all roles. The framework must also set high standards for professional performance and distinguish the specialized skills and knowledge of the early childhood profession from those of other professions (*The Early Childhood Career Lattice: Perspectives on Professional Development,* by J. Johnson and J.B. McCracken, [Washington, DC: National Association for the Education of Young Children], p. 11. © by NAEYC.)

1989
Code of Ethical Conduct is published by NAEYC.

Figure 10-7	**The Career Lattice: no longer the old model of a career ladder.**

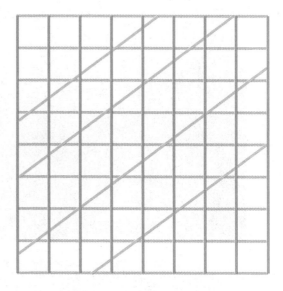

Career Lattice: Term used to refer to diversity of educational backgrounds, entry points, and employment opportunities within the early childhood field.

Aide: Person, usually without professional training, employed under supervision of a professional in the classroom.

The symbol of a **career lattice** (See Fig. 10-7) is used to convey the needed combination of diversity and development. The career lattice includes the idea of the multiple roles and levels (horizontal strands) and settings (vertical strands) within early childhood education, and diverse entry points and bridges between roles and settings in terms of professional preparation and responsibility (diagonals). It allows for the concept that there may be upward movement with increasing responsibility and compensation within that role, as well as for intersecting movement across the various roles. This seems like a better image for a field as diverse as early childhood education than the more traditional ladder, that implies just one clearly defined path to professional development where one must proceed in one defined direction, stepping over others to advance.

Instead, the lattice allows for the scenario of someone who is employed as a child care **aide** without any preservice training. After two years of experience, she is given a promotion to lead teacher, and encouraged to enter a program at a community college where she completes a two-year degree in early childhood education. Some time later, she seeks employment as a lead teacher in a Head Start program, where she is encouraged to continue her education in a baccalaureate program. A number of years later, she applies for the assistant director position at her original child care center (see Fig. 10-8). The career lattice concept also allows for the scenario of a parent in a Head Start program who is hired as bus driver/aide. He begins work to prepare for CDA credentialing, and after a number of years and after credentialing, becomes a lead teacher in a Head Start program. While continuing to teach in the program, he continues his education to obtain his state's prekindergarten certification, and later becomes a kindergarten teacher in a local elementary school.

The lattice allows for the entry of these individuals into the profession, and their individual continued professional growth and movement into various

1989

United Nations Convention on the Rights of the Child is adopted by 159 member states of the United Nations General Assembly.

Figure 10-8 This teacher, newly employed without credentials, is at a beginning point on the career lattice. Her plan to begin working on an associate degree at night will move her on the lattice, and open up new possibilities for her career.

roles, as well as for those who followed more traditionally defined routes of enrolling in a teacher certification program or associate degree program immediately after high school graduation and obtaining preservice credentials before gaining employment in the field, and then perhaps making several changes in the early childhood settings chosen for employment.

The lattice distinguishes the early childhood field from the early childhood profession; the field includes anyone engaged in providing early childhood services, while the profession includes those who have acquired some professional training and are on a professional path. It defines six distinct early childhood professional categories on a continuum of professional development. The levels identify levels of preparation programs for which standards have been established nationally (see Fig. 10-9).

The task of theory is to help teachers understand better the nature of their problems

—Loris Malaguzzi

Core Knowledge

One of the essential prerequisites to defining professional program standards is identifying the core of shared knowledge that defines the early childhood profession. As discussed in Chapter Nine, a distinguishing characteristic of any profession is a specialized body of knowledge and skills shared by all its members, and not shared by others. As this core of common knowledge is defined, it results from answering these two questions: (1) "Is this knowledge

1990

President George Bush vetoes the Family and Medical Leave Bill, which would have provided for many working parents to take up to twelve weeks of unpaid leave after the birth or adoption of a child, or for family illness.

EARLY CHILDHOOD PROFESSIONAL LEVEL VI

Successful completion of a Ph.D. or Ed.D. in a program conforming to NAEYC guidelines; *or*
Successful demonstration of the knowledge, performance, and dispositions expected as outcomes of a doctoral degree program conforming to NAEYC guidelines.

EARLY CHILDHOOD PROFESSIONAL LEVEL V

Successful completion of a master's degree in a program that conforms to NAEYC guidelines; *or*
Successful demonstration of the knowledge, performance, and dispositions expected as outcomes of a master's degree program conforming to NAEYC guidelines.

EARLY CHILDHOOD PROFESSIONAL LEVEL IV

Successful completion of a baccalaureate degree from a program conforming to NAEYC guidelines; *or*
State certification meeting NAEYC/ATE certification guidelines; *or*
Successful completion of a baccalaureate degree in another field with more than 30 professional units in early childhood development/education including 300 hours of supervised teaching experience, including 150 hours each for two of the following three age groups: infants and toddlers, three- to five-year olds, or the primary grades; *or*
Successful demonstration of the knowledge, performance, and dispositions expected as outcomes of a baccalaureate degree program conforming to NAEYC guidelines.

EARLY CHILDHOOD PROFESSIONAL LEVEL III

Successful completion of an associate degree from a program conforming to NAEYC guidelines; *or*
Successful completion of an associate degree in a related field, plus 30 units of professional studies in early childhood development/education including 300 hours of supervised teaching experience in an early childhood program; *or*
Successful demonstration of the knowledge, performance, and dispositions expected as outcomes of an associate degree program conforming to NAEYC guidelines.

EARLY CHILDHOOD PROFESSIONAL LEVEL II

II. B. Successful completion of a one-year early childhood certificate program.
II. A. Successful completion of the CDA Professional Preparation Program or completion of a systematic, comprehensive training program that prepares an individual to successfully acquire the CDA Credential through direct assessment.

EARLY CHILDHOOD PROFESSIONAL LEVEL I

Individuals who are employed in an early childhood professional role working under supervision or with support (linkages with provider association or network or enrollment in supervised practicum) and participating in training designed to lead to the assessment of individual competencies or acquisition of a degree (Willer, 1994, p. 16).

The Early Childhood Career Lattice: Perspectives on Professional Development, by J. Johnson and J.B. McCraken, (Washington, DC: National Association for the Education of Young Children) p. 11. © by NAEYC.

Figure 10-9 **The six distinct early childhood professional categories indicate the continuum of professional development.**

Core Knowledge: The basic knowledge the professional group acknowledges to be needed by all its members. A body of core knowledge has been defined by the NAEYC position statement on early childhood professional development.

or skill required of every early childhood professional, regardless of level or setting or professional role?" (Willer, 1994, p. 13). That is, does every early childhood teacher have to know and be able to do this in order to be effective? (2) "Does the sum of this body of knowledge and competencies uniquely distinguish the early childhood professional from all other professionals?" (p. 13). That is, despite the fact that other professionals may share some of this knowledge, is most of this knowlege different from that required by other professionals?

The **core knowledge** has been identified by comparing common elements in the guidelines for various structures of professional teacher preparation programs at the associate and baccalaureate levels (NAEYC, 1985; 1991; 1995) and in the Child Development Associate Professional Preparation Program (Phillips, 1991) (see Fig. 10-10). These common components suggest that all early educators should know and be able to do the following:

1990
30,000 CDA's have been awarded.

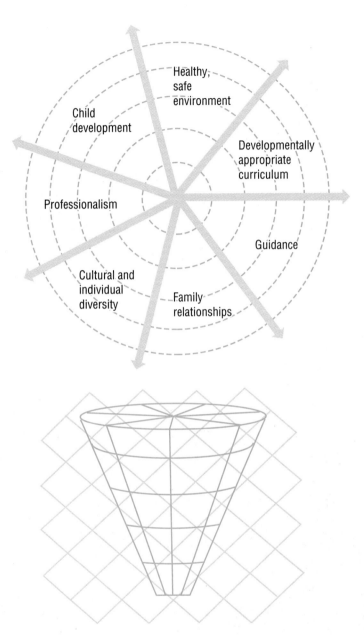

Used by permission of NAEYC

Figure 10-10

a. Core Knowledge in the Early Childhood Profession. Note that the dotted lines indicate stages of professional development marked by attaining recognized credentials. The innermost circle represents the pre-credential level; the next represents the knowledge required for the CDA credential, followed by associate, bachelors, and advanced degrees.

b. The Expanding Knowledge Base. If the core content of Fig. 10-10a is seen as a three-dimensional figure, it forms a cone of shared knowledge inherent in the career lattice. The "leaky funnel" demonstrates the increasingly specialized knowledge base that leads to expanded career options.

▶ demonstrate an understanding of *child development* and apply this knowledge in practice;

▶ *observe and assess children's behavior* in planning and individualizing teaching practices and curriculum;

▶ establish and maintain a *safe and healthy environment* for children;

▶ *plan and implement developmentally appropriate curriculum* that advances all areas of children's learning and development, including social, emotional, intellectual, and physical competence;

▶ establish supportive relationships with children and implement developmentally appropriate techniques of *guidance and group management;*

▶ establish and maintain positive and productive *relationships with families;*

▶ support the development and learning of individual children, recognizing that children are best understood in the context of *family, culture, and society;* and

▶ demonstrate an understanding of the early childhood profession and make a commitment to *professionalism.* (Willer, 1994, p. 13 in *The Early Childhood Career Lattice: Perspectives on Professional Development* by J. Johnson and J.B. McCracken. Washington, DC: NAEYC, © by NAEYC).

Figure 10-11   **Some roles require that teachers gain deeper knowledge to be effective, such as greater knowledge for working in classrooms where children have multiple special needs (Courtesy of Christie Shamel)**

1990

For Head Start's twenty-fifth anniversary celebration, it is announced that 11,394,800 children have been served, including 11 to 13 percent with special needs.

Phillips (1994) identifies five themes that address content that every professional in the field should know: (1) children develop in context; (2) strategies for working with children are constructed each day; (3) effective practice requires a comprehensive set of skills, described by the six CDA competencies and 13 functional areas which will be discussed shortly; (4) early childhood professionals know they belong to a profession; and (5) even skilled professionals have limitations.

In order to be able to do all this, professional education programs must expose students to general knowledge and specific competencies associated with all groups within the early childhood span–infants, toddlers, preschoolers, and primary-aged children. Students must learn about children with needs beyond those of the typically developing child. They must also have coursework and practicums that particularize their knowledge about some of these age-groups.

In addition to what all early educators must know, there is also specialized knowledge necessary only for some professionals in particular roles, such as a director of an early childhood program, or a family child care provider; some roles also will require greater depth of knowledge for teachers to be effective, such as learning more about special education or language delays (see Fig. 10-11.) And because of the complexity of early educators' roles, professional knowledge must reach beyond child development and early education to learning the communication skills that allow them to work effectively with colleagues on the teaching team and on more extended professional teams, with parents and others in families, and with the community beyond (see Fig. 10-12). At each successive level of preparation, from the CDA cre-

> *Teachers–like children and everyone else–feel the need to grow in their competences; they want to transform experiences into thoughts, thoughts into reflections, and reflections into new thoughts and new actions*
>
> —Loris Malaguzzi

Figure 10-12 **Communication skills to work effectively with families is one of the components of the core knowledge identified as necessary for all professionals.**

1990
First national educational goal is formulated: "By the year 2000 all children will start school ready to learn."

Figure 10-13   **A recent change in guidelines for early childhood degrees is increased emphasis and specificity on cultural and linguistic diversity.**

Please think of the children first. If you ever have anything to do with their entertainment, their food, their toys, their custody, their child care, their health care, their education–listen to the children, learn about them, learn from them. Think of the children first

–Fred Rogers

dential through graduate degree levels, professionals become increasingly able to apply, analyze, and refine the core knowledge to improve practices. In addition to the professional knowledge, it is recognized that higher levels of general education are linked to quality in programs for children, as professionals are able to see their specialized knowledge in the context of, and with applications of, general knowledge. General knowledge also helps early childhood teachers create learning experiences for children that draw on the broad content of general studies in the arts and sciences.

NAEYC has just revised and expanded the guidelines of associate and baccalaureate professional preparation programs (1995). (This term itself is one of the most "profound changes in the guidelines . . . reflecting the variety of roles, in addition to classroom teacher, that may be open to early childhood educators at various levels of preparation" [Bredekamp, 1992, p. 68].) Other changes reflect a clear emphasis on preparing practitioners for working in environments for children that fully include children with disabilities and special learning and developmental needs with typically developing children. In addition, the revised guidelines include a greater depth of preparation for working with families, and a more family-centered approach, as well as more in-depth preparation for working collaboratively with other adults. A final area of change in the guidelines is increased emphasis and specificity on cultural and linguistic diversity, with emphasis on individualization of curriculum and assessment (Bredekamp, 1995) (see Fig. 10-13).

Everything that is learned is used, as professionals increasingly refine their skills and broaden their knowledge. This ongoing discussion about what

1990
Passage of Americans with Disabilities Act (ADA), PL 101-336, providing Americans with disabilities the same freedoms and privileges as nondisabled Americans, including issues beyond educational.

early childhood professionals need to know will enrich and include, rather than stagnate and exclude.

CHILD DEVELOPMENT ASSOCIATE CREDENTIAL

In fact, the early childhood profession has a long history of attempting to include, rather than exclude. In the early 1970s, primarily as a result of Head Start expansion, it was recognized that the increasing national need for child care practitioners demanded more personnel than were currently available. In addition, as the need for more personnel increased, concerns about quality of care grew. It was recognized that the early childhood field would be employing individuals who had not had the time or resources to follow traditional preparation routes. A consortium of organizations concerned with the care and welfare of children developed a system to assess and credential individuals who had gained much of their knowledge through experience and practice. Thus the Child Development Associate credential was begun as an in-service program, based on proven competency at functioning in the classroom. Six broad competency areas were adopted as the basis for proving competence. These six competency goals continue to guide the program standards today:

1. to establish and maintain a safe, healthy learning environment;
2. to advance physical and intellectual competency;
3. to support social and emotional development and provide positive guidance;
4. to establish positive and productive relationships with families;
5. to ensure a well-run, purposeful program responsive to participant needs; and
6. to maintain a commitment to professionalism.

Each goal is subdivided and further defined to create thirteen functional areas for which each teacher is held accountable. For example, the first goal includes (i) safe, (ii) healthy, and (iii) learning environment, or three functional areas (see Fig. 10-14 for the functional areas.)

In the first fifteen years of the credentialing process, candidates for the CDA were responsible for creating several kinds of written documentation of competency. One was the portfolio, produced by the candidates, indicating evidence of what was happening in the classroom, an explanation of why the individual teachers did what they did, and how it showed they are competent teachers of young children (see Fig. 10-15 for an example of a portfolio entry.)

A CDA advisor/trainer produces documentation based on observations of the candidate working in the classroom. A local parent/community representative produces documentation that includes responses to questionnaires by parents of the children in the classroom, as well as observations of the candidates. Finally, a representative of the National CDA Credentialing program visits to complete required observations in the classroom and an extensive interview with the can-

1990

PL 101-576 reauthorized the Education for all Handicapped Children Act (PL94-142), renaming it Individuals with Disabilities Education Act (IDEA).

CDA COMPETENCY GOALS AND FUNCTIONAL AREAS

I. **To establish and maintain a safe, healthy learning environment**
1. **Safe:** Candidate provides a safe environment to prevent and reduce injuries.
2. **Health:** Candidate promotes good health and nutrition and provides an environment that contributes to the prevention of illness.
3. **Learning environment:** Candidate uses space, relationships, materials, and routines as resources for constructing an interesting, secure, and enjoyable environment that encourages play, exploration, and learning.

II. **To advance physical and intellectual competence**
4. **Physical:** Candidate provides a variety of equipment, activities, and opportunities to promote the physical development of children.
5. **Cognitive:** Candidate provides activities and opportunities that encourage curiosity, exploration, and problem–solving appropriate to the developmental levels and learning styles of children.
6. **Communication:** Candidate actively communicates with children and provides opportunities and support for children to understand, acquire, and use, verbal and nonverbal means of communicating thoughts and feelings.
7. **Creative:** Candidate provides opportunities that stimulate children to play with sound, rhythm, language, materials, space, and ideas in individual ways to express their creative abilities.

III. **To support social and emotional development and provide positive guidance**
8. **Self:** Candidate provides physical and emotional development and security for each child and helps each child to know, accept, and take pride in himself or herself and to develop a sense of independence.
9. **Social:** Candidate helps each child feel accepted in the group, helps each child learn to communicate and get along with others, and encourages feelings of empathy and mutual respect among children and adults.
10. **Guidance:** Candidate provides a supportive environment in which children can begin to learn and practice appropriate and acceptable behaviors as individuals and as a group.

IV. **To establish positive and productive relationships with families**
11. **Families:** Candidate maintains an open, friendly, and cooperative relationship with each child's family, encourages their involvement in the program, and supports the child's relationship with his or her family.

V. **To ensure a well-run, purposeful program responsive to participant needs**
12. **Program management:** Candidate is a manager who uses all available resources to ensure an effective operation. The candidate is a competent organizer, planner, recordkeeper, communicator, and a cooperative co-worker.

VI. **To maintain a commitment to professionalism**
13. **Professionalism:** Candidate makes decisions based on knowledge of early childhood theories and practices, promotes quality in child care services, and takes advantage of opportunities to improve competence, both for personal and professional growth and for the benefit of children and families. (Reprinted from Phillips, 1991, p. 466 by permission of the Council of Early Childhood Professional Recognition.)

Reprinted from "At the Core: What Every Early Childhood Professional Should Know" by permission of the Council for Early Childhood Professional Recognition

Figure 10-14 **Child Development Associate (CDA) Functional Areas.**

didate. After all the documentation is thoroughly discussed at a meeting where all these representatives are present, the team members vote on the candidate's competence, and the national credential is issued. As you will see from the Timeline, the credentialing process allowed many members of the early childhood profession who had entered through nontraditional routes to use their knowledge gained through experience to earn recognition for their competence.

1990
National Committee for Prevention of Child Abuse reports that approximately 2.5 million children were abused and neglected.

| FUNCTIONAL AREA : COMMUNICATION | ENTRY #1 |

Story Time

    I read stories that are familiar to the children in my class to develop their communication and language skills. As I read the stories, if the children know what will happen next, they will say the words with me. I often ask the children about the different events described in the stories and in what sequence they occurred.

    When I observe the children playing out the different roles in the stories, I know they are communicating in a relaxed and comfortable atmosphere.

    I read stories to stimulate the children's language and vocabulary. I know that it is important for them to have language stimulation so that they can learn to communicate their own thoughts and feelings.

—From the portfolio of Amy Loretta, CDA Jicarilla Apache Head Start
(Beers, David. 1993, p. 10, in *Growing Teachers*. E. Jones, Ed.).

Figure 10-15   **Sample portfolio entry. (Used with permission of Elizabeth Jones)**

Over 30,000 CDA credentials have been awarded to date, since the first in 1975; 46 states and the District of Columbia recognize the credential as evidence of professional preparation in their licensing requirements. Since Head Start mandated that the CDA credential (or higher degree) would be a requirement for all lead teachers in Head Start classrooms by 1994, over 80 percent of the CDA credentialed teachers are employed in Head Start class-rooms (Phillips, 1990). Individuals who work in various settings with different age-groups–preschools, infant/toddler programs, and family child care–may be credentialed, as well as those who are fluent in both English and Spanish (see Fig. 10-16).

Since 1985, the CDA National Credentialing Program has been administered by the **Council for Early Childhood Professional Recognition**, a permanent national body created by NAEYC, and now an independent entity. In 1991, the Council announced a new model that linked training and assessment. There are two parts to the new Council Model. One is for individuals who have no prior experience with children. The process involves a one-year training program leading to the CDA credential, with a first phase of guided field experiences with young children on a daily basis; then a phase of instructional coursework provided by a local college or other postsecondary educational institution monitored by the Council; with a last phase of integrated field work with instructional coursework. During this time, the student completes a performance-based assessment, interview and review of written documents with a Council representative. After the Council reviews all documents, successful candidates receive a CDA credential. In addition to this preparation program, the Council continues to offer direct assessment to candidates, with competency-based evaluation of performance and written assessments of knowledge of good early childhood practice (see Fig. 10-17).

The CDA Professional Recognition system continues to offer an alternative route for beginning professional preparation for early educators. Many who

Council for Early Childhood Professional Recognition: Independent body that supervises awarding of the Child Development Associate (CDA) credential.

1990

Legislation for the Child Care and Development Block Grants (called the ABC bill during the years when proponents were lobbying for its passage) is approved and funded by Congress.

Figure 10-16 **Practitioners who work with infants and toddlers may be credentialed in those settings.**

have been traditionally excluded from higher education because of socioeconomic reasons can still begin their journey to professionalism via the CDA. For many, the credential may be the beginning on the career lattice.

> Working on my CDA credential, I've found that I'm able to do college-level work in early childhood education courses offered here in Dulce by San Juan College. Going back to school was a real thrill. I never even came close to thinking I'd ever go back to school. I am amazed at all the information I've learned about the ways of teaching and talking with children since I started with Head Start. I believe that earning my CDA credential is the first step in earning my master's degree in early childhood education. Judith L. (Beers, 1993, p. 3).

In this teacher's statement, you can see not only the reflection of knowledge that helps create higher quality programs for children, but also the sense of personal and professional growth that is vital for early childhood teachers. It is crucial for the growing professionalism of early childhood education that efforts continue to help CDA credentialed teachers articulate with other higher education programs. For many, this is an important example of adults needing choices and alternative routes, as well as the children they teach.

MENTORING

During the past several years, a new pattern has been added to opportunities for professional growth and learning in many early childhood communities. It is possible that you will have an opportunity to benefit from a mentoring program, either as a student or as a professional. In mentoring programs, experienced and effective early educators are given specialized training, to help beginning teachers gain skills and become more effective practitioners. Students

1990

The National Education Association issues a policy statement that public schools should be a primary provider of high-quality early childhood education programs for children ages three to eight.

Figure 10-17	**Photos such as these may be included in candidates' proofs of knowledge of good early childhood practice.**

or beginning teachers—often called protégés, mentees, or apprentices—are paired with the mentor teacher, generally in the mentor's classroom. Here, during experiential learning, mentors act as backup support, offering feedback that allows the beginner to move to a higher level of skilled performance.

Who does such an arrangement benefit? Obviously, both participants gain. Experienced teachers receive recognition, advanced education, and increased salaries as they participate as mentors. They can remain in their classrooms with children, using their developed skills and expertise, and yet feel that they have advanced in their own professional careers, taking on new positions of leadership in their centers and community. They are more likely to remain in the field, with the new status and enhanced salaries, as well as the new interest in leader-

All real learning requires activity on some level
—William Ayers

1991
The number of preschool children with employed mothers has doubled since 1977.

ship and professional development. Their own practice is likely to improve, as the mentors increase their reflection about their teaching to share with the protégé. The protégé is also more likely to remain in the field over time, having been given the opportunity to develop the skills needed to prevent the overwhelming frustration of the unskilled. Having formed a relationship with an experienced teacher, they see that early childhood is a viable profession over time. They have received the coaching, guidance, and counseling that helps during the initial adjustments to any new experience. In lessening the probability of staff turnover and by developing more educated and skilled practitioners, mentor programs are making important contributions to communities and early childhood programs. Thus the quality of services to children and families is directly impacted by the development of such opportunities.

There are diverse ways to structure mentor programs, according to community resources and needs. For examples of successful mentor programs, see Whitebook et al., 1994.

From the discussions about the various issues regarding professional education programs, you may have a clearer perspective on where your own goals and training fit into the larger picture. It is important that you understand the options open to you, and also comprehend the purposes behind the design of your current program, as you are using this text. A well-prepared early childhood professional can contribute most to these continuing discussions.

CAREER DIRECTIONS

As you look ahead to your professional career, you may be looking towards thirty or more productive years. During that period, you may be involved in different kinds of work in the early education field. Today, as the field continues to grow and expand, there are numerous possibilities for those who choose to make their life's work focus on early childhood.

> As larger numbers of children live in families where both parents work, more early childhood professionals are needed to care for and teach these children. Families also need people to help them find care and assistance paying for this care. In addition, our society has become more concerned about how this care affects young children and what quality child care really means. These concerns have led to more jobs. We need more family and early intervention specialists to help families find the kind of care they need; we need more researchers to find out what produces quality child care programs; we need more trainers and consultants to make sure child care programs are meeting the quality requirements; and we need more administrators to help organize all these people and projects.[1]

I was neither a good listener nor an able storyteller when my name became Teacher. What I doubtless knew as a child was buried under piles of disconnected information. I was a stranger in the classroom, grown distant from the thinking of children. I knew myself no better than I did the children. How was I to behave? How could I know what to say to so many children when I could hardly recall anything a teacher ever said to me?
—Vivian Paley

---

[1]From *Careers in Early Childhood,* (p.1), by Sue Russell and Teresa M. Derrick, 1993, Chapel Hill, NC: Day Care Services, Inc. Used with permission.

1991
The number of preschool children who are cared for in organized child care programs is now almost 25 percent.

It is exciting to know that there are possibilities that allow for individuals with particular talents and interests, and for movement and continuing challenge that will utilize your growing professional knowledge.

Careers in the early childhood field include: those that serve children directly; those that serve families directly; those that organize services for children and families; those that provide information about children and families; and those that provide goods and services affecting children and families. We will explore some of these here. Remember that within each type of position, there are many different job positions, and that the particular responsibilities and requirements, as well as salary ranges, will also vary with specific organizations.

Careers that Serve Children Directly

Teaching in Center-Based Programs. Teaching in **center-based** classrooms will likely be a starting point for many of you. Almost every other related career suggests that professionals have some direct experience with young children. Many of you may decide this is where you want to stay for many years; others of you may consider the classroom experience an important foundation experience for other goals. From your reading of earlier chapters, you will know that there are many different kinds of center-based programs in which to teach, depending on your educational preparation. These may include: public programs, such as **Chapter One Prekindergarten** programs, developmental day programs, kindergartens or primary grades; before- and after-school care programs; Head Start programs; child care centers that may be operated by churches, not-for-profit corporations, for-profit organizations or owners; employer-sponsored, or government agencies; and part-day preschools. Sometimes teachers may operate out of a center-based program, but teach in children's homes, as home visitors working with children and entire families.

Teachers in Home-Based Programs. Teachers may work with young children in their own home, or in the child's home. **In-home childcare specialists**, sometimes referred to as nannies, may be hired by individual families. You will recall our earlier discussions about family child care programs that may serve as many as twelve children, and may be licensed or registered with the state. Many teachers choose to teach in their own homes for matters of both convenience to their own families, and preference for the types of relationships fostered in the homelike setting. Obviously conditions are controlled closely in each individual situation.

There are many programs nationally organized around a home-visitor format. When professionals work with children in the child's own home, the arrangements are again quite individual with each family and agency.

Child Development Specialist on Health Team. Professionals with child development background are often included on the assessment and education teams that may be part of providing services to children with special needs. Education specialists may interact with children during screening

Center-Based: Refers to those programs where care and education is organized in classrooms in a child care center, away from the child's home.

Chapter One Prekindergarten: Programs for four-year-olds, supported by Chapter One Funds, and held under the auspices of school systems to prepare children considered at risk for kindergarten success.

In-Home Child Care Specialist: Provision of child care by an individual within the child's own home. Also called "nanny." This position may or may not be a full-time live-in situation.

1991
The first Worthy Wage Day, organized by the Child Care Employee Project, is held on April 9th.

or assessment sessions, may help provide appropriate stimulation for children in small group therapy sessions, or may provide appropriate knowledge and guidance for family members. Some health departments include child development specialists on their teams to include well-baby information about typical development of young children for parents. Other child development specialists may be part of the staff facilitating children's play in the play therapy room in hospital pediatric units. Some health agencies, such as the Red Cross, employ early childhood practitioners in their community education programs.

Recreation Leaders.   Some recreation facilities, such as city park and recreation programs and residential camps, employ early childhood-trained teachers to staff and administer their recreation programs for children. There are companies who sponsor exercise, dance, and fitness programs for children, and others that provide child care for parents who participate. Some library systems employ individuals with early childhood backgrounds to be storytellers and provide other services in children's rooms.

Careers that Serve Families Directly

Family Specialists.   Family specialists include a broad spectrum of early childhood professionals who help families gain access to the services they need to care for their children. Many community agencies support families in doing the complex tasks of parenting and finding the resources they need to do this. A family specialist may provide information and education, may refer families to services, may help them gain access for funds to pay for services, or give direct support services. Family specialists may deliver services in agency offices, in child care programs, or in the family's home. Some have specialized expertise, such as child care referral counselors, social workers, or family counselors. Examples of programs that employ family specialists are child care resource and referral agencies, Head Start programs and Parent-Child centers, community mental health and child abuse prevention agencies, and health departments.

Early Intervention Specialists.   **Early intervention** is an interdisciplinary field that includes health, human services, and educational services for young children with special needs and their families. These specialists work directly with children and their families, in both homes and child care programs. They also work with other specialists who provide direct services to children and their families, such as child care providers, speech and language diagnosticians and therapists, physical and occupational therapists, medical personnel, and social workers. As the special needs of each child and the concerns of the family are identified, early interventionists and other service providers work with the family on creating a plan to meet those needs. This plan is called an **Individualized Education Plan (IEP)** or **Individualized Family Services Plan (IFSP)**, depending on the age of the child. (You will learn much more about this terminology and this entire process in your later coursework on children with special needs.)

Early Intervention Programs: Programs that work with children whose development is delayed or at-risk, often offering comprehensive services.

Individualized Educational Plan (IEP): Written plan for children with special needs over the age of three, specifying what will be done for the child, and how and when it will be done. Mandated by 1976 Education for all Handicapped Children Act.

Individualized Family Service Plan (IFSP): Written plan for children with special needs under age three, developed by a multidisciplinary team and the child's parents. Outlines the family's strengths for enhancing the child's development, and the intervention services needed to meet the needs of child and family. Mandated by 1986 Amendments to the Education for all Handicapped Children Act.

1992
1,824 early childhood programs have been accredited by the National Academy of Early Childhood Programs.

Early intervention specialists coordinate activities between the family and the other professionals working with the child, and help plan and deliver services. In these positions, individuals utilize not only their knowledge of child development, assessment, and family needs. They must also be skillful in working with other professionals, in communicating with parents, and in techniques for working successfully with children.

Careers that Organize Services

Child Care Program Administrators.   Program administrators usually have several years of teaching experience, as well as specialized studies in administration and business matters. These individuals have responsibility for: ensuring that programs offer developmentally appropriate experiences for children that also meet all legal standards; helping teachers to grow and develop professionally; supporting the needs of families, and involving them in their children's lives at the center; and supervising the daily flow of all center operations, including maintaining staffing, collecting fees, meeting nutritional needs, and ordering equipment, materials, and supplies. Fiscal management is an additional challenge, and some may also have responsibilities for fund-raising. Because the director is usually the one who handles crises, the job may include plumbing, first aid in emergencies, social work, and counseling on any given day. The differences in center-based programs help determine what is expected of directors. Some very large centers also have an assistant director to help meet these responsibilities.

In very large early childhood settings, program administrators may have much greater responsibility for arranging wider goals and priorities, and less with the day-to-day minute details of operating a program. For example, an upper-level manager may be the executive director of a child care resource and referral agency or a director of a multisite Head Start program. Program or project coordinators often have responsibility for managing a single specialty area, such as the education coordinator of a Head Start program, or a day care coordinator in a local department of social services.

Regulators.   Regulators, or licensing specialists, are the individuals who have the task of overseeing the compliance of early childhood programs with various federal, state, or local requirements. Regulators visit programs to examine for compliance with particular standards. In addition, many regulators assist directors and teachers with technical assistance and/or training to help them meet the standards. Some regulators also have the task of visiting programs that have been suspected of noncompliance with regulations. The knowledge required by regulators is quite comprehensive: they must know child development, appropriate programming and curriculum, effective guidance, and health and safety precautions. In addition, communication skills for working in the often difficult situation of monitoring others' practice are required. Most regulators are employed by state or local government agencies. Some monitor child care centers or homes; others monitor food programs, or complaints of abuse or neglect.

The best way to grow as a teacher is to study something interesting to you that is far removed from your usual teaching, like gardening, pantomime, juggling, massage, or belly dance. Watch yourself as you learn something new and hard, and you'll find out more about learning and teaching
—Syndey Gurewitz-Clemens

1992
2.2 million couples receive Lamaze training for childbirth.

Consultants.   Early childhood consultants provide assistance and information to businesses, communities, and other organizations to help them develop child care programs or meet various standards. Usually consultants work on site with the organization in need of their services to help them assess their current program and resources and future plans. A growing need is for consultants to help employers work out methods of providing for their employees' child care needs. In addition to knowledge of child development and child care program administration, consultants who work with the corporate community likely need specialized knowledge about market research and employee benefits.

Careers that Provide Information

Researchers.   As programs and policies regarding children continue to expand, there is an ever-increasing need to understand the various aspects of children's development and programming. Researchers generally focus attention on specific service aspects, such as child care, health services, early intervention programs, or nutrition. Much research focuses on children at various stages of development, and on family variables and needs. Employment opportunities are with colleges or universities, research institutes that may be affiliated with universities, government agencies, foundations, professional associations, or advocacy organizations. In addition to having a wide background in child and family development knowledge, many researchers need knowledge of various observation and other data collection methods, as well as data anyalysis techniques. Many researchers begin their careers as part-time research assistants or interns.

Trainers and Instructors.   Those who work with practitioners have an important responsibility of helping those adults gain the knowledge and skills they need to work effectively with young children and their families. In addition to having a depth of knowledge in child development and all aspects of effective early childhood education and programming, they must understand adult development and learning, and effective teaching strategies. Effective trainers and instructors have generally had considerable firsthand experience in classrooms with children. Many experienced early childhood professionals train others on a part-time basis at the same time that they work in the classroom with young children, by participating in workshops or at local conferences, or teaching part-time at a local college. This is a satisfying way of making a larger contribution to the field, while still maintaining the connection to the classroom.

You will recall from the discussion of mentors earlier in this chapter that many classroom teachers are able to work in their own classrooms with children while supporting students and other new teachers in learning effective teaching practice through mentoring. Others, such as regulators, family specialists, or early intervention specialists, also occasionally provide training as part of their jobs. Still others, such as college and university early childhood education faculty or high school child development teachers, are

1992
Overall infant mortality rate is 8.5 infant deaths per 1,000 live births; black infants die at the rate of 17 per 1,000.

Figure 10-18 **Although most of us think of working with children like these as early childhood careers, some decide to move to other careers in early childhood education besides direct classroom services to children. (Courtesy of Connie Glass and Tracie O'Hara)**

involved full time in educating other practitioners. Some very large child care programs with multiple centers employ their own educational specialists to work with their staff.

Authors/Editors. There are a number of local and national publications devoted entirely to children's and family issues. These vary from the large, glossy magazines sold nationally on newsstands and by subscription, to local publications sometimes distributed free of charge in doctors' offices and

1992
32 states support prekindergarten initiatives.

schools. All of these publications offer professionals opportunities to share their knowledge about children and families in print.

Careers that Provide Goods and Services

Merchandisers.   There is a large consumer market for developmentally appropriate toys and materials, books, teaching materials, clothing, and other items used for the care and teaching of young children. People who merchandise items used by children, their families, and their programs may sell their products in stores, or at local or national conferences. Many corporations prefer to have their items marketed by individuals with a knowledge of child development.

Legislators and Lobbyists.   While child development background or experience is not a prerequisite, gaining a voice in the legislature is one way that many who care about children's and family issues can be effective. Legislators have a direct impact on creating the laws and policy that influence lives of families, and of childhood education programs. In our modern world of increasing organization to deal with the complexities of the legislative process, others with early childhood interests may find there are opportunities to influence others by working with advocacy groups, as lobbyists. Here again, child development and other professional knowledge can make legislators and lobbyists far more effective.

This is by no means an exhaustive list, but it should suggest to you that your interests and talents may move you in multiple directions, as you gain more education and experience. Use every opportunity to find out what other early childhood professionals do in your community (see Fig. 10-18).

Where is your thinking now? What might be your next move? Where do you see yourself five or ten years from now?

1993
President Bill Clinton signs the Family and Medical Leave Bill into law.

SUMMARY

In this chapter, the varying methods of preparing for professional roles in the early childhood field have been described. There is little uniformity in current knowledge or requirements, due to the dual nature of the regulatory bodies for training requirements, and due to variations within individual state requirements of certification and licensing. Currently attempts are being made, by NAEYC's National Institute for Professional Development and other organizations, to create comprehensive plans for teacher preparation. These plans provide both flexibility of entry point and preparation options, as well as increase the level of professional education in the defined core knowledge that is essential for all early childhood practitioners.

Within the early childhood field, there are increasing numbers of possible career options, and more will come with time. Those entering the field should investigate the possibilities in both education and employment that match their personal and professional goals.

QUESTIONS FOR REVIEW

1. Discuss the differences between licensing and certification.

2. Identify reasons for diversity in early childhood preparation requirements.

3. Identify and discuss the reasons for forming NAEYC's National Institute for Professional Development.

4. Discuss what is meant by a "career lattice" and its significance for the early childhood field.

5. Describe the Child Development Associate credential, and how it fits into early childhood professional preparation.

6. Discuss the concept of "mentoring" as it is currently being used in early education professional development.

7. Discuss various career options within the early childhood field, under the headings of: working directly with children, working directly with families, organizing services for children and families, providing information about children and families, and providing goods and services affecting children and families.

ACTIVITIES FOR FURTHER STUDY

1. Find the section in your state's child care program licensing regulations that stipulate training requirements for early childhood personnel. Discuss these requirements in class, with regard to ideas about effective personnel. Compare them to NAEYC's guidelines. Draw up a set of recommendations for training that you feel would strengthen the quality of programs for children.

2. Investigate the various types of early childhood certification currently available in your state, and what kinds of coursework and/or practicum experiences these involve. Again, draw up a set of recommendations that would align the certification requirements with NAEYC guidelines.

3. Analyze your early childhood program to see how the various courses provide the kinds of knowledge recommended by the NAEYC statement on core knowledge for early childhood professionals, practical experience, and general knowledge.

4. If possible, interview an early childhood teacher who has received a CDA credential. Talk about the experience, and examine any available documentation. (You may want to contact a local Head Start office to get information on successful candidates in your area.)

5. Learn whether mentoring programs exist in your area, and how you can be involved.

6. From the careers listed in the chapter, work with friends to identify people in as many of these positions as you can. Choose three careers that you would like to investigate further. Where possible, make an appointment to discuss the work with an individual currently involved in it.

REFERENCES

Author. (1991b, September). NAEYC to launch new professional development initiative. *Young Children, 46,* (6), 37-39.

Author. (1991a, November). Early childhood teacher certification: A position statement of the association of teacher educators and the National Association for the Education of Young Children. *Young Children, 47,* (1), 16-21.

Author. (1995). *Guidelines for preparation of early childhood professionals associate, baccalaureate, and advanced levels. Position statement.* Washington, DC: NAEYC.

Beers, C. David. (1993). Telling our stories: The CDA process in Native American Head Start. In Elizabeth Jones (Ed.). *Growing teachers: Partnerships in staff development.* Washington, DC: NAEYC.

Bredekamp, Sue. (1992, January). Composing a profession. *Young Children 47,* (2), 52-54.

Bredekamp, Sue. (1995, January). What do early childhood professionals need to know and be able to do? *Young Children, 50,* (2), 67-69.

Corsini, David A., Wisensale, Steven, & Caruso, Grace-Ann. (1988, September). Family day care: System issues and regulatory models. *Young Children, 43,* (6), 17-23.

Morgan, Gwen, Azer, Sheri L., Costley, Joan B., Genser, Andrea, Goodman, Irene R., Lombardi, Joan, McGimsey, Bettina. (1993). *Making a career of it. The state of the states report on career development in early care and education.* Boston MA: The Center for Career Development in Early Care and Education at Wheelock College.

Phillips, Carol Brunson. (1990, March). The child development associate program: Entering a new era. *Young Children, 45,* (3), 24-27.

Phillips, Carol Brunson, (Ed.). (1991). *Essentials for child development associates working with young children.* Washington, DC: Council for Early Childhood Professional Recognition.

Phillips, Carol Brunson. (1994). At the core: What every early childhood professional should know. In Julienne Johnson, & Janet B. McCracken (Eds.), *The early childhood career lattice: Perspectives on professional development.* Washington, DC: NAEYC.

Russell, Sue, & Derrick, Teresa M. (1993). *Careers in early childhood.* Chapel Hill, NC: Day Care Services, Inc..

Spodek, Bernard. (1994). The knowledge base for baccalaureate early childhood teacher education programs. In Julienne Johnson, & Janet B. McCracken (Eds.), *The early childhood career lattice: Perspectives on professional development.* Washington, DC: NAEYC.

Willer, Barbara, (Ed.). (1994). A conceptual framework for early childhood professional development. NAEYC position statement. In Julienne Johnson, & Janet B. McCracken (Eds.), *The early childhood career lattice: Perspectives on professional development.* Washington, DC: NAEYC.

Whitebook, Marcy, Hnatiuk, Patty, & Bellm, Dan. (1994). *Mentoring in early care and education: Refining an emerging career path.* Washington, DC: National Center for the Early Childhood Work Force.

SUGGESTIONS FOR READING

Author. (1991, November). A vision for early childhood professional development. *Young Children, 47,* (1), 35-37.

Bredekamp, Sue. (1992, September). The early childhood profession coming together. *Young Children, 47,* (6), 36-39.

Greenough, Kathrin. (1993). Moving out of silence: The CDA process with Alaska native reachers. In Elizabeth Jones (Ed.). *Growing teachers: Partnerships in staff development.* Washington, DC: NAEYC.

Johnson, Julienne, & McCracken, Janet B. (1994). *The early childhood career lattice: Perspectives on professional development.* Washington, DC: NAEYC.

Seaver, Judith A., Cartwright, Carol A., Ward, Cecilia, B., & Heasley, C. Annette. *Careers with young children.* Washington, DC: NAEYC.

Willer, Barbara, & Bredekamp, Sue. (1993, May). A "new" paradigm of early childhood professional development. *Young Children, 48,* (4), 63-66.

11

CURRENT ISSUES IN EARLY EDUCATION

OBJECTIVES

After studying this chapter, students will be able to:

1. discuss the relationship between compensation and economic conditions for teachers and quality programs for children, and identify what is meant by the "Worthy Wage Campaign," discussing its significance to increasing professionalism;

2. describe what is meant by "burnout," identifying several specific teacher actions that can prevent burnout;

3. discuss common concerns regarding early academics, readiness, and achievement testing;

4. identify what is meant by "inclusion," and discuss the benefits for all children and adults involved;

As you proceed through your professional preparation and early education program, you will study the theories and research applications of developmentally appropriate practice. You will also encounter the most current thinking and trends that influence the profession today. As you are introduced to early education, it is important that you consider the complexity of the issues early educators face. Consequently, you gain an initial appreciation of ideas that invite your participation and efforts.

In this rapidly expanding profession, responses to needs of children, families, and teachers are propelling changes that will impact us all. Some of these trends will strengthen the profession itself, making it more likely that you who are now joining the ranks of professionals will see enormous changes during your entire active career. Other trends will create improved learning environments and conditions for children, demanding growth, expanded knowledge, and change in the teachers who care for them. So consider this chapter as an overview of important issues that you will encounter as you progress. Knowing that these trends exist may help you appreciate the dynamic nature of the profession of early education.

Before you read any further, it would be interesting for you to note down those ideas that you believe might be included in this discussion of issues. Think about the ideas you have encountered earlier in this book that seem to be of likely importance to all early childhood professionals. Think also of the issues that have been referred to in the conversations you have had with early educators as you pursued further learning activities. Obviously no list of issues can be completely comprehensive, but the summaries that follow suggest some of the important areas of discussion and work in the early childhood profession today. You will discover also that solutions to the issues are beyond the scope of this chapter; here you will find a brief consideration of a particular issue, and current activities involving the issue. It is hoped that you, your instructor, and your fellow classmates will use the references at chapter end to guide deeper learning and discussion about some of these issues, in addition to the wider learning opportunities you will have in subsequent coursework. As you continue your professional development, you will be involved in working on some of the processes that move towards solutions, resolutions, and further action. There are many exciting developments in our immediate and distant futures.

5. discuss the concepts that lie behind the antibias curriculum;

6. describe some of the benefits of mixed-age groupings in early education classrooms; and

7. discuss some ideas regarding the use of technology in early childhood classrooms.

ISSUES THAT IMPACT ON THE EARLY CHILDHOOD PROFESSION

Quality and Compensation

Perhaps like most of the rest of Americans, you were jolted by newspaper and television news feature stories in early 1995. "Most Day Care Poor to Just OK" announced USA Today (USA Today 2/6/95); "Child Care is Worse Than Believed, with Safety Jeopardized, Study Suggests" proclaimed the Wall Street Journal (Wall Street Journal 2/6/95); "Child Care Attacked," summed up Connie Chung on the CBS Evening News. Behind these worrisome headlines is a complicated report of studies that once again linked the quality of the child care in the four states studied (400 randomly selected centers in California, Colorado, Connecticut, and North Carolina) to specific variables, most of which are related to economic factors. To be specific, the study found that, while there were wide variations among states and individual programs within states, the care at the majority of the centers studied was poor to mediocre when rated according to standards of provisions for health and safety, of relationships characterized by warmth and support of adults, and of attention to children's learning needs. In fact, 40 percent of infant and toddler care was rated at less-than-minimal quality (see Fig. 11-1). Another finding of the study indicates that children's later cognitive and social development are positively related to the quality of their child care experiences, no matter what the variables in maternal education, ethnicity,

1993
Percentage of child support cases in which states collect any payment reaches 18.7 percent.

Figure 11-1 **The most recent study on child care quality indicates that the majority of children are in centers that offer poor or mediocre quality in specific areas.**

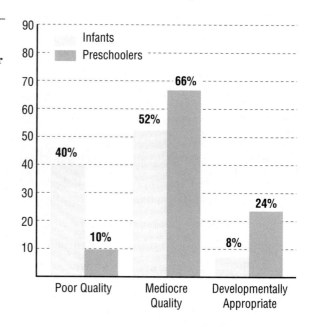

or child gender. Therefore, it seems imperative that quality child care be part of every child's optimum early experiences. Yet the finding that so few children have this quality child care is certainly shocking in a nation that at least verbalizes its concern and recognition of the importance of early childhood experiences. It is even more disturbing that the study points out that quality is linked to specific variables that are significantly related to economic factors.

Before this study, previous research had already linked quality and factors related to economic and education conditions of early childhood teachers. In 1989, the National Child Care Staffing Study reported some significant findings relating quality in child care and adult work environment variables. Major findings of this study were that:

(1) the education of child care teaching staff and the arrangement of their work environments are essential determinants of the quality of programs for children. As you might expect after reading the earlier discussions in this text, teachers provided more responsive and appropriate care for children if they had had formal training in early childhood at the college level, earned higher wages and better benefits, and worked in centers whose budgets used a higher percentage of their funds for teacher salaries and benefits.

(2) the most important predictor of the quality of care children receive, among all the variables related to adult work environments, is staff wages. Better quality centers had higher wages for teachers, and, consequently, lower rates of teaching staff turnover.

(3) child care teaching staff earn very low wages, especially considering the fact that they have higher levels of formal education than the average American worker. At the time of the study, early childhood teachers were earning less than one-half of what women with comparable education levels were earning in the general work force, and less than one-third of what men with comparable educa-

1993
The National Alliance of Multi-age Educators holds its first national conference; multi-age early childhood education programs exist in almost every school district in the nation.

tion were earning. Even worse, the salaries were going backwards; in the previous decade, child care teacher wages had decreased more than 20 percent, when adjusted for inflation. Employment benefits were minimal: fewer than half of the teachers in the study received medical coverage, and only a small percentage had a retirement plan. Other than sick leave and paid holidays for some, the only other benefit for most staff was reduced child care fees for their own children.

(4) the turnover rate of teaching staff in child centers had nearly tripled from the late 70s to the late 80s; by the late 80s, the annual turnover rate for early childhood teachers was about 41 percent. To underscore the fact that the turnover rate was absolutely related to the salary level, the study found that the turnover rate for teachers earning the lowest wages was about twice that of teachers with the highest wages.

THEORY INTO PRACTICE

This is Natasha England. She has worked in child care for four years, primarily with infants. She is presently the lead teacher in an infant room at a child care center that is part of an intergenerational program on the campus of a nursing home, used primarily by employees of the nursing home. She is working to complete an associate degree program in early childhood education.

What has been a significant frustration for you in early education? How do you deal with it?

A significant frustration for me has been coming to understand why parents do things the way they sometimes do. For example, why they don't take their children to the doctor when it is noticeable that the child is sick. I usually talk to my director about it and let my frustrations out with her.

What is one thing you learned in classes that you really discovered to be true when you started working with children?

I have discovered that teachers must have patience, and the ability to communicate with parents in an open-minded, though difficult, situation.

What is an area you are working on now to learn more about?

I want to learn more about administration, as that is a career goal.

Why have you stayed in early education?

I have stayed because it's something that I enjoy doing, and there are kids who need that special attention. I feel I can meet the needs of those children.

What is a comment or piece of advice you would give to those beginning to work in early childhood education?

I would say only do it if it's in your heart. It's not an easy job and you have to have patience to really stick with it. If you have the care to give, there are those out there who want it. You'll need to be understanding as well as sympathetic. If you're looking for a challenge, then you're in the right field. You'll also be able to work out difficult situations without blowing up.

Teachers are expected to reach unattainable goals with inadequate tools. The miracle is that at times they accomplish this impossible task

–Fred Rogers

When this study was published in 1989, The National Child Care Staffing Study recommended that:

(1) child care teacher salaries be raised as a means of recruiting and retaining a qualified professional work force;

(2) opportunities for formal education and training be provided for teachers to enhance their ability to offer developmentally appropriate learning experiences for young children;

(3) state and federal regulations regarding adult-child ratios, staff education, and compensation be adopted as a means of raising the quality in the United States' child care programs;

(4) standards for the adult work environment be developed within the child care industry to minimize differences in quality between various types of programs; and

(5) public education about the crucial importance of well-trained and adequately compensated teachers be promoted, to gain community support for the **full cost of quality** care.

That these recommendations have not yet succeeded is evidenced by the findings of an update of the study (Whitebook et al., 1993). Four years later, less than 20 percent of the centers included in the original study offered full health benefits for all staff. In 1993, the average highest paid child care center teacher was earning $15,400, even though about 75 percent of them had at least some college level training or a B.A. degree. This was revealed at the same time that average salaries for women with college degrees or some college training was $33,300, and that for males with degrees was $51,804. The lack of changes over the four-year period affected their retention in the field: indeed, only 30 percent of the teachers and assistants interviewed in the original study were still employed in the same setting, and of the 227 centers in the original study, 34 had closed (Bellm et al., 1994).

Let's return to that phrase "full cost of quality." The issue of affordability for families is directly tied to the issue of teachers' compensation, since in non-profit centers, by far the largest percentage of the budget that drives parent fees is the salaries and benefits for the professional staff. Another aspect of budgetary costs that impacts quality is the adult-child ratio, the number of children that are cared for by one adult. Obviously lower adult-child ratios are more costly, as well as more effective for quality programs. While parents find their budgets strained by the cost of their child care, what the average parent or policymaker does not realize is that quality child care actually costs more than is apparent from the fees that parents pay. The full cost includes hidden costs, such as goods and services that may be donated, occupancy of the facility, donations, and, most importantly for this discussion, foregone wages and benefits–that is, the difference in wages between the actual wage received as an early childhood teacher, and the amount the individual could have earned in another occupation. As you can see in Fig. 11-2, foregone wages amount to nearly 20 percent of the full cost of quality. By accepting low wages, child care professionals are in fact subsidizing the child care costs of the families in their communities. (See more about this in the discussion of NAEYC's full cost of quality campaign, designed to heighten community awareness of this hidden subsidy [Willer, 1990].)

1993

Perry Project publishes its data on the now 27-year-olds who were once in its preschool programs, showing the continued benefits in social adjustments and proving economic effectiveness of preschool education.

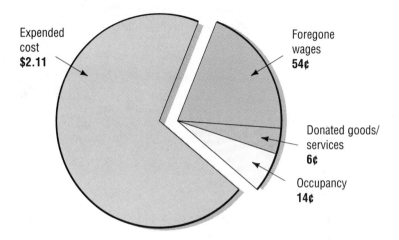

Average full cost = $2.83/child hour

Average hidden cost = 72¢/child hour (represented by cut slice)

Expended cost $2.11

Foregone wages 54¢

Donated goods/ services 6¢

Occupancy 14¢

Figure 11-2 | **Foregone wages (those amounts teachers could have earned in other comparable work) account for nearly 20% of the cost of quality.**

Early childhood teachers' habit of caring for others extends even to this form of sacrificing their own incomes. But awareness has been growing that this sacrifice hurts those who teachers have been trying to protect in the long run—children and families experience the impact of teacher dissatisfaction in the form of staff turnover.

Clearly there is a connection between the low staff wages and teacher turnover. In too many communities, teachers discover that they literally cannot pay all their bills on the salaries they earn as early childhood teachers. Some teachers discover they need to take on an additional job to meet their financial responsibilities. Working with young children all day long is already physically exhausting, and emotionally and cognitively challenging; to have to then go on to a different job puts heavy burdens on teachers, to say nothing of strains on their personal lives. And there is more to it than that: the low salaries imply a lack of societal support and respect for the importance of what teachers do that ultimately eats away at self-esteem and a sense of professional worth.

One teacher who chose other career directions after five years of working with four-year-olds said, "I got tired of always being broke days before my next paycheck. And hoping against hope that I wouldn't get sick enough to have to go to a doctor, let alone take time off my job, since sick days weren't one of our center's benefits. And most of all I got tired of seeing the friends I had gone to college with be able to go on trips and stuff that I knew I'd never be able to do if I stayed in that job. I miss the work, and the kids, but I decided if changes were coming, they weren't coming soon enough to suit me." It is not hard to imagine the feelings of frustration, hurt, and disappointment that lie behind

Readiness is a special mixture of both power and desire
                            —James Hymes

1993
Teenage births account for about 25 percent of American births.

Figure 11-3   **Disruptions in style of care, relationships and routines are disturbing to children's security, especially with young children.**

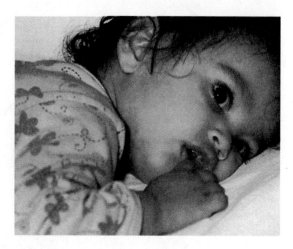

such words, and behind such a final act as leaving the early childhood profession. (See Jalongo, 1991, for one teacher's similar story.)

But we do not have to only imagine the impact of the departure of this, and many thousands of other teachers, from the centers they worked in. What this most recent study on *Cost, Quality, and Child Outcomes in Child Care Centers* documents is that quality suffers with these high rates of teacher turnover. Quality is a result of many things, but several characteristics are directly related to the issues of teacher compensation. The study found that good-quality centers shared these characteristics: small groups of children were assigned to each adult; college-educated teachers worked competently with children, basing their actions on child development knowledge; experienced administrators managed the programs; staff stability existed, resulting from the programs' ability to recruit and retain good staff; and mechanisms existed to meet high standards, such as strong licensing requirements and voluntary accreditation.

Training is important. But it is quite unreasonable to expect the high level of professional preparation that results in excellent situations for children without the matched levels of compensation. When trained teachers cannot be recruited to staff child care programs, the administrators' desperation to hire individuals to at least maintain the adult-child ratios may result in lowering standards for teachers, with a resulting drop in the quality of experiences for children. Without the training, children's development suffers: it is clearly shown in all the studies.

And even with the training, and without the compensation that should accompany it, children and families still suffer, because of the high rates of staff turnover. When children are left in the care of adults other than their parents, it is critical that they be able to form trusting, warm relationships with those caregivers. Learning and stimulation, we have said, occurs within the context of relationships, with teaching embedded in interaction. Learning to feel safe and secure with adults is an important developmental task for young children. It is just about impossible to accomplish this task when a young child's question is, "Mommy, who's going to be my teacher today?" (Whitebook and Granger,

1993
Only three in five teen mothers received early prenatal care; one in 10 received late or no prenatal care.

1989). The disruptions in style of care and in routines are disturbing to children's security, and the more so, the younger the children (see Fig. 11-3).

Just consider all the changes children must adapt to when a teacher leaves. The daily schedule may be different; there are likely new rules and expectations; the new teacher will not know, at least for some time, each child's individual needs, likes, and style; and the songs she sings or the things he says just seem oddly unfamiliar to the young child. The security of the daily rituals, and the person who was associated with them, is gone, shaking children's sense of safe belonging. And for parents who are already struggling with turning the care of their children over to others, having to learn to trust still another adult takes time, energy, and a feeling that it may not be worthwhile to invest much into building yet another relationship. This is an attitude that will not facilitate the comfortable communication that benefits children, parents, and teachers. The center as a whole is disrupted when staff members leave, with those who remain having to take on additional responsibilities, including orienting another new teacher, while wondering how much longer they themselves can remain or grow in this context of continual disruption. The dilemma, to paraphrase Marcy Whitebook, is that it is obvious many teachers cannot afford to stay, while the children cannot afford to have them leave (Whitebook, in Whitebook and Granger, 1989).

It is obvious that the issues related to inadequate compensation are pervasive, and completely counterproductive to overall quality, professional growth and development of individuals (as we discussed in earlier chapters), and to increase public recognition of early childhood professionals. As we have seen, there is a vicious cycle at work here: there are many factors related to compensation that push teachers out of the field, and this results in replacing them with less qualified staff, therefore diminishing the quality of programs for children. When the public perceives this poor quality–and indeed reads only headlines such as those we saw earlier that reported the recent study, without seeing the complexity and interrelatedness of factors that result in quality–their response is to devalue the work of teachers. Then we're right back at the low status, one of those factors that related to compensation and decreased sense of professionalism in the first place!

This is the cycle that must be broken, if there are to be viable futures for all of us, including you who are just entering the profession. And the cycle must be broken because the healthy future of children and families also depends on it. Actually, the headlines *should* read, as Marcy Whitebook (1995) said, "What's Good for Child Care Teachers is Good for Our Country's Children." In the past, teachers have been reluctant to lobby for their own interests, thinking it made them appear less professional and more self-centered, rather than focused on serving others and worrying about the increased costs of care for parents. But the study included here makes it clear that it is necessary to lobby for conditions that affect quality for children and themselves, simultaneously. In addition, because parents have a clear interest in obtaining the highest possible quality of care for their children, they should understand that supporting teachers' efforts to establish higher standards in regulations, and for finding access to extra resources beyond parent fees will benefit their own children.

> *It is hard not to feel that there must be something very wrong with much of what we do in school, if we feel the need to worry so much about what many people call "motivation." A child has no stronger desire than to make sense of the world, to move freely in it, to do things that he sees bigger people doing*
>
> –John Holt

1993

15.7 million United States children are poor–the highest number in thirty years.

Figure 11-4 **At a Worthy Wage rally in Charlotte, N.C., teacher Connie Glass presents a "check" to State Senator Leslie Winner, who had spent a morning job shadowing in Connie's classroom. The large "check" is written out for $6.25, the typical hourly take-home salary for child care teachers in Connie's center. (Courtesy of Tracie O'Hara)**

This focus on the issue of quality may bring parents into the battle for fair compensation as cosupporters in ways that have not yet happened with other initiatives. For some time now, it has seemed to many teachers that they were going to have to "face the harsh reality of the economic marketplace. No one else is going to solve our problem for us. We must become more and more assertive on our own behalf. It is child care employees themselves who hold the key to improving compensation" (Morin, 1989, p. 18). A group of child care teachers in the San Francisco Bay area concerned about the low pay and status of their work established an organization called the Child Care Employee Project in 1977. This was the force behind the National Child Care Staffing Studies of 1988 and 1993 that have so clearly linked the issues of compensation and quality. Now called the **National Center for the Early Childhood Work Force**, this is the most powerful voice for advocating for fair and decent employment conditions for early childhood professionals. It is under this organization that the Worthy Wage Campaign efforts are organized. This is a grassroots attempt to mobilize child care professionals, parents, and others, to fight for solutions to the issues of low compensation and resultant turnover.

In recent years, the efforts of the campaign have focused on various local and national activities on Worthy Wage Day, held on a day during the Week of

National Center for the Early Childhood Work Force: Organization dedicated to improving compensation and retention in the early childhood field.

1993
More than one million cases of child abuse or neglect are confirmed for the year.

Figure 11-5   **Quality for teachers' employment situations means corresponding quality for children and programs. (Courtesy of Tracie O'Hara)**

the Young Child in April. It attempts to draw community attention to the facts of compensation and advocate for improving conditions (see Fig. 11-4). For example, in April 1995, for the fourth annual Worthy Wage event, hundreds of citizens nationwide were invited to participate in a "Job Shadow." They worked alongside an early educator in a classroom or family child care home, and then received a check that was equal to the teacher's real wage for that period. In such ways, the Worthy Wage Campaign is trying to support community efforts to improve working conditions for teachers.

And real avenues for improving both training and compensation are coming with funding from the federal government. With the passage of the Child Care and Development Block Grant (CCDBG) in 1990, states were given funds to create some improvements in compensation and quality. Under the guidelines, a state must spend at least 5 percent of its funds on the improvement of child care quality, with such activities as increasing provider compensation, training, upgrading licensing requirements, and offering resource and referral services. Some states used Block Grant funds to survey salaries, initiate grant programs, and raise reimbursement rates–those amounts that are paid for children whose care is subsidized by the state.

Others have used funds to reward professionals who receive advanced training (such as in the mentor programs discussed in Chapter Ten), and for scholarships to expand access to training. There have been some very promising developments in improving both compensation and quality. Read about some of the specific initiatives in various states in Bellm et al., 1994.

> Each time a state CCDBG planning group succeeds in making headway in some area of compensation and training, it becomes easier for other groups

You can't solve a problem on the same level that it was created. You have to rise above it to the next level
—Albert Einstein

1993
There are 4,500 employer-sponsored child care centers in the United States.

to convince their state policymakers to take a step forward. Each experiment is an important building block to help others design increasingly sophisticated and comprehensive models. Despite the obstacles, the prospects have never been brighter to finally make early childhood education a well-recognized and well-rewarded profession (Bellm et al., 1994, p. 168).

The expanded understanding that we now have is that the link between increasing compensation and increasing parent fees can and must be broken. Consumers simply cannot bear the burden for an appropriate income for all early childhood teachers. Serious commitments of public and private funds will be essential, and recent efforts show progress in this direction. By removing the link between teacher salaries and parent fees, both teachers and parents will be able to approach the matter without trying to protect personal vested interests, focusing only on the idea that quality for teachers will mean corresponding quality for children and programs (see Fig. 11-5).

You can clearly see the importance of the compensation issue, to the profession, to children, families, and communities, and to you yourself. Progress is being made, slowly, yet more every year. These efforts will not succeed unless all teachers make it their business to understand the issues and the solutions, and to recruit others, both parents and teachers, to join in the effort. Make it your concern, now as a student and later as a trained professional, to find out about Worthy Wage campaign efforts in your community. You can get more information about activities and publications from:

> National Center for the Early Childhood Work Force
> 733 15th Street NW, Suite 1037
> Washington, DC 20005-2112.

Alice in Wonderland: "Can you tell me please which direction to take?" Cheshire Cat: "That depends a good deal on where you want to go"
—Lewis Carroll

Teacher Burnout

When the school year ends, I'm leaving. I don't know yet what I'm going to do, but all I know is that I can't teach any more. I can barely drag myself out of bed to go to work in the morning. The littlest things that the children do get on my nerves. I'm honestly afraid I could lose it with one of them. It seems to me to be a thankless job. Instead of telling me they appreciate what I've done, all I get from parents is challenges about my curriculum and complaints.

I had been teaching for thirteen years and felt it was time to leave the classroom. Part of it was the money, but I also felt I was losing my enthusiasm for the work. Then the mentor program came around and I decided to stay and give it a try.

I was at the point of burn-out when I heard about the Mentor Teacher Program.

I was so frustrated as a preschool teacher. I felt that nobody cared about my work, and I was planning to go back to school so I could go into a "real" profession. Then I got involved in the mentor teacher program (Whitebook et al., 1994, p. 17–18).

1994

A 1994 report from the Institute of Medicine said more than 7.5 million American children suffer from psychiatric illnesses or no fault brain disorders, including Conduct Disorders.

Teaching is not the only profession whose practitioners experience **burnout**. But the complexity of the multiple roles teachers of young children are asked to fill, compounded with low salaries and lack of respect, means that teachers have to be aware of this potential condition. Burnout is characterized by losing one's enthusiasm for the work, feeling **stressed**, feeling physically exhausted and energy-depleted, and feeling exploited. It is an incapacity to put much effort into the work, or an emotional withdrawal from the relationships within the work. It creates unhappy environments for children and for adults. When teachers burn out, they either leave the classroom, contributing to the overall problem of impermanence in the profession, or, worse still, they remain, doing their jobs mechanically and joylessly.

Happily, many teachers find ways to avoid reaching the point of ultimate burnout, and they do this by being aware of ways of preventing it. Even though you are just embarking on your professional journey, now is the time to set patterns that will help you keep your professional enthusiasm. Some of the teachers quoted above discovered ways of setting new goals for themselves by learning new skills and taking on new roles as mentors. Burnout usually is avoided when teachers are able to learn new things, try new ideas, play new roles. Listen to some ideas from experienced teachers on things they have found helpful:

> It helps to pull back and look at the long range. Whenever I do this I find a fresh outlook which seems to give more purpose to what I am doing. The day-to-day can get you down, but if you know where you are going it helps (Joan D.).
>
> It helps to focus on our mission, our original grass roots motivation (Linda L.).
>
> I find I can maintain my motivation if I spend some time each month in study and research (Jeanne C.).
>
> I keep involved with new ideas, new projects (Carl S.).
>
> I periodically alter my role in order to avoid boredom or burnout (RoseAnn D.).
>
> I always keep myself involved in at least one project that is exploring unfamiliar, or better yet, uncharted waters (Peter S.).
>
> Visiting other programs, attending conferences and workshops, and reading . . . helps me to keep excited about my job (Rick P.).
>
> One of my chief sources of renewal is our directors' support group which meets every other month to discuss ideas, problems, and solutions (Sumako M.).
>
> To keep upbeat, I join in community efforts that engage in the larger picture (Ethel S.).
>
> I find it very important to face each and every day as a new and exciting experience (Anne D.).
>
> All of these early education professionals are quoted in Exchange, 1988.

Burnout: Stress related to work, indicated by physical and emotional weariness.

Stress: The physical and emotional responses associated with coping with situations beyond one's capacities.

Total selflessness on the part of the caregiver may actually impede her ability to care, as she loses herself in the process. One challenge presented for caregivers, then, centers on their ability to maintain their own sense of well-being while caring for the children

—Robin Leavitt

1994
Fisher Price Toy Company sells $800 million worth of toys.

Figure 11-6 | **Developmentally appropriate classroom practices help develop all domains of the child's development, not purely focusing on the cognitive.**

These excellent suggestions point out that finding support from others, gaining new information, creating new challenges, expanding roles, and focusing on larger goals helps teachers maintain their freshness.

ISSUES THAT AFFECT PROGRAMS

Early Academics, Readiness and Achievement Tests

Since the beginning of the modern era of early education in the 1960s, one particular issue has generated a good deal of debate, and that is how much academic content and method is appropriate for children in their early years. While many professional early childhood teachers understand and support developmentally appropriate practices for young children, there are those less grounded in developmental knowledge. They are more easily influenced by administrators, parents, and policymakers who push for academic experiences for young children, that look a good deal like those presented to older children. You will need to be prepared to offer convincing and solid rationales for structuring the kinds of environments and learning experiences where children initiate their own active learning through play. These environments and experiences are supported by facilitators who recognize that teaching opportunities that occur within the context of active learning are opportunities to develop all domains of the child's development, and are not purely focused on the cognitive (see Fig. 11-6).

There are a number of underlying reasons for this concern about accelerating young children's acquisition of academic skills. When it was acknowledged that the Russians had won the competition to launch a satellite into space (see Sputnik on Timeline), the entire educational system was given close scrutiny. One of the explanations offered for what was seen as failure on the part of the public education systems was that many young children, particularly those from socially and economically disadvantaged backgrounds, were beginning school unprepared for the rigors of academic learning. Among the many

It is as much good to a child to know his three R's by rote, to have been poured full of knowledge of skills without the ability to use them, as it is to a man to know the principles of swimming and not be able to save himself from drowning
–Caroline Pratt

Figure 11-7 **These children in a developmentally appropriate classroom are learning to use language actively, not being drilled in isolated skills by rote.**

programs that proliferated during the years following this initial concern were some that stressed academics in a highly stuctured, teacher-controlled system.

In many cases, programs for preschool children were established within the structure of the school system to try to facilitate their early learning. School systems were used to dealing with the development and learning of older children, and often based these new programs for the youngest ones on a dribbled-down version of what the older ones were doing, rather than recognizing that all those years between the ages of one and six are there for a reason (Greenberg, 1990), and that reason is quite different from what is good for older children. Based largely on the work of behavioral learning theorists (see Skinner in Chapter Eight), these programs for preschools and kindergartens emphasized helping children learn earlier the isolated skills that they would need for later learning. The methods employed by teachers in these academically oriented programs look suspiciously like those used by teachers in classrooms for much older children, where teachers tended to take on the primary role of instructing, drilling, assigning, directing, and testing for knowledge retained (see Fig. 11-7).

In fact, proponents of academic emphasis in early education have basically moved down the academic curriculum. What was once taught in first grade is now frequently expected to be mastered in kindergarten, which means the preschool years must be spent learning the subskills for reading and math that would bring success at that later stage. In many cases administrators of

1994
Loris Malaguzzi, founder of the schools in Reggio Emilia, Italy, dies, while the philosophy of the schools continues to influence programs around the world.

Figure 11-8   **It is difficult for many parents to see the valuable learning embedded in play activities. (Courtesy of Tracie O'Hara)**

school programs were being pressured by the policymakers to whom they were accountable to produce measurable evidence that learning was proceeding, and the kinds of academic knowledge that can be drilled and taught by rote are more easily measured and quantified. So one reason that educational systems moved to earlier academics was to attempt to answer some of the system's own questions about how best to achieve learning results and how to define their role in serving very young children.

But why have parents accepted and supported the need for this academic pressure on their young children? You may recall that, beginning in the 1960s, women in increasing numbers were joining the work force, necessitating substitute care for their very young children. Today most parents, unfamiliar with child development knowledge, are comfortable in finding a program that looks like what they remember of their education experiences, rather than with the appearance of good early education. "What are you teaching them?" they ask. "Do they just play here?" (see Fig. 11-8). And as consumers who want to be assured that they are receiving their full money's worth, they too want to see measurable results, which unfortunately for developmentally appropriate practice, may be more concrete and obvious when a preschooler has a worksheet to take home than when he has spent a productive morning building in the block area. Modern families have been under stress, as the statistics on divorce and single parent families on the Timeline indicate, and when parents are contending with their own concerns, it has often been easier and necessary for parents to assume that their young children are more mature and capable than they really are. "This assumption has enabled parents to accept the commonly held view that today's children are ready for learning earlier than in past generations" (Gestwicki, 1995, p. 21).

One last factor influencing parental attitudes about early academics is the contemporary emphasis on competition, achievement, and success that underlies much of our current culture. If parents are concerned about giving their

1995
Congress allocates $3.53 billion for the Head Start budget.

children the "competitive edge," getting them started off on the right track and in a hurry should logically enable their later acceptance into the right school or program. This leaves parents vulnerable to accepting the influence of both professionals and entrepreneurs who promote ideas for early teaching.

Where is the real danger for young children in being caught between the opposite poles of this debate on developmentally appropriate practices and formally structured academic experiences? By ignoring the active nature of the young child's real learning style, children's healthy development may be jeopardized.

> Infants and young children are not just sitting twiddling their thumbs, waiting for their parents to teach them to read and do math. They are expending a vast amount of time and effort in exploring and understanding their immediate world. Healthy education supports and encourages this spontaneous learning. Early instruction miseducates, not because it attempts to teach, but because it attempts to teach the wrong things at the wrong time. When we ignore what the child has to learn and instead impose what we want to teach, we put infants and young children at risk for no purpose (Elkind, 1988, p. 25).

What sort of risks do many experts see when children are exposed prematurely to academic learning? There are several. One is a widespread concern about the effects on self-esteem if children are unable to succeed at the tasks that seem so important to the adults. Many children, and especially young children, just cannot learn in the ways that academic instruction uses, no matter how hard they try. They cannot sit still, comprehend or use the material they have learned by rote, or even see its importance. They feel incompetent, as they realize they have failed to meet the adult's standards, without understanding that they have failed at something that is alien to their nature and learning style. When these kinds of learning are not meaningful to them, there is no sense of self-worth even when there is some mastery (see Fig. 11-9).

Another component of healthy development that is thought to be at risk in academic preschool programs is self-control (Greenberg, 1990). Learning to make good choices is an important component of self-discipline. In a teacher-directed and teacher-managed environment, young children have few opportunities to make choices. The longitudinal studies of the preschool programs in Ypsilanti, Michigan (Schweinhart et al., 1986; Schweinhart and Weikart, 1993) suggest more positive social and emotional adjustment of adolescents and adults who participated as children in preschool programs that allowed them to choose and initiate their activities.

> The results call into question the advisability of pushing formal academics on four-year-olds. In particular, such programs, focusing on teacher-directed activities, may not be the best way to improve a disadvantaged child's chance for a successful life. To overcome obstacles to success, disadvantaged children must have opportunities to chart their own course. To be self-directed, they must initiate their own learning, follow through with their own plans, and evaluate the outcomes (Schweinhart et al., 1986, p. 43).

We need only say one thing to young children: come as you are! Come with your age-level characteristics. Come with those qualities that make you a unique and special person. Schools can have the flexibility and imagination and sensitivity to be ready for the children to come

—James Hymes

1995
NAEYC membership is approximately 90,000, with over 20,000 attending the annual conference.

Figure 11-9   **The evident self-esteem in a child who has selected his own activity contrasts with children asked to learn with more formal academic instruction. (Courtesy of Connie Glass)**

If you want truly to understand something, try to change it

–Kurt Lewin

Still another concern is the stress that "is a common risk seen in children when excessive and inappropriate demands are made on them through formal instruction" (Bullock, 1990, p. 15). A number of studies corroborate that there is increased stress on children in developmentally inappropriate learning situations (Burts et al., 1992).

Lastly, it seems likely that the long-term effects of rushing children prematurely into formal academics may in fact be less than positive in any case. Frequently children's attitudes and dispositions to learning are negatively impacted by the stress and circumstances of those first learning experiences. Evidence also suggests that children whose introduction to academic content and methods has been delayed past preschool and kindergarten have had at least equally positive results in later learning, rather than being handicapped when compared with their peers whose academics began earlier (Burts et al., 1992). This seems to support the notion that waiting until children are developmentally ready for later kinds of school learning is in fact beneficial.

It is significant that moving academic kinds of learning ever earlier in children's lives has created the concept of "readiness," with the resultant required assessment by testing, of young children. As children are asked to be "ready" for school–which means ready for the academic demands of the primary classroom–they are expected to enter school already knowing what they formerly were taught during the first year's curriculum. Now, as schools move to measure the quality of their instruction, it is increasingly important to them that children have achieved particular standards of learning at specific points, frequently before entering kindergarten or first grade. This has meant that children who are assessed as not ready for the next learning step are asked to wait a year, or perhaps attend a transitional year program (Brewer, 1990; Uphoff, 1990; Bredekamp, 1990).

1995
Over 4,300 early childhood centers in 50 states nationwide and in 16 foreign countries have been accredited by NAEYC.

Figure 11-10   **The NAEYC position statement on school readiness emphasizes making schools responsive to individual needs and learning abilities, as demonstrated in this group of four–year–olds.
(Courtesy of Connie Glass)**

Since tests tend to focus on the single dimension of narrowly cognitive
tasks, the overall development and strengths of young children are not given
equal importance in making decisions about readiness. And since young children do not have the basic requisites for successful test-taking–sitting still, following directions, writing or making specific marks–the test results are very
often inadequate measures of what they truly know and who they truly are. In
having particular expectations for what children should already know before
they enter or progress in school, the concept of readiness really becomes a
method of gatekeeping–excluding those children who cannot be expected to
adjust to the demands of school (Willer and Bredekamp, 1990).

What many early childhood professionals call into question is the concept
that young children must be ready to adapt to the schools' requirements, rather
than schools being prepared to adapt to the unique variations in children's development and learning. The NAEYC position statement on school readiness
emphasizes making schools responsive to individual needs, rather than demanding that children be ready to fit into "rigid, lock-step distinctions between grades"
(NAEYC, 1990, p. 23) (see Fig. 11-10). The variety of methods of making valid
assessments of children's development, beyond narrow achievement tests, is
encouraged as appropriate to our understanding of children's development.

You should understand that early childhood professionals are not unanimous in this position. There are those who believe that early direct instruction
enhances children's later academic success, and that the earlier this direct

1995
Over 400 NAEYC affiliate groups are active.

instruction is started, the better (Gersten and Keating 1987, in Jensen and Chevalier, 1990). It will be important for you to immerse yourself in understanding the research and statements of both viewpoints. Only teachers who have truly formed a personal philosophy about appropriate practices for children will be able to adequately defend their position to others.

Inclusion in Early Childhood Classrooms

It is entirely likely that there will be at least one young child with special developmental or learning needs enrolled in the first early childhood program you work in as a student or a graduate; the majority of early childhood programs of various types report enrolling at least one child with developmental delays and disabilities (Wollery and Wilbers, 1994). While the inclusion (also called integration, and formerly more commonly known as mainstreaming) of children began in the mid-70s, only recently have we seen integrated programs become common in many communities.

There are numerous reasons for this pattern. Foremost are the benefits that have been identified for all the children involved, both those whose development follows typical patterns and those with needs that require special supports and adaptations. Research shows that children with disabilities in non-segregated classrooms are provided with competent models that allow them to learn and practice many new skills through imitation and reinforcement of their peers. They demonstrate higher levels of social play and initiate more appropriate social interactions with peers than do children in self-contained special education preschool classes (Diamond et al., 1994). The gains in language, cognitive, and motor-skill development made by children in integrated classrooms are comparable to peers in special education classrooms. Thus they are able to take advantage of the activities that promote development while gaining an advantage in levels of play. More realistic expectations are placed on children with special needs who attend the same programs as children with typical abilities (Chandler, 1994). Children with special needs will be perceived as "less different" if they are not excluded from the environments with other children, and so be more easily accepted by family, peers, and community (see Fig. 11-11).

Studies also show that children without disabilities benefit from the inclusion of children with special needs in preschool classrooms. In addition to making developmental gains that are at least equivalent to children in nonintegrated classrooms (Diamond et al., 1994), they have opportunities to learn more realistic and accurate views about individuals with disabilities, and to develop positive attitudes instead of prejudices toward others who are different from themselves. In integrated settings, children are able to develop responsive, helpful behaviors towards others, becoming sensitive to the needs of others.

Parents of children with and without special needs generally support the concept of integration, but express concerns about whether the needs of all children within the classroom will be met (Galant and Hanline, 1993). However, after experience in such classrooms, both groups of parents are far more positive about the impact on their children. For parents of children with special

If adults have thought of 1,000 hypotheses, then it is easy to accept the fact that there can be 1,001 or 2,000 hypotheses. The unknown is easier to accept and adults are more open to new ideas when they have generated many potentialities themselves
—Carlina Rinaldi

1995
The number of mothers of children under six in the work force increases to 61.7 percent.

| Figure 11-11 | **Children with special needs often benefit from inclusion in classrooms with typically developing children.** |

needs, their child's integration may help them feel less isolated within the community, and more hopeful about their child's future.

What has inclusion been like for early education professionals who have been trained to work with children whose development follows typical patterns? As you might imagine, initially teachers react with caution, fear, or negative responses, wondering whether the placement is wise for the child and fair to all the children. But in two recent studies (Giangreco and Kontos, reported in Diamond, 1994), teachers reported that the children had become part of the class, without the disability being their most important characteristic. Teachers who had the experience of working in inclusive classrooms reported they had become more confident and flexible in their teaching, reflecting more on the needs of all the children in their class (see Fig. 11-12).

There can be barriers to successful inclusion. One is that there are philosophical and methodological differences between early childhood special education and regular early childhood education. The individualized teaching plans of early special education emphasize skill acquisition, structured use of instructional time, a strong behavioral orientation, and more teacher direction than is considered good practice in regular early childhood education. There are various turf issues that are created by these differences, with many special educators feeling they can provide the best education for children with disabilities. However, it has been noted that "cooperation, collaboration, and mutual

1995

The number of children under age five in organized child care increases 67 percent from 1986 to 1995.

| Figure 11-12 | **Teachers report that when children with special needs are included, they become part of the class, without their disability being their most important characteristic.** |

respect between regular and special education early childhood teachers and therapists was an important component of successful integrated programs" (Diamond et al., 1994, p. 71). When regular classroom teachers have the support of an intervention team who supports their expertise and respects their educational approaches, most believe that they can meet the needs of the children with disabilities in their classrooms.

It is most helpful to successful inclusion if the intervention work with the specialists is provided within naturally occurring situations in the classroom, rather than disrupting the curriculum and routines. So the speech therapist comes in to present a group activity to all the children or interact conversationally or in a game with small groups during free play time, rather than coming in to remove the young child with special language needs to go out for an individual therapy session. So too the physical therapist encourages all the children to try rolling on her giant ball, realizing that the participation of children without physical limitations may encourage the child with cerebral palsy who is her special responsibility. This prevents disruption of the classroom routine, as well as avoids sending a message to the other children that the child is not really a member of their classroom. The regular classroom teacher feels supported when the members of the special intervention team share the common framework and goals.

Effective integration programs use naturalistic teaching strategies within the context of regular classroom routines. "Activity-based intervention" strategies involve exactly the kinds of teaching we have discussed earlier in our considerations of developmentally appropriate practice. This happens where teacher

1995

Congress makes cuts in appropriations for fiscal year 1996 for programs serving children and families, eliminating 171 programs, including programs for planning, administrative support, and professional preparation of teachers and human services providers.

awareness of goals for individual children helps teachers plan appropriate active learning experiences. Thus, a child who is using the variety of fasteners on the dress-up clothes is working on a fine-motor goal, and one who is invited to use the puppets is working on a language goal. Because each child's goals are addressed within the context of classroom activities, teachers have the responsibilities of targeting goals, planning materials and activities to further those goals, and regularly assessing progress towards those goals. Doesn't this sound exactly like the planning cycle that is part of good practice in every excellent early education classroom, no matter what the ability of each participating child? The difference in integrated classrooms is that special education teachers or therapists are available to consult with the teacher, and help plan modifications in the environment or activity to facilitate involvement of children with special needs.

As early educators understand fully the implication of individualizing programs and curriculum decisions, they will see that inclusion of children with special needs in early childhood classrooms is simply an extension of this developmentally appropriate practice of individualization. They will be supported in their efforts to help the children with special needs by the active ongoing involvement of parents, special education teachers and interventionists, and administrators. There has been much learning about inclusion in the past ten years. The task that lies before you as you enter the profession is to continue learning how to provide education that respects the special uniqueness of all children.

Anti-Bias Curriculum

When you first work with young children in programs, you may be working in large urban areas, smaller towns, or rural communities. You may work with children and families who look very much like yourself, having grown up in similar cultural and community settings, of the same racial heritage, and sharing the same religious and historical traditions. However, given the diversity of the American population, it is more probable that your classroom will include families composed of varying structures, including two parents of different genders, two of the same gender, single parents of either gender, families headed by grandparents, adoptive parents, or foster parents. They may be families of varying income and educational levels. There may be homeless families, families where children are abused or neglected, and others where children are well cared for. They may represent one of any number of the religious, racial, and ethnic groups that comprise the tapestry of America today. You may work with children whose linguistic background includes learning English as a second language. And, as we just discussed, you may also work with children whose physical or mental abilities are impaired. What an amazing and enriching diversity we find in American society. If your classroom children presently live in a more homogeneous community, you know that the United States is anything but homogeneous, and they need to be prepared to interact comfortably and respectfully with this diversity. But differences make people uncomfortable, particularly when those differences seem threatening, as they do when no one talks about the reason for the differences, and the similarities that exist along

If we are to weave a richer culture we must weave one in which each diverse human gift will find a fitting place
—Margaret Mead

1995

The Head Start budget for fiscal year 1996 is cut by 4 percent, providing $3.3 billion, ending more than five years of funding increases.

Figure 11-13   **Young children need to be prepared to interact comfortably and respectfully with the diversity that is obvious in our society.**

with the differences. This is exactly the rationale for discussions in the early education community about the need for anti-bias education with young children (see Fig. 11-13).

Very young children are busily constructing their own self-identity, and attitudes about that identity, by observing the ways they are different from and similar to other people, and by absorbing the verbal and nonverbal messages from others about the differences. Identity and attitudes of young children are constructed through the interaction of three factors:

▶ experience with their bodies. Questions that are being explored include: What does my body look like, and how is it different from that of others? What can my body do? Do I like my body?

▶ experience with their social environments. What messages do I get, either explicitly or implicitly, that help me accept the facts and differences that I observe about myself or others? What is my environment telling me about society's acceptance–its evaluation of worth or worthlessness–of the identity I'm forming?

▶ children's cognitive functioning. Young children's method of thinking produces some confused or illogical conclusions, like assuming that genital identification or color might be open to change, or disability open to catching by contagion.

In this process of identity, children need the help of adults who can help them explore some of their questions and curiosity about differences. We know

1995
Nineteen children died in a child care center when the Oklahoma City Federal Building was bombed on April 19.

Figure 11-14 | **Young children exploring identity issues need the support of adults who can help them explore some of their questions and curiosity about differences.**

that even very young children can perceive and uncritically absorb the negative messages about diversity in the world, and that these messages can be both powerful and harmful in producing bias. Prejudice and bias are destructive forces, and they can hurt all children (see Fig. 11-14).

> On the one hand, struggling against bias that declares a person inferior because of gender, race, ethnicity, or disability sucks energy from and undercuts a child's full development. On the other hand, learning to believe they are superior because they are White, or male, or able-bodied, dehumanizes and distorts reality for growing children (Derman-Sparks, 1989, p. ix).

Children need adults who can help them develop positive attitudes about their own identity and that of others, and can help them to deal with the reality of the world, while learning that they can also participate in changing past ideas which we do not want in their future. The goals of the **anti-bias curriculum** are to enable all children "to consuct a knowledgeable, confident self-identity; to develop comfortable, empathetic, and just interaction with diversity; and to develop critical thinking and the skills for standing up for oneself and others in the face of injustice" (Derman-Sparks, 1989, p. ix).

Although this is called the "anti-bias curriculum" by those who see this work as an integral part of what classroom teachers do, they are quick to explain that this is an aim, an approach, that permeates the existing environment and curriculum, rather than being something that is added on. It is looking at everything teachers do and say, and the children's interaction and classroom life, "through an anti-bias lens." The attitude of respect for all people that lies behind the anti-bias attitude is completely consistent with the sensitivity to individual children and families. Furthermore, their cultural diversity and values are a declared principle of developmentally appropriate practice. But the thinking behind the anti-bias curriculum argues that it is important to go beyond respect, and create an environment in which children can actively explore questions about disabilities,

Anti-Bias Curriculum: The philosophical approach developed by Louise Derman Sparks, to use classroom practices and materials that (1) foster each child's construction of a knowledgeable, confident self-identity; (2) foster each child's comfortable, empathetic interaction with diversity among people; (3) foster each child's critical thinking about bias; and (4) foster each child's ability to stand up for self and others in the face of bias.

1996
Special education child development settings are now approved by the Council for Early Childhood as eligible settings for CDA assessment.

Figure 11-15   **Classrooms that promote anti-bias attitudes go beyond just racial differences to encourage all children to explore all materials, free of gender-bias or stereotypes of any kind.**

The central organizing goal in our schools should be the creation of communities of care and compassion
–Mara Sapon-Shevin

gender, and race, in order to understand differences and appreciate similarities, and to recognize and confront ideas and behaviors that are biased.

In other reading, you will likely come across the term "multicultural curriculum." This refers to teaching children about other peoples' cultures, in the hope that they will learn to respect each other and not develop prejudice. This is obviously a similar positive intent to the anti-bias approach, but those who practice anti-bias curriculum suggest that the multicultural approach too frequently deteriorates into a "tourist curriculum" (Derman-Sparks, p. 7). This happens because, generally, other cultures are presented as something exotic and foreign, with different food, holiday celebrations, clothing and so on, rather than dealing with peoples' real life experiences. "Children 'visit' non-White cultures, and then 'go home' to the daily classroom, which reflects only the dominant culture" (Derman-Sparks, p. 7). The danger here is that such experiences fail to communicate real understanding, and stereotypes about differences may actually be reinforced. In addition, multicultural curriculum usually focuses on other countries–China, for example, or Mexico–rather than focusing on the diversity of people in our own country that children actually come in contact with. Anti-bias tries to avoid some of the dangers of this tourist approach. It retains some of the positive ideas from multicultural curriculum, and at the same time includes diversity other than just cultural. Anti-bias curriculum addresses ability, age, and gender differences, as well as the problem of stereotypical or biased behavior in children's interactions (see Fig. 11-15).

1996
Kindercare Learning Centers begin a major initiative toward NAEYC accreditation in selected geographic areas.

ACTIVITIES TO RAISE TEACHER CONSCIOUSNESS ABOUT BIASES

a. Share your earliest memories related to learning your racial/ethnic identity, your gender identity, and your physical abilities and limitations. What was good or painful as you learned about these aspects of your identity?

b. Share how you agree or disagree with your parents' views on race, ethnicity, gender, and abledness. If you disagree, how did you develop your own ideas? If you are a parent, what do you plan to teach your children?

c. Write down your list of acceptable and nonacceptable behaviors for males and females. Compare with others.

d. Take one of the popular European fairy tales *(Cinderella, Snow White)* and rewrite it, switching genders of the characters.

e. Tell about an incident where you experienced prejudice or discrimination against yourself, or observed it against another person. What did you do? How did you feel?

f. Experience a day being differently abled (using a wheelchair, having the use of only one arm). Notice what changes would have to be made in your environment to allow you to be more independent. Pay attention to how people respond to you.

g. List what you want others to know about and what you don't want people to say about your racial/ethnic heritage.

Ideas suggested in Louise Derman-Sparks and the Anti-Bias Task Force (1989) *Anti-Bias Curriculum: Tools for Empowering Young Children,* National Association for the Education of Young Children, Washington, DC.

Figure 11-16   **Sample activities for teacher consciousness-raising.**

There are those who feel that these concepts are beyond the capacity of young children to absorb. Yet there are others who feel that young children themselves are interested in questions about diversity, and that they may exhibit fearful, or prejudiced behavior when they are not encouraged to understand differences in a positive way.

How do teachers prepare themselves to deal with anti-bias issues with young children? A first, and ongoing, step is to themselves confront their own attitudes and discomforts, to become self-aware of how their own identities and attitudes were formed by early experiences. See Fig. 11-16 for sample activities for consciousness-raising from Louise Derman-Sparks' book. This is a process that may bring pain as well as awareness, but it helps teachers identify their prejudices that need to be uncovered before they will be able to do anti-bias work with children.

Teachers then examine their environments, materials, and curriculum activities, to find and eliminate sterotypical messages, messages of omission, and to answer the question, "What am I currently doing in curriculum about gender/race/culture/different physical abilities/stereotyping and discriminatory behavior? and what can I add?" (see Fig. 11-17). They observe their children and discover the issues in the community that affect their lives, as well as learn the family and community resources for doing specific anti-bias activities. Teachers watch for opportunities when children's spoken and unspoken questions show

1996
As of January, 13,258 programs from 54 states, U.S. territories and commonwealths, and 13 foreign countries are enrolled in the accreditation process, including 8,731 in self-study, and 4,527 accredited.

Figure 11-17   **Teachers begin by examining the toys and materials available in the classroom, to ensure that children will find items they can identify with, such as these babies to be washed in the water table.**

We think of a school for young children as an integral living organism, as a place of shared lives and relationships among many adults and very many children
–Loris Malaguzzi

that they need help to understand differences, or to be supported to confront unfair treatment.

Such examination and reflection help teachers discover the steps they will take to slowly make their classrooms into environments where diversity is accepted, and where children know they can explore these important issues with supportive adults. Teachers and parents work together to explore how to handle sensitive and emotional issues, like how to celebrate holidays, and which holidays to celebrate, or whether holidays should even be celebrated at all in early education programs. These are deeply felt concerns, and it is through dialogue that adults support one another to help children develop healthy self-identity and attitudes of acceptance of diversity. As America's diversity grows, children moving towards the twenty-first century will be empowered and enriched to interact comfortably with those whose lives, appearance, and experiences are unlike their own. Issues raised in the discussion of multicultural and anti-bias education free all early educators to find new and positive answers. Involve yourself in these dialogues, in later reading, coursework, and experiences. We will all benefit.

Mixed-Age Groupings

Those of you who have listened to grandparents and great-grandparents tell of their experiences in attending one-room schoolhouses will understand that mixed-age groupings in education are not a new phenomenon. But the concept is receiving new attention in early education programs in many parts of the country, in addition to being used successfully in England, Canada, Sweden, and Italy. At this time when we are striving to meet standards of indi-

1996
President Clinton signs a telecommunications act that requires manufacturers of television sets to include "V-chip" microchips, enabling adults to block out violent programming from children's viewing, and establishing violence rating systems.

Figure 11-18   **Older children have an opportunity to develop leadership skills, responsibility, and self-regulation of behavior when they are part of a mixed-age grouping.**

vidualization in developmentally appropriate practice, rethinking the concepts of mixed-age groupings may assist this effort.

A mixed-age grouping combines children across at least two, preferably three, chronological years. Usually the grouping remains together for much of the time, with the oldest children moving on each year, and a new cohort of youngest children joining the group. This means that children are in a group for three years, are generally together for at least two years, and remain also with the same teacher over this time. Such an arrangement is more like a typical family or neighborhood setting, with opportunities for interage contact, instead of the classroom that has been said to be educating children in "litters," with only age-mates.

There are some clear social advantages to such a system. One is that, over extended time, relationships among children, and between children, teachers, and parents can develop and provide security and deeper knowledge. Another is that older children have opportunities to exhibit leadership skills with less threatening younger children, and to develop their assumption of responsibility (see Fig. 11-18). Older children in mixed-age groupings seem to increase their own regulation of their behavior, perhaps taking seriously their roles as models for the younger children. Their prosocial, caring skills also increase. Younger children also benefit by participating in the more complex forms of play developed by the older children, in imitating their behaviors, and in then

1996

The April-May issue of Molecular Psychiatry reported that attention deficit hyperactivity disorder (ADHD) in children was probably linked to a gene that is yet-to-be identified.

Figure 11-19 **Parents come to see the advantages to children of mixed-age groupings.**

being able to also become the oldest in the group. Cooperative behaviors increase for all children (Katz et al., 1991).

There are cognitive benefits for children in these groupings also. Rigid curricula with age-graded expectations must necessarily be relaxed in mixed-age settings. All children are then allowed to develop and learn at their own rates without fear of failure and a lessened danger of competition. Children's unique needs are more easily identified when teachers are not considering group goals; curriculum is more likely to be matched to children's needs and skill learning levels. Children whose knowledge is similar but different stimulate one another's mental growth and thinking. Therefore, cooperative learning and peer tutoring situations generally abound in multi-age settings.

Many parents are initially opposed to the concept of mixed-age groupings. Their concerns include the worry that older children will be held back or even regress when they are placed with young ones, and that young ones will become victims of older children. Some parents also dislike the idea of their children having the same teacher over a period of time. Generally, as parents are involved in dialogue with teachers and other parents, and involved in the classroom life, they learn more about the advantages to their children (see Fig. 11-19).

Teachers are the key in how effectively mixed-age groupings actually work to benefit children. Simply putting children of different ages together does not guarantee these benefits without teachers carefully structuring the environment, planning curriculum, and playing particular roles. As teachers learn about children's interests, abilities, learning style, and choices for play partners they can support individual growth. They plan activities for children that are child-initiated, so that children can find their own place on the developmental ladder.

1996

In April, the U.S. Congress tentatively agreed to require states to begin testing of newborns for HIV.

Figure 11-20 | **Until fairly recently, the closest most young children got to technology was an old typewriter! (Courtesy of Tracie O'Hara)**

By freeing themselves from the role of director, they are free to step in to facilitate as children need their interaction. They may consciously create opportunities for children who are different from each other to work together, make suggestions about how children can help each other, or frame thought-provoking questions that suggest ways of working with others who are younger or older. Children, with teacher guidance, can learn much about democratic practices by jointly solving the problems that naturally arise in a multi-age grouping, such as what to do when the younger ones don't want to listen to the longer books that the older ones love to have read chapter by chapter.

Frequently teachers resist the move to mixed-age groupings at first, fearing it will be too impossible a task to plan for great differences, and that individual age-stage behaviors won't mix. But, as in the case of parents, teachers usually change their opinions, after some experience. They discover they are teaching better, more responsively and appropriately. They benefit by having the opportunities to truly learn about individual differences in new ways, and by questioning their stereotypes and prejudices about particular behaviors that they may have assumed were products of age-level behavior. They discover that the teaching and learning in their classrooms is shared among all participants. Perhaps this innovation will be in your professional future.

Technology in Early Education

There was a time, not so very long ago, when there was almost universal horror when computers and young children were mentioned in the same sentence. The image of children sitting staring at computer screens suggested a passive learning mode. Most felt this passive mode conflicted with the idea that children construct their understandings of the world by manipulating objects and interacting actively with others within their environments. It was felt that the com-

1996

June 1 is designated as a time to Stand for Children at the Lincoln Memorial, Washington, D.C. Conceived by Marian Wright Edelman of the Children's Defense Fund, and endorsed by more than 500 national organizations, this day of commitment to children is attended by over 200,000 people.

puter screen could only offer two-dimensional symbolic representation, instead of the sensory experience and social interaction needed for real early childhood learning (see Fig. 11-20). The general sentiment of many early educators is expressed in this letter sent to NAEYC in response to an article about computers:

> Let us not let our adult excitement with what computers can do in the adult workplace deter us from offering to children the squishiness of making mud pies, the scent of peppermint extract when making cookies, and the feel of balancing a block at the top of a tower. Children deserve to have a rich and varied childhood. The adult world of the plastic workplace comes all too soon (Bredekamp and Rosegrant, 1994, p. 54).

Educators are currently attempting to come to terms with the idea that **technology** can be an effective and interesting additional choice in early childhood curriculum. Indeed, sometimes it is their own "technophobia" that causes professionals to dismiss computers so abruptly. In fact, research and observation of children using computers suggest that computers offer children another way to play, enhancing social, emotional, and cognitive development. To be sure that computers in early childhood classrooms support ideas of developmentally appropriate practice and nurture overall child development, certain assumptions about computers are helpful:

1. Computer use is a social activity.
2. Computer use is a child-initiated and child-directed activity.
3. Computer software is selected that allows children to explore, experiment, and solve problems.
4. Computers are one of many materials in a classroom (adapted from Davidson and Wright, 1994).

In fact, while adults are struggling to keep up with, and feel comfortable with, technology, young children accept it as a normal part of their environment. Observers note that they are quite comfortable with computers, exhibiting only curiosity and no fear when given a new software program. Much research that has been done in recent years indicates that there are generally positive indications regarding children's learning on computers. There are increased opportunities for social interaction, with many children preferring to work with one or two partners over working alone, and those making more requests for help from peers than from the teacher (see Fig. 11-21).

There are also high levels of spoken communication and cooperation at the computer. "They interact more frequently and in different ways than they interact when engaged with traditional activities, such as puzzles or blocks. Whereas in sociodramatic play there tends to be a 'leader' of communication, children share leadership roles on the computer" (Clements, 1994, p. 43). Computer use has also been shown to enhance children's attitudes about their own competency, and about academic subjects such as reading (Orabuchi, in Clements, 1994).

Obviously the benefits of computer usage depend on the kinds of software used, and its developmental appropriateness for young children's thinking abilities. Much research has also been done on this recently, and those of

Technology: Refers to modern technical knowledge that drives machines, particularly computers.

With the loss of tradition we have lost the thread which safely guided us through the vast realms of the past, but this thread was also the chain fettering each successive generation to a predetermined aspect of the past. It could be that only now will the past open up to us with unexpected freshness and tell us things that no one as yet had ears to hear

—Hannah Arendt

1996
In the fall, Democrat Bill Clinton ran for re-election as the "Education President" against Republican Bob Dole.

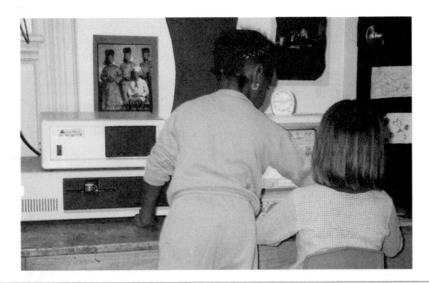

Figure 11-21 Computers become a social activity, with preschoolers cooperating and helping each other.

Figure 11-22 A criterion for appropriate software is that young children should be able to use it independently, even before they can read.

you who are interested in exploring this subject more thoroughly will be able to find helpful lists (see lists and discussion in Wright and Shade, 1994, and Hohmann et al., 1995.) Criteria for appropriateness suggest overall principles of developmentally appropriate practice:

1. Children can use the program independently, without asking for help, and no matter what their reading ability (see Fig. 11-22).

2. Children can control the pace and direction of the program.

3. There are opportunities for children to explore a number of concepts on different levels.

4. There is prompt feedback given to children, and children feel successful.

5. There is multisensory capacity for children's natural learning style.

6. The program is enjoyable, fun to use, and takes imagination to explore (Adapted from Narodick, 1992, in Bowman and Beyer, 1994).

Other warnings regarding the use of technology include the caution that inequities must not be repeated. That is, children of both genders, and all racial and linguistic backgrounds, must be encouraged equally to use software that conveys no biases about their interests or abilities, so that children have the same opportunities to advance in their comfort with using technology (Thouvenelle et al., 1994). Technology may also be very useful for young children with special needs (Behrmann and Lahn, 1994).

It appears probable that technology will be used increasingly in early education programs as we approach the next century. You will have opportunities during your program of professional preparation to explore these issues in depth (Hyson and Eyman, 1986), so that you do not become one of those professionals who resists the use of computers without exploring how much they can offer, as an option, in active learning environments.

SUMMARY

QUESTIONS FOR REVIEW

1. Discuss the relationships between teacher compensation and quality in programs for children.

2. Identify the "Worthy Wage Campaign." How does it influence increasing professionalism?

3. Discuss the phenomenon of teacher burnout, identifying several specific actions teachers can take to prevent it.

4. Describe some of the issues involved in the profession's discussion of early academics, readiness, and achievement testing.

5. Discuss what is meant by "inclusion," and benefits for the children and adults who are part of integrated early education classrooms.

6. Describe what is meant by an "anti-bias curriculum," and the rationale for it. How does an anti-bias approach differ from a multicultural approach?

7. Identify what is meant by "mixed-age groupings" in early education, and what are some of the advantages for children and adults.

8. Describe current thinking about the appropriateness of using technology in the classroom in early education.

ACTIVITIES FOR FURTHER STUDY

1. Do some informal research on the relationship between factors associated with quality in your community. Where possible, compare three different kinds of settings: a nonprofit center, a for-profit center, and one that is accredited by NAEYC.

   a. Determine the adult-child ratios in each.

   b. Compare the salaries and benefits paid to early childhood professionals. Try to compare positions that might be similar, such as lead teachers or assistant teachers. Learn if there is a differential paid for training or advanced degrees.

   c. Through conversations, try to learn how long teachers have been in their positions at the center. You may want to cooperate on gathering this information with other students and combine your data. Draw up a table to allow you to juxtapose this information. Do your findings support the correlations found in the studies referred to in this chapter?

2. Discover whether there is a local Worthy Wage Campaign in your community. If there is, find out how you can become involved. If there is not, contact the National Center for the Early Childhood Work Force to obtain their curriculum *Working for Quality Child Care*, to help you organize efforts to improve employment conditions in your locality.

There are many issues that are the focus of dialogue and study in early education today. Some of these–such as compensation for teachers and burnout–directly impact teacher effectiveness and professional futures. Other subjects under discussion–such as concerns about academics and the related conditions of "readiness" and achievement testing, inclusion, anti-bias curriculum, mixed-age groupings, and technology in early childhood classrooms– have direct impact on the kinds of programs offered to young children. It should be very obvious to you that this list of issues is by no means exhaustive. Many others will be presented to you in the course of your studies. You probably thought of some new topics as you began reading this chapter. In addition, many professionals are concerned with topics like the effects of full-time child care on infant development, whole language vs. more traditional methods of teaching literacy–and far more. This should suggest that you are entering a dynamic and developing profession, with much yet to be learned and done by us all.

3. Talk with several experienced teachers about burnout, asking them what they do to consciously prevent it.

4. Select one of the references or suggested readings on the subject of early academics, readiness, or achievement testing to read. Discuss it with your classmates, to learn more about one of these issues.

5. Visit a classroom in your community that includes young children with special learning or developmental needs. Talk with the teacher about the experience of working in this setting–what are the advantages and/or disadvantages for the children and adults involved? What, if any, obvious modifications do you see that have been made in the physical environment to meet the needs of children, and why? What other specialists are involved in planning and/or therapy for the children?

6. Go to the library and find several books that a classroom teacher could use to help raise children's awareness and positive acceptance of diversity in various forms. Share these books with fellow classmates. There is a helpful list in Derman-Sparks' book to get you started.

7. Learn if your community has any early childhood programs or mixed-age groupings in the school system. If so, try to visit, to observe the interaction of the children and the differences in learning environment and curriculum that distinguish the programs.

8. Try to observe young children using computers. How does the software encourage: creativity; problem-solving and logical thinking; social interaction; independence? What questions about technology does this observation suggest to you for further study?

REFERENCES

Quality and Compensation

Bellm, Dan, Gnezda, Terry, Whitebook, Marcy, & Breunig, Gretchen Stahr. (1994). Policy initiatives to enhance child care staff compensation. In Julienne Johnson & Janet B. McCracken (Eds.). *The early childhood career lattice: Perspectives on professional development.* Washington, DC: NAEYC.

Cost, Quality, and Outcomes Study Team. (1995, May). Cost, quality, and child outcomes in child care centers: Key findings and recommendations. *Young Children, 50,* (4), 40-50.

Jalongo, Mary Renck. (1991, September). Stephanie: One teacher's story. *Young Children, 46,* (6), 62-64.

Morin, Jim, (1989, September). We can force a solution to the staffing crisis. *Young Children, 44,* (6), 18-19.

Whitebook, Marcy. (1995, May). What's good for child care teachers is good for our country's children. *Young Children, 50,* (4), 49-50.

Whitebook, Marcy, & Granger, Robert C. (1989, May) Mommy, who's going to be my teacher today? Assessing teacher turnover. *Young Children, 44,* (4), 11-14.

Whitebook, M., Howes, C., & Phillips, D. (1989). *Who cares? Child care teachers and the quality of care in America.* Final report of the National Child Care Staffing Study. Oakland CA: Child Care Employee Project.

Whitebook, M., Phillips, D., & Howes, C. (1993). *The national child care staffing study revisited: Four years in the life of center-based child care.* Oakland, CA: Child Care Employee Project.

Willer, B., (Ed.). (1990). *Reaching the full cost of quality in early childhood programs.* Washington, DC: NAEYC.

Burnout

Author. (1988, May). Nourishing your enthusiasm: Staying excited about your job. *Child Care Information Exchange.* (61), 9-10.

Whitebook, Marcy, Hnatiuk, Patty, & Bellm, Dan. (1994). *Mentoring in early care and education: Refining an emerging career path.* Washington, DC: National Center for the Early Childhood Work Force.

Early Academics, Readiness, and Testing

Bredekamp, Sue. (1990, September). Extra-year programs: A response to Brewer and Uphoff. *Young Children, 45,* (6), 20-21.

Brewer, Jo Ann. (1990, September). Transitional programs: Boon or bane? *Young Children, 45,* (6), 15-18.

Burts, D.C., Charlesworth, R., & Fleege, P.O. (1992). Observed activities and stress behaviors in developmentally appropriate and inappropriate kindergarten classrooms. *Early Childhood Research Quarterly, 7,* 297-318.

Elkind, David. (1988). *Miseducation: Preschoolers at risk.* New York: Alfred A. Knopf.

Gersten, Russell, & Keating, Thomas. (1990). Long-term benefits from direct instruction. In Mary A. Jensen & Zelda W. Chevalier (Eds.). *Issues and advocacy in early education.* Boston: Allyn and Bacon.

Gestwicki, Carol. (1995). *Developmentally appropriate practice: Curriculum and development in early education.* Albany, NY: Delmar Publishers Inc.

Greenberg, Polly. (1990, January). Why not academic preschool? (Part 1). *Young Children, 45,* (2), 70-80.

NAEYC. (1990, November). Position statement on school readiness. *Young Children, 46,* (1), 21-23.

Schweinhart, L., Weikart, D., & Larner, M. (1986). Consequences of three preschool curriculum models through age 15. *Early Childhood Research Quarterly, 1,* 15-45.

Uphoff, James. (1990, September). Extra-year programs: An argument for transitional programs during transitional times. *Young Children, 45,* (6), 19-20.

Willer, Barbara, & Bredekamp, Sue. (1990, July). Redefining readiness: An essential requisite for educational reform. *Young Children, 45,* (5), 22-24.

Inclusion

Chandler, Phyllis A. (1994). *A place for me: Including children with special needs in early care and education settings.* Washington, DC: NAEYC.

Diamond, Karen E., Hestenes, Linda L., & O'Connor, Caryn E. (1994, January). Integrating young children with disabilities in preschool: Problems and promise. *Young Children, 49,* (2), 68-73.

Galant, Kim, & Hanline, Mary Frances. (1993). Parental attitudes toward mainstreaming young children with disabilities." *Childhood Education, 69,* (5), 293-297.

Wolery, Mark, & Wilbers, Jan S. (Eds.). *Including children with special needs in early childhood programs.* Washington, DC: NAEYC.

Anti-Bias Curriculum

Derman-Sparks, Louise. (1989). *Anti-bias curriculum: Tools for empowering young children*. Washington, DC: NAEYC.

Mixed-Age Groupings

Katz, Lilian G., Evangelou, Demetra, & Hartman, Jeanette Allison. (1991). *The case for mixed-age grouping in early education*. Washington DC: NAEYC.

Technology

Behrmann, Michael M., & Lahm, Elizabeth A. (1994). Computer applications in early childhood special education. In *Young children: Active learners in a technological age*. Washington DC: NAEYC.

Bowman, Barbara T., & Beyer, Elizabeth R. (1994). Thoughts on technology and early childhood education. In *Young children: Active learners in a technological age*. Washington, DC: NAEYC.

Bredekamp, Sue, & Rosegrant, Teresa. (1994). Learning and teaching with technology. In *Young children: Active learners in a technological age*. Washington DC: NAEYC.

Clements, Douglas. (1994). The uniqueness of the computer as a learning tool: Insights from research and practice. In *Young children: Active learners in a technological age*. Washington DC: NAEYC.

Davidson, Jane, & Wright, June L. (1994). The potential of the microcomputer in the early childhood classroom. In *Young Children: Active Learners in a Technological Age*. Washington DC: NAEYC.

Hohmann, C., Carmody, B., & McCabe-Branz, C. (1995). *High/Scope buyer's guide to children's software*. (11th Ed.). Ypsilanti, MI: High/Scope Press.

Hyson, Marion C., & Eyman, Alice P. (1986, September) Approaches to computer literacy in early childhood teacher education. *Young Children, 41,* (6), 54-59.

SUGGESTIONS FOR READING

Quality and Compensation

Author. (1993, January). The effects of group size, ratios, and staff training on child care quality. *Young Children, 48,* (2), 65-67.

Author. (1990, November). NAEYC position statement on guidelines for compensation of early childhood professionals. *Young Children, 46,* (1), 30-32.

Bloom, Paula Jorde. (1993, March). But I'm worth more than that! *Young Children, 48,* (3), 65-68.

Bloom, Paula Jorde. (1993, May). But I'm worth more than that!: Implementing a comprehensive compensation system. (Part 2) *Young Children, 48,* (4), 67-72.

Modigliani, Kathy. (1988, March). Twelve reasons for the low wages in child care. *Young Children, 43,* (3), 14-15.

Russell, Sue. (1993, July). Linking education and compensation: A wholistic model. *Young Children, 48,* (5), 64-68.

Early Academics, Readiness, and Testing

Bredekamp, Sue, & Rosegrant, Teresa, (Eds.). (1992). *Reaching potentials: Appropriate curriculum and assessment for young children*. Washington, DC: NAEYC.

Charlesworth, Rosalind. (1989, March). Behind before they start? Deciding how to deal with the risk of kindergarten failure. *Young Children, 44,* (3), 5-13.

Kamii, Constance. (1990). *Achievement testing in the early grades: The games grownups play.* Washington, DC: NAEYC.

Meisels, Samuel. (1987, January). Uses and abuses of developmental screening and school readiness testing. *Young Children, 42,* (2), 4-6, 68-73.

Puckett, Margaret B., & Black, Janet K. (1994). *Authentic assessment of the young child: Celebrating development and learning.* New York: Merrill.

Inclusion

Rose, Deborah F., & Smith, Barbara J. (1993, May). Preschool mainstreaming: attitude barriers and strategies for addressing them. *Young Children, 48,* (4), 59-62.

Spodek, Bernard, & Saracho, Olivia N. (1994). *Dealing with individual differences in the early childhood classroom.* New York: Longman.

Widerstrom, A.H. (1986, December). Educating young handicapped children: What can early childhood education contribute? *Childhood Education, 63,* 78-83.

Wolery, Mark, Holcombe, Ariane, Venn, Martha L., Brookfield, Jeffri, Huffman, Kay, Schroeder, Carol, Martin, Catherine G., & Fleming, Lucy A. (1993, November). Mainstreaming in early childhood programs: Current status and relevant issues. *Young Children, 49,* (1), 78-84.

Anti-Bias Curriculum

Clark, Leilani, DeWolf, Sheridan, & Clark, Carl. (1992, July). Teaching teachers to avoid having culturally assaultive classrooms. *Young Children, 47,* (5), 42-49.

Jones, Elizabeth, & Derman-Sparks, Louise. (1992, January). Meeting the challenge of diversity. *Young Children, 47,* (2), 12-17.

Sheldon, Amy. (1990, January). Kings are royaler than queens: Language and socialization. *Young Children, 45,* (2), 4-9.

Mixed-Age Grouping

Stone, Sandra. (1994/1995, Winter). Strategies for teaching children in multiage classrooms. *Childhood Education, 71,* (2), 102-105.

Theilheimer, Rachel. (1993, July). Something for everyone: Benefits of mixed-age grouping for children, parents, and teachers. *Young Children, 48,* (5), 82-87.

Technology

Burns, Susan M., Goin, Laura, & Donlon, Jan Tribble. (1990, January). A computer in my room. *Young Children, 45,* (2), 62-67.

Clements, Douglas H., Nastasi, Bonnie K., & Swaminathan, Sudha. (1993, January). Young children and computers: Crossroads and directions from research. *Young Children, 48,* (2), 56-64.

Clements, Douglas H., & Swaminathan, Sudha. (1995). Technology and school change: New lamps for old? *Childhood Education, Annual Theme Issue, 71,* (5), 275-281.

Wright, June L., & Shade, Daniel D. (Eds.). (1994). *Young children: Active learners in a technological age.* Washington, DC: NAEYC.

12

THE ROAD AHEAD

As you conclude your reading and study of the essentials of early education, you have arrived at a fork in the road. In one direction lies the field of early education and the plan for professional preparation and growth that will allow you to take your place among the ranks of the committed women and men who, over many years, have seen the education and care of young children to be their way of making a mark on the world. In the other direction lies other work that you may have decided is better suited for you and your life. Should you decide that this second road is the one for you, you go with our good wishes and gratitude for realizing now that this is not a commitment you want to make.

Nevertheless, this study and reflection about good early childhood education will help you as you make decisions as a citizen and for your own children. Never again will you be unaware of the importance of the educational experiences of the early years, or of the need for qualified and committed early educators. You will know that when children's and family issues are discussed in our legislative bodies, you can play an important role as a knowledgeable advocate, recognizing that a nation shows its moral sense as it supports its youngest citizens for a positive and strong beginning in life.

As you stand here looking in both directions, you are reminded again that the children of our nation and world need and deserve the support of parents, teachers, and administrators who are dedicated to providing optimum life experiences for the early years. For those of you deciding to undertake the journey on the road of early education, know that, while the path you take will be uniquely your own, you will benefit by following some markers laid down by those who have successfully negotiated the road before. In this chapter we will consider some of the guidelines that will help you move successfully down the road in early education.

ESSENTIALS FOR EARLY EDUCATORS

Having decided that working with young children is the career for you, you will now continue in a planned program of professional preparation at a college or university. This course of study has been designed to offer you both the knowledge base that you will need to provide developmentally appropriate responses, environments, and learning activities for the children you will work with, as well as giving you opportunities to develop your skills in supervised practicum situations. The path through your coursework has been designed quite clearly for you, to offer the most appropriate sequence of learning experiences. But how you travel that path is up to you. It is important to understand that the same principles that we recognize as optimum for children's learning apply equally well to adults. We know that children learn best when they take initiative, make choices among interesting possibilities, act on materials, and interact with people. So too, adults construct their increasingly sophisticated new ideas by interaction with the concepts and experiences they encounter. Whether your past learning environments have encouraged you to play this active role of a learner or not, allow yourself now to assume an active role.

If you are to be a successful early educator, you are going to have to invent your own way of teaching; you will use the knowledge and experience you gain, and reflect on your own meanings and experiences. You will come out of your professional preparation program ready to assume your own teaching identity, only if you have done more than passively meet the assigned requirements and little beyond, to create your own knowledge and increase your own self-understanding (see Fig. 12-1).

Begin this now, by framing some of your own questions and using some of the additional resources suggested at the end of each chapter to delve further into the material than the basic assigned reading from the text. Use every encounter and opportunity to create your expanded understanding of what it means to be an early childhood educator, and how you will do it.

Lesson 13: Be confident that you can make a difference. Don't get overwhelmed
—Marian Wright Edelman

Attitudes and Dispositions

The attitudes and dispositions that you now begin to form will guide you as you become an effective professional educator. Let us consider those that are crucial from this point on.

Figure 12-1	**You will create your own identity as a teacher, from your knowledge and experience, and your reflections on meaning and experience.**

The mediocre teacher tells. The good teacher explains. The superior teacher demonstrates. The great teacher inspires
—William Arthur Ward

In general, you will need to have a positive attitude: towards yourself, towards the children you work with as students, toward their parents, your supervising teachers and other administrators, your colleagues as a student and later as an employee. This positive attitude provides the ability and desire to see the potential in any situation or person, rather than narrowly focusing on limits and restrictions. Teachers who nurture this perspective find less frustration and greater pleasure in their working situations.

In acknowledging that there is no one right way to teach and that there are always unknowns, the disposition of remaining open to new ideas and possibilities develops. It is important that you realize that completing a professional preparation program is not the end of something, but only another step along the path. So many students seem to feel that graduation and the awarding of a degree means that the learning aspect of their career is over, and they are now moving into the practice aspect. It is vital that you understand that continual learning comes *from* the practice, if teachers are to remain able to grow and adapt to new demands. Learning becomes a passion for open, growing teachers: "the exceptional teachers I know are passionate about learning. . . . They see connecting points everywhere" (Perrone, 1991, p. 117).

Along with this disposition to remain open to insights and learning goes the disposition of risk-taking. You must dare to try new things, to risk the mistakes and failure that sometimes accompany new directions, and to learn from what you have risked. These are characteristics that you will want to cultivate. Students are often unnecessarily hard on themselves, expecting the polished

THEORY INTO PRACTICE

This is Michelle Pope. Michelle worked at a learning center as an assistant teacher for one year, then another year as a full-time teacher of two-year-olds, and as an assistant manager trainee. She then became a full-time student, completing an associate degree, that included 693 hours of hands-on internship with a variety of ages. Currently she is a lead teacher in a class of three-year-olds in a church-sponsored NAEYC-accredited child care center.

What has been a significant frustration for you in early education? How do you deal with it?

My most significant frustration has been dealing with parents and families who are disinterested in the emotional, social, and cognitive growth of their children, not wanting to hear the things that are significant in their child's day–to–day experiences at preschool. They continue to treat us teachers as simple "babysitters," someone there to only make sure their child is safe. I deal with it on a day-to-day basis by doing what I can, but with the realization that I can't make parents see what I see. I simply make sure they have plenty of literature on different subjects relating to their child, such as effects of television, health and developmental issues, and our philosophy of developmentally appropriate practices.

What is one thing you learned in classes that you really discovered to be true when you started working with children?

The thing I learned from my classes that I have found to be true is that coteaching is an ongoing job itself. Children see and feel tension between coworkers, and their stresses are already so overwhelming as young children of the 90s. I find that a full–day child–care center needs to be the safest, securest, and nonthreatening environment from the moment the children enter the building.

What is an area you are working on now to learn more about?

There are several areas that I am continuing to learn more about. One is a deeper look into a child's growth and development, as well as a further look into specific problem areas for children and families. Another area I am working on is furthering my professional development as a role model for both parents and upcoming early childhood teachers.

Why have you stayed in early education?

I have stayed in early education because I love what I do; I love to come to work every day. Secondly, children in today's world are growing up with so many stresses and are rushed through each day; I hope to encourage some sense of stability along with encouraging their independence and love of themselves, so they will have the potential to grow up as healthy, happy, strong individuals.

What is a comment or piece of advice you would give to those beginning to work in early childhood education?

My advice is to learn good communication skills with coworkers, parents, and children. Continue your own professional growth; it keeps you focused, as well as allows you to become a stronger, more self-confident teacher. Most important, I would advise you to always laugh, always be flexible, and enjoy each child each day for his or her own characteristics, realizing every day does not have to go perfectly.

Figure 12-2   **Delighting in children's ability to learn is important for teachers.**

Keep in mind always the present you are constructing. It should be the future you want
—Alice Walker

performances that they see when visiting the classrooms of mentor teachers. Recognize now that much of your learning as a student will come in evaluating experiences afterwards–figuring out what you will do differently the next time. Mistakes and less than positive experiences are a necessary part of this learning.

Closely related to risk-taking is the disposition of restlessness: the inability to accept and drift with the status quo. For your healthy professional future, it is important that you not be lulled into any rut, but maintain a perspective of restless searching for what step, idea, or experience comes next–for you and for your classroom.

Another disposition to develop is what Van Arsdell (1994) describes as "seeing themselves less as managers of learning and more as witnesses to learning" (p. 94). Being able to see the excitement in others' active learning, and not feel one has to control the directions of that learning allows teachers to retain true excitement about children's learning and growth (see Fig. 12-2).

Perhaps the most important disposition is the capacity to be passionate about what you do. To retain the edge of excitement and freshness, teachers develop strong convictions about what is appropriate for children's healthy growth. That underlying passion propels teachers with determination that doesn't falter, even in the face of frustrating circumstances. Care about what you do, and keep caring. These attitudes and dispositions will be indispensable as you travel your professional path.

1996
According to the Urban Institute, welfare reform or "The Personal Responsibility and Work Opportunity Act of 1996," is expected to impoverish 1.1 million more children.

Collegiality and Connection

Your growth and learning as a professional will have to be in the context of dialogue with other teachers. For those of you planning to do family child care, this will be harder than for the others, but the principle remains the same. It is within those professional relationships that you will find the support, the challenges, the ideas that you will need. When you find yourself within a community of others who care about common issues as well as for each other's welfare, you will be encouraged in the difficult periods and fortified in the good times of teaching. Where are you going to find these connections?

First, deliberately seek employment in a school or center that values collegiality. You will be able to tell if this is so by asking questions about staff meetings and staff development opportunities, by looking at the staff bulletin board, reading job descriptions, and talking with teachers. Some programs make collegiality and **team-teaching** a vital part of their day-to-day life, and it is evident in the relationships of the coworkers.

When newly employed, convey an attitude of openness to others, by asking their assistance and opinions about issues that will occur. New teachers are often so anxious to prove themselves and their competence to others that they put up invisible barriers that prevent getting the support and assistance that they really need. Seek out the experienced teachers whose classrooms you admire, and let them know you would value their ideas and help in designing your practice. Find out if there are formal mentoring programs in your program; many communities have designed such pairings to support new teachers in their first year or two of teaching. If there is such a system, volunteer to become involved. Not only will this relationship foster your developmental growth as a teacher, but it also benefits the experienced colleague. If such systems do not exist, read about and promote discussion of mentoring systems.

Make sure that you become involved in whatever local professional organization is available to you. Here you will find a ready-made group of individuals who have similar interests and commitment to children's issues. You will find members with a cross section of experience, job description, and training; within such diversity you will find others to support you. Take the initiative to seek out what you need. If you gain more by talking with experienced teachers, do so. Or if talking with other novice teachers who are undergoing the same kinds of adjustments to teaching that you are is more helpful, create these opportunities.

There are several ways to form teacher support groups. If a number of graduates from your program are working in the same area, you may be able to form the core for a group for regular meetings to discuss common concerns. Or the professional association may offer such options. Both new and experienced teachers benefit from the exchange of questions and ideas in such a group. Sometimes groups read and discuss a common book; others simply raise issues of personal or classroom concern. Sometimes such groups work on community early childhood issues, finding a common voice together, but for beginning teachers, their main benefit is support for professional growth. Whatever form it takes, teachers who expect to grow and learn, through good times and bad, will discover they must find ways of **networking**, making connections to colleagues.

Knowing is not enough; we must apply! Willing is not enough; we must do
—Goethe

Team-Teaching: Status and responsibility of teachers in a classroom is equal, rather than hierarchical.

Networking: Making connections with others in the profession for mutual support and information, for professional development and advancement.

1997

In September, the Federal Communications Commission will require television broadcasters to air at least three hours of educational programming for children per week.

Reflective Teaching

Reflective Teaching: The process of thinking back over teaching experiences to form questions, set goals, and grow as a teacher.

Throughout this text, you have been encouraged to discover the importance of reflection on your relationship to teaching, **reflective teaching** and your life. As you move on into early childhood classrooms, it will continue to be important for you to use your daily experience as material for you to consider, muse and meditate upon, contemplate and speculate upon. "The basic and comprehensive question during reflection is, 'What am I doing and why?'" (Valverde in Cruickshank, 1987, p. 3).

Many teachers find that recording events and questions to reflect upon in a personal journal allows them to gain different perspectives for approaching their work. Finding a few minutes when children are napping or at the end of the day may seem too difficult for new teachers who are overwhelmed with lesson plans, material preparations, and classroom maintainence. But it is likely one of the most important things you can do to help keep your focus on your professional development. Through using a reflective journal, teachers record their "experiences within and outside of the classroom that bear directly on classroom life" (Cruickshank, 1987, p. 10). This record of thoughts, actions, beliefs, and attitudes will help teachers learn much from the children and the classroom. When ideas and experiences are recorded, they provide a frame of reference for teachers to refer back to and see growth, or see patterns of questions that will identify needs for additional research. Make it your resolution to begin a journal on the first day of your new job, and to record in it regularly. Keeping a journal forces a teacher to assume the posture of reflection. The teacher asks: "How did I come to do it this way? What might I do differently?" Teacher growth and development lie in the answers.

Fine-Tuning Skills and Deepening Knowledge Base

One must learn by doing the thing; though you think you know it, you have no certainty until you try

—Sophocles

As has been stated, completing a program of professional preparation at a college or university is a beginning. During the early years of your teaching practice, you will discover that there are many classroom skills that must be fine-tuned. There are many things that you learned in theory, and likely had limited opportunities to practice, in your early education courses and practicums.

However, it is only through regular and frequent use of these skills in the context of your own classroom that you will become comfortable, confident, and proficient in their use, and that you will discover what additional knowledge you need. Instead of purely concentrating on survival during your first months and years in the classroom, you will benefit from consciously identifying skills that need to be developed, and setting small goals for each on a regular basis. For example, you will likely need to develop your skills of observation and organization of your record-keeping, of communication, and of decision-making.

A beginning teacher might set the goal of recording an observation on every child at least once a week. Recognizing that the teacher preparation program was just a beginning, good teachers continue to develop their own goals and skills.

From our discussions of the developments of the profession in Chapter Nine and the issues facing the profession in Chapter Eleven, you know that your knowledge must grow in these two areas in order to remain current.

2005

By 2005, 250,000 more child care workers will be needed, according to The Bureau of Labor Statistics.

Self-Evaluation

One of the most difficult things for many new teachers is to develop the skill of self-evaluation (Duff et al., 1995). Perhaps because so many life experiences depend on others to tell us how well (or not) we are doing, most beginning teachers have not had a great deal of experience in evaluating their own performance. Any well-run program will provide you with evaluation from your supervisor, but usually such feedback is so occasional that teachers must instead rely on their own evaluation of their performance to determine their particular strengths and set their own goals for improvement. Your personal reflections and your journal can be helpful in starting this process. You will likely discover a number of evaluation tools in the course of your studies, and as you visit various centers. The questions at the end of each chapter in Carol Hillman's *Teaching Four-Year-Olds* (1988) act as useful informal self-evaluation guides on the various aspects of a teacher's practice. Don't hesitate to evaluate yourself honestly and fairly; your professional growth depends on this.

Personal Philosophy of Education

In order to evaluate how close you are keeping to your personal pathway, it is important that you have the guideline of your personal philosophy of education. As your last act in this preliminary examination of early education, organize your thoughts about what you believe about teaching and learning into a written statement. (See assignment under "Activities for Further Study.") No doubt this document will grow and be adapted as you proceed through subsequent coursework in your professional preparation. Plan to review it at the end of each semester or year. And take it with you, making it something you refer to and reflect on as you complete each school year, or evaluation session, or some regular period in your classroom life. As you evaluate your day-to-day practice in the light of your vision and philosophy, you may be able to keep your ideals and realities aligned.

Listen to the mustn'ts, child,
Listen to the don'ts
Listen to the shouldn'ts
The impossibles, the won'ts
Listen to the never haves
Then listen to me—
Anything can happen, child
A N Y T H I N G
can be done
                    –Shel Silverstein

Rhythms of Teaching

As is true of so many things in life, there is a rhythm, pacing, and pattern to teaching, ranging from the excitement and exhilaration of the first experiences, to the plateaus of sameness and day-to-day duties, to the depths of frustration. Recall the stages of teacher development that we discussed in Chapter Nine, and give yourself the benefit of time to grow, to develop, to become. Be aware that the first year of teaching is generally recognized as difficult for most new teachers. Don't be afraid to admit your dissatisfactions and disappointments, and to seek the help and support you need during this difficult time. As you will be patient with your children's progress, so too be patient with your own (see Fig. 12-3). You won't be the same teacher in the first month that you will be in your twelfth and then in your twentieth. Know that your decision was right and good, find the supports you need, and watch your own growth and development as a teacher. Don't let discouragements take you from the field. Stay, for all the reasons that brought you here.

2005

54 percent more teachers of kindergarten and preschool children will be needed by 2005, according to The Bureau of Labor Statistics.

Figure 12-3   **Be patient with your progress. Know that you will continue to grow as a teacher.**

Teaching is a challenging profession with many wonderful aspects. It provides a way to stay young at heart, to maintain a lifetime of active learning, to be a special part of the world of the present *and* the future while having opportunities to delve into the past. It is in every respect a profession of hope (Perrone, 1991, p. 131).

Join yourself to this hope. As you join, realize the commitment you are making, as embodied in NAEYC's Statement of Commitment.

As an individual who works with young children, I commit myself to furthering the values of early childhood education as they are reflected in the NAEYC Code of Ethical Conduct.
To the best of my ability I will
–Ensure that programs for young children are based on current knowledge of child development and early childhood education.
–Respect and support families in their task of nurturing children.
–Respect colleagues in early childhood education and support them in maintaining the NAEYC Code of Ethical Conduct.
–Serve as an advocate for children, their families, and their teachers in community and society.
–Maintain high standards of professional conduct.
–Recognize how personal values, opinions, and biases can affect professional judgment.
–Be open to new ideas and be willing to learn from the suggestions of others.
–Continue to learn, grow, and contribute as a professional.
–Honor the ideas and principles of the NAEYC Code of Ethical Conduct.
(Reprinted with permission from NAEYC.)

Keep this commitment before you, and grow as a teacher with joy.

In endings there are beginnings
—Carol Hillman

2005
74 percent more special education teachers will be needed by 2005, according to The Bureau of Labor Statistics.

Figure 12-4 **Could some of these children be in your teaching future? (Courtesy of Tracie O'Hara, Cathy Mowrey and Jeffrey Meyer)**

A story is told of two men visiting an ocean. They saw, much to their amazement, that a storm had tossed thousands, perhaps, millions, of starfish up on the shore. As far as the eye could see, piles of starfish lay there out of the water in the sunshine; it was obvious that very soon, they would begin to die. One of the men stooped down and began to pick up starfish and throw them back into the water. "What are you doing?" cried his friend. "Don't you see that it is hopeless? There are millions of starfish here, and they are all going to die!" Picking up another and throwing it back into the waves, the first man replied, "Not that one." Keep your eyes firmly fixed on the lives you can touch (see Fig. 12-4).

Make a difference, and make your mark in the future of early education.

SUMMARY

Beginning teachers will have much professional development ahead of them. As they grow professionally, they will be helped by: forming particular attitudes and dispositions; collegiality and connections; reflective teaching; fine-tuning skills and a deepening knowledge base; self-evaluation; developing a personal philosophy of education; and recognizing the rhythms of teaching, including the difficulties of the first year.

QUESTIONS FOR REVIEW

1. Discuss several actions that will be helpful to your professional development.

ACTIVITIES FOR FURTHER STUDY

1. Write a comprehensive personal statement of your thoughts and aims in education, including such ideas as your beliefs about effective teaching and optimum learning situations for young children.

2. Examine your own suitability for teaching. List your strengths and weaknesses. Set some goals for yourself. Sketch out a tentative plan for specific actions you will take to begin your professional development: (a) as a student; (b) in your first year of teaching.

3. Read one of the personal accounts of beginning teachers listed under "Suggested Readings."

REFERENCES

Cruickshank, Donald R. (1987). *Reflective teaching: The preparation of students of teaching.* Reston, VA: Association of Teacher Educators.

Duff, R. Eleanor, Brown, Mac H., & Van Scoy, Irma J. Reflection and self-evaluation keys to professional development." *Young Children, 50,* (4), 81-88.

Hillman, Carol B. (1988). *Teaching four-year-olds: A personal journey.* Bloomington, IN: Phi Delta Kappa Educational Foundation.

Perrone, Vito. (1991). *A letter to teachers: Reflections of schooling and the art of teaching.* San Francisco: Jossey-Bass Publishers.

Van Arsdell, Marian. (1994). Preparing early childhood teachers for careers in learning. In *New perspectives in early childhood teacher education: Bringing practitioners into the debate.* New York: Teachers College Press.

SUGGESTIONS FOR READING

Brand, Susan F. (1990, January) Undergraduates and beginning preschool teachers working with young children: Educational and developmental issues. *Young Children, 45,* (2), 19-24.

Dollase, Richard H. (1992). *Voices of beginning teachers: Visions and realities.* New York: Teachers College Press.

Goffin, Stacie G., & Day, David E. (Eds.). (1994). *New perspectives in early childhood teacher education: Bringing practitioners into the debate.* New York: Teachers College Press.

Kane, Pearl Rock. (Ed.). (1991). *The first year of teaching: Real world stories from America's teachers.* New York: Penguin Books.

Raphael, Ray. (1985). *The teacher's voice: A sense of who we are.* Portsmouth, NH: Heinemann.

INDEX

Note: Page numbers followed by an *f* indicate a figure reference.